Italy and the USA
Cultural Change Through Language and Narrative

LEGENDA

LEGENDA is the Modern Humanities Research Association's book imprint for new research in the Humanities. Founded in 1995 by Malcolm Bowie and others within the University of Oxford, Legenda has always been a collaborative publishing enterprise, directly governed by scholars. The Modern Humanities Research Association (MHRA) joined this collaboration in 1998, became half-owner in 2004, in partnership with Maney Publishing and then Routledge, and has since 2016 been sole owner. Titles range from medieval texts to contemporary cinema and form a widely comparative view of the modern humanities, including works on Arabic, Catalan, English, French, German, Greek, Italian, Portuguese, Russian, Spanish, and Yiddish literature. Editorial boards and committees of more than 60 leading academic specialists work in collaboration with bodies such as the Society for French Studies, the British Comparative Literature Association and the Association of Hispanists of Great Britain & Ireland.

The MHRA encourages and promotes advanced study and research in the field of the modern humanities, especially modern European languages and literature, including English, and also cinema. It aims to break down the barriers between scholars working in different disciplines and to maintain the unity of humanistic scholarship. The Association fulfils this purpose through the publication of journals, bibliographies, monographs, critical editions, and the MHRA Style Guide, and by making grants in support of research. Membership is open to all who work in the Humanities, whether independent or in a University post, and the participation of younger colleagues entering the field is especially welcomed.

ALSO PUBLISHED BY THE ASSOCIATION

Critical Texts
Tudor and Stuart Translations • New Translations • European Translations
MHRA Library of Medieval Welsh Literature

MHRA Bibliographies
Publications of the Modern Humanities Research Association

The Annual Bibliography of English Language & Literature
Austrian Studies
Modern Language Review
Portuguese Studies
The Slavonic and East European Review
Working Papers in the Humanities
The Yearbook of English Studies

www.mhra.org.uk
www.legendabooks.com

ITALIAN PERSPECTIVES

Editorial Committee
Professor Simon Gilson, University of Warwick (General Editor)
Dr Francesca Billiani, University of Manchester
Professor Manuele Gragnolati, Université Paris-Sorbonne
Dr Catherine Keen, University College London
Professor Martin McLaughlin, Magdalen College, Oxford

Founding Editors
Professor Zygmunt Barański and Professor Anna Laura Lepschy

In the light of growing academic interest in Italy and the reorganization of many university courses in Italian along interdisciplinary lines, this book series, founded by Maney Publishing under the imprint of the Northern Universities Press and now continuing under the Legenda imprint, aims to bring together different scholarly perspectives on Italy and its culture. *Italian Perspectives* publishes books and collections of essays on any period of Italian literature, language, history, culture, politics, art, and media, as well as studies which take an interdisciplinary approach and are methodologically innovative.

APPEARING IN THIS SERIES

20. *Ugo Foscolo and English Culture*, by Sandra Parmegiani
21. *The Printed Media in Fin-de-siècle Italy: Publishers, Writers, and Readers*, ed. by Ann Hallamore Caesar, Gabriella Romani, and Jennifer Burns
22. *Giraffes in the Garden of Italian Literature: Modernist Embodiment in Italo Svevo, Federigo Tozzi and Carlo Emilio Gadda*, by Deborah Amberson
23. *Remembering Aldo Moro: The Cultural Legacy of the 1978 Kidnapping and Murder*, ed. by Ruth Glynn and Giancarlo Lombardi
24. *Disrupted Narratives: Illness, Silence and Identity in Svevo, Pressburger and Morandini*, by Emma Bond
25. *Dante and Epicurus: A Dualistic Vision of Secular and Spiritual Fulfilment*, by George Corbett
26. *Edoardo Sanguineti: Literature, Ideology and the Avant-Garde*, ed. by Paolo Chirumbolo and John Picchione
27. *The Tradition of the Actor-Author in Italian Theatre*, ed. by Donatella Fischer
28. *Leopardi's Nymphs: Grace, Melancholy, and the Uncanny*, by Fabio A. Camilletti
29. *Gadda and Beckett: Storytelling, Subjectivity and Fracture*, by Katrin Wehling-Giorgi
30. *Caravaggio in Film and Literature: Popular Culture's Appropriation of a Baroque Genius*, by Laura Rorato
31. *The Italian Academies 1525-1700: Networks of Culture, Innovation and Dissent*, ed. by Jane E. Everson, Denis V. Reidy and Lisa Sampson
32. *Rome Eternal: The City As Fatherland*, by Guy Lanoue
33. *The Somali Within: Language, Race and Belonging in 'Minor' Italian Literature*, by Simone Brioni
34. *Laughter from Realism to Modernism: Misfits and Humorists in Pirandello, Svevo, Palazzeschi, and Gadda*, by Alberto Godioli
35. *Pasolini after Dante: The 'Divine Mimesis' and the Politics of Representation*, by Emanuela Patti

Managing Editor
Dr Graham Nelson, 41 Wellington Square, Oxford OX1 2JF, UK
www.legendabooks.com

Italy and the USA

Cultural Change Through Language and Narrative

❖

Edited by Guido Bonsaver,
Alessandro Carlucci and Matthew Reza

LEGENDA

Italian Perspectives 44
Modern Humanities Research Association
2019

Published by Legenda
an imprint of the Modern Humanities Research Association
Salisbury House, Station Road, Cambridge CB1 2LA

ISBN 978-1-78188-875-9 (HB)
ISBN 978-1-78188-876-6 (PB)

First published 2019

All rights reserved. No part of this publication may be reproduced or disseminated or transmitted in any form or by any means, electronic, mechanical, photocopying, recording or otherwise, or stored in any retrieval system, or otherwise used in any manner whatsoever without written permission of the copyright owner, except in accordance with the provisions of the Copyright, Designs and Patents Act 1988, or under the terms of a licence permitting restricted copying issued in the UK by the Copyright Licensing Agency Ltd, Saffron House, 6–10 Kirby Street, London EC1N 8TS, *England, or in the USA by the Copyright Clearance Center, 222 Rosewood Drive, Danvers MA 01923. Application for the written permission of the copyright owner to reproduce any part of this publication must be made by email to legenda@mhra.org.uk.*

Disclaimer: Statements of fact and opinion contained in this book are those of the author and not of the editors or the Modern Humanities Research Association. The publisher makes no representation, express or implied, in respect of the accuracy of the material in this book and cannot accept any legal responsibility or liability for any errors or omissions that may be made.

Trademark notice: Product or corporate names may be trademarks or registered trademarks, and are used only for identification and explanation without intent to infringe.

© *Modern Humanities Research Association 2019*

Copy-Editor: Dr Nigel Hope

CONTENTS

	Acknowledgements	ix
	Notes on the Contributors	x
	Introduction: Mapping Cultural Change: Italy and the USA during the 'Long American Century'	1
	PART I: HISTORICAL CONTEXTS AND CHANNELS OF CONTACT	
1	Italian Storytelling Memories: Personal Recollections of Fairy and Folk Tales in the USA MATTHEW REZA	17
2	The English Language and Anglo-American Culture in Twentieth-Century Italy VIRGINIA PULCINI	31
3	English in Italian Education: Between Europeanization and Americanization GIANCARLO SCHIRRU	47
4	Modern Throwbacks: Screening Italians in the USA — The First Fifty Years GIORGIO BERTELLINI	59
5	Narrating New Italianness in the USA in the Early Twenty-First Century TERESA FIORE	72
	PART II: FROM THE LATE NINETEENTH CENTURY TO THE SECOND WORLD WAR	
6	Buffalo Bill and the Italian Myth of the American West LUCA COTTINI	89
7	Turin between French and US Culture: The Film and Car Industries in 1904–1914 GUIDO BONSAVER	103
8	US Culture and Fascist Italy: The Case of *Omnibus* (1937–1939) MANUELA DI FRANCO	123
	PART III: FROM THE SECOND WORLD WAR TO THE TWENTY-FIRST CENTURY	
9	The Forbidden City: Tombolo between American Occupation and Italian Imagination CHARLES L. LEAVITT IV	143

10 The Other America: Contact and Exchange in the Italian Folk Revival   156
    RACHEL E. LOVE

11 PC or not PC? Some Reflections upon Political Correctness and its
    Influence on the Italian Language   174
    FEDERICO FALOPPA

    PART IV: LONG-TERM INFLUENCES AND EFFECTS

12 'Little Italy' on the Move: The Birth and Transatlantic Relocation of a
    Cultural Myth   201
    MATTIA LENTO

13 Italianisms in US English: Past and Present   216
    LAURA PINNAVAIA

14 A Century of Americanisms   232
    MASSIMO FANFANI

15 Contact, Change, and Translation: A Theoretical and Empirical
    Assessment of Non-Lexical Anglicisms   246
    ALESSANDRO CARLUCCI

    Index   262

ACKNOWLEDGEMENTS

This book is based on research conducted by all contributors between 2015 and 2017 as part of the project *Cultures on the Move: Italy and the USA*. We are grateful to the John Fell Fund, University of Oxford for their financial support, and to Italian Studies at Oxford for hosting this initiative. We are also grateful to the participants in the international conference which was central to this project: *Cultures on the Move: Italy and the USA. Language, Literature, Cinema* (Oxford, 23–24 September 2016). The conference was generously supported by the Faculty of Medieval and Modern Languages at the University of Oxford, and the Society for Italian Studies. For reasons of space, this volume could not host all the many, stimulating contributions to the conference.

Finally, we are grateful to Graham Nelson, our editor at Legenda, and to our copy-editor, Nigel Hope, who have seen this manuscript through to press. The back cover image was very kindly provided by PadovaOggi (http://www.padovaoggi.it).

NOTES ON THE CONTRIBUTORS

Giorgio Bertellini is Professor of Media History at the University of Michigan. He is the author and editor of the award-winning volumes *Italy in Early American Cinema: Race, Landscape and the Picturesque* (2010) and *Italian Silent Cinema: A Reader* (2013). His monograph on Emir Kusturica, published in Italian (2011) and English (2015), is also available in Romanian (2017) and, in part, in Japanese translation (2018). He is currently Associate Editor of the *Journal of Italian Cinema and Media Studies* and co-editor of the University of California Press book series *Cinema Cultures in Contact*. His latest volume is *The Divo and the Duce: Promoting Film Stardom and Political Leadership in 1920s America* (Oakland: University of California Press, 2019).

Guido Bonsaver is Professor of Italian Cultural History at Oxford University and a Fellow of Pembroke College. His research interests lie at the interface of political and social history, literature and film. He is currently working on the influence of US culture in Italy. He is the author of a number of publications among which are: *Elio Vittorini* (2000), *Censorship and Literature in Fascist Italy* (2007), *Vita e omicidio di Gaetano Pilati* (2010) and *Mussolini censore* (2013); and co-editor of: with R. Gordon, *Culture, Censorship and the State in Twentieth-Century Italy* (2005); with M. McLaughlin and F. Pellegrini, *Sinergie narrative: cinema e letteratura nell'Italia contemporanea* (2008); with E. Bond and F. Faloppa, *Destination Italy: Representing Migration in Contemporary Media and Narrative* (2015); and, with B. Richardson and G. Stellardi, *Cultural Reception, Translation and Transformation from Medieval to Modern Italy* (2017).

Alessandro Carlucci is a Research Fellow of the University of Bergen. From 2017 to 2019 he was an MHRA Research Associate at the University of Oxford, where he worked on the AHRC-funded project 'Creative Multilingualism'. He is also a consultant to the *Oxford English Dictionary* (with particular responsibility for entries of Italian or Italo-Romance origin). His research focuses on the history of the Italian language, Tuscan dialectology, language contact, Italian cultural and intellectual history, and the history of linguistic thought. His articles on English influences in Italian have appeared in *Modern Language Review* and *Lingua Nostra*. He is the author of *The Impact of the English Language in Italy: Linguistic Outcomes and Political Implications* (Lincom, 2018) and *Gramsci and Languages: Unification, Diversity, Hegemony* (Brill, 2013; Haymarket, 2015), co-winner of the Giuseppe Sormani International Prize for the best monograph on Antonio Gramsci (4th edition, 2012–17).

Luca Cottini is a scholar of modern Italian literature and a cultural historian. He received his training in Classical Philology at the University of Milan (BA, 2003), and later specialized in Italian modernist literature and early industrial culture, first at Notre Dame (MA, 2007), then at Harvard (PhD, 2012). His research on the nineteenth and twentieth centuries combines a traditional literary focus (as in his work on D'Annunzio, De Amicis, Palazzeschi, Papini, Alvaro, Calvino, and Fenoglio) with a broader interdisciplinary horizon, including visual studies (with publications on early Italian photography, silent cinema, and the modernist rediscovery of the Baroque) and social history (with a specific focus on universal expositions, the birth of advertising, and the development of industrial design). He published a study on Italo Calvino's autobiographical writings for Longo (*I passaggi obbligati di Italo Calvino: autobiografia, memoria, identità*, 2017), and a monograph on the birth of Italian design for University of Toronto Press (*The Art of Objects: The Birth of Italian Industrial Culture, 1878–1928*, 2018).

Manuela Di Franco is a PhD candidate in the Italian department at the University of Cambridge. Her research interests include the development of the popular press in Fascist Italy and the influence of modern American culture on Italian society. Her current research focuses on the influence of foreign models on Italian popular magazines in the 1930s, and in particular the presence of American culture and its impact on Italian culture. More specifically, her work examines the multicultural dialogue within Europe and the USA in the shaping of the Italian illustrated popular press in the Fascist era. She graduated cum laude from the University of Roma Tre in 2013 in International Relations with a thesis in American History, 'The Transformation of the United States and Fascist Italy, 1922–1942'. The dissertation analyses the main changes that occurred in American society during the interwar years, investigating how Fascist Italy viewed the USA and how it interpreted its cultural productions and models.

Federico Faloppa teaches history of the language, linguistics and discourse analysis at the Department of Modern Languages of the University of Reading, where he is the Programme Director of Italian Studies. He has published extensively on the representation of otherness in language, media representation of migrants and minorities, hate speech, and racism in language. His publications include: *Parole contro* (2004); *Razzisti a parole (per tacer dei fatti)* (2011); *Sbiancare un etiope. La pelle cangiante di un topos antico* (Aracne, 2013); 'Per un linguaggio non razzista', in Marco Aime (ed.), *Contro il razzismo. Quattro ragionamenti* (2016); 'Rimuovere "razza" dalla Costituzione? Alcune riflessioni linguistiche', in Manuela Monti and Carlo Alberto Redi (eds), *No razza Sì cittadinanza* (2017). He is currently working on a monograph on the *politicamente corretto* (2019), and he is a consultant on hate speech and discrimination for Amnesty International Italy, the Alexander Langer Foundation in Bozen, and the association of journalists Carta di Roma.

Massimo Fanfani was born in Florence in 1953. Formerly Secretary of the Accademia della Crusca, he is Associate Professor of Italian Linguistics at the University of Florence, and senior editor of the journal *Lingua Nostra*. His research focuses mainly on the historical lexicology and semantics of Italian. He has published extensively on the history of individual words and morphological structures, on the influence of foreign languages (especially American English and Russian) on Italian, and also on the terminology and history of modern linguistic thought.

Teresa Fiore holds the Theresa and Lawrence R. Inserra Chair in Italian and Italian American Studies at Montclair State University (USA). The recipient of several fellowships (De Bosis, Rockefeller, and Fulbright), she was Visiting Assistant Professor at Harvard University, NYU, and Rutgers University. She is the author of *Pre-Occupied Spaces: Remapping Italy's Transnational Migrations and Colonial Legacies* (Fordham University Press 2017) and the editor of the 2006 issue of *Quaderni del '900*, devoted to John Fante. Her numerous articles on migration to/from Italy linked to twentieth- and twenty-first-century Italian literature and cinema have been published in Italian, English, and Spanish in journals (*Bollettino d'italianistica*, *Annali d'Italianistica*, *Studi italiani*, *El hilo de la fabula*, *Diaspora*, *Zibaldone*, *Journal of Italian Media and Cinema Studies*) and edited collections (*Postcolonial Italy*; *Teaching Italian American Literature, Film, and Popular Culture*; *The Cultures of Italian Migration*). Two articles by her on new migration flows from Italy were recently published in *The Routledge History of Italian Americans* (2017) and *New Italian Migrations to the United States*, II: *Art and Culture Since 1945* (2018). She coordinates a regular programme of cultural events and educational initiatives on campus that focus on the circulation of people, ideas, and products from/to Italy.

Charles L. Leavitt IV is Assistant Professor of Italian Studies at the University of Notre Dame. He studies modern Italian literature and cinema in a comparative context. He is currently completing a monograph on Italian neorealism, while also continuing to pursue research on a range of topics, and in particular on intersections between Italian and African American culture. He is co-editor of *The Italianist* Film Issue, and his work has appeared in publications such as *Modern Language Notes*, *Italian Culture*, *Journal of Modern Italian Studies*, *California Italian Studies*, *Tre Corone*, and *The Italianist*.

Mattia Lento is Advanced Postdoctoral Mobility Fellow at the Swiss National Science Foundation (SNSF) and Senior Researcher at the University of Lausanne. Mattia holds a joint PhD in Film Studies from the University of Zurich and the University of Milan. He has taught courses on film experience, film acting, and transnational cinema at the Universities of Zurich, Westminster, and Innsbruck. His main research interests include the relationship between Italian diasporas and international cinema. He has attended different international conferences and has published academic articles and book chapters in English, German, and Italian. His PhD thesis was published in 2017 by ETS. He works also as a freelance journalist for the Italian Swiss Radio (RSI/SRG-SSR).

Rachel E. Love is a Core Postdoctoral Fellow at New York University (NYU), having earned her PhD from NYU in Italian Studies in May 2018. Her essays on twentieth-century Italian politics and culture have appeared in the journals *Popular Music*, *Modern Italy*, and *Interventions*. Her current book project, 'Songbook for a Revolution: Popular Culture and the New Left in 1960s Italy', analyses the political use of folk music in 1960s Italy through the history of a leftist musical collective, the Nuovo Canzoniere Italiano (NCI). Her interdisciplinary research interests move between contemporary Italian history and literature, cultural studies, postcolonial studies, and oral history.

Laura Pinnavaia is Full Professor of English Language and Linguistics at the University of Milan (Italy). Her research interests in lexicology and lexicography have resulted in the publication of over forty articles; one edited volume, *Insights into English and Germanic Lexicology and Lexicography: Past and Present Perspectives* (2010); and four authored monographs: *The Italian Borrowings in the OED: A Lexicographic, Linguistic and Cultural Analysis* (2001), *Sugar and Spice ... Exploring Food and Drink Idioms in English* (2010), *Introduzione alla Linguistica Inglese* (2015), *Food and Drink Idioms in English: A Little Bit More Sugar and Lots More Spice* (2018). She is currently working on English seventeenth-century travelogues of Italy and on the compilation of an *Italian–English Dictionary of Collocations*.

Virginia Pulcini is Full Professor of English Language and Linguistics at the University of Turin, Italy (Department of Foreign Languages, Literature and Modern Cultures). She has had a thirty-year-long career as university lecturer in English language and linguistics in Italy and published extensively in several fields of English linguistics. She contributed to the Italian entries of the *Dictionary of European Anglicisms* (2001) and to the volume *English in Europe* (2002), both published by Oxford University Press. Her most productive research area is the lexical influence of English on Italian. In this field she has co-edited the volume *The Anglicization of European Lexis* in 2012. She is currently involved in the Erasmus+ Project 'Transnational Alignment of English Competences for University Lecturers' (2017–20).

Matthew Reza is a sessional lecturer and Italian language tutor at the University of Oxford, and the events coordinator for the research network Italian Studies at Oxford. His research focuses on Italian fantastic literature and utopian narratives. Within Italian American Studies, he works on the migration of Italian oral narratives — particularly the fairy and folk tale — to the USA during the twentieth century. His work has appeared in *Forum for Modern Language Studies*, *The Italianist*, and *Modern Language Notes*.

Giancarlo Schirru is Full Professor of General and Historical Linguistics in the Department of Asian, African, and Mediterranean Studies (DAAM) at the University of Naples 'L'Orientale'. He has published in major linguistics journals such as *Studi linguistici italiani*, *L'Italia dialettale*, and *Archivio glottologico italiano*. He has also published extensively on the linguistic ideas of the Italian philosopher and political leader Antonio Gramsci, including their reception in the USA, and on educational linguistics. He has recently edited Gramsci's *Appunti di glottologia 1912–1913* (2016).

INTRODUCTION

Mapping Cultural Change: Italy and the USA during the 'Long American Century'

A Theoretical and Methodological Note

The multi-disciplinary, composite structure of this book is the result of a number of theoretical and pragmatic premises. Together, they combine to produce the frame which both hosts the individual chapters and uses them to suggest a macrotextual cohesion. For this reason, it is important to address these premises right at the start. The method will follow a linear, although unorthodox, form of reasoning: each single expression chosen for the title of this introductory chapter will be used as a stepping stone, from the verb 'Mapping' to the phrase 'Long American Century'. After this, a few pages will be devoted to the individual contributions of the fifteen chapters which constitute the book, and a concluding section will suggest future developments and point to still uncultivated areas of study.

The intention to 'map' a field is in itself a declaration of intent. It suggests an interest in defining and categorizing phenomena. The challenge, as always, is to find the right balance between the inevitable simplifications of the 'bigger picture' and the need to respect the variety and complexity of each individual case. The latter is, we hope, well-evidenced by the rich and overflowing content of the fifteen chapters. The former is a more contentious issue. This book is the product of a collective endeavour for which each of the fifteen contributors was free to choose the parameters of their own specialist study. It would be foolish to expect a tightly-knit pattern from such an operation. The fragmentation is even more inevitable as a consequence of the different disciplines involved and the different objects of study. At the same time, the attempt at 'mapping' a phenomenon is indicative of the intention to favour a historical approach and a systematic use of data, capable of suggesting trends and tendencies. The presence of a substantial number of linguistic studies is a corollary to this. Within the humanities, the quantitative approach which is typical of the social and hard sciences has been adopted especially in linguistic studies. Although this is no magic wand to the study of the complexities of human culture, it is nonetheless a reminder of the need to produce hard data, systematically collected, in order to try to understand the main developments within a certain community, however fluidly defined. Each chapter, within its confines, attempts to do that.

'Cultural change' is the object of our study. Human evolution is marked by a constant process of change at both an individual and a social level. The factors at play are innumerable, hence the challenge of trying to define the set of influences which drive development in a certain direction. When it comes to cultural change the challenge is twofold. The first relates to the definition of 'culture'. The concept we envision here is a trade between the anthropological notion of culture — as the distinctive customs, social behaviour and products of a certain community — and the one traditionally associated with the humanities, where culture relates to a more specific ambit, that is, the artistic and intellectual products of said community. This is a well-trodden territory, first defined by the Cultural Studies 'turn' of Stuart Hall's Birmingham School in 1960s Britain and, with regard to Italy, already set out by Antonio Gramsci thirty years earlier, with his reflections on popular culture and on the key notion of hegemony.[1] Our approach does not aim at a discussion of the economic and political dimension which subsumes the approach of Cultural Studies: a choice dictated by the scholarly boundaries of this volume, certainly not because this dimension is not part of the relationship between Italy and the USA. As already mentioned, the historical element is the one which drives our approach, hence the field of Cultural History, as more recently defined by Peter Burke, is the one which probably best reflects the theoretical premises of this book.[2] A multi-disciplinary approach is necessary in any such study, but equally necessary is defining its disciplinary spread. Language is at the centre as the most evident cultural trait defining an individual's identity (however multilingual and subjectively conceived). Around it, we have imagined a wider field loosely defined as narrative. By narrative we mean storytelling in its more traditional manifestations — that is, tales told through written as much as visual and performative means — but also other forms through which the story of a community takes shape. This line of approach has produced scholarly forays into relatively less institutionalised areas of study such as itinerant shows, the car industry, folk music, and the study of places as 'contact zones' between different cultures.[3]

The second challenge concerns the study of 'change'. Nobody would deny that individuals and societies change over time. They also change in space, and within this discourse we are comfortable with a fluid definition of space as proposed by Doreen Massey.[4] The definition of change, however, has not received much theoretical attention. Once again, we thought that the discipline of linguistics could provide some inspiration. Contact linguistics aims to study the consequences of the reciprocal influence of languages when, for a number of different reasons, they come into contact with each other. One must distinguish between two different categories of contacts: those involving human mobility, and the cases of indirect cultural influence and exchange. Languages — and, we implicitly argue, cultures — can change both as a result of their encounter with other languages and cultures, through direct speaker interaction, and as a result of the indirect influence exerted by other languages or cultures thanks to their perceived prestige but without regular, large-scale speaker interaction (here most Cultural Studies theorists would warn us of the unequal economic and political prestige of the languages and cultures in contact: and, once again, the Italy/USA case would provide fertile ground).[5]

This eventually takes us to the core of this book: the choice of 'Italy and the United States of America'. The previous comments about contact linguistics indirectly suggest that a most stimulating field of study should contain examples of both direct and indirect contact. The cultural history of the interaction between Italy and the USA during the twentieth century provides precisely that context. On the one hand we have the transnational phenomenon of Italian migration to — and return from — the USA, and on the other the influence of US culture on Italian society, which was based on political, economic and technological factors, but did not involve large-scale human mobility. There is therefore a methodological attraction to this two-way relationship. This, moreover, is amply strengthened by the importance of the cultural relation in both directions. On the one hand, the recent fortune of the transnational approach to the study of culture makes it particularly relevant to reflect on the case of the impact of Italian culture (again, however, accurately sub-defined) in a country, the USA, which has built its own identity under the continuous cultural stimulation from new waves of migrants from all over the world. At the other end of the spectrum, it would be difficult to deny that so-called 'Americanization' was a major, possibly the biggest cultural influence on Italian society in the twentieth century. The actual presence of the US army during the liberation of Italy in 1943–45 and the subsequent presence of US troops in various bases throughout the country was certainly a factor at play, as Charles L. Leavitt IV's chapter on Tombolo in this book shows. At the same time, other chapters will show how the influence of US culture began to permeate Italian culture well before the Second World War, and even in the second half of the twentieth century, its influence acted well beyond the effect of the direct contact with the few thousand US troops on Italian soil.

Finally, the notion of a 'long American century' is no foolish attempt to mimic Eric Hobsbawm's erudite and paradigm-shifting notion of a 'long nineteenth century', nor to compete with his later definition of a 'short twentieth century'. Our rationale is more pragmatic, dictated first and foremost by the chronological boundaries marked by some of the fifteen chapters in this volume. At the same time, this has revealed a logic which has historical and cultural implications too. At one end, when considering the rise of the USA as a world-leading economy, historians would agree that the expansion of the use of electricity in the latter part of the nineteenth century coincided with the capacity of US entrepreneurs to embrace this new technology in order to bring industrial production in all sorts of different fields to levels which progressively left the European continent behind. In other words, the century of US economic supremacy has its roots in the last years of the nineteenth century.[6] At the other end of the spectrum, one could argue that it is in the early years of the twenty-first century that the USA has begun to lose its dominant position. In economic terms, according to the International Monetary Fund, in 2014 China began to overtake the USA as the country with the largest

Purchasing Power Parity (PPP).[7] Culturally, however, the process is far from having reached a tipping point. If nothing else, the English language (imposed by US President Woodrow Wilson as the language of diplomacy back in the aftermath of the First World War) is today even more pervasive than in the previous century. Within the confines of our study, it is also evident that the reciprocal influence of Italian and US culture is far from over. At the same time it is taking different shapes, with new waves of Italian migrants arriving in the USA with levels of education and skills which were unthinkable during most of the twentieth century. Equally, the global economy in which the USA as much as Italy has to operate is producing effects which, once again, seemed impossible only a couple of decades ago. A symbolic episode is the *de facto* acquisition of a giant of the US car industry, Chrysler, by the Turin-based firm FIAT, and the subsequent merger and 'globalization' of Fiat Chrysler Automobiles as a London-based corporation. Once again, it would be tempting to allow the political and economic discourse to be part of the conversation. As shall be mentioned in the concluding considerations of this Introduction, it is a dimension which might well be part of future studies stemming from this volume. However, within the linguistic and narrative confines of this book, a passing comment related to this episode can be made in relation to storytelling. A highly popular animation film produced by Pixar in 2006, *Cars*, contains an endearing narrative featuring anthropomorphic cars. The plot is entirely set in the most iconic of US settings, a fictional Monument Valley, and the characters display a variety of personalities associated with types of cars. In one case, two characters are explicitly associated with their migrant origin: they are Luigi and Guido, proud owners of a tyre shop, and comically presented in the humble shape of a yellow Fiat 500 and a small forklift. Only at the end of the film, the more glamorous side of the Italian car industry makes a brief cameo appearance when a Ferrari turns up (voiced by Michael Schumacher himself) to the irrepressible excitement of the two Italian migrants who end up fainting on the spot. One could suggest that what is at play here is a fairly old-fashioned representation of US society, with the Italian migrant playing a minor, comic role (it is a 'functional' use of the migrant as Giorgio Bertellini convincingly shows in his chapter). Very interestingly, when the sequel *Cars 2* came out in 2010, an Italian character played a much more central role, and this time it was not a migrant: Francesco Bernoulli (voiced by Italian American actor John Turturro) is an Italian Formula One champion who challenges the US hero of *Cars* to a world grand prix. The fact that the year before, in June 2009, Sergio Marchionne added to his role of Chief Executive Officer of FIAT that of CEO of the Chrysler Group (the major step which led to the merger in 2014) is an indication of a tell-tale coincidence (in the literal sense) between history and fiction which might inspire further insights.

Finally, the twentieth century is sometimes called 'the American century', and it is from there that we have borrowed the term for our title.[8] This, however, should also be complemented with a clarification. Throughout this book we have endeavoured to offer a homogeneous use of the abbreviation and acronyms used to define the United States of America. In particular, the adjective 'American' and the noun 'America' imply a degree of ambiguity since they can be equally used to define the wider concept and geographical reality of the two American continents. For this reason, unless it is imposed by specialist usage or, naturally, when part of a solidified expression — such as 'American Dream' — we have decided to propose uniformity and overall clarity with the adoption of two simple acronyms: 'USA' as a noun, and 'US' as an adjective. It goes without saying that there is also an ideological dimension behind this choice. The use of 'American' as referring strictly to the USA somehow imposes a hegemonic stamp on the expression. Since unambiguous and ideologically neutral expressions are at hand, we thought we should rely on them.

Fifteen Takes on Cultural Change

As already suggested, this collection of chapters explores the impact of cultural contact and human mobility on two countries which reciprocally influenced each other. It brings together a series of overviews and specific case studies of the relationship and exchanges — linguistic, literary and visual — between Italy and the USA, from the last years of the nineteenth century to the first two decades of the twenty-first. The cross-disciplinary and transnational approach brings it into a number of different directions but in other ways they all address the same question, namely, how and to what extent cultural contact can affect long-term historical change.

As far as language is concerned, several studies have suggested that Anglo-American influences increased during the second half of the twentieth century, but no book-length contribution exists that takes a detailed diachronic approach to this expansion: our volume focuses on a period which is long enough to study the gradual transformation of the Italian language as a whole, but also specific enough to assess the impact of contacts with English in particular varieties of the language, and in different communicative domains, socio-cultural milieus and historical contexts. Another understudied aspect of the contacts between Italian and English is the role of US English — in other words, the question of how and to what extent a distinction can be made between the influence of the USA and that of Britain and other English-speaking countries.[9] Addressing this question and weighing up US influences are indeed two of the aims of our volume.

With regard to literary and visual narratives, the radically different kind of contact between mass migration of Italians to the USA and the great influence of US culture in twentieth-century Italy comes to the fore. In the first case, a number of chapters tackle a range of issues related to the movement, preservation and transformation of Italy's national and regional heritage once Italian migrants settled and integrated in the USA. In the latter case, the challenge is to examine the channels through which US culture has been progressively perceived as a model — to adopt as much as to contrast with — in different fields, such as popular culture, literature, cinema, etc. Again, a diachronic approach allows for a better perception of the varying speeds with which different areas of culture reacted to this phenomenon. A fundamental issue which concerns language but has powerful wider implications with regard to the absorption of US culture concerns the field of education, that is the slow process through which English replaced French as the first foreign language of study.

The fifteen chapters are divided into four parts. In the first, 'Historical contexts and channels of contact', five chapters introduce the role of language, education, literature and film, and their importance for a discussion of cultural contact and change between Italy and the USA. The following three sections open up to a wide range of case studies. Parts II and III are divided into broadly defined chronological sub-periods: 'From the late nineteenth century to the Second World War' and 'From the Second World War to the twenty-first century'. The distinction between the two halves of the century is adopted not only because of the periodizing value of the Second World War in modern history at large, but also because of the widely recognized role of the war and its aftermath as a turning point for the Americanization of Italian society (which, in itself, has been the object of a considerable amount of scholarship in a number of disciplines).[10] The fourth and final part focuses on 'Long-term influences and effects', providing wider perspectives over the course of the twentieth century and in some case touching upon more recent, ongoing trends.

Our approach is not to group the chapters by discipline, but rather to order them chronologically and according to scope, to better allow a dialogue between topics, and provide a clearer picture of the processes of cultural contact that have been taking place. The volume also showcases new research — quantitative, interpretative and archival — which can illuminate basic questions of cultural contact in an original way and are inspiring beyond their disciplinary boundaries.

Part I opens with Matthew Reza's broad study of oral narrative culture in Italian migrant communities in the USA during the twentieth century. Drawing from a range of sources from the Eastern and North-Eastern States — New Jersey, New York State, Minnesota and Illinois — as well as the West Coast, and California, Reza's chapter addresses the question of the survival of Italian fairy and folk tales and the influence of written and non-Italian sources in the documented stories. Reza also focuses on changing generational attitudes to heritage through accounts of Americans learning about their Italian forebears through college assignments, all of which argues for a coexistence of literary, non-literary, oral and written cultures.

Virginia Pulcini's chapter addresses the attitudes towards the English language in twentieth-century and early twenty-first-century Italy. These linguistic attitudes have been influenced by different views on Anglo-American culture and lifestyles, ranging from a mixture of fascination and wariness at the beginning of the twentieth century, to overt political opposition during the Fascist regime, and finally to generally welcoming and favourable sentiments since the Second World War. Pulcini's overview focuses especially on the stances taken by lexicographers and linguists engaged in the compilation of Italian dictionaries and in the description of the state of the language vis-à-vis the substantial inflow of Anglicisms. Finally,

Pulcini considers recent debates on the adoption of English as a language of instruction in Italian universities, which have stirred new hostile feelings against the expanding role of English.

The following chapter, by Giancarlo Schirru, looks at the process through which Italy's educational system moved away from French as the traditional foreign language being taught in schools at all levels. Through a historical narrative supported by an original set of statistical data, Schirru shows the complex progress of English teaching in Italian schools during the twentieth century within the context of the national debate on language education and foreign-language teaching. Particular attention is paid to the development of lower secondary education and, overall, on how the political and intellectual debate influenced the particular field of educational policies. The chapter also shows how this influence reflected Italy's geopolitical position between the European and US spheres of influence.

The discussion then moves on to film studies with Giorgio Bertellini's stimulating overview of the ways in which US cinema portrayed Italy and Italians during the first half-century of its existence. The identification of four key moments, with the early representations in silent movies and Italian neorealist cinema at the two ends of the spectrum, provides a stimulating analysis of the ways in which the binary notion of Italians as either migrants in the USA or citizens in their homeland has evolved. Bertellini's original contribution lies in moving beyond the erudite, historical outline in order to offer an insight into continuities which somehow question received scholarly opinions. In particular, an issue such as the reception of Italian neorealist cinema in the USA, which one would take as uncontroversially settled, is revealed to be intricately attached to the wider discourse of US policies and a general tendency toward 'US-centric liberal compassion' in the early post-Second World War years.

The final chapter brings us into the twenty-first century, with Teresa Fiore's chapter that draws a distinction from the first phase of the migration of Italians to the USA, and considers the highly educated 'New Italians' of the new century. Fiore focuses closely on work by Elena Attala-Perazzini, Chiara Marchelli and Tiziana Rinaldi Castro, showing how their narratives resist easy categorization and labels by belonging both to Italian literature abroad and to American literature in Italian. Fiore's analysis goes beyond a simple binary approach of looking at the interactions of two cultures, and engages with the interplay of numerous cultures on the level of the individual. Fiore reveals the complexity bound up in the issue of the migration of New Italians, and the need for a plethora of labels to reflect the variety in their experiences, a plurality of identities for a nexus of numerous cultures, interactions and atypical migration experiences, all of which questions and reconsiders the traditional narratives of Italian migration to the USA.

Part II presents some specific cases related to the first half of the so-called long twentieth century. Luca Cottini looks at the impact of the first arrival of US culture on Italian soil through the itinerant show which the legendary Bill Cody, otherwise known as Buffalo Bill, took to Italy on a European Tour in 1890 and 1906. This is a cultural event which achieved the rare objective of impacting on both popular imagination and the Italian intelligentsia. The first is indicated by the sheer popularity of the show, thanks also to Bill Cody's sophisticated use of publicity and to his organizational skills which, it could be argued, were in themselves an example of the emergence of the USA as a great entrepreneurial superpower. At the same time, Cottini expands on the fertile influence of the *Wild West* show on the work of authors as different as Filippo Tommaso Marinetti, Emilio Salgari and the composer Giacomo Puccini.

With Guido Bonsaver's chapter on Turin in the early years of the century, the focus on the influence of US culture on Italy is maintained. However, in his analysis of the film and car industries in their early years, Bonsaver's chapter shows the extent to which, first of all, there was an early perception of the rising importance of the USA as a world-leading economy, and, secondly, that Italian entrepreneurs in both industries had no qualms in taking the fight to US soil. The rationale of pairing films and cars is carefully argued in the opening pages, and the parallel analysis produces a substantial study which proves the fruitfulness of comparing different ambits in order to understand dramatic shifts in national culture such as, in this case, the move from France to the USA as an influential foreign model.

Manuela di Franco's chapter focuses on the publishing industry in Italy and the case of *Omnibus*, a weekly cultural magazine founded by Leo Longanesi in 1937. Rather than departing from a stance of labelling *Omnibus* according to its alleged Fascist or anti-Fascist traits, di Franco instead analyses the ambivalent and contradictory nature of articles in *Omnibus* on the USA, and the heavy presence of US cultural products in the magazine. Di Franco highlights how Hollywood, in particular, is depicted both in its glitzy and aspirational appeal but also as a space of violence and greed which is used to ridicule US society. Despite this negative representation, di Franco argues that the sheer space dedicated to the USA in *Omnibus* responded to an undeniable fascination that the USA inspired in the minds of Italians.

Part III moves beyond the watershed marked by the Second World War. After Italy's liberation, the presence of US troops became an inevitable source of contact, which could and was interpreted in very different ways. Charles L. Leavitt IV's study examines one of the hot spots of these encounters, a US military encampment near Livorno in Tombolo. Drawing from Pratt, Leavitt argues that Tombolo serves as a 'cultural contact zone', as a space of enforced cross-cultural interaction between on the one hand the racial US and Italian regimes of Jim Crow and Fascism, and on the other the corresponding Civil Rights and Italian anti-Fascist movements. Leavitt furthers the discussion on the interactions between Italian and US cultures where he argues that the presence of African American soldiers at Tombolo had a profound impact on life in Italy and on the post-war African American experience in the USA, and which revises the *mito dell'America* for Italians as well as a *mito dell'Italia* for Blacks in the USA.

The second chapter of this section is the only one entering the territory of music history, folk music in this case. Rachel E. Love's study of the interaction between some leading figures in Italy's 'folk revival' of the 1960s argues that US popular culture provided a rich yet problematic source of inspiration for leftist musicians and intellectuals. After a discussion of the friendship between two key figures, Alan Lomax and Roberto Leydi, the chapter examines how various artists of the Italian folk revival — and in particular Giovanna Marini — adapted styles borrowed from American folk traditions to critique US politics and culture. Particular focus is given to how Marini's experiences at the Folkstudio influenced her musical style and fostered her growing disillusionment with US politics.

The section continues with Federico Faloppa's richly documented chapter on the fortunes and misfortunes of political correctness and the related expression *politically correct* (or *PC*) in both English and Italian. This chapter traces the history of the notion of political correctness from its origins in the international communist movement during 1920s to its use as part of the struggle against ethnic, sexual and social discrimination in the USA, and finally to its rejection by the political Right in the 1980s and 1990s. With the help of substantial textual evidence, Faloppa reconstructs the history of *political(ly) correct(ness)* in US English, as well as its adoption and adaptation in Italian (where it has given rise to *politicamente corretto*) and its perception by Italian speakers especially since the 1990s. As in other chapters on language, the outcomes of linguistic and cultural contact are analysed by Faloppa in connection with the work of lexicographers and other specialists; in his chapter, however, they are also linked to more general debates on the notion of political correctness in contemporary Italian society.

The final four chapters comprising Part IV deal with phenomena which are traced through a chronological trajectory which spans the entire 'American' century. Unsurprisingly three out of four of them concern the world of language history. As already suggested at the beginning, linguistic changes are often slower than in other walks of cultural production. Equally interesting, however, is Mattia Lento's study of the geographical and symbolic journey of the expression used to define the areas of a city in which Italians settled in large quantities: 'Little Italy'. Lento retraces the history of the term, first in the USA and then its emergence in Europe, and argues that this movement across the Atlantic plays a significant role in the valorization of the historical experience of Italian migration of the late nineteenth and twentieth centuries. Lento then explores in greater depth the case study of Little Italy in the Aussersihl quarter of Zurich, one of the most important European cities in the history of Italian migration. Through the medium of film, Lento analyses the interactions of Swiss and Italian cultures, and demonstrates the shift over time of the term 'Little Italy' from one with negative connotations to one with more positive associations, particularly stylishness.

In her chapter, Laura Pinnavaia describes the influence that the Italian language has had on the English language in Britain and in the USA. She does so by examining the number, type and semantic area of Italian borrowings attested in two important dictionaries, the *Oxford English Dictionary* for British English and the *Merriam-Webster* dictionary for US English. Pinnavaia's analysis shows that, since the 1900s, owing among other things to the strong presence of Italians in the USA, not only British English but also and possibly more so US English has become influenced by Italian, with numerous borrowings that refer to matters regarding scientific and cultural life, including the world of food. Pinnavaia's chapter complements other linguistic chapters which look at influences going in the opposite direction (i.e. from English to Italian). At the same time, it mirrors Fanfani's chapter, which immediately follows it, in that they both gather new evidence by focusing on contact between Italian and a particular variety of English — namely US English.

Finally, both Fanfani's and Carlucci's chapters add to the existing scholarship on the influence of the English language on Italian, which has so far focused almost exclusively on lexical influence. In his chapter, Massimo Fanfani does not deal with Anglicisms in general, but with words and expressions which have appeared in Italian under the specific influence of US English. Although it is not always possible to separate completely the linguistic influence of the USA from that of Britain and other English-speaking countries, Fanfani's move in this direction enables him to provide fresh and original insights into the spread of lexical Anglicisms — or, as he calls them in his chapter, of 'Americanisms'. He reconstructs the history of a significant number of words of US provenance and shows how their adoption by Italian speakers was linked to historical phenomena and events affecting various semantic fields (from the economy and work relationships, as in the case of *boss, business, contractor, trust* and so on, to politics and society, as exemplified by *abolizionismo* 'abolitionism' and *piattaforma* 'programme of a political movement').

Alessandro Carlucci's chapter moves beyond the lexicon by exploring how and to what extent Italian grammar is also changing under the influence of English. Drawing on recent discussions of linguistic contact and change, the chapter offers a definition of contact-influenced change, whereby internal development and contact with other languages are not seen as mutually exclusive factors but can in fact combine to lead to change — including changes in the frequency and productivity of an existing feature in the affected language. Through a combination of quantitative and qualitative analyses, this conception of change is applied to two features of Italian grammar. Special attention is paid to the role of translation as a source of contact-influenced change, with the inclusion within the analysed texts of both literary and non-literary translations from English.

An Open Conclusion

The complex nature of this book no doubt requires some final considerations on the areas — theoretical, methodological and discipline-specific — which have been explored and on the directions of further research that they might be signalling towards. There is a popular saying that sometimes one should 'throw away the map' and proceed following one's own instincts. This is far from what we might want to argue, but at the same time it is a fact that a map, any map, is the result of particular choice, that is, the adoption of a number of conventions — to the exclusion of others — through which the subject matter under scrutiny is examined and signified in a particular fashion. Since childhood, we all have been mesmerized by the different results of mapping planet Earth according to one or other cartographer's system.

Does this make all maps useless and *de facto* 'wrong'? Of course, the answer is not a simple yes or no. Similarly, in our case we have been trying to adhere to a number of conventions in order to suggest how the complexity of the question of cultural influence can be addressed in order to facilitate dialogue beyond disciplinary confines. Language, as we mentioned at the beginning of this introductory chapter, has been put at the centre for both conceptual and methodological reasons. It was one of many options; but we thought that, for our aim, it provided a solid ground and allowed us to build our working practice around it. The systematic use of data in linguistic studies has proved to be a sobering reminder of the need for a similar approach if our aim is to historicise and properly contextualize cultural events. At the same time, if language, narrative and history were our disciplinary points of reference, it is revealing to note the recurrence of two more areas of study which kept re-emerging and implicitly asking for an examination of their role in the process. We are referring to politics and economics. The relative role of the Italian American community in forging what we might want to call the collective cultural values of the USA — however imaginary and kaleidoscopic — is certainly linked to its political and economic weight in US public life. What links eleven unknown Sicilian immigrants lynched in Louisiana in 1891 to the rise of public Italian American figures such as those of Rudolph Valentino and Alphonse Capone in the 1920s and, later, the first generation of Italian American politicians spurred by the career of Fiorello La Guardia, and the first Italian American banker, Amadeo Giannini, whose Californian banking empire grew into the largest in the USA? It is the narrative of an immigrant community which generation after generation climbed up the social ladder of US society. Giannini founded his first bank in 1904 — called Bank of Italy — aiming to serve the local immigrant community. By 1930 he came to the conclusion that Bank of America was a better trading name, and his financial services helped the post-Depression recovery of the US film industry. If animation cinema was mentioned earlier, it is perhaps appropriate to remember that Giannini's Bank of America was behind what in 1937 was considered Hollywood's maddest film production to date: the creation of Walt Disney's first long animation film, *Snow White and the Seven Dwarfs*. The film simply made cultural history; and so, one should argue, did Amadeo Giannini.

Similar considerations can be made at the other end of the geographical span of this volume. The history of the reception and influence of US culture in Italy cannot be fully understood unless one addresses the political and economic issues which shaped the boundaries through which it developed. The mass-scale expansion of the culture industry in the twentieth century implied the escalation of the commercial revenues — and conflicts — attached to cultural production. This is easily shown if one thinks of specific markets such as the film industry. After the arrival of sound cinema, the European national industries could only rival US competition through protectionist policies and state funding. And this is equally true of more traditional, 'nobler' arts such as literature. Particularly during the Fascist period, the translation and diffusion of American literature was constrained by the regime's cultural policies. Shrewd publishers such as Arnoldo Mondadori were fully aware of the advantages linked to a close and friendly relationship with Benito Mussolini. Politics and economics were at the centre of Mondadori's considerations whenever he made a case for certain novels to be translated and published. He argued that translations should be published for two main reasons: in order prevent foreign publishers from benefitting from a ban (he would recurrently state that educated Italians would either read those novels in French translation, or some Swiss publishing house would enter the frame); and as a compensation for the nationalistic contribution of his publishing house to the publication of contemporary Italian authors (who, with rare exceptions, sold far fewer copies than the foreign authors he translated).

As for politics and economics in the post-Second World War years, it is simply impossible to reach an adequate understanding of the influence of US culture without taking into account the pervasive way in which the US administration took the initiative — and the US cultural industry followed suit — in shaping the new, republican Italy which rose from the ashes of the Fascist dictatorship. Cultural history, in other words, needs the help of experts in the political and economic fields. The multi-disciplinary boundaries of this volume do not extend as wide, but future initiatives of this kind should perhaps do so more systematically.

One other question to be addressed in this concluding section is the level of the overall contribution of this volume to the understanding of cultural change. As already said, the adoption of the USA/Italy case addresses two very different cases of cultural influence — that is, cultural change in the presence or absence of human mobility on a large scale. This in itself provides, we hope, a contribution to the debate, showing the complexity of the interaction and the many different factors at play. At the same time, no single chapter in this volume attempted a theorization of the differences between these two types of cultural influence. Linguistic studies are probably the most advanced in placing this distinction at the centre of their analyses and, indeed, the distinction is mentioned in some of the chapters penned by linguists. However, a fully-fledged theorization pertaining more widely to cultural history is still to come. It is not present here any more than it is present, to our knowledge, in the wider scholarly debate. This is another area in which we hope that this volume will provide useful case study material which, in the future, can be used as a source of inspiration for a theoretical discussion.

Finally, with reference to the position of this volume within the field of Italian American studies, our hope is that the clear parallel drawn here between the two sides of the USA/Italy cultural relations will alert all scholars in the field to the need of always keeping this perspective in the back of their mind. It goes without saying that in many instances, works on specific cases of cultural contact and change do not require this double-take to be methodologically present. This is what happens, after all, in many chapters in this volume too. However, we hope that readers will agree with the notion that the cultural history of Italians in the USA and that of Italian society during the long 'American' century are interconnected at so many different levels as to make their parallel study a welcome approach.

Notes to the Introduction

1. See Kate Crehan, *Gramsci, Culture and Anthropology* (London: Pluto Press, 2002) and Tullio de Mauro, 'Una certa concezione della cultura', in *Tornare a Gramsci. Una cultura per l'Italia*, ed. by Gaspare Polizzi (Rome: Avverbi, 2010), pp. 117–25.
2. Peter Burke, *What Is Cultural History?* (Cambridge: Polity, 2004). See also Anne Showstack Sassoon, 'Raymond Williams, Stuart Hall, Gramsci e noi', in *Gramsci, le culture e il mondo*, ed. by Giancarlo Schirru (Rome: Viella, 2009), pp. 73–87.
3. The obvious reference here is to Marie-Louise Pratt's *Imperial Eyes: Travel Writing and Transculturation* (London: Routledge, 1992).
4. Doreen Massey, *For Space* (London: SAGE Publications, 2005).
5. See Arturo Tosi, 'Languages in Contact with and without Speaker Interaction', in A. L. Lepschy and A. Tosi, eds, *Rethinking Languages in Contact* (Oxford: Legenda, 2006), pp. 160–72.
6. See for example Robert Rydell and Rob Kroes, *Buffalo Bill in Bologna: The Americanization of the World 1869–1922* (Chicago: University of Chicago Press, 2005); David Ellwood, *The Shock of America: Europe and the Challenge of the Century* (Oxford: Oxford University Press, 2012).
7. See the IMF World Economic Outlook Database, published in October 2014. <http://www.imf.org/external/pubs/ft/weo/2014/02/weodata/index.aspx> [last accessed 23 March 2018].
8. The expression, made famous by Henry Luce in his 1941 essay, has recently been adopted by historian Alfred McCoy in his book *In the Shadow of the American Century: The Rise and Decline of U.S. Global Power* (Chicago: Haymarket, 2017).
9. In literature on English as a global language, it is widely accepted that British English and US English are the two most prominent native varieties, because of their widely recognized role in political, economic and artistic life, as well as in language teaching. This role is confirmed — and at the same time further enhanced — by their prestigious tradition of grammatical and lexicographic codification.
10. See for example: Umberto Eco, Gian Paolo Ceserani and Beniamino Placido, *La riscoperta dell'America* (Bari: Laterza 1984); Victoria De Grazia, *Irresistible Empire: America's Advance through Twentieth Century Europe* (Cambridge, MA: Harvard University Press, 2006); David Ellwood, 'Containing Modernity, Domesticating America in Italy', in A. Stephan, ed., *The Americanization of Europe* (New York and Oxford: Berghahn, 2006), pp. 253–76; Antonio Cardini, ed., *Il miracolo economico italiano: 1958–1963* (Bologna: Il Mulino, 2007); Stefano Cavazza, Emanuela Scarpellini, eds, *La rivoluzione dei consumi. Società di massa e benessere in Europa 1945–2000* (Bologna: Il Mulino, 2010).

PART I

Historical Contexts and Channels of Contact

CHAPTER 1

Italian Storytelling Memories: Personal Recollections of Fairy and Folk Tales in the USA*

Matthew Reza

Introduction

In the latter part of the nineteenth century and the first half of the twentieth century, millions of Italians left Italy in search of a better life, many of whom crossed the Atlantic bound for the USA. This chapter will focus on how the oral tradition of telling stories — namely fairy and folk tales — that came across to the new world can be traced and their survival or disappearance over the course of the twentieth century analysed.[1] The following questions bear consideration: do first-generation Italian migrants to the USA tell their children or each other fairy and folk tales and other oral narratives? Does the second generation pass on its cultural knowledge, either in dialect, regional Italian or English, or does the process stop? Do third-generation Italian Americans — or, more accurately, Americans with Italian heritage — maintain a tradition or indeed recall their family stories?

Underpinning such avenues of inquiry is the fact that in Italy storytelling in rural communities was a ubiquitous practice until midway through the twentieth century,[2] and the question of what happens to the stories that migrants bring with them starts with the recognition that they heard and learnt such tales in a community setting in Italy. The question of the trajectory of tales in the USA is therefore bound up with the question of the changing nature of Italian and Italian American circumstance and identity, but to consider such identities as unified is simplistic and rejects the arguments for a plurality of Italian identities from all over Italy.

This chapter will discuss some of the fates that befall fairy and folk tales in the case of a number of Italians and Italian Americans, and through a variety of recorded formats, such as autobiographies, family histories, and interviews (not my

---

* I would like to thank the John Fell Fund of the University of Oxford, thanks to whose funding this chapter was made possible. I would also like to thank the staff at the Immigration History Research Center Archives at the University of Minnesota, the Walter P. Reuther Library, Wayne State University, and Princeton University Library, for their invaluable help.

own). Materials from Italians and Italian Americans come from the Eastern and North-Eastern States — New Jersey, New York State, Minnesota, and Illinois — as well as the West Coast, and California. The terms folk tale and fairy tale are sometimes used interchangeably, but one way to distinguish the two is through the use of magic: the former usually without magic, the latter with. For my purposes here, I am not drawing a particular distinction between the two. Rather, I am more concerned with how either or both feature in the life of the Italian or Italian American, also given the scarcity of references, which in turn fall into three main categories. Firstly, there are passing references to storytelling practices or stories told many years ago recalled in either positive or negative terms. This category predominantly serves to confirm whether storytelling takes place, but rarely indicates more than that. Secondly, there are recollections of the content of stories, the odd detail, perhaps a title, which shows a more in-depth recall. Many of the examples here bear this level of detail. Occasionally, however, there are instances of the third category: the entire story is recalled and retold.

The question of literacy plays an important role in this study as does the primary use of English in nearly all the sources. In the accounts that follow, the second- or third-generation migrants often recall illiterate parents and grandparents while they have themselves been to school in the USA and learnt English. Some cases demonstrate a high level of literacy, which is relevant for a number of reasons. Firstly, it brings into focus the question of education, and secondly, in some cases it disrupts the process of oral transmission of older generations handing down and telling stories to a younger one because of the addition of literary and written sources.

This chapter is divided into two sections. In the first, I look at recollections from second-generation migrants who remember their parents and in some cases grandparents. In the second, I look at the case of Americans learning about their Italian heritage through the lens of a college assignment. I will proceed broadly speaking chronologically, not by date of birth but by approximate date when the stories were told over the course of the century, from the first years to the final decades of the twentieth century, and on a case by case basis, each of which features varied family, personal and linguistic circumstances.

C'era una volta?

In his short autobiography, published in English, Joseph Fucilla — who would go on be a university professor and an early editor of *Italica*[3] — begins by tracing his family roots. He presumes that his grandfather (b. c. 1840), an elementary school-teacher in Cosenza, was middle-class, otherwise he would never have been able to enjoy his years of schooling, when, as Fucilla notes, illiteracy rates were high. Fucilla's father Giovanni (b. 1871, La Motte) was trained as a shoemaker,[4] but worked on the railroads in New York State after he arrived in 1892 (a common job for Italian immigrant workers), then worked in a stone quarry in Chicago. Joseph himself, born in Chicago, is sent to school, and in his words, 'I was a good student and a voracious reader not only devouring all the books I was allowed to withdraw from the school library, but also those I was allowed to take out of the public library at any one time'.[5]

> But perhaps the most important event during my grade-school days was my learning Italian. On cold winter evenings my father used to read aloud semi-popular stories such as the *Paladini di Francia*, *I Cavalieri della Tavola Rotonda* and *Guerino detto il Meschino* [. . .]. He read principally for the benefit of my mother, my older sister and myself. The other children were too young or did not understand Italian (Tuscan) well enough to be interested. Instead of sitting down to listen, I used to stand behind him as he sat with his legs in the open oven of our kitchen stove and watched him read. Before the first winter was over I asked him to allow me to do the family reading. He reluctantly consented, and on finding that I did reasonably well surrendered the task to me, which I continued for the two or three ensuing winters.[6]

Fucilla's literacy, within the immediate context of his family history, is perhaps not all that surprising. What is noteworthy is that storytelling here draws from a written not oral source (stories of the Paladini, for example), and that after practising his Italian, he is rewarded with being a reader or storyteller at home.[7] However, it is in a footnote about his grandmother early on that a fairy and folk tale reference can be found:

> I might mention here that grandmother Maria Francesca was a most lovable old lady, everybody's friend. Though illiterate she had an amazingly retentive memory. She knew scores of popular folk tales by heart, and, in retelling them, had the uncanny ability of dramatizing their action giving the tales life and appeal. We grandchildren so enjoyed them that we used to ask her to tell them again and again. She never failed to oblige.[8]

Fucilla makes no further mention of his grandmother, but her illiteracy and fast recall from a repository of tales learnt by heart is in keeping with the habits of Italians in the late nineteenth and early twentieth centuries.[9]

The question of the interplay between literacy and illiteracy also emerges in the account of the life of Anna Maria Beraducci, born in Petarano, Italy, in 1906 to parents Ferdinando and Francesca, and who emigrated from L'Aquila in 1908 to Chisholm, Minnesota. Her father Ferdinando was a coal worker (both a transporter and then later a miner) and the family goes back and forth from the USA a number of times before settling in 1920 after the end of the First World War. Anna recounts how her father used to draw on her reading skills to provide him with storytelling inspiration:

> he used to tell stories and you just sit around him, you know, and he used to tell all kind a stories of, you know. . . I used to get books, you know. So he said, 'Tell me — read me that book,' because he couldn't read. Well, he didn't had a chance to go to school there. So he says, it was all for Italian, you know, he say, 'Read me a book,' he says, 'I want to see, read that story in that book.' So I read to him. I started to finish, you know, if I don't finish one night, next night, he says, 'Come on, Annie,' he says, 'you start again,' and where I left off, you know. Okay, after I get done with that book he called all of us, then he says, 'Now I'm gonna tell you that story that your sister read in that book.'

> And he used to start from the beginning to the end without a missing a word (as transcribed).[10]

When asked about the type of story and language, Anna replies, 'Oh, you know, fairy tale story, you know [. . .] All in Italian.'[11] At the time Anna says that she must have been between ten and twelve years old,[12] and that she was more linguistically capable with Italian than with English. Moreover, her father, clearly an accomplished storyteller, demonstrates his skill by drawing on published work — even if they were fairy tales — rather than from any oral narratives from his own past or personal Italian heritage. In other words, this is no longer a case of orally transmitted folklore, but of reformulating a literary transcription of tales, in a manner which mirrors Fucilla's grandmother in that she too is illiterate with a highly retentive memory.

Still in the 1920s but further east, Baladino Ferrara, a second-generation Italian American born in 1909 in Rocky Hill, New Jersey, provides details of more 'traditional' (read: old world) storytelling memories. His father Antonio first went to the USA in 1905, and worked as a labourer in a quarry and on the railways. His mother Carmela remained in Montefalcone until she joined them. After detailing how the family moved a few times, and the occasional school anecdote, Baladino (or Bill as he introduces himself and indeed as the title of his memoir states, 'Just call me Bill') discusses cold winters evenings when he was a child, probably around the early 1920s.

> In the summer time we could always find plenty to do. Winters were tougher. Evenings, Mom and Pop would get us together in the parlor and tell us stories. [. . .] Mom often told us the story of Sister Fox and Brother Wolf. She would sit in the dim light of the oil lamp, flickering shadows and light playing across her face. Sometimes she nursed a cup of coffee as she talked.[13] Sometimes she would sit quietly, her hands folded in her lap. She would give a little laugh and her eyes would crinkle at the corners, then she would begin. 'A una volte un Volpe,' [sic] At one time a Fox. . .[14]

It is worth mentioning a few points before giving details of the actual stories. Firstly, nearly a quarter of the memoir is dedicated to transcribing the tales Bill heard as a boy, suggesting the importance that these stories hold for Bill as a part of his family memory and his upbringing; secondly, there is barely any indication of the Italian language. Even in episodes when Italian women meet Bill's Italian mother,[15] their interactions are recorded in English apart from the odd key phrase. While all the stories appear in English, the rhythmic beginning to the first animal story — 'A una volte un Volpe' [sic] — suggests that Bill heard the stories in Italian, which he recalled and wrote down many years later in English, the language with which Bill feels most at ease.

The first is an animal tale about two enemies — Brother Wolf and Sister Fox — who steal cheese. The Wolf is caught and beaten because he eats too much, whereas the Fox eats enough so that she can also escape. Sister Fox then puts some cheese on her head to feign injury, and Brother Wolf carries her. When they visit the king of the animals, both try to denounce the other. The fox is successful when the king kills the wolf and wears the wolf hide to cure his fever.[16] As Caprettini makes clear, not only is this a common plot of wolf stories, but also many aspects have differing regional variations. 'La più vasta gamma di aneddoti riguardanti il lupo è senza dubbio quella costituita dagli episodi che vedono questo animale alle prese con i brutti tiri giocatigli dalla volpe' [The widest range of anecdotes that deal with the wolf concern without doubt episodes that portray this animal struggling against the fox's horrible tricks].[17] The first part of the story adheres to Aarne-Thompson category 41, 'The Wolf Overeats in the Cellar', which has variants in Friuli, Molise and Tuscany. The next part of Bill's story, where 'La volpe, che è riuscita a sfuggire alle bastonate che invece hanno colpito il lupo, si finge ferita e si fa portare in groppa dal lupo' [The fox, who has been able to escape the beating which instead the wolf receives, pretends to be wounded and get the wolf to carry it on its back] has Campana and Tuscany variants. Finally, with variants from Campana, Calabria and Basilicata, and Tuscany, the wolf's downfall: 'La volpe inganna il lupo credulone e gli fa compiere azioni che lo danneggiano a volte fino alla morte' [The fox deceives the gullible wolf and makes it carry out tasks that harm it, which sometimes results in death].[18] The widespread nature of this tale (it is also a Grimm story entitled 'Der Wolf und der Fuchs' [The Wolf and the Fox]) shows that Carmela, Bill's mother, retells the story across the Atlantic with little divergence from its common variants back in Italy.[19]

The second story, which Antonio the father — 'Pop' — used to enjoy telling, is about a man who wishes to return home after seeking his fortune. His employer gives him some advice: not to leave the old road for the new road; whatever he sees and hears, he should keep to himself; and to make sure he is right before he makes any kind of move. He gives his employee a pizza and cautions him not to open it until there are three happy hearts. On his journey, the man does not stray from the road and so avoids robbers, and when he sees his wife sitting with a priest, he first asks around in the village only to discover it is her (and therefore his) son. When they are reunited as three happy hearts, they break apart the pizza and gold coins come out.[20]

Third, a tale often told by a John Cordisco (perhaps a family friend), talks of a family celebrating the daughter's engagement. The daughter goes to the cellar to get some wine and sees a loose brick above a barrel that she fears will fall and kill her future son Diazeel. The mother and then the father come down and wring their hands at the terrible fate of their as-of-yet-unborn grandson. The fiancé comes down and after such a fuss, pulls out the brick and throws it in the yard.[21]

The last two stories are tales which resonate with Bill Ferrara's own history or any Italian family. Certainly 'the three hearts' could be the story of any returning Italian migrant after a period of work in the USA, and indeed contains the same structure and tripartite advice (AT 910b) as a tale by James Mancina, an immigrant from Calabria in 1911.[22] It also features in Italo Calvino's anthology as 'I consigli di Salomone'.[23] The measured response and repression of a quick temper lead the worker to a happy reunion with his wife and the son he did not see grow up, as well as a financial reward. The distress over the threat towards an unborn son which can easily be resolved is clearly intended for comic purposes, and variations of this story appear recorded elsewhere by Italian Americans.[24]

Family dynamics underpin the accounts of storytelling, and Jerre Mangione's famous work *Mount Allegro* (1942) is no exception. Born in 1909, Mangione chronicles events, traditions and conflicts within his extended Sicilian family in Rochester, New York. There are numerous examples of the practice of storytelling, but two in particular stand out. Firstly, early on, in describing Donna Maricchia who is nearly entirely deaf, Mangione writes, 'Joe and I, under the recent influence of some of Grimm's grimmer fairy tales, called her the Witch, and she figured in some of our more remarkable nightmares.'[25] This passing reference does not reveal whether these Grimm tales are read out loud or read from a book, by whom and when, but it demonstrates an engagement with non-Italian literary culture.[26] There is, moreover, a storytelling tradition within the family, the most elaborate example of which, Mangione relates, is a story told by his uncle Nino. The tale opens with Baron Albertini, who decides to take a weaver's daughter, Annichia, as his bride. Her widowed mother, however, insists on her being educated at the Baron's expense. He accepts and they marry. The Baron's rich friend Benito looks down upon her, and wagers the Baron that he can prove her unfaithfulness. When the Baron is away in Palermo for business, Benito attempts to seduce Annichia, but he is outsmarted and finds himself instead locked up and forced to spin wool for his food. A week later, Antonio Luppo, a friend of Benito's, who knows about the wager, decides to prove Annichia unfaithful, but he also ends up in Benito's prison spinning wool. Finally, the Notary tries his luck and is also outsmarted. When the Baron returns, Benito pays out, the three are set free, but Annichia makes sure the whole town knows. The humiliation drives the three out of town and the Baron and Annichia live happily ever after.[27]

There are numerous fairy tale motifs here: the testing of virtue, the three tempters (one of whom bears the allusive animalistic name Luppo, albeit with a double *p*), the punishment — to spin yarn for their food — and the happy ending, but more than that, the morals. As Gans notes in the introduction to *Mount Allegro*, the tale 'not only demonstrates that peasants are smarter than noblemen, but also justifies upward mobility as long as the status-seeker has the strength of character to retain peasant values'.[28] To put the tale in the terms of the migrant experience, seeking one's fortune is acceptable if old-world values are retained, yet these are values that are necessarily challenged in *Mount Allegro* when immigrants are gradually scattered and integrate into US life far afield although always with an albeit dwindling connection back to Rochester.[29]

With similarly traditional fairy tale motifs, Joan Stefano, a teacher, recalls her childhood and the stories her father told her. Joan was born in 1935 in Crosby, Minnesota, to an Italian father Pietro (born 1893 in Savelli, Calabria) who came to the USA when he was twelve years old, around 1905, and worked as a miner in Minnesota; and a second-generation Croatian mother Anna (born 1909 in Copper, Michigan). When asked about stories, Joan replies,

He told many, many stories. When we were children he used to put us up on his lap and he would tell stories about kings and queens and he always ended, *'and they stayed there and I came over here'*.[30]

She continues,

they were usually about royalty and my memory is not very good and all I can remember [is] that it wasn't so much what he said but how he said it and he was so expressive. I don't think they were old Italian folk tales, I think they may have been stories maybe that his parents, his mother told him and his grandpa, and that he just told us. But what impressed me the most was that he always ended it the same way, *'They stayed there and I came over here'*.[31]

When pressed on the significance of this personalized finish, Anna suggests a sense of nostalgia, and of the memories of missing what was left behind after leaving for the USA at the age of twelve.[32] However, there is more to garner from this linguistic inflection: Pietro's language constrains and delimits the tales of kings and queens to an old world across the Atlantic. While Pietro might well draw from his memories of stories passed down from his family, he reminds his children of the separation between his life now in the USA and what he left behind, not only in terms of the story but also in terms of language: as Joan recalls, Pietro did not speak in Italian at home except when he was angry.[33] The new common language of English reinforces the new life away from the old world with its echoes of monarchy. Moreover, by leaving the kings and queens behind, Pietro inserts himself as the brave adventurer in the stories, crossing the Atlantic on a quest for a new life.

While the focus here is broadly on storytelling as a participatory practice, there is another associated consideration: bedtime stories and bedtime reading. Virginia and Elios Anderlini, an Italian American couple who lived in Telegraph Hill, San Francisco, explain how they did not have a bedtime story environment around the early 1920s. Virginia (b. 1913, San Francisco) and Elios (known as Andy, b. 1908, Kansas) both with parents from Italy, show their different families' responses.

Virginia remembers how her family 'still had that immigrant mentality to work to help the family', meaning that education was minimal, including those of her parents: 'We didn't have bedtime stories because our parents didn't read to us. They couldn't read English, and they never told us bedtime stories, never. I don't even remember books.'[34] With hindsight, Virginia expresses regret that she did not ask lots of questions about stories from Italy, but she posits an explanation why such stories never came up: 'they didn't have very happy memories of Italy. Like my mother in the north, they were starving most of the time. And they couldn't wait to get out of there once they had the opportunity to come here.'[35] Andy also shows that English and schooling created a barrier.

They [it is assumed in reference to his parents] spoke Italian at home. And the education was strictly the school. [. . .] They had an Italian tradition, but we were in school in English so there was no storytelling at bedtime.[36]

While Andy also admits his own lack of interest in the old country, in contrast to Virginia — 'It's too bad we didn't ask a lot of questions'[37] — he provides the second-generation perspective: 'They didn't volunteer anything and we weren't curious about it. *This* was our country'.[38] Old world stories did not play a role in Andy's life because he considered himself more closely related to the USA than to Italy, and in the cases of Virginia and Andy, literacy in English creates a barrier to storytelling. In later decades, a further obstacle would undermine storytelling. From his (by no means unique) perspective Mangione additionally argues that there is a change to tale-telling from the 1950s onwards due in part to the frequency with which a television features in the home. 'The storytelling sessions had virtually disappeared, either because they had run out of stories or, more likely, because television by then had reared its voracious head and seemingly swallowed their tongues.'[39]

Reclaiming and documenting a tradition

Between 1961 and 1976 Catherine Ainsworth collected tales and stories from young Italian Americans in the New York area, the majority of whom were aged between eighteen and nineteen years old, and who spoke to their parents or grandparents about their Italian heritage. The tales range in source — a family story, a tale handed down through the generations, a personal experience narrative,[40] a legend that dates back a few centuries — and date heard (one of the first stories of the collection (not chronologically), for example, is entitled *The Little Devil*, recorded in 1970, and was first heard when the informant, a Frank Fasso of Niagara, New York, was around ten in the early 1960s. All are written in English, and Ainsworth makes the following observation:

> The present-day tellers of oral tales are no longer illiterate, but many good purveyors of folktales in the past have been far from illiterate, also. They illustrate well the existence in the United States of an oral tradition, sublimated it is true, alongside a rather highly literate one. Folklore in the oral tradition must have, along the long road from its pre-literate beginnings, coexisted and survived and been propagated by a folk that could, in the main, also read and write.[41]

The coexistence of a literate tradition alongside an oral tradition is a salient point to raise because it recognizes a transition from an illiterate generation to a literate one, not a mutual exclusivity, and acknowledges English as the medium that translates, both literally and figuratively, as it 'carries across' an oral tradition from Italy to the United States of America from dialect or regional Italian into English. It also legitimates the position of literate storytellers who emerge from a predominantly illiterate Italian context (such as Joseph Fucilla's father or Anna Beraducci). Moreover, while tracing a solely oral tradition is inherently flawed due to the passing of time and tellers, literacy allows for written fairy tales to enter the discussion, not necessarily as folklore *sensu strictu*, but as a record of stories told in the family.

Within a college context, for an assignment in 1975, Marina Amici interviewed her Italian relatives from Montegiadino [sic], San Marino. Together with recalling a few animal fables after an admittedly leading question — 'Nona, do you know any Cinderella stories or any fairy tales that your nona taught you?' — Marina's grandmother Stefania Carloni (b. c.1902, Montegiadino) also remembers the famous tale:

> There is a story about 'Cenenertola' [sic] that I remember. It's about a prince whose wife died and left him a daughter named Zezolla. The prince remarried and during the ceremony a dove flew in and talked to Zezolla. The dove told her if she was unhappy, he would grant her a wish through the magic date tree.
>
> One day the King gave a great ball. Everyone was invited except Zezolla, who was now called Cenenertola because she worked in the kitchen trying to please her six stepsisters.[42]

The summary continues for another paragraph, but in short reveals a very close match to Giambattista Basile's 1634 *Cenerentola*, that is, a written version of an oral fairy tale, which at first glance might problematize the legitimacy of an oral tradition. However, Lavinio posits an explanation:

> La fiaba può essere considerata un genere che permette di affrontare in maniera esemplare il problema della circolazione culturale delle forme letterarie dall'oralità alla scrittura e, viceversa, dalla scrittura all'oralità. All'origine di molte novelle — e quindi di testi scritti — della nostra tradizione letteraria si sono individuati motivi e tempi tipici della tradizione orale (si pensi per esempio al *Novellino* o al *Decameron*); ma, viceversa, molti racconti orali e popolari possono avere avuto origine da una fonte scritta, introdotta solo in un secondo tempo nel circuito orale e popolare.
>
> [The fairy tale can be considered a genre that allows us in an exemplary way to grapple with the problem of the cultural circulation of literary forms from orality to writing, and vice versa, from writing to orality. At the root of many tales — and thus of written texts — of our literary tradition, motifs and eras typical of the oral tradition have been singled out (think for example of the *Tuscan Novellas* or the *Decameron*); but, vice versa, many oral and popular stories could have originated from a written source, introduced only a second time around into oral and popular circulation.][43]

While there is no further information in Stefania's account, Lavinio's model of interplay between oral and written cultures suggests how Basile's version features as part of Stefania's family memory, where the written version is introduced into the family storytelling, something which Beraducci's father (above) likewise does explicitly. Moreover, Lavinio suggests how Judith Cassai (b. 1907, Highwood, Illinois, whose family came to the USA in 1904[44]), in her account of stories from her childhood, could hint at non-Italian and published sources of stories, spoken in Italian by her parents or uncle.

> I: What kinds of stories would they tell?
> N: Well, it was in Italian. [. . .] They got to learn English, you know, as time went on. They didn't have no schooling. They hardly had any schooling in Italy. [. . .].
> I: Do you remember what the stories were about that they would tell?
> N: Oh, about a little, white duck and the wolf comes. . . something like that. . . something like a Little Red Riding Hood. . . something like that.[45]

Judith Cassai's frequent use of simile ('something like') is on the one hand used rhetorically as filler, but on the other, also suggests that she does not recall Little Red Riding Hood precisely, but rather similar fairy tales: 'Little Red Riding Hood' is a synecdoche that stands for a vague memory of non-specific tales. Alternatively, over a long period of time — and the interview date of 1980 is approximately sixty years after the childhood moment in question — her recollection of the actual fairy tales has perhaps been subsumed under the more popular fairy tales that she heard since then, perhaps a Grimm or Perrault version of Little Red Riding Hood. Caprettini points out that an Italian version favours animal–animal rather than animal–human fables, '[i]l lupo delle nostre fiabe preferisce stare con gli animali più che misurarsi con gli uomini' [the wolf of our fairy tales prefers to be with animals more than pit itself against humans],[46] as in the above example of Brother Wolf and Sister Fox. On the other hand, Aprile documents numerous cases of the 'fanciulla e il lupo (o l'orco)' [girl and wolf (or bogeyman)] story in Italy (AT 333).[47] In other words, it is unclear whether Cassai is recalling an Italian version, or non-Italian version, and it is moreover ambiguous whether or not, in accordance with Lavinio's argument, Cassai encounters this tale though a published version that documents an originally oral source.

In another student paper submitted in 1977, William Marinelli interviews his maternal grandmother Elvira Tiani (b. c. 1902, Setti Fratti) for reasons of personal interest and to learn about his family history. William acknowledges the linguistic difficulty in both understanding and transcribing the tales, 'I do not understand this dialect [of Monte Cassino] and the informant has only a fair ability in English; therefore she and I had to work together and translate this folklore.'[48] This, together with the infrequency with which he has heard these stories ('I have always had an interest in the stories she occasionally told me as I grew up'),[49] suggests a process on his part of reclaiming a tradition of oral narratives through translation rather than being the bearer of a tradition handed down. Indeed, he readily acknowledges that he will learn more about his heritage through documenting it from the perspective of a college assignment:

> Since I have been so busy lately and have not had much time to visit with my grandmother, this was a beautiful opportunity to spend time with her, help her recall her earlier years, and *thereby learn more about my own particular heritage.*[50]

In the preface to her own investigation for a student paper carried out in 1974 Deborah LaFrate (perhaps erroneously) suggests that 'One would have expected to find that in these groups, tales or anecdotes which had been passed down through generations and would continue to flow into future ones.'[51] Her sources provide personal narratives, sketches of stories heard, and superstitions, but she has to coax them out for the purposes of preservation. All of LaFrate's informants are (all being in their forties and fifties) second-generation Italian Americans, whose heritage did not appear to include folk tales in any significant way. They recall tales but not in the same profuse manner of William Marinelli's grandmother. LaFrate notes:

> I find it difficult to believe that the people interviewed did not recall any folktales. I felt that they knew many stories originating from their people, but

for some reason did not feel comfortable relating them to me. The few folktales I did hear were not told in story form.[52]

Her exasperation might be warranted given that she recalls having heard stories at past gatherings, but one of her informants, a Josephine Jeane Pacelli LaLama, hints at a possible explanation for the silence of LaFrate's other informants when she 'seemed some what [sic] ashamed to talk of her ethnic background. She stressed the difference between true Italians and Italian Americans.'[53] For reasons ranging from apprehension, to shame in showing such links to the old world, to undoubted lapses in memory, collecting tales as a college assignment provides obstacles, even when framed as an exercise in family and cultural preservation.

Conclusions

These examples of fairy and folk tales come from a variety of records, and not all Italians and Italian Americans share the same sense of preserving old-world culture. Some reject the practice, and indeed, out of many collections of Italian American folklore, fairy tales feature very rarely when compared to other considerations such as foodways, language, family dynamics, work, marriage, and death. Beyond the record of a fairy tale in a family, interviewees provide little to suggest that it is actively passed down. Perhaps for reasons of simply failing to raise the issue, interview respondents and authors mention their own upbringing but neglect mentioning if they in turn told their own children stories from the old country. What the later studies such as those by LaFrate, Marinelli and Ainsworth suggest is that by the third generation — Americans with Italian heritage — fairy tales do not play a role in family upbringing or in contributing to forming an identity (or at least it has an ephemeral and elusive character); rather, participants express an interest in reconnecting with their lost heritage. They are no longer the bearers of a tradition but learn about it with a more objective focus through cataloguing tales as part of a university assignment. Yet this disconnection from the original tale is also true of some second-generation Italian Americans as in the case of the Anderlinis. In examples from the earlier part of the twentieth century, such as Joseph Fucilla and Anna Beraducci, the fairy tale tradition is already being modified by the literacy of a younger generation. As Gardaphé notes,

> In less than three generations, Italian Americans have assimilated so rapidly and so well into the American way that they have become strangers, not only to contemporary Italians, but strangers unto themselves [. . .]. In terms of processes, the stories of our past, especially when told by our elders, has been the major vehicle by which our heritage is transmitted from generation to generation. But this process became endangered when Italians migrated to America. Loss of shared primary languages, lack of shared environments (as children leave not only their homes, but the neighborhoods and often the states of their upbringing), contributed to the distortion of our heritage. When our families relinquished the task of storytelling to radio, television and film, the inside stories remained locked away and only the outside stories were accessible.[54]

From the beginning of the century, literacy features in the upbringing of second-generation Italian Americans, in either Italian, regional Italian, or English, which results in a trait shared across many of the examples above: a coexistence of written and oral cultures, where the first parent generation retells the folk tales of their communities back in Italy, while the second generation reads new material, and even informs the storytelling practices of the family. This disrupts a neat handing down of stories from one generation to another, and rather suggests a more complex discourse of stories between family members, not a simple top-down approach. This is not, however, to deny a strong sense of hierarchy present in other sources where the mother and father, or grandparents, dutifully tell stories to children.

Together with literacy, the common factor in all of these sources is the presence of English. In some cases, the interviewer is a native speaker of English and so Italian culture has to be mediated through English; in others, the Italian American feels more comfortable in English. Even if the original source material is in dialect or standard or regional Italian, English is used to recover the tales, which means they are more readily accessible to the Anglophone environment which encloses such Italian culture in the USA. English in fact proves to be the medium to preserve an Italian fairy and folk tale tradition as shown in Bill Ferrara's case or in the case of the student assignments by LaFrate and Marinelli together with all of Ainsworth's collected stories. Indeed Anthony Navarra questions the importance of telling stories in their original Sicilian (in his case): 'Let them be told in our glorious English tongue. The tellers pass on and the tongues change, but the tales remain.'[55] This is not to undermine the validity of the material, but simply to note that education (read: literacy) and the English language, rather than replace the fairy and folk tale, records it, and allows a tradition to survive, but in a fundamentally changed state: no longer as family lore but in a written form available more widely in a different language. Not only is the fairy tale 'carried across' the Atlantic, but it is translated both into English and onto the written page.

Notes to Chapter 1

1. For previous work on the Italian fairy tale in the USA, see Carla Bianco, *The Two Rosetos* (Bloomington: Indiana University Press, 1974); Frances M. Malpezzi and William M. Clements, 'Stories and Storytelling', in *Italian-American Folklore* (Little Rock: August House, 1992), pp. 163–97; Elizabeth Mathias and Richard Raspa, *Italian Folktales in America: The Verbal Art of an Immigrant Woman* (Detroit: Wayne State University Press, 1985). Smaller collections of tales appear in: Rosemary Agonito, 'Il Paisano: Italian Immigrant Folktales of Central New York', *New York Folklore Quarterly*, 23 (1967), 52–64; Violet Forchi, 'Folktales: 4. Fortune', *West Virginia Folklore*, 5 (Spring 1955), 49–59; Alexander Garofalo, 'The Oven of the Seven Montelli', *New York Folklore Quarterly*, 2 (1946), 273–75; Dan G. Hoffman, 'Stregas, Ghosts, and Werewolves', *New York Folklore Quarterly*, 3 (1947), 325–28; M. Jagendorf, 'Italian Tales in New York City', *New York Folklore Quarterly*, 11 (1955), 177–82; Louis C. Jones, 'Italian Werewolves', *New York Folklore Quarterly*, 6 (1950), 133–38; Melia Rose Maiolo, 'Italian Tales Told in Shinnston', *West Virginia Folklore*, 8 (1957), 8–12; Ruth Ann Musick, 'European Folktales in West Virginia', *Midwest Folklore*, 6 (1956), 27–37; idem, 'Tales Told by Mr Rocco Pantalone of Fairmont', *West Virginia Folklore*, 11 (1960), 2–16; Lydia Pietropaoli, 'Folklore from the Heart of Italy, Part I', *New York Folklore Quarterly*, 19 (1963), 163–82; idem, 'Folklore from the Heart of Italy, Part II',

New York Folklore Quarterly, 19 (1963), 283–95; Leonard Roberts, 'Folktales from the Italian Alps', *Tennessee Folklore Society Bulletin*, 12 (1956), 99–108; idem, 'More Folktales from the Italian Alps', *Tennessee Folklore Society Bulletin*, 13 (1957), 95–104; Sylvia Trop, 'An Italian Rip Van Winkle', *New York Folklore Quarterly*, 1 (1945), 101–05.

2. Giuseppe Gatto, *La fiaba di tradizione orale* (Milano: LED, 2006), p. 33.
3. Joseph G. Fucilla, *My Autobiography*, The Joseph Fucilla Papers, Immigration History Research Center Archives, University of Minnesota, p. 35.
4. Ibid., p. 2.
5. Ibid., p. 4.
6. Ibid., pp. 6–7.
7. Fucilla is not the only Italian migrant to reference the *Paladini di Francia*. Another Italian, Dominic Crea, born in 1910 in Malia, Calabria, mentions his father telling him stories from the *Palladini di Franchi* [sic] when Dominic was between ten and twelve years old (in the early 1920s): 'he'd read 'em and then tell us kids the story'. Crea also notes that his father's literacy was a rare occurrence in Calabria (Dominic Crea Interview, interviewed by Mary Ellen Mancina-Batinich, The Mary Ellen Mancina Batinich Papers, Immigration History Research Center Archives, University of Minnesota, Box 31, pp. 10–12). Anthony Navarra also recalls that his grandfather's favourite stories were from the Carolingian cycle, and mentions the Duke of Mayence and Roland (Anthony Navarra, 'Old Tales and New Tongues', *New York Folklore Quarterly*, 18 (1962), 12–15 (p. 13)).
8. Fucilla, *My Autobiography*, p. 3.
9. 'Most of the Italians who immigrated to America between 1880 and 1920 came from a peasant culture based on oral traditions. Books were not among the possessions they carried along in the move to America' (Fred L. Gardaphé, *Italian Signs, American Streets: The Evolution of Italian American Narrative* (Durham, NC: Duke University Press, 1996), p. 26). Del Giudice echoes this point: 'The vast majority were peasants and laborers, illiterate (or modestly educated) dialect speakers, firmly rooted in regional *oral* cultures' (Luisa Del Giudice, 'Speaking Memory: Oral History, Oral Culture, and Italians in America', in *Oral History, Oral Culture, and Italian Americans*, ed. by Luisa Del Giudice (New York: Palgrave Macmillan, 2009), pp. 3–18 (pp. 3–4, original emphasis)). See also Antonio Canovi, in Linda Barrett Osborne, and Paolo Battaglia, *Explorers Emigrants Citizens: A Visual History of the Italian American Experience from the Collections of the Library of Congress* (Modena: Anniversary Books, 2013), pp. 70–79 (p. 75).
10. Anna Beraducci Interview, interviewed by Mary Ellen Mancina-Batinich, The Mary Ellen Mancina Batinich Papers, Immigration History Research Center Archive, University of Minnesota, Box 30, pp. 23–24 (as transcribed).
11. Ibid., p. 24.
12. Ibid.
13. Anthony Navarra shares a very similar experience: 'How can I recapture the sense of warmth and love as, on a cold December night in Auburn, New York, we huddled around the coal stove, with hot faces and cold backs. Then, impatiently waiting for a few chestnuts or filberts to roast, we would urge her [mother] to tell us another story.' (Navarra, 'Old Tales and New Tongues', p. 14)
14. Baladino Ferrara, 'Just Call me Bill', Princeton Archives, 1 Box, pp. 25–26.
15. 'The Italian ladies from town would often come out to the farm to Mom to get her to cure their headaches. They blamed the pain of the 'Male Occio' [sic] — Evil Eye. | "Carmela," they pleaded, "Lift the spells. Cast out the Male Occio"' (Ferrara, 'Just Call me Bill', p. 38).
16. Ibid., pp. 26–31 (my summary).
17. Gian Paolo Caprettini, *Dizionario della fiaba italiana: simboli, personaggi, storie delle fiabe regionali* (Roma: Meltemi, 2000), p. 224.
18. Ibid., p. 225.
19. Indeed Carla Bianco records a version of this in her *Two Rosetos*, called 'The Fox and the Ricotta', pp. 176–79.
20. Ferrara, 'Just Call me Bill', pp. 31–33 (my summary).
21. Ibid., pp. 33–35 (my summary).

22. See Mary Ellen Mancina-Batinich, *Italian Voices: Making Minnesota Our Home* (St Paul: Minnesota Historical Society Press, 2007), pp. 285–87. For further work on James and his storytelling, see Matthew Reza, 'A Calabrian in Minnesota: The Tales of James Mancina', *Italian Americana*, 36.1 (2018), 9–28.
23. Italo Calvino, *Fiabe italiane* (Turin: Einaudi, 1956), pp. 938–40.
24. See 'The Foolish Girl', in Catherine Harris Ainsworth, *Italian-American Folktales* (Buffalo: Clyde Press, 1977), p. 119. Ainsworth also notes that this story is AA type 1450.
25. Jerre Mangione, *Mount Allegro: A Memoir of Italian American Life/Jerre Mangione; Introduction by Herbert J. Gans* (New York; Guildford: Columbia University Press, [1942] 1981), p. 8.
26. Insofar as the Grimm tales are written versions of oral tales. See also Lavinio in this chapter.
27. Mangione, *Mount Allegro*, pp. 142–51 (my summary).
28. Ibid., p. xii.
29. Ibid., pp. 308–09.
30. Joan Stefano Interview, interviewed by Mary Ellen Mancina-Batinich, The Mary Ellen Mancina Batinich Papers, Immigration History Research Center Archives, University of Minnesota, Box 36, p. 30 (original emphasis).
31. Ibid., p. 31 (original emphasis).
32. Ibid.
33. Ibid., pp. 25–26.
34. Virginia and Elios Anderlini Interview, interviewed by Audrey Tomaselli, Telegraph Hill Dwellers Oral History, consulted at the Immigration History Research Center Archives, University of Minnesota, Box 1, p. 31, 58.
35. Ibid., pp. 58–59.
36. Ibid., pp. 31, 58.
37. Ibid., p. 58.
38. Ibid. (original emphasis).
39. Mangione, *Mount Allegro*, p. 301. Bianco makes a similar argument regarding Roseto, Pennsylvania, during the 1960s (Bianco, *The Two Rosetos*, pp. 76–77).
40. See also Matthew Reza, 'Telling New Tales in New Spaces: La fiaba in America', *Italian Canadiana*, Special Issue, 31 (2017), 141–55.
41. Catherine Harris Ainsworth, *Italian-American Folktales* (Buffalo: Clyde Press, 1977), p. vi.
42. Marina Amici, *Italian Folklore* (1975), Walter P. Reuther Library, Wayne State University, pp. 17–18.
43. Cristina Lavinio, *La magia della fiaba: tra oralità e scrittura* (Scandicci: La Nuova Italia, 1993), p. 1 (my translation).
44. Judith Cassai Interview, interviewed by Anthony Mansueto, Italians in Chicago Project, University of Illinois, consulted at the Center for Migration Studies, New York, p. 1.
45. Ibid., p. 12.
46. Caprettini, *Dizionario della fiaba italiana*, p. 224.
47. Renato Aprile, *Indice delle fiabe popolari italiane di magia*, 2 vols (Florence: Olschki, 2000), II, 500–20.
48. William Marinelli, *Folklore of Settefrati, Italy in Use from 1902–1937* (1977), Walter P. Reuther Library, Wayne State University, p. 49.
49. Ibid., p. 2.
50. Ibid. (my emphasis).
51. Deborah A. LaFrate, *Italian-American Folklore*, Walter P. Reuther Library, Wayne State University, p. 2.
52. Ibid., pp. 2–3.
53. Ibid., p. 9.
54. Fred L. Gardaphé, 'Identical Difference: Notes on Italian and Italian American Identities', in *The Essence of Italian Culture and the Challenge of a Global Age*, ed. by Paolo Janni and George F. McLean (Washington, DC: Council for Research in Values and Philosophy, 2003), pp. 99–102.
55. Navarra, 'Old Tales and New Tongues', p. 15.

CHAPTER 2

The English Language and Anglo-American Culture in Twentieth-Century Italy

Virginia Pulcini

Introduction: The Spread of English and the Americanization of Italian Society

The attitudes of Italians to the influence of British and American societies have changed in the course of time, moulded by the social events that influenced the political, economic and cultural relations between them. In the twentieth century contacts between Italy and the English-speaking nations — mainly Great Britain and the USA — were both direct and indirect: the former involved the physical movement of individuals and communities across the countries involved (chiefly from Italy to the USA), while the latter took place through the exchange of cultural and material products. From a social and political point of view, in the first half of the twentieth century, the European arena was devastated by two World Wars, and Italy experienced twenty years of the Fascist regime. In the second half of the twentieth century, a period of peace and prosperity set in: the USA, the victor in the Second World War, took the leadership in the material and moral reconstruction of the ravaged European countries. These historical events are largely responsible for the political, economic and cultural Americanization of Western Europe.

During this century Italy underwent profound transformations in its economy and in its social fabric: from a mainly agricultural society with about 50% of the population illiterate in early 1900, Italy experienced an economic boom in the 1950s and 1960s, and, at the turn of the third millennium, is now one of the largest industrialized countries in the world with illiteracy reduced almost to zero.[1] The Americanization of Italian society, which started in the years following the Second World War, had strong effects not only on the economic and political sphere but also on people's habits and lifestyles, spreading the ideology of well-being and consumerism. Fascination with the English language is largely, though not exclusively, due to the attraction to the American 'way of life' and to anything that was associated with modernity, progress and glamour.

Appreciation for the English-speaking world, however, was already present and intense two centuries before, when the cultural phenomenon called 'Anglomania' by the Italian poet and scholar Arturo Graf began, which continued thereafter in the following centuries.[2] Although France and the French language were greatly influential as cultural models in Italy in the eighteenth and nineteenth centuries, British society was admired for its parliamentary institutions, which were considered the source of its economic prosperity and political power, and also for its literary, scientific and philosophical achievements, as evidence of technical expertise and cultural distinction. In fact, it was in Britain where the industrial revolution had begun, spreading technological innovation for industrial production everywhere in the world. As pointed out by Stammerjohann,[3] both Britain and the United States of America were also a political harbour for many Europeans escaping from persecution and conflicts, as in the case of the French writer Voltaire, who was exiled in England between 1726 and 1729 and wrote that English was the language of free people, of 'une nation libre et savante' [a free and learned nation]. Goethe, the great German literary figure, admired the ideals of freedom and independence inspired by the American revolution, and dedicated the much-quoted poem *Den Vereinigten Staaten* to the USA, containing the famous verse 'Amerika, du hast es besser' [America, you have it better].[4] In the following century, many exiles from the 1848 revolutions that swept through European countries landed in Britain, including key figures of the Italian *Risorgimento* such as the political activist Giuseppe Mazzini, and in the USA the patriot and soldier Giuseppe Garibaldi.

Following the phenomenon of 'Anglomania', in the nineteenth century the representations of the new world across the Atlantic began to fire the imagination of Italian readers, thanks to translations of US novels,[5] which triggered a fertile production of narrative staged on the North American frontier, populated by Indians and cowboys. As explained by Tosi: '[t]he early borrowings of American origin show a picture of a country perceived as being between life in the wild and a futuristic society',[6] like *Far West*, *cowboy*, *barman*, *cocktail*, *globetrotter* and *skyscraper* (initially translated into *grattanuvole*, later into *grattacielo*). Direct contacts between the USA and Italian society began with the massive phenomenon of the emigration of millions of Italians, especially from southern Italy, to the New World. Between 1876 and 1930, about 5 million Italian immigrants arrived in the United States of America, mainly labourers, in search of better job opportunities. The USA was seen as a 'promised land' of freedom and democracy, in spite of the hardships suffered by immigrants. The roots of the American myth lie in this period, and so does borrowing from American English.[7]

The influence of US society became more and more pervasive in Italy after the end of the Second World War, developing into the massive phenomenon of Americanization, as forecast by the British journalist William Stead,[8] a victim of the Titanic disaster in 1912, who, with remarkable foresight, labelled this global event as the worldwide 'trend of the 20th century'.

In extreme synthesis, the historical facts mentioned above provide some essential extra-linguistic background to the analysis of attitudes of Italians to the spread and influence of the English language in Italy and the input of English loanwords in the twentieth century into the Italian language. In this chapter, we will look at different and changing attitudes towards the influence of the Anglo-American culture and language[9] and reactions to the phenomenon of borrowing from English into Italian. Mirroring the changing sentiments toward British and US societies before and after the historical divide of the Second World War, attitudes to English gradually changed from the overt political opposition of the Fascist regime and the mild disapproval of neo-purist scholars in the first half of the twentieth century, to enthusiastic acceptance from the post-war years to present-day Italian society. Although the success of a language is largely due to the political, economic and cultural prestige of the speech communities that speak it, sociolinguists recognize the contribution of attitudes in strengthening the power of a language as well as in supporting or counterbalancing official policies on language matters. As discussed by Peter Garret,[10] social attitudes to language are widespread in all societies and have a crucial role in influencing common sentiments, acting as an invisible but decisive factor for social advantage or discrimination.

Many scholars have described and weighed up the borrowing of Anglicisms in Italian resulting from centuries-old cultural contact between the Italian peninsula and English-speaking countries, with particular emphasis on the cultural and linguistic impact of the USA in the post-Second World War decades.[11] Overall, the lexical impact of English on the Italian language is rather low (c. 2%) and is even more inconsequential on the general language. In spite of this, many Italian scholars have complained about the supposed 'flood' of Anglicisms in the Italian language and the negative consequences of the massive 'Anglicization' of Italian vocabulary. A look at some recent articles devoted to this issue reveals that many Italian linguists have taken a critical stance towards the impact of English, starting from the often-quoted definition of the spread of English as a 'morbus anglicus', a real disease of Italian society, given by Arrigo Castellani.[12] Bolelli recommends 'surveillance' but not 'crusades' against English.[13] Riccardo Gualdo and Cristina Scarpino wonder how much this influence actually 'weighs' on Italian,[14] whereas Claudio Giovanardi asks whether there may be a 'peaceful cohabitation' of English and Italian words,[15] and Francesco Sabatini thinks that Italian has been too permissive and argues in favour of a common strategy to face the ongoing Anglicization of modern European languages.[16] Finally, Nicoletta Maraschio and Domenico De Martino envisage a catastrophic future in which Italian is banned from Italian universities.[17]

In the following sections, some old and new attitudes of linguists, lexicographers, language experts and observers towards the assimilation of Anglicisms in Italian will be examined. This overview will consider the socio-political context against which English-Italian language contact took place in the twentieth century and, in particular, the leadership of the USA as a donor of cultural products and loanwords in Italian society and language. Finally, we will report on a new wave of negative reactions against the growing adoption of English as a medium of instruction in Italian higher education.

Lexicographic Evidence in the Early Twentieth Century

As pointed out above, the contacts between Italy and English-speaking countries were both direct and indirect. Lexical borrowing, however, witnessing the outcome of cultural contacts, initially took place indirectly through the written language (books and printed media), but from the beginning of the twentieth century also through radio, television, cinema, and over the last few decades through the Internet and social media. As explained by Ivan Klajn, personal interaction, like the presence of foreign residents or tourists, may only give rise to ephemeral types of borrowings.[18]

At the turn of the twentieth century Italy had only just become a united nation (in 1861) and was above all committed to the consolidation of its national identity and of the national language, the latter in competition with local dialects. Neologisms and especially the use of foreign words were considered a deterioration of the purity of the language and an offence to national pride. A first record of twenty unadapted Anglicisms appeared in Fanfani and Arlìa's dictionary,[19] whose title, *Lessico dell'infima e corrotta italianità* [*The Lexicon of the Vulgar and Corrupted Italian Spirit*], well expresses the purist intent of the authors, namely to collect those words that were considered improper, particularly foreign (mainly French) and bureaucratic terms, and propose Italian acceptable substitutes. The borrowing of Anglicisms gradually intensified in early 1900, although the socio-cultural elites did not seem to be competent in English, because French was the foreign language normally learnt by educated people, and therefore undesirable lexical intrusion was attributed to French.

A further phase, according to Iamartino,[20] goes from the 1930s to the end of the Second World War, in which the language policy adopted by the Fascist regime strengthened the nationalistic ideals of the previous decades, and made them even more radical. An example of a gradual change in attitude towards foreignisms can be seen in Panzini's *Dizionario Moderno*, published in 1905 and re-edited ten times up to 1963.[21] Panzini considered his dictionary an addition to general dictionaries (hence the subtitle *Supplemento ai dizionari italiani*), but he aimed at collecting new words in Italian, in particular foreignisms, regional and dialectal words and thieves' cant (*gergo furbesco*), which he named 'monsters and little monsters' (*mostri e mostricini*).[22] The first edition contains an appendix of letters of appreciation or criticism sent by scholars and readers of this dictionary, fuelling a debate on the possible negative outcome of a collection of neologisms, namely to encourage 'improper use'. Panzini reacted to criticism saying that keeping track of the evolution and renovation of Italian was more important than judging the correctness or otherwise of new lexical items or of new senses attached to old words. He further explained in the preface to the third edition that his intention had been both literary and patriotic, because he wanted to provide an account of the 'health' of Italian. In his own words, he declared: 'Nella mia prima idea era, o mi pareva, una collezione di anomalie e di brutture, germinate sul bellissimo idioma in cui Dante scolpì la sua Commedia' [In my initial idea it was, or I imagined it to be, a collection of oddities and blots, sprouting on the beautiful Italian language in which Dante crafted his Comedy].[23]

However, in the following editions he eliminated some rare foreign terms, added comments discouraging their use and provided acceptable Italian equivalents. Nevertheless, Panzini distanced himself from those 'purist' opponents of foreign words, and took the following stance on the matter:

> Dunque io penso che è inutile opporsi all'accettazione tanto dei così detti barbarismi e gallicismi come delle nude voci straniere, giacché la loro forza è maggiore. E né meno penso che per questo soltanto la lingua italiana vada in rovina.
>
> [In fact, I think that it is useless to counter the acceptance of both the so-called barbarisms and gallicisms and plain foreign words, because their strength is greater. Neither do I believe that the Italian language will deteriorate only for this reason.][24]

Panzini's attitude appears quite progressive for his age, considering that in the 1920s several legislative measures had already been taken by the newly born Fascist regime in order to impose a policy of 'language self-sufficiency' (*autarchia linguistica*). Yet, as a lexicographer, he acted as an independent thinker and compiled the entries of his dictionary in a rather personal and ironic way, freely expressing his opinions on the adoption or otherwise of new words, which he considered necessary if they denoted something new. See, for example, the comment that accompanies the entry for *Foot-ball*:

> Qui ricorderemo soltanto come nella patria del *Calcio* e della *Pallacorda* si giochino i detti giuochi con denominazioni inglesi ed i maestri insegnino in inglese, e i vecchi nomi italiani sono obliati. Dicono gli intenditori che il nuovo *foot-ball* non corrisponde all'antico e perciò i nuovi nomi hanno ragione di essere.
>
> [Here we will only remind you that in the homeland of *calcio* and *pallacorda*, these games are played with English denominations and coaches train in English, and the old Italian terms are forgotten. Experts say that the new *football* does not match with the old one and therefore the existence of the new terms is fully justified.][25]

Panzini is, however, critical towards many scientists and scholars of his time, the former for their excessively succinct style and the latter for their pedantic decoration of speech, both categories being inclined to use foreign words just for snobbery or to sound more 'intellectual'.

Equally personal and radically committed to 'cleaning up' the Italian language from 'infamous barbarisms', in support of the pride and dignity of the Italian language, is another dictionary of foreign words, namely *Barbaro dominio* by Paolo Monelli.[26] The author welcomed the campaign against foreign words promoted by a column in a newspaper of his time (*Gazzetta del Popolo*) expressing openly nationalistic views on the purity of the Italian language. Most of the entries of this dictionary (about 500) are French words. Only about 100 are Anglicisms, many from the field of sport (e.g. *dribbling, tennis, knock-out, match, set, game*) and fashion (e.g. *pullover, tight, trenchcoat*), for which he recommends Italian equivalents. He also expressed criticism of foreign behaviours and lifestyles, making anti-foreign and sexist comments about Americans and women, among others. For example, in his discussion of the term *vamp*, of American origin, he ironically states that, rather than 'vampires', American women are better defined as 'bloodsuckers'. Furthermore, for the term *sex-appeal* Monelli says that there is no Italian equivalent for it, beside the inadequate expression 'richiamo al sesso', but this term is anyway an American invention, because ladies in this country must move and speak in a 'strange' way in order to be noted by athletic American gentlemen, who seem to be too busy and cold to pay attention to them. Monelli concludes that this term is not necessary (a 'tautology', a 'duplicate') for Italian women!

Fascism and Neo-Purism

The Fascist regime (1922–45) transformed purist concerns into a xenophobic campaign, intensifying the battle against foreign words in public signs and advertisements, introducing taxes and later fines and even imprisonment for those who violated these norms. Names of towns and hotels that sounded foreign had to be changed and harmonized to Italian. A special Commission of the Regia Accademia d'Italia would post on its Bulletin lists of forbidden words and their substitutes, especially French loanwords but also Anglicisms, among which we can quote *breakfast, beefsteack* (*beefsteak*), *lunch, box, hall*, and terms of commerce and industry (e.g. *agreement, bill, budget*). Because of legislative measures in the 1930s and 1940s, many Anglicisms, especially sports terms, were permanently replaced by Italian equivalents, but the purist campaigns to encourage the use of Italian substitutes did not bring the desired effects. An interesting episode quoted by Sergio Raffaelli[27] regards a competition addressed to readers and promoted by a newspaper in 1932, which aimed to find substitutions for foreign loanwords, including fifteen Anglicisms. This event resulted in the disappearance of the hybrid phrase *five o'clock* 'tè' (*il tè delle cinque*), the maintenance of six (*jazz, smoking, tight, bar, klacson/clacson, film*) and the survival of the rest together with Italian equivalents (*copyright, dancing, raid, flirt, golf, record, sandwich, taxi*).[28]

In spite of the ideological propaganda and the legislative intervention of the Fascist regime, Anglicisms continued to be used by Italians and many of the rather awkward, even ridiculous, proposals were not adopted: for example 'arlecchino' (*cocktail*), 'arresto' (*stop*), 'obbligata' (*slalom*), 'lista' (*menu*), 'mescita', 'quisibeve', 'taberna potatoria' and several others (*bar*), 'festivale' (*festival*), 'tramvia' (*tram*), 'pellicola' (*film*). The following, instead, were considered 'untranslatable': *bridge, poker, golf* and *tennis*. Many linguists of the period did not agree with this extreme form of purism based on the rhetoric of cultural isolation, and preferred to take a comparatively moderate position, which was named 'Neo-Purism' by its founder Bruno Migliorini in 1942. On the one hand, scholars professionally engaged in language matters were in favour of the protection of Italian from foreign influence, especially in the case of structural divergence which could prevent the harmonious assimilation of neologisms into Italian. On the other hand, linguists did not deny the historical dimension of language and its need to renew itself through contacts with other language and cultures. Also the role of the Accademia della Crusca changed in the Fascist decades. As explained by Francesco Sabatini,[29] conflict arose between the century-old Crusca and the new Accademia d'Italia appointed by the Fascist regime; as a consequence the Crusca turned to historical and philological research and abandoned its normative action on the state of the contemporary language, which would be resumed later on by the journal *Lingua Nostra* (founded in 1939 by Bruno Migliorini and Giacomo Devoto).

The American Model in Post-War Italy

In the post-war decades linguistic censorship was removed and a new, open attitude to linguistic innovation swept through Italy, 'liberated' from Nazism by the US troops. A complex of political, economic and sociolinguistic factors, which included the unifying impact of the mass media, much higher levels of literacy and competence in Italian in the majority of the population, favoured the diffusion of Anglo-American culture and interest in the English language in this part of the century. The desire to learn English as a foreign language for professional purposes has also greatly increased in time, replacing French from the 1960s as the most popular foreign language in Italian education from elementary school onwards (see Schirru in this volume).

The cultural impact of the 'American way of life' in post-war Italy was strong and pervasive. The economic expansion of the USA on the European market brought new exciting products that became icons of modernity, like Coca-Cola and Levi's blue jeans. New consumer goods such as household appliances (televisions, dishwashers, vacuum cleaners) and social habits (shopping in supermarkets, mail order, coin-operated machines, take-away restaurants and fast food), leisure activities (lotteries, gambling) were a cultural shock for many Italians. While the appeal of Hollywood stars sparked awe and admiration, the glamorous American style was often considered excessive, ridiculous, even transgressive, as the Italian derogatory word '*americanata*' would express for behaviour characterized by naïve grandiosity and exhibitionism, typically attributed to Americans.

The input of Anglicisms in the second half of the twentieth century increased exponentially. Table 1 shows the number of Anglicisms recorded by *il Devoto-Oli. Vocabolario della lingua italiana 2017*.[30] In the first decades of the century the highest number of English loanwords were in the fields of sport, music, cinema, games, whereas in the post-war period the incidence of scientific and technical terms increased, especially in the domain of information technology, overtaking sport, the economy, music and finance as the richest field in Anglicisms.[31] The provenance of many Anglicisms may be attributed to US society on social and historical grounds, so that we can say that British English also has renewed its lexicon thanks to the input of American English.

Lexicographers of these decades observed and recorded the assimilation of Anglicisms into Italian, without objecting to their increase, inspired by the academic goal to describe the dynamic innovation of the Italian language. A comparison between different counts is limited by conflicting criteria of inclusion, i.e. whether the category of Anglicism includes only words whose form is

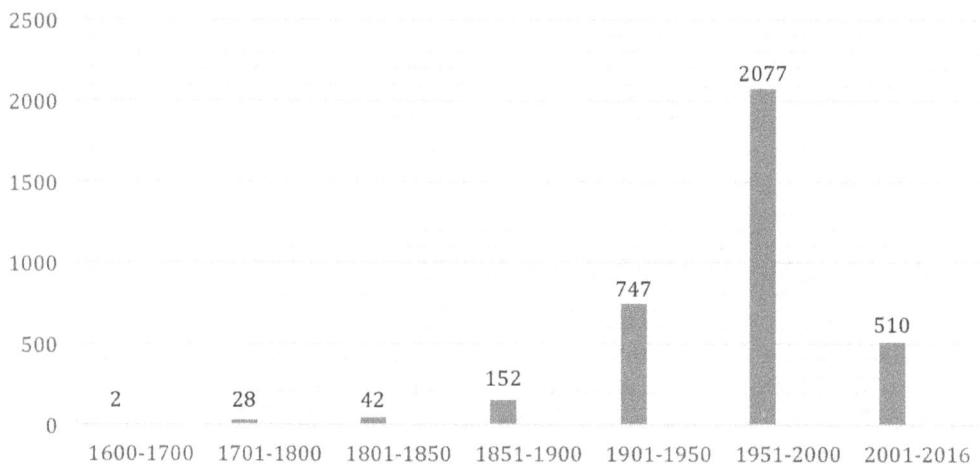

Fig. 2-1. Number of Anglicisms recorded in Italian from the seventeenth century to 2016. Source: Devoto-Oli 2017.

recognizable as English, or also adapted forms, calques and semantic loans (in some cases proper names, brand names, and abbreviations are also considered). We can find 2,300 entries in Gaetano Rando,[32] 5,850 recorded by the GDU,[33] 4,320 in Tullio De Mauro and Marco Mancini,[34] 2,761 in the most recent edition of lo Zingarelli 2017,[35] and 3,522 in the Italian dictionary Devoto-Oli.[36] The attitude taken by lexicographers and dictionary publishers in general is simply descriptive, in contrast with the prescriptive standpoint of the lexicographers of the beginning of the century. Moreover, there seems to be a competition among different dictionaries to expand their word-lists and include as many neologisms as possible, and as soon as possible, preferably every year, a policy that has become feasible thanks to the electronic format of present-day dictionaries. The risk of this open attitude is to include new words just because they have enjoyed popularity for some time, or indicate an event highlighted by the media, while their actual currency in everyday use is very low. On the incidence of Anglicisms in Italian, a word of caution has been expressed by Tullio De Mauro, one of the wisest and most far-sighted scholars in Italian academia. Commenting on the average 2% impact of Anglicisms on the total Italian lexicon, De Mauro observed that the most frequent Anglicism in spoken Italian is the word *okay* and, apart from that, only some ten Anglicisms feature among the 5,000 most frequently used words in spoken Italian. This information should reassure those speakers who cry out against the invasion of Anglicisms and the 'pidginization' of the Italian language. Yet, De Mauro explains, there are some social groups who use Anglicisms more frequently, like managers, economists, IT experts, and young people, and the number of English 'casuals' and 'quotation words'[37] in today's media (especially newspapers) is huge, which makes any numerical account of how many Anglicisms are actually present in Italian particularly difficult.[38]

Since the end of the Second World War, Italy has become quite open to English words and linguists are aware that imposition from above, such as the intervention of an academy, is not the right way to safeguard the national language. For this reason, Italian has been defined as a 'democratic language', open to borrowing from other languages, as opposed to its sister languages, French and Spanish, whose language academies exercise the right to decide on language matters. Further evidence of this welcoming attitude of present-day Italian comes from Manfred Görlach's *Dictionary of European Anglicisms*, which compares the presence of Anglicisms in sixteen European languages.[39] From a numerical count, Italian ranks in fourth position after Dutch, Norwegian and German among the most 'Anglicized' European languages (actually, Italian appears to be the most 'Anglicized' of the Romance languages).[40]

In a cultural context which is today openly 'Anglophile', the job of lexicographers over the last decades has concentrated on the collections of neologisms and foreign words in order to record and describe the expansion of Italian vocabulary.[41] By contrast, the volume written by Claudio Giovanardi and Riccardo Gualdo[42] continues the tradition established by previous linguists to collect English loanwords and propose Italian substitutes. The editors declare their neutral stand between 'Anglo-skepticals and Anglo-enthusiasts' and identify thirteen linguistic parameters on which the fortune of an Anglicism and the possibility of replacing it may be measured: age (old or recent borrowing), degree of integration (common or rare), domain of use (general or specialized), register (formality), degree of technicality, semantic status (monosemic, polysemic), expressive value, spelling and pronunciation, semantic divergence (false Anglicism), diffusion in French and Spanish, equivalence in Italian, number of possible Italian substitutes, and compositionality. Within this framework, a selection of Anglicisms is carefully assessed and a final statement about their chance of replacement is made: for example, It. *allegato* is given as a successful substitute for Eng. *attachment*, but the brevity and phonetic expressivity of Eng. *aquagym*, *blog*, *chat line*, *cookie*, *flop* and *tag* do not offer much chance to Italian competitors. Some proposals made by the authors sound awkward (*giallino* for *post-it*, or *fusopatia* for *jet lag*), whereas *tour promozionale* (note that *tour* is a French word) is regarded as a possible successful replacement for *road show*, quite an opaque compound in Italian. It is interesting to point out that Slow Food (for which the authors suggest *mangiar bene* as an Italian alternative) is the Italian brand name of the movement founded in the Piedmont region of Italy in 1986. Despite its formal 'Englishness', which is modelled on the term *fast food*, the manifesto of Slow Food promotes values — that is, appreciation for local food heritage, responsible agriculture and respect for the environment — that are totally unrelated and in contrast with globalization and consumerism.

The economic and socio-cultural transformation of Italian society in the second half of the twentieth century is not free from contradictions, also with respect to language matters. As explained by Tosi: 'Italy is a country where a great passion for eccentric neologisms and radical manifestations of political correctness cohabits with a widespread tolerance for linguistic sexism and racist connotations in the language of the media.'[43] While many families are firmly convinced that investing in English tuition for their children will guarantee a better professional future for them,[44] campaigns are launched in the media in the name of linguistic nationalism and against the 'flood' of Anglicisms in Italian (see below). Many observers, in fact, have deplored the excessive use of English in the press, advertisements and shop signs, which have made English part of the Italian urban cityscape. The overuse of Anglicisms by some categories of speakers, especially managers, economists and IT experts, is criticized as a form of snobbery, an intentional form of 'exhibitionism', or even a 'a mental vice inherited by centuries of servitude' (a comment made by the Italian journalist Indro Montanelli), 'a lack of effort by the layman's press to find the corresponding Italian terms'.[45] In political discourse, politicians have been accused of using too many Anglicisms not only for snobbery, but also to cover up unpleasant measures (*spending review*, with the meaning of 'cuts to expenses') or to make humiliating allowances sound like benefits (*social card*). Further criticism is addressed against the naïve assumption of Italian speakers that English is an easy language, with short, high-impact words, and plasticity in word formation, and that, because it has the role of an international lingua franca, pronunciation and morpho-syntactic infelicities can be tolerated. This carefree attitude toward the use of English has given rise to a host of speakers of '*Itangliano*' and '*Italiese*' (by analogy with *Franglais*), a jocular term coined to indicate the overuse or misuse of English terms for the purpose of adding a touch of class to Italian discourse, especially in some managerial careers.[46]

Across the New Millennium: EMI and New Preoccupations

A new wave of criticisms has recently arisen in the humanities quarters of Italian academia about the introduction of English as a medium of instruction (EMI) in Italian universities. The ensuing debate among linguists and opinion-makers also created quite a strong echo in the media. EMI was introduced in Italy in the 1990s, in compliance with the directives of the Bologna process, i.e. to integrate European education, to increase student and staff mobility, to enhance international knowledge transfer and to make graduates more competitive in a growing globalized market. The number of degree programmes offered by universities has constantly grown, hailed, on the one hand, as a great opportunity for professional success, especially in the fields of engineering, science and economics, while, on the other hand, it has also been criticized as an extra hurdle for students (and also for lecturers) whose competence may not meet minimum standards.

A legal case regarding EMI, which stirred much popular sensation, was brought by some professors of the Polytechnic of Milan against the decision to offer all postgraduate and doctoral courses in English from the academic year 2013–14. The appeal was initially admitted by the Regional Administrative Court (in June 2013) on the principle that lecturers are free to teach in Italian and no linguistic discrimination should be practised in education. However, the Polytechnic's own appeal against this first judgment was admitted by the State Court on the grounds that higher education institutions, by virtue of their 'autonomous status', have the right to offer degree programmes entirely taught in English to strengthen internationalization.[47]

The EMI controversy has been a turning point for the Accademia della Crusca, which had hardly ever taken a clear stand on language policy. In 2013, a volume was published with the challenging title *Fuori l'italiano dall'università?*,[48] in which the question of whether one's mother tongue should be abandoned in higher education was commented upon by members of the academy, and by other Italian scholars and intellectuals. The prevalent opinion is that the importance of English as an essential tool for scientific and professional interaction in today's world cannot be denied, but Italian students should anyway acquire the technical and scientific terminology of their specialization in their mother tongue. In recent times, these debates have revived national sentiments, and given rise to a new form of 'moderate' purism in Italian society. Scholars have felt the need to counter the enthusiastic, welcoming attitude to the English language and to an 'Anglocentric', entrepreneurial vision of education, whereby priority is given to 'quello che serve e non quello che è utile per la formazione della personalità e la cultura dell'immaginazione' [what is needed and not to what is useful for the development of your personality and the culture of imagination].[49]

Reacting against Anglomania, some journalists have once again joined in the chorus against people's excessive recourse to Anglicisms, accusing them of 'parochialism, inferiority complex, exhibitionism, sloppiness, laziness'.[50] In 2015 the online petition #dilloinitaliano[51] was launched by a journalist and addressed to the Italian government and to the board of the Accademica della Crusca, asking for support. The objective was to encourage speakers to use Italian words, in order to speak clearly and strengthen Italian identity. According to the promoters of this movement, bilingualism is desirable, but sprinkling Italian speech with unnecessary English words is not a good practice, especially by people playing public roles on the national stage. Italians, the petition highlights, should become more respectful of their national language and more aware of the cultural, historical and artistic heritage that they miss out on when they use a foreign language rather than their own mother tongue. In the same year, the President of the Accademia della Crusca organized a symposium devoted to neologisms and foreign borrowings in Italian and in other Romance languages in times of globalization, and how to protect the national languages.[52]

The Italian linguist Tullio De Mauro, who has always expressed very open attitudes to the influence of English on Italian, has argued that a shared language for communication is needed in Europe, not only to simplify bureaucracy and institutional matters, but especially to build a strong democratic community. In this respect, as a 'Latinized' (or only partly Germanic) language, English appears to be the most qualified candidate for this important role in multilingual Europe, which would not jeopardize the status and identity of the other national languages. Nevertheless, in the book *In Europa son già 103. Troppe lingue per una democrazia?*, De Mauro stated that everybody should learn English and use it as a European lingua franca, but it is important to keep all levels of education in Italian to preserve our language and people's full competence in their mother tongue.[53]

Conclusion

Attitudes to the spread of English in Italy throughout the twentieth century have changed in different historical periods, depending on more or less favourable contexts for cultural exchanges. Forms of purism or prescriptivism embraced by linguists or academies have been rather mild, both in the past and in the present. Even during the Fascist regime, language imposition from above did not manage to eliminate quite a few already integrated Anglicisms. In contrast to the moderate resistance to English of Italian linguists, nowadays the public response is overwhelmingly favourable. Most Italians believe that English is indeed the most important language in contemporary society and learning English is a priority in education. English is considered indispensable for professional purposes, to travel and communicate on an international level, to access knowledge in many strategic fields but also, especially for digital natives, to feel part of an international community through the Internet and social media, sharing forms of popular culture (cinema, music, games), which are nowadays dominated by English. This positive, welcoming attitude of present-day Italian society is rooted in the historical phenomenon of 'Anglomania', i.e. the fascination for the Anglo-American culture, which was already at work in the centuries before the twentieth.

The Americanization of Italy after the end of the Second World War was a socio-cultural phenomenon that affected many areas of Italian society. The linguistic outcome was the donation of a remarkable stock of general and specialized vocabulary to the Italian language. Recent research has shown that, although British and American English have been developing side by side, American English has been the most influential variety in the twentieth century and up to the present day has also affected British English to some extent.[54] Other recent findings have shown that most of the Anglicisms imported into Italian at the turn of the millennium belong to the fields of information technology, the Internet and social media.[55]

After Brexit and the establishment of Donald Trump's administration, observers have hypothesized that there will be a decline in the Anglo-American influence in Europe (even the expunction of English from the official languages of the EU). Predicting the future is impossible but we may envisage that, as far as English is concerned, globalization has favoured the circulation of hundreds of English words and terms, many of them imported from US society, which are likely to stay in the vocabularies of European languages as international Anglicisms as long as their referents continue to exist.

Notes to Chapter 2

1. <http://www.istat.it/it/files/2011/03/Italia-in-cifre.pdf> [accessed July 2017].
2. Arturo Graf, *L'Anglomania e l'influsso inglese in Italia nel sec. XVIII* (Turin: Loescher, 1911) <www.opal.unito.it>; Paolo Zolli, *Le parole straniere* (Bologna: Zanichelli, 1991); Giovanni Iamartino, 'La contrastività italiano-inglese in prospettiva storica', *Rassegna Italiana di Linguistica Applicata (RILA)*, 33.2–3 (2001), 7–130; Virginia Pulcini, 'Anglicisms in Italian: Moving on into the Third Millennium', in *English in Italy: Linguistic, Educational and Professional Challenges*, ed. by Cecilia Boggio and Alessandra Molino (Milan: FrancoAngeli, 2017), pp. 15–37.
3. Harro Stammerjohann, 'L'italiano e altre lingue di fronte all'anglicizzazione', in *Italia linguistica anno Mille. Italia linguistica anno Duemila. Atti del XXXIV congresso internazionale di studi della Società di Linguistica Italiana (SLI). Firenze, 19–21 ottobre 2000*, ed. by Nicoletta Maraschio and Teresa Poggi-Salani (Rome: Bulzoni, 2003), pp. 77–101.
4. Quoted by Stammerjohann, ibid., p. 80.
5. E.g. James Fenimore Cooper's *The Last of the Mohicans* (1826).
6. Arturo Tosi, *Language and Society in a Changing Italy* (Clevedon: Multilingual Matters, 2001), p. 209.
7. See Iamartino, 'La contrastività italiano-inglese in prospettiva storica', pp. 62–63.
8. William Stead, *The Americanization of the World or the Trend of the 20th Century* (London: H. Marckley, 1902).
9. In this chapter the term 'Anglo-American' is used to refer to the general influence of English, without any specific reference to the USA or to the UK. British English and American English (instead of US English) are preferred as they are generally used in the literature to refer to the two main standard varieties of English in the world. The term 'America' is used to denote the new world from a European perspective; the 'USA' or 'US' are adopted for specific references to this nation as a political entity.
10. Peter Garret, in *Attitudes to Language* (Cambridge: Cambridge University Press, 2010), presents data on the use of foreign languages in advertisements (quoting Harald Haarmann, 'The Role of Ethnocultural Stereotypes and Foreign Languages in Japanese Commercials', *International Journal of the Sociology of Language*, 50 (1984), 101–20), showing that foreign languages carry stereotypical 'ethnocultural' associations and are strategically exploited in product advertising to provoke positive reactions in audiences. For example, English is a marker of international appreciation and is preferred in particular in advertisements of cars, televisions, sportswear and alcoholic drinks.
11. Ivan Klajn, *Influssi inglesi nella lingua italiana* (Florence: Olschki, 1972); Virginia Pulcini, 'Italian', in *English in Europe*, ed. by Manfred Görlach (Oxford: Oxford University Press, 2002), pp. 151–67; Tullio De Mauro and Marco Mancini, *Parole straniere nella lingua italiana* (Turin: Garzanti, 2003 [2001]); Riccardo Gualdo and Cristina Scarpino, 'Quanto pesa l'inglese? Anglicismi nella vita quotidiana e proposte per la coabitazione', in *Identità e diversità nella lingua e nella letteratura italiana. Atti del XVIII Congresso dell'Associazione Internazionale per gli Studi di Lingua e Letteratura Italiana (AISLLI). Lovanio, Louvain-la-Neuve, Anversa, Bruxelles, 16–19 luglio 2003*, ed. by Serge Vanvolsem, Stefania Marzo, Manuela Caniato and Gigliola Mavolo, 3 vols (Florence: Franco Cesati, 2007), I, 257–81; Andrea Bistarelli, 'L'interferenza dell'inglese sull'italiano in tre dei maggiori repertori di anglicismi degli ultimi 20 anni', *inTRAlinea* 10, 2008. <http://www.intralinea.org/archive/article/Linterferenza_dellinglese_sullitaliano> [accessed July 2017]; Virginia Pulcini, Cristiano Furiassi and Félix Rodríguez González, 'The Lexical Influence of English on European Languages: From Words to Phraseology', in *The Anglicization of European Lexis*, ed. by Cristiano Furiassi, Virginia Pulcini and Félix Rodríguez González (Amsterdam & Philadelphia John Benjamins, 2012), pp. 1–24; Virginia Pulcini, 'Anglicisms in Italian: Moving on into the Third Millennium'.
12. Arrigo Castellani, 'Morbus Anglicus', *Studi Linguistici Italiani*, 10 (1987), 137–53 <http://www.italianourgente.it/files/morbus-anglicus-5562d24be0aa734270100f2f.pdf>.
13. Tristano Bolelli, 'Non crociate ma vigilanza', in *Dove va la lingua italiana?*, ed. by Jader Jacobelli (Rome and Bari: Laterza, 1987), pp. 23–28.

14. Gualdo and Scarpino, 'Quanto pesa l'inglese?'.
15. Claudio Giovanardi, 'Italiano e inglese: convivenza pacifica?', in *Inglese-Italiano 1 a 1. Tradurre o non tradurre le parole inglesi?*, ed. by Claudio Giovanardi, Riccardo Gualdo and Alessandra Coco (San Cesario di Lecce: Piero Manni, 2008, 2nd edn [2003]), pp. 9–27.
16. Francesco Sabatini, 'L'italiano, lingua permissiva? Proposte per una strategia comune delle lingue europee verso l'anglicismo', in *Sprachkontakt und Mehrsprachigkeit. Zur Anglizismendiskussion in Deutschland, Österreich, der Schweiz und Italien*, ed. by Sandro M. Moraldo (Heidelberg: Winter Universitätsverlag, 2008), pp. 267–75. See also Massimo Fanfani, 'Reazioni italiane agli anglicismi', in *L'inglese e le altre lingue europee. Studi sull'interferenza linguistica*, ed. by Félix San Vicente (Bologna: CLUEB, 2000), pp. 215–31.
17. Nicoletta Maraschio and Domenico De Martino, *Fuori l'italiano dall'università? Inglese, internazionalizzazione, politica linguistica* (Rome and Bari: Laterza, 2013).
18. Klajn (in *Influssi inglesi nella lingua italiana*) quotes the exceptional case of *sciuscià*, the Italian popular pronunciation of English *shoeshine*, a term referring to the humble job done by some Italian youths in the post-war years and used to communicate with US soldiers. It became the title of the homonymous Oscar-winning film (1946).
19. Pietro Fanfani and Costantino Arlia, *Lessico dell'infima e corrotta italianità* (Milan: P. Carrara, 1877), reprinted in 1881, 1890, 1998, 1907, with additions in 1884, 1896.
20. Iamartino, 'La contrastività italiano-inglese in prospettiva storica', p. 62.
21. Alfredo Panzini, *Dizionario moderno. Supplemento ai dizionari italiani* (Milan: Hoepli), editions: 1905, 1908; 1918; 1923; 1927; 1931; 1935; 1942 with an Appendix edited by B. Migliorini; reprinted in 1950, 1963); Bruno Migliorini, *Parole nuove: appendice di dodicimila voci al "Dizionario moderno" di Alfredo Panzini* (Milan: Hoepli, 1963).
22. The percentage of Anglicisms recorded in Panzini's *Dizionario* was examined by Gaetano Rando in 'Anglicismi nel "Dizionario Moderno" dalla quarta alla decima edizione', *Lingua nostra*, 30 (1969), 107–12, in order to quantify the input of Anglicisms from the fourth to the tenth edition and explain the historical reasons which influenced increases and decreases. He noticed a decline between the third edition (1918) and the fourth (1923, 8.5%) which can be explained by the political tension between Italy and Great Britain in the post-First World War years, and another decline between the seventh (1935, over 9%) and the eighth (1942, 8.5%), which can be ascribed to the Fascist campaign against the use of foreign words. Overall, however, the number of Anglicisms rose from 8.5% in 1923 to over 11% in 1963. The Anglicisms included were not only non-adapted forms (e.g. *nursery, outsider, ping-pong, tea-room, trainer*) but also adaptations (*telepatico, vegetariano, pressurizzare*), calques ('allenamento', from *training*; 'dissolvenza', from the cinema term *fade-out*), phraseologisms (*business is business*), Anglo-Latinisms ('interferenza' in physics; 'ultimatum'), and semantic loans, like the political term 'aggiornare' (to postpone a session).
23. Panzini, *Dizionario moderno* (1918), p. xiii.
24. Ibid., p. xxviii.
25. Ibid., p. 190.
26. Paolo Monelli, *Barbaro dominio. Seicentocinquanta esotismi esaminati, combattuti e banditi dalla lingua con antichi e nuovi argomenti. Storia ed etimologia delle parole e aneddoti per svagare il lettore* (Milan: Hoepli, 1943). The title comes from a quotation taken from the Italian politician and scholar Niccolò Machiavelli's *Il principe* [*The Prince*] (Chapter XXVI: 'An Exhortation to Liberate Italy from the Barbarians') in which the writer says: 'Ad ognuno puzza questo barbaro dominio' [To all of us this barbarous dominion stinks]. See *Opere di Niccolò Machiavelli* (Milan: Società Tipografica de' Classici italiani, 1804), p. 128 (available in digitalized version at <www.opal.unito.it>).
27. Sergio Raffaelli, *Le parole proibite. Purismo di Stato e regolamentazione della pubblicità in Italia (1812–1945)* (Bologna: Il Mulino, 1983).
28. Virginia Pulcini, 'Attitudes toward the Spread of English in Italy', *World Englishes*, 16.1 (1997), 77–85.
29. Francesco Sabatini, 'L'italiano, lingua permissiva? Proposte per una strategia comune delle lingue europee verso l'anglicismo', in *Sprachkontakt und Mehrsprachigkeit* (Heidelberg: Winter

Universitätsverlag, 2008), pp. 267–75. F. Sabatini was President of the Accademia della Crusca from 2000 to 2008.
30. Giacomo Devoto and Gian Carlo Oli, *il Devoto-Oli. Vocabolario della lingua italiana 2017*, ed. by L. Serianni and M. Trifone (Milan: Le Monnier, 2016).
31. Pulcini, 'Anglicisms in Italian: Moving on into the Third Millennium'. See Fanfani (in this volume) about loanwords from American English.
32. Gaetano Rando, *Dizionario degli anglicismi nell'italiano postunitario* (Florence: Olschki, 1987).
33. Tullio De Mauro, *Grande dizionario italiano dell'uso*, 6 vols. + CD-ROM (Turin: UTET, 2007).
34. Tullio De Mauro and Marco Mancini, *Parole straniere nella lingua italiana* (Turin: Garzanti, 2003 [2001]).
35. Nicola Zingarelli, *lo Zingarelli 2017. Vocabolario della lingua italiana*, ed. by M. Cannella and B. Lazzarini (Bologna: Zanichelli, 2016).
36. Devoto and Oli, *il Devoto-Oli. Vocabolario della lingua italiana 2017*.
37. Casuals and quotation words are English words used in journalism and advertising for playful or stylistic reasons, or as instances of 'code-switching', but not likely to become true borrowings (cf. Virginia Pulcini, 'A Dictionary of Italian Anglicisms: Criteria of Inclusion and Exclusion', in *Insights into English and Germanic Lexicology and Lexicography*, ed. by Laura Pinnavaia and Nicolas Brownlees (Monza: Polimetrica, 2010), pp. 319–34). They are also called *pérégrinismes* or *xénismes* (Klajn, *Influssi inglesi nella lingua italiana*).
38. Virginia Pulcini, 'A New Dictionary of Italian Anglicisms: The Aid of Corpora', in *Proceedings XII EURALEX International Congress*, ed. by Elisa Corino, Carla Marello and Cristina Onesti, I (Alessandria: Edizioni dell'Orso, 2006), pp. 313–22; Virginia Pulcini, 'Lexical Obsolescence among Italian Anglicisms', in *Thou sittest at another boke. . . Studies in Honour of Domenico Pezzini*, ed. by Giovanni Iamartino, Roberta Facchinetti and Maria Luisa Maggioni (Monza: Polimetrica, 2008), pp. 471–88.
39. Manfred Görlach, ed., *A Dictionary of European Anglicisms* (Oxford: Oxford University Press, 2001).
40. Manfred Görlach, 'Usage in the Usage Dictionary of Anglicisms in Selected European Languages', *Studia Anglica Posnaniensia*, 31 (2001), 67–77.
41. Antonio Amato, Francesca M. Andreoni and Rita Salvi, *Prestiti linguistici dal mondo anglofono. Una tassonomia* (Rome: Bulzoni, 1990); Bona Schmid, *New words, new trends. Le parole nuovissime del 'Villaggio Globale'* (Florence: Sansoni, 1992); Cristiano Furiassi, *False Anglicisms in Italian* (Monza: Polimetrica, 2010); Gloria Italiano, *Parole a buon rendere, ovvero l'invasione dei termini anglo-italiani* (Fiesole: Cadmo Edizioni, 1999); Domenico Torretta, *Anglicismi nell'italiano dell'economia e della finanza* (Modugno: Ariete, 2002); Fabrizia Venuta, *E-finance e dintorni. Il lessico dell'economia e dell'informatica: inglese e italiano a confronto* (Napoli: Edizioni Scientifiche Italiane, 2004).
42. Claudio Giovanardi and Riccardo Gualdo, eds, *Inglese–Italiano 1 a 1. Tradurre o non tradurre le parole inglesi?* (San Cesario di Lecce: Piero Manni, 2003).
43. Tosi, *Language and Society in a Changing Italy*, p. ix.
44. Data from the Eurobarometer (2012) about 'Europeans and their Languages' reveal that 70% of Italians say that English is the most important language for their own personal success (11% indicated French) and 84% say that English is the most important language for their children's future (14% indicated French).
45. Maurizio Dardano, *Sparliamo italiano? Storia, costume, mode, virtù e peccati della nostra lingua* (Milan: Curcio, 1978).
46. Giacomo Elliot, *Parliamo itang'liano. Ovvero le 400 parole inglesi che deve sapere chi vuole fare carriera* (Milan: Rizzoli, 1977).
47. On the English-medium instruction debate, see: Nicoletta Maraschio and Domenico De Martino, eds, *Fuori l'italiano dall'università? Inglese, internazionalizzazione, politica linguistica* (Rome and Bari: Laterza, 2013); Alessandra Molino and Sandra Campagna, 'English-Mediated Instruction in Italian Universities: Conflicting Views', *Sociolinguistica*, 28 (2014), 155–71; Sandra Campagna and Virginia Pulcini, 'English as a Medium of Instruction in Italian Universities: Linguistic Policies, Pedagogical Implications', *Textus. English Studies in Italy. Perspectives on English as a Lingua Franca*, ed. by Mariagrazia Guido and Barbara Seidlhofer, 27 (2014), 173–90;

Virginia Pulcini and Sandra Campagna, 'Internationalisation and the EMI Controversy in Italian Higher Education', in *English-Medium Instruction in European Higher Education*, ed. by Slobodanka Dimova, Anna Kristina Hultgren and Christian Jensen (Berlin: Mouton De Gruyter, 2015), pp. 65–87.

48. Maraschio and De Martino, *Fuori l'italiano dall'università?*.
49. Gian Luigi Beccaria and Andrea Graziosi, *Lingua Madre: italiano e inglese nel mondo globale* (Rome: Aracne).
50. <https://www.change.org/p/un-intervento-per-la-lingua-italiana-dilloinitaliano>.
51. <https://www.internazionale.it/opinione/annamaria-testa/2015/02/17/dillo-in-italiano>.
52. Claudio Marazzini and Alessio Petralli, eds, *La lingua italiana e le lingue romanze di fronte agli anglicismi* (Florence: goWare and Accademia della Crusca).
53. Tullio De Mauro, *In Europa son già 103. Troppe lingue per una democrazia?* (Bari: Laterza, 2014).
54. Paul Baker, *American and British English: Divided by a Common Language?* (Cambridge: Cambridge University Press, 2017).
55. Pulcini, 'Anglicisms in Italian: Moving on into the Third Millennium'.

CHAPTER 3

English in Italian Education: Between Europeanization and Americanization

Giancarlo Schirru

The History of a Relationship

This chapter aims to illustrate a particular aspect of the relationship between Italy and the USA: a particular but not completely marginal aspect. It intends to summarize the development of the English language within the Italian school system. The final part of this chapter, including the statistics provided in the appendixes, will offer original data on the lower secondary school system (scuola media inferiore) for use in future research. Education policies may be considered among the main tools employed by Italian language planning with regard to foreign languages. At the same time, they can be examined as important aspects of the country's international orientation. Obviously, the English language concerns not only the USA, but the United Kingdom as well: more precisely, the relative position of the two main English-speaking countries will be the object of reflection in this chapter. However, with regard to the Italian situation, it is clear that, from the mid-twentieth century onwards, the spread of English has largely been developing in parallel with the importance of the USA in culture and in political institutions.

Nowadays, the Italian education system is clearly oriented towards English: it is classifiable as an English-first system. This means that English is not only the foreign language taught most widely in schools, but it is also the first foreign language studied by all pupils: English is universally taught in primary school, and only in secondary school can students ask to begin to study a second or even a third foreign language (depending on their curricula), chosen from a range offered by each institution, normally comprising three other European languages (French, Spanish, German). Only in the upper secondary school years are other languages — such as Russian, Arabic and Chinese — offered by some schools.

Such a system was designed only in recent years, and cannot be considered as a mere reflection of the wide dissemination of English in the contemporary world. It represents the end point of a long and complex development, which cannot be summarized as a linear and progressive process. It has been part of the history of Italy since the country was unified a century and a half ago, and has seen many different phases, many steps backwards, and some decisive turning points. Like all convoluted stories resembling a saga, this one, too, has its heroes and deserves to be told.

The French-Oriented Italian School

The Italian education system marks its starting point with the school reform that was implemented in 1859 in the Kingdom of Sardinia, the small state originally including Piedmont, Liguria and Sardinia (but which at that time already extended to Lombardy and part of the northern Italian peninsula), ruled by the royal dynasty of Savoy. The reform is known as the 'Casati Law', taking its name from Gabrio Casati, the Lombard minister of education who promoted and signed it into law. The reform was passed just two years prior to the transformation of the Kingdom of Sardinia into the Kingdom of Italy, with the country's unification in 1861: the Casati Law was then inherited by the unified state as the basis for the new Italian national education system.[1]

The position of foreign languages within the school designed by the Casati reform can be understood considering the particular linguistic position of Savoy-Piedmont — the actual political core of the Kingdom of Sardinia: the French language occupied a position of strong prestige in this region, with a wide dissemination among both the leadership and popular classes. One case to take as a meaningful example is that of the political leader who was to become the triumphant minister of Italian unification, Camillo Benso Cavour. He had been educated in French and, according to contemporary descriptions, the prospect of making speeches in Italian at the first sitting of the Italian parliament in Turin caused him anxiety and presented him with difficulties.[2] Moreover, within the Kingdom of Sardinia, in the Duchy of Aosta (now the Valle d'Aosta Region), French was the official language of administration and the schools, due to an old feudal privilege.[3] In that area, and in sections of Piedmont, French, Occitan and Franco-Provençal had at that time — and still have — a large local and popular spread as primary languages.

The Casati reform is clearly oriented towards the adoption of the French language; it may be called 'French first', since French occupied a dominant position among foreign languages. This may be considered not only as the result of the role French played as an international vehicular language at that time, but is also due to more contingent reasons. The Kingdom of Savoy long fluctuated between two different languages and political environments as it oscillated between the two sides of the Alps, the French and the Italian; only in the late nineteenth century did it make its clear choice in favour of the latter.[4]

The school designed by Casati may be compared to a tree with two large branches. The central trunk represents the four years of common primary school, of which only the first two were obligatory. After that, the educational path came to a fork. On one side was the classical school, which adopted the international models: the first five years were named *ginnasio* and were inspired by the Austrian *Gymnasium*; the subsequent three years were labelled *liceo*, and were patterned after the French *lycée*. In this way, Casati merged the French tradition of Piedmont and the Austrian one of Lombardy, now joined together in the new kingdom. On the other hand, there were three years of technical school, which represented at that time — and still do to this day — the system's true weak spot. In secondary schools, a foreign language course was introduced, represented everywhere by French: only in some sections of the technical school was a second foreign language — English or German — introduced.[5]

Therefore, English entered Italian schools at their beginning, but in a clearly subordinate position, and only as a technical language, as a reflex of the dominant position of English industry at that time, and not as a language of culture.

Until the Second World War, the later evolution of the Italian education system may be summarized as a continuous branching of the originally binary secondary school model of Casati.[6] In the reform designed in 1923, at the start of the Fascist Era, by minister of education Giovanni Gentile, a large improvement in secondary school orientations can be observed. Nevertheless, these new orientations are all the result of the distinction between the classical schools on the one hand and the technical schools on the other. Nor did any noteworthy innovation occur for foreign language education. French was introduced as the first foreign language in all the different branches of secondary school, and only in technical school was a second foreign language occasionally offered, represented by English or German.

The real innovations taking place after the First World War may be found in the teaching methods and the increased total hours of foreign language instruction in the curricula: this greater attention to foreign languages took place during the first years of Fascism as well. But Italian language policy changed radically in the mid-1930s. Giuseppe Bottai, minister of education from 1936 to 1943, was called upon to pursue a policy of open hostility, by schools and other public institutions, to foreign languages, as a reflex of the general politics of autarchy and closure promoted by the government during that phase. In 1940, the Italian government closed even private language schools, such as Berlitz.[7]

A New Direction

The Second World War marked the main turning point in this history: as soon as the Anglo-American troops landed in Sicily, a sub-commission on education was set up within the Allied government commission. By a particularly fortuitous circumstance, the commission included a highly motivated and competent educator serving in the US Army at that time. Colonel Carleton W. Washburne was born in Chicago, and was deeply influenced by the pedagogical ideas of John Dewey, a family acquaintance. Washburne began his career as a schoolteacher in California, and had been subsequently named supervisor of public schools in Winnetka County, Illinois. Here, he introduced the new principles of the active school, and experimented with his philosophy of education based on the individualization of student-based curricula, creative group activity, and the development of social responsibility.[8]

At the outset, the commission operated with the aim of deleting fascist propaganda from schoolbooks and public education. But quite soon, Washburne focused on the need for powerful action in the field of foreign language teaching as a tool for rebuilding a nation destroyed by war. The sensitivity to the importance of foreign languages had been a key feature characterizing the US war mobilization: at that time all the main scientific forces of US linguistics were active in the description of languages diffused in areas of strategic relevance, and in the development of the new methodologies for teaching them to the servicemen. A similar attention to the linguistic aspect of the war effort was completely missed by the Italian institutions. The commission led by Washburne began a reflection on the methodologies of language teaching inspired by new educational principles.[9] At the end of the war, Washburne did not return to the USA, but stayed in Italy for many years as a counsellor to the Italian Ministry of Education, and as president of USIS (United States Information Service).[10] According to Paolo Balboni, doyen of foreign language education in Italy, the USIS was the main inspiration for the Special Project on Foreign Languages (Progetto speciale lingue straniere) launched by the Department of Education during the 1970s.[11]

However, the figure from the Italian ruling classes who played the most important role in the development of the English language in Italian schools was the Christian Democrat politician Aldo Moro. In 1958, as a young minister of education, Moro signed a new Development plan for schools (Piano di sviluppo per la scuola nel decennio dal 1959 al 1969), which laid the groundwork for the later radical reform of the lower secondary school of 1962. This plan devoted great attention to the teaching of foreign languages, the culmination of reflection that had begun many years earlier. An initial result was the increased number of hours dedicated to foreign language instruction in lower secondary schools. As a second consequence, a general revision of the teaching methodologies for foreign languages was promoted. Thirdly, the plan overcame the monopoly of French in Italian schools, which was replaced by a choice between four languages in lower secondary school. This is the crucial segment in the education system for the choice of the foreign language, since it even determines the language a pupil will continue to study in the upper secondary school. The four languages were French, English, German and Spanish.[12] Therefore, foreign language teaching was legitimated from the perspective of Italy's European choice: eventually, English found a role in the Italian school as one of the main languages of Western Europe, the area in which the country was placed after the war.

Even if at the beginning the possibility of choosing among different languages was actually implemented only in a minority of schools, it had a long-term effect for the development of the English language in Italian schools. The actual result of this decision was the beginning of the progressive prevalence of English over French. Such a change took place from the bottom up, as a result of the intentional choice by individual families, and within about twenty years inverted the positions of these two languages in Italian schools.

A second effect of this decision concerned universities, since it legitimated the diversification of curricula for foreign language teaching and supported the expansion of English, German and Spanish within the Italian university (although Spanish did not seem to meet favour with families in the first years).[13]

Therefore, in the early 1960s, the English language changed its status in the Italian school system, passing from its function as a technical-commercial language, to the position of one of the cultural languages of the new Atlantic Europe.

Decades of Experiments

The lower secondary school reform, which introduced the unified middle school in 1962, opened the age of militant debate on education. The new 'language question' was broached by the writer Pier Paolo Pasolini, with a 1964 article entitled 'Nuove questioni linguistiche' [New Language Questions], which provoked many reactions from scholars, journalists and writers.[14] But several years later, in May 1967, the explosive book entitled *Letter to a Teacher* was published; signed by the 'Barbiana school' (Scuola di Barbiana), it was presented as the result of a collective effort by a group of pupils at the school, but was largely inspired by the thoughts of its founder, the priest Don Lorenzo Milani.[15] The text marks one of the most notable points in the controversy against the 'school of grammar' in both Italian and foreign languages. It literally called for a destruction of traditional grammatical education, the banning of literary Italian from schools, and the adoption of inductive methodologies for foreign language learning, for example based on listening to records.

The book was published a few months before the explosion of the student protests of 1968. It suddenly became one of the books of the student movement, and was perhaps one that was most representative of them.

Many students involved in the 1968 demonstrations became schoolteachers or university professors. For a long period, two different fronts were active for the expansion of foreign languages in education. The first was the institutional one, and was represented by the Ministry of Education's already cited special project for foreign languages (Progetto speciale lingue straniere), based largely on trialling new methodologies. The plan had been discussed for more than a decade, and was passed by the Ministry in 1977, in response to the Modern Language Project elaborated by the European Council in 1967.[16]

The second front was represented by the spontaneous activism of the teachers, organized in trade unions and many associations. One of the more active of them was GISCEL (Gruppo di Intervento e Studio nel Campo dell'Educazione Linguistica [Intervention and Study Group in the Field of Language Education]), created within the activity of the Società italiana di linguistica (Italian Language Society), which was in turn founded in 1967, and had its first conference at the Center for American Studies of Rome. In 1975, in Rome, GISCEL presented *Ten Theses for Democratic Linguistic Education* (Dieci tesi sull'educazione linguistica democratica): this text, originally developed by the linguist Tullio De Mauro, joined *Letter to a Teacher* as the other radical criticism against a traditional language teaching methodology.[17]

These decades of militant discussions were also characterized by experiments: for the first time, in 1974, a second foreign language was experimentally introduced in some secondary schools.

As may be observed, the expansion of the English language in the education system was connected with the general change in teaching methodologies, with the activism of schoolteachers and scholars, and with the growing importance of foreign languages in the perception of all the actors. Such an evolution met the indications of the European Community in support of multilingualism in education, formulated for example in article 126 of the Maastricht Treaty of 1992.

This is the context of the more recent evolution, which may be defined as a period of 'permanent reform', given the high number of school reforms passed starting in 2000. With the reform developed by the ministers Luigi Berlinguer and Tullio De Mauro, the principle of autonomy was introduced into the education system. In the field of linguistics, the reform absorbed the European principle establishing education with two EU foreign languages. The main attention then shifted to the second language; this condition encouraged the spread of the Spanish language, until that time confined to a marginal position.

Nevertheless, from 2003 to 2009, a series of decisions partially corrected the principle of a generic European multilingualism, assuming the position of the so-called 'English first' language policy. This development sanctioned the fact that in Italy multilingualism is based on the centrality of English as a foreign language, thus accepting at the institutional level the development which had been spontaneously taking place in society.

The relevant decisions in this regard were the following:

> (a) in 2003, under minister Letizia Moratti, English was introduced as an obligatory subject in primary school: after a long trial period, foreign languages entered all primary school programs, but the only language was in fact English;[18]
>
> (b) the reform of the university programs of 2007, signed by minister Fabio Mussi, included an obligatory English language and translation exam for all first-level courses of study;
>
> (c) the school reform of 2009, promoted by minister Mariastella Gelmini, stated the clear predominance of English in Italian education, introducing the principle that, in all the curricula with only one foreign language, that language had to be English.

As may be observed, in recent years the Italian education system completed a deep and long-term transformation in its foreign language orientation: at the moment of its foundation, with Italian unification, it was exclusively oriented towards French; one and a half centuries later, it is clearly oriented towards English. This slow evolution was accomplished after the Second World War during an initial first period as the result of a liberalization process, and only in more recent times as an explicit target of education policies.

Italy, United States of America, United Kingdom

The spread of English in Italian schools is not a generic reference to the English-speaking world: it is the result of an explicit undertaking of the US government, and took shape as an effect of Italy's entry into the North Atlantic sphere of influence. It is clearly a topic having to do with the international relationships between Italy and the USA.

Nevertheless, it must be stressed that the Italian ruling classes never interpreted such a relationship in a bilateral way, as one between two nations, and between two sets of state, security, education and cultural systems. On the contrary, the transatlantic relationship was always read in a multilateral way, as an alliance also comprising many other realities, and as an overcoming of the inadequacy of bilateral relations, which depended largely on secret diplomacy and were therefore considered responsible for the outbreak of the Second World War.

Italy took part in building transatlantic relations by engaging in building European institutions. Therefore, in the linguistic field as well, the adoption of English as the foreign language of reference for schools was not motivated as a consequence of the special role that the USA played for Italy, or with reference to the function of English as a global vehicular language, but, crucially, it was considered an aspect of the country's integration into the new European framework.

From this perspective, the relationship between Italy and the USA required the United Kingdom's entry into the European Community for full development. In recent decades, the road from Rome to Washington has passed through London.

Appendix: Foreign Languages in Italian Schools

In this appendix, the available data from institutional sources, concerning the distribution of the different foreign languages in the lower secondary school, is summarized:

- until the school year 1994–95 data are taken from the yearbooks of the Istituto nazionale di statistica — Istat (The National Institute for Statistics) (until 1989 Istituto centrale di statistica [The Central Institute for Statistics]);

- for the school years comprising 1995–96 and 2000–2001, reference is made to: Ministero dell'Istruzione, dell'Università e della Ricerca, *Quadro informativo sulle lingue straniere*, September 2001 (downloaded from the URL: <http://www.edscuola.it/archivio/statistiche/lingue01.pdf> [accessed 7 January 2018]);

- for the school years 2001–02 and 2002–03 data are not available because of the migration of the statistics survey;

- for subsequent school years, data are directly provided by the statistics service of the Minister of Education.

Data are presented only for lower secondary schools because the distribution of foreign languages in this crucial segment was reformed in 1962, and was only subsequently reflected in upper secondary schools.

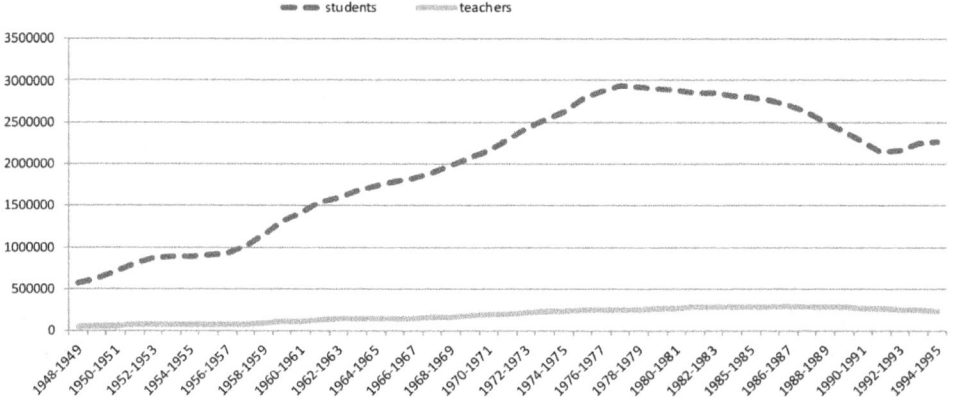

FIG. 3.1. Total students enrolled and teachers in lower secondary schools (Scuola media inferiore)

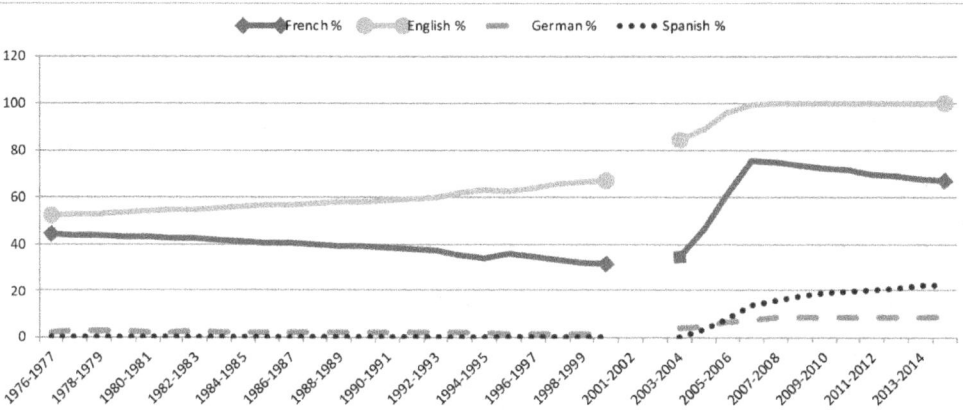

FIG. 3.2. Percentage of lower secondary school students by modern foreign language studied (the diffusion of the second foreign language became relevant from the school years 1993–94 onward)

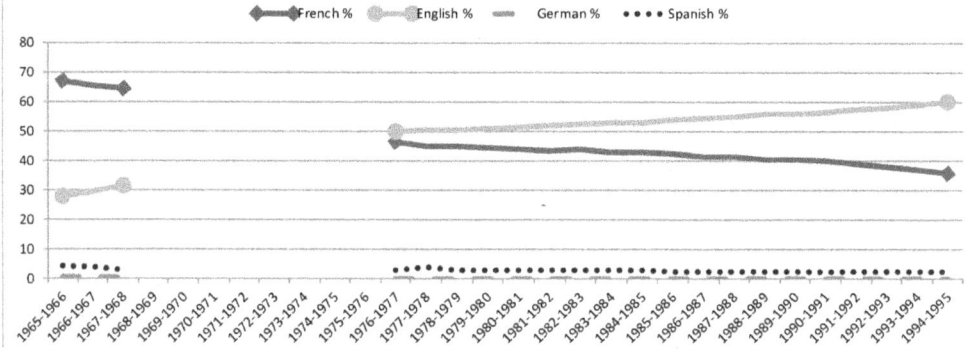

FIG. 3.3. Percentage of foreign language teachers in lower secondary schools by language

TABLE 3.1. Students in lower secondary schools by modern foreign language studied

School Year	French	English	German	Spanish	Total Enrolled
1976–77	1,278,137	1,497,191	71,000	4,508	2,869,593
1977–78	1,287,484	1,554,217	81,753	4,769	2,938,791
1978–79	1,278,667	1,541,400	79,103	4,966	2,923,974
1979–80	1,254,926	1,540,661	80,028	5,146	2,900,220
1980–81	1,234,792	1,556,137	71,520	3,807	2,884,759
1981–82	1,209,523	1,554,988	69,992	3,507	2,856,441
1982–83	1,201,436	1,553,533	75,723	3,404	2,849,898
1983–84	1,175,651	1,552,908	66,311	3,332	2,815,922
1984–85	1,149,987	1,553,319	64,670	2,649	2,788,584
1985–86	1,120,248	1,553,858	62,930	2,574	2,756,577
1986–87	1,087,083	1,539,143	60,787	2,858	2,704,940
1987–88	1,035,725	1,503,064	57,125	2,311	2,613,635
1988–89	985,656	1,448,931	52,774	2,133	2,503,799
1989–90	931,617	1,390,876	49,495	2,652	2,388,910
1990–91	870,871	1,328,991	45,109	1,921	2,261,569
1991–92	812,089	1,277,889	43,782	1,765	2,150,676
1992–93	798,319	1,300,315	47,303	1,745	2,163,880
1993–94	790,024	1,394,550	49,876	1,716	2,251,375
1994–95	773,461	1,421,118	48,025	1,737	2,258,614
1995–96★	749,739	1,312,991	30,393	1,844	2,094,967
1996–97	717,033	1,305,894	29,882	1,815	2,055,524
1997–98	674,543	1,333,620	30,454	1,846	2,040,463
1998–99	657,526	1,349,174	30,436	1,851	2,038,987
1999–2000	641,501	1,360,925	30,074	1,814	2,034,314
2001–02	—	—	—	—	—
2002–03	—	—	—	—	—
2003–04★	619,938	1,528,170	68,947	9,121	1,805,001
2004–05	830,671	1,596,194	87,316	64,474	1,792,244
2005–06	1,081,126	1,693,252	120,755	141,789	1,764,230
2006–07	1,304,747	1,719,649	132,316	235,810	1,730,031
2007–08	1,294,015	1,723,615	148,470	276,298	1,727,339
2008–09	1,288,631	1,756,989	150,795	310,140	1,758,384
2009–10	1,285,598	1,777,562	153,916	334,204	1,777,834

★ Change of the data series (see above).

2010–11	1,276,538	1,786,449	152,204	349,959	1,787,467
2011–12	1,252,016	1,791,992	152,804	367,318	1,792,379
2012–13	1,222,553	1,779,563	152,970	378,830	1,779,758
2013–14	1,192,114	1,761,142	154,478	387,476	1,760,766
2014–15	1,159,940	1,738,448	155,767	389,904	1,738,729

TABLE 3.2. Foreign language teachers in lower secondary schools by language

school year	French	English	Spanish	German	Total foreign language
1965–66	9,551	3,974	90	610	14,225
1966–67	9,739	4,428	92	623	14,882
1967–68	9,899	4,861	97	486	15,343
1968–69*					
1969–70*					
1970–71*					
1971–72*					
1972–73*					
1973–74*					
1974–75*					
1975–76*					
1976–77	11,703	12,558	48	692	25,105
1977–78	11,597	12,963	49	1,005	25,729
1978–79	11,551	12,981	50	776	25,645
1979–80	11,294	12,993	50	763	25,420
1980–81	11,484	13,480	42	762	26,062
1981–82	11,608	13,847	39	785	26,579
1982–83	11,699	13,995	38	798	26,704
1983–84	11,484	14,036	40	723	26,581
1984–85	11,953	14,889	36	757	27,939
1985–86	12,046	15,333	33	733	28,444
1986–87	12,015	15,771	46	750	28,860
1987–88	11,971	15,986	26	726	28,987
1988–89	10,996	15,080	25	664	27,019
1989–90	10,812	15,039	33	644	26,799
1990–91	10,415	14,810	26	611	26,135
1991–92	10,225	15,053	30	632	26,248

* Data not surveyed

1992–93	10,038	15,469	33	697	26,536
1993–94	9,741	15,506	30	711	26,275
1994–95	9,291	15,611	37	672	25,933
1995–96	8,362	13,420	18	595	
1996–97	7,887	13,288	17	577	

Notes to Chapter 3

1. For the importance of the Casati reform as the birth of the Italian education system, see Giuseppe Talamo, *La scuola. Dalla Legge Casati all'Inchiesta del 1864* (Milan: Giuffré, 1960); Marino Raicich, *Scuola, cultura e politica da De Sanctis a Gentile* (Pisa: Nistri Lischi, 1981), pp. 29–54, 170–284; Adolfo Scotto di Luzio, *La scuola degli italiani* (Bologna: Il Mulino, 2007), pp. 19–40, 57–63.
2. Cavour's mother tongue was the Piedmontese dialect, but like all the other members of the Subalpine aristocracy, he spoke French as a cultivated language. He encountered many difficulties in his progress in Italian; see the biography of Rosario Romeo, *Cavour e il suo tempo*, I: *1810–1842*, 3rd edn (Rome and Bari: Laterza, 2012), pp. 186–876; and the linguistic observations in Luca Serianni, 'Cavour e la conquista dell'Italiano', in *Atlante della letteratura italiana*, III: *Dal Romanticismo a oggi*, ed. by Sergio Luzzatto and Gabriele Pedullà (Turin: Einaudi, 2012), pp. 256–60.
3. See Paolo E. Balboni, *Gli insegnamenti linguistici nella scuola italiana* (Padua: Liviana, 1988), p. 11.
4. On this topic, see the historical reconstruction offered in Claudio Marazzini, *Il Piemonte e la Valle d'Aosta* (Turin: UTET, 1991); Claudio Marazzini, *Storia linguistica della città di Torino* (Rome: Carocci, 2012). See also Tullio De Mauro, *Storia linguistica dell'Italia unita*, 6th edn (Rome and Bari: Laterza, 2011), pp. 286–89.
5. See Balboni, *Gli insegnamenti linguistici*, pp. 13–15; Paolo E. Balboni, *Storia dell'educazione linguistica in Italia. Dalla legge Casati alla Riforma Gelmini* (Turin: UTET, 2009), pp. 24–25.
6. The institution of the *liceo moderno*, in 1911, can be mentioned here as a partial attempt to open up the study of modern foreign languages in the secondary school. The experiment met with limited success, and was abandoned in the years of Fascism; see Balboni, *Storia dell'educazione linguistica*, pp. 40–41.
7. See Balboni, *Gli insegnamenti linguistici*, pp. 43–53; Balboni, *Storia dell'educazione linguistica*, pp. 59–61; Scotto di Luzio, *La scuola degli italiani*, pp. 195–99. On the language policy of Fascism, see Sergio Raffaelli, *Le parole proibite. Purismo di stato e regolamentazione della pubblicità in Italia (1812–1945)* (Bologna: Il Mulino, 1983), pp. 133–225; Gabriella Klein, *La politica linguistica del fascismo* (Bologna: Il Mulino, 1986); Pier Vincenzo Mengaldo, *Storia della lingua italiana. Il Novecento* (Bologna: Il Mulino, 1994), pp. 13–16; Riccardo Tesi, *Storia dell'italiano. La lingua moderna e contemporanea* (Bologna: Zanichelli, 2005), pp. 199–214.
8. For a summary of this experience, which was soon translated into Italian, see Carleton W. Washburne and Sidney P. Marland Jr., *Winnetka: The History and Significance of an Educational Experiment* (Englewood Cliffs, NJ: Prentice-Hall, 1963); It. trans. *Winnetka. Storia e significato di un esperimento pedagogico* (Florence: La Nuova Italia, 1960). See also Carleton W. Washburne, *The World's Good: Education for World-Mindedness* (New York: Day, 1954); It. trans. *Il bene del mondo* (Florence: La Nuova Italia, 1965).
9. On the school reorganization promoted by the Allied government commission in Italy, see Sara Tomasi, *La scuola italiana dalla dittatura alla Repubblica, 1943–1948* (Rome: Editori Riuniti, 1976), pp. 14–19; Balboni, *Gli insegnamenti linguistici*, pp. 70–71; Balboni, *Storia dell'educazione linguistica*, pp. 62–64.
10. In an autobiographical sketch on the activity he devoted to Italy, Washburne recalls:

    During the war I accepted a commission from the army and was put in charge of the reopening and the 'defascizing' of the schools and the universities in Italy. Later, I took an active part in combating Communism in Italy as a Public Affairs Officer of the United States

Department of State. (Carleton W. Washburne, *What is Progressive Education: A Book for Parents and Others* (New York: Day, 1952), p. 9)

On the role he played in the reorganization of the Italian school system during the Allied military occupation, and his activity in the country in subsequent years, see also Carleton W. Washburne, 'La riorganizzazione della scuola in Italia', *Scuola e città*, 21 (1970), 273–92.

11. See Balboni, *Gli insegnamenti linguistici*, p. 71; Balboni, *Storia dell'educazione linguistica*, p. 69.
12. See Balboni, *Gli insegnamenti linguistici*, p. 82.
13. For a brief reconstruction of English teaching in Italian universities, see *The Study of English Language in Italian Universities: Papers of the National Conference* (Turin, 17–20 January 1990), ed. by Maria Teresa Prat Zagrebelsky (Alessandria: Edizioni dell'Orso, 1991), pp. 5–10.
14. The article was published on 16 December 1964 in the communist magazine *Rinascita*, and subsequently republished in Pier Paolo Pasolini, *Empirismo eretico* (Milan: Garzanti, 1972), pp. 5–24; the main texts in this debate are collected in *La nuova questione della lingua*, ed. by Oronzo Parlangeli (Brescia: Paideia, 1971).
15. Scuola di Barbiana, *Lettera a una professoressa* (Florence: Libreria editrice fiorentina, 1967); Engl. trans. by Nora Rossi and Tom Cole, with postscripts of Robert Coles and John Holt, Boys of Barbiana, *Letter to a Teacher* (New York: Random House, 1970).
16. See Balboni, *Gli insegnamenti linguistici*, pp. 124–26; Balboni, *Storia dell'educazione linguistica*, p. 83.
17. The *Theses* can now be read on the GISCEL website (<http://giscel.it> [accessed 7 January 2018]), and, in French and English translation, in Silvana Ferreri, *Dieci tesi per l'educazione linguistica democratica* (Viterbo: Sette città, 2007).
18. On the experimentation of foreign language teaching in primary school from 1977 to the present day, see Balboni, *Gli insegnamenti linguistici*, pp. 129–31, 146–69.

CHAPTER 4

❖

Modern Throwbacks: Screening Italians in the USA — The First Fifty Years*

Giorgio Bertellini

> '[the gangster] speaks for us, expressing that part of the American psyche which rejects the qualities and the demands of modern life, which rejects 'Americanism' itself.'
> ROBERT WARSHOW, 'The Gangster as Tragic Hero', 1948.[1]

In this chapter I discuss how US film culture — which comprises films produced *and* screened in the USA — responded to, and reworked, images of Italy and Italians from the turn of the twentieth century to the early 1950s. Throughout this half-century, several momentous historical events structured the traffic of Italian people and their representations across the Atlantic — from mass migration and the rise of fascism to the country's post-war shift from monarchy to republic. In the same period, US film culture also underwent radical historical transformations that deeply affected both the film representation of Italians and the overall experience of Americans as film spectators. These occurrences related to the emergence of the star and studio systems, the introduction of synchronized sound, and the enforcing of a censorship code.

In this overview, I combine two different critical approaches in the study of how national film cultures engage with foreign worlds or subjects — whether through settings, genres, or characters. The most common method tends to subsume foreignness as a *functional* resource, both commercially and ideologically, within the hegemonic borders of a nation's cinematic ethos. In the specific context of my research, I have sought to assess the *function* of the representations of Italians to master US cultural and dramaturgic narratives. A second, more ambitious method flips the critical perspective: it asks what we can discover about a national film

---

* I wish to thank Guido Bonsaver, Alessandro Carlucci, and Matthew Reza for organizing and running an exceptionally productive conference that brought together scholars from very different disciplines and geographies, and for editing this volume with impeccable grace. I also would like to express my gratitude for their most helpful feedback on my own contribution. Theirs is a model of scholarly dialogue and service.

culture when we view it *through* the lens of its foreign constituencies, that is when we study the *transformative work* that these foreign representations perform inside a national culture, and when we identify what novel historiographical reframing they encourage. In this chapter I thus look also beyond questions of function to consider whether and how the films that I regard as particularly relevant to the representation of Italy and Italians contributed to *disrupt*, rather than to reinforce, familiar narratives about US film culture.

For both approaches, I have operated under a working assumption — actually, a structuring prejudice — which generally associates cinema, and specifically US cinema, with *what is modern*, namely with enlightened and forward-looking subjects, efficient narratives, and innovative market strategies, and associates Italy and Italians with *what is not*. It is a prejudice that the representation of Italians in early twentieth-century USA inaugurated, shaped, and consolidated and that, as an influential primal scene, informed the historical function of Italians as icons of primitive inadequacy or bracing authenticity — on and off screen. On a critical level, namely in relationship to US film historiography, the study of the prejudicial representation of Italians may be distinctively revealing: it ought to expose the antinomies, or contradictions, undergirding the notion of Hollywood history as an inevitable index of modernity.

Led by this assumption I have identified four historical moments that, defined in relation to distinct historical junctures, variously juxtaposed modernity with backward Italianness (hereafter simply named 'Italianness'). In each period 'Italianness' is either identified with 'Italians in Italy' or 'Italians in America', more rarely with both. The first moment pertains to early cinema, that is, to the period conventionally encompassing the years between 1895 and 1915, when Italianness referred to both Italians *and* Italian immigrants. The second one pertains to the cinema of the post-First World War years, when Italianness mainly referred to the representation of Italians *and not* of immigrants. The third one, encompassing post-Depression gangster films, returned Italianness to a dominant representation of Italian immigrants and their descendants. The final one, coinciding with the season of Neorealism, saw another shift, with Italianness once again mainly referencing Italians.

Early Cinema: Characters of the Picturesque

Scholars of early cinema have long held that motion pictures, in their combined ability to absorb technological innovations and appeal to masses of interclass spectators, constituted a symptom of, and a catalyst to, modernity. Film historians have been able to posit such convenient interlocking of cinema with modernity by defining the latter in terms of turn-of-the-twentieth-century industrial and technological development and related radical changes in mass urbanization and transportation. Perhaps unsurprisingly, film historian Ben Singer has described the historical pairing of cinema with modernity in terms of a 'nexus'. He writes:

> The emergence of cinema was predicated on a *specific* convergence of modern technology [. . .] industrial rationalization applied to the efficient manufacture

and distribution of amusement; on massive urbanization; on the subsequent coalescence of a mass audience [in possession of] a modicum of expendable income [. . .]; on the cultural permissibility of heterosocial public circulation [. . .] on extensive transportation and communications networks.[2]

While referring to the works of both early twentieth-century critics and current film scholars, and after comparing 'film-viewing' to 'the perceptual intensity of quotidian experience in the metropolitan environment', Singer concluded with a lapidary statement — 'cinema was the mirror of modern life'.[3]

Film historians have productively embraced this approach by illustrating the medium's ground-breaking impact on the lives of millions of Americans beyond the terms of mere amusement. Scholars have reflected on *how* cinema provided a new form of experience and knowledge of the world, but have tended to describe such experiences through the isomorphic terms of modernity's radical innovations — expanded access to rapidity, mobility, and information.[4] The very literalness of an approach that defines cinema *qua* modernity and modernity *qua* cinema, however, has presented shortcomings. It has failed to account for key historical phenomena — from the circulation of foreign films in the USA to mass immigration — and for their cultural and aesthetic import, particularly in relation to the representation of national and racial difference.[5] For the purposes of this chapter, suffice it to say that the same modernist emphasis has not accounted for the US popularity of foreign historical re-enactments and of productions about Italian immigrants — the latter often indebted to the so-called picturesque mode. In brief, the most glaring blind spot in the aforementioned notion of cinematic modernity pertains to the representation of subjects not immediately assimilable to the modern world — past figures and foreign immigrants.[6]

In early US film culture, the most visible and successful display of Italian filmmaking was repeatedly associated with the representation of history, whether related to ancient Rome, the Middle Ages, or the Renaissance. The fame of stunning epic re-enactments, including *The Last Days of Pompeii* (1908 and 1913), *Quo Vadis?* (1913), and *Cabiria* (1914), effortlessly aligned Italy (and Italians living in Italy) with a fervent vocation for antiquity and a resilient passéist taste.[7] Secondly, a narrowly defined matching of cinema with modern life has dealt with mass migration not as one of the USA's master narratives, but as an accidental occurrence, morphologically extraneous to the phenomenon of modernity. Admittedly, film historians have acknowledged the large presence of immigrants in US movie theatres. But they treated them as 'throwback' subjects, carriers of anti-modern or pre-modern culture, and thus destined to be passive receivers of cinema's modernity and not in any way as its contributors. Yet, US cinema devoted a considerable number of productions to immigrants, and particularly to those coming from Italy. This was certainly in relationship to the massive size of the Italian colony in the film capital of New York City. But it was also because the pre-circulating aesthetic tradition of the picturesque, for centuries devoted to Southern Italians, provided a ready-made visual referent for their representation. Other immigrant groups, including Jewish, Slavic, or Greek, did not enjoy the same aesthetic position.

US films' subsumption of Italian immigrants aestheticized their difference on the basis of the picturesque's remarkable encyclopaedia of images and narratives which had been circulating among European painters and image-makers since the late seventeenth century. The key to such a modern aestheticizing process, which granted appeal to the allegedly primitive Southern Italian populations, can be found in the words of one of the picturesque's earlier theoreticians. In 1792, the Anglican cleric William Gilpin noted that advanced countries' industrial modernity came at an aesthetic loss. While 'in a moral view, the industrious mechanic is a more pleasing object than the loitering peasant', in a picturesque light, he claimed, it is otherwise: 'The arts of industry are rejected; and even idleness, if I may so speak, adds dignity to a character.'[8] To both foreign travellers to Italy and film spectators in the USA, the backwardness of Italians as idle shepherds, artists, or blackhanders was a source of aesthetic delectation. It did not matter whether these throwback characters were meandering in ruin-dotted landscapes or in the Little Italies of the USA. Films like *Little Italy* (1909), *The Chord of Life* (1909), and *The Italian Blood* (1911) displayed those 'conditions of destitution and disorder', which, as photographer Jacob Riis had argued in 1890, 'are the delight of the artist', because they 'lend a tinge of color to the otherwise dull monotony of the slums they inhabit'.[9] Immigrants' 'filth', as critic and poet Sadakichi Hartmann added in 1903 referring to New York's Italian sections, is 'the wizard who renders every scene and object — even the humblest one — picturesque'.[10] It was exactly this notion of charming, Old World authenticity that US actor George Beban exploited in his blockbusters *The Italian* and *The Name of the Rose* (both 1915) before describing the reason for his popular characterizations of Italians in terms of their 'picturesqueness'.[11]

On a historical level, the picturesque representations of Italians as charming throwback subjects helped US cinema translate the challenging and divisive issue of national and racial diversity into entertainment value. As their most loyal customers, immigrants in general and Italians in particular had to be screened in an 'agreeable light', but the celebration of their pristine humanity, not yet poisoned by the neurasthenia of modern life, could become most serviceable if it domesticated their otherness in reconciling and entertaining terms. On a critical level, when read through the lens of the picturesque representation, the aforementioned definition of cinematic modernity reveals quite glaringly its failure to address the inner contradiction of cinema's modernity — namely, the tension between the newness of its mass cultural impact and the country's resilient national diversity. As a contradiction that was central to the history of film production and consumption in early twentieth-century USA, it ought to prompt scholars to expand the familiar trope of industrial and technological modernity to include an appreciation of the ways, on and off screen, immigrants contributed to the new form of mass representation and communication.

Novel and Unmodern Leading Men

While less central in the scholarly interventions about the 1920s, the notion of modernity for the decade has often relied on utopian accounts.[12] The 1920s, the argument went, saw a mass expansion of civic and consumer participation, evident in the granting of the right to vote to women, the rise of wages across classes, and the ensuing emergence of new democratic and subversive models of gender behaviour — most obviously represented by the figure of the 'flapper'. Such positive gains also revealed a less-known flip side. The decade saw strenuous efforts to channel and manage such expansion of rights and opportunities not just through restrictions over immigration and leisure time (i.e. the Johnson Quota Act and Prohibition), but also through the emerging professional practices of publicity and public relations.[13] It is no coincidence that in this period Hollywood expanded the star system into the industry's key vector for managing attendance and commercial success, and in the process granting the medium a most influential role within the country's public culture. Stars had existed before 1917, obviously, but the co-optation of Mary Pickford, Douglas Fairbanks, and William S. Hart in the Liberty Bond Drives in 1917 and 1918 effort taught Hollywood that stars could sell more than films. They could market ideas of personal conduct, gender relationship, and even political convictions — at home and abroad.

Further, the war had internationalized US popular culture. The direct or vicarious exposure to the world by millions of individuals following war news or fighting 'over there' had opened most Americans to unbeknownst geographies, characters, and customs. The explosion of mass consumption in the roaring twenties also relied on the wide circulation of foreign products, styles, and idols. With disposable income, young Americans appeared to showcase a novel cosmopolitan taste. Restrictive immigration laws passed in 1921 and 1924 further weakened the association of foreigners with immigrants. It was in this context that two Italians from Italy came to figure prominently in US 1920s celebrity culture — Rodolfo 'Rudolph' Valentino and Benito Mussolini — beyond the older appeal of the picturesque.[14]

Gaining the spotlight in 1921 and 1922, respectively, the Divo and the Duce coexisted in US public culture as individuals rather different from one another, at least until Valentino's untimely death in 1926. In his films, from *The Sheik* (1921) to *The Son of the Sheik* (1926), and in numerous interviews and profiles, the sophisticated Valentino appeared to be a Southern Italian aristocratic man of passion, who effortlessly impersonated the Latin-lover type as tango dancer, Arab sheik, or Spanish toreador, and who was prone to heroic deeds as signs of devotion to a woman. Mussolini instead appeared to be a Northern Italian man of humble origins but of vigorous action, whose anti-egalitarian masculinity was moulded on the political and discursive repression of the feminine and on the Caesarian subjugation of his opponents. On another level, however, the two celebrities' reputation seemingly converged onto their masterful ability to stoke and manage public opinion. While their path to stardom was controversially unmodern — on various occasions the two stars voiced reactionary opinions about gender differences

— their well-promoted status as leaders over masses of ordinary people was anything but passé.

Through the long-ignored work of publicity mediators, Valentino was made to voice peculiar anti-modern views of leadership in both romantic and political affairs. In his first interview in 1921, shortly after the passing of the Nineteenth Amendment, he allegedly told his interviewer-publicist Herbert Howe:

> In America democracy has been carried even to the home, and you see the consequences. *There must be a leader for a nation, for a state, for a home. There is no such thing as equality.* The woman is not the equal of the man, intellectually or any other way.[15]

The aspiration for strong male authority in both domestic and governmental matters amounted to an early motif in his well-curated interviews and ghost-written autobiographical writings. Frequent references to his authoritative competence in romance and politics positioned him as an idealized model of sexuality and citizenship: he appeared capable of displaying forceful confidence over women and unwavering support of monarchic governments.[16] He even described Bolshevism as 'just another democratic theory' that was destined to fail.[17]

Mussolini's position was not dissimilar even though his main cinematic domain of excellence was the newsreel — with the exception of a Goldwyn production, *The Eternal City* (1924), in which he acted as himself. The Duce's remarkable publicity machine had its centre in a lobbying association named 'Italy America Society', with ties to Wall Street, the State Department, and the Italian Embassy.[18] The promotion of his autocratic leadership was meant to legitimize the pursuing of business investments in Italy and broader geopolitical interests in the Mediterranean. Mediated by modern promotional initiatives, from serialized biographies to newsreel segments, Mussolini's histrionic performative style embodied a model of government arrangement that challenged democracy from an aggressively anti-Bolshevik stance. Film magazines marvelled at the Duce's forceful acting style, and in press, financial, and political circles the dictator became an idol of public order and personal discipline. At least for a decade or so, his model of authoritarian and charismatic leadership appeared suitable to a country that badly needed to do away with its folkloric backwardness. But his undemocratic authority also represented, in the words of the dean of US political science Charles Merriam, a 'striking experiment', and an inspiring one against the frequent impasse of US presidential power.[19]

From a historical perspective, the stardom of the Italian duo in the USA during the 1920s is significant on many levels. It enacted a form of spectatorial reception that went beyond aesthetic delectation or emotional sympathy — such as the one exuded by Beban's picturesque characters. Instead, their celebrity pioneered a mass experience of idolization, romantic appeal, and even erotic desire for Italian figures. The foreignness of the Divo and the Duce was made to index a captivating Latin bluntness that granted them rhetorical licence and promotional possibilities unavailable to all-American stars. As such, their popularity also indexed the 1920s modernity's darker side. In a country that at the end of the 1910s was experiencing both mass consumerism and tumultuous social protests, Valentino and Mussolini's exotically forceful leadership catalysed a safe admiration for an unapologetic charismatic authority capable of both stirring and managing modern crowds. On a critical level, the study of these two modern throwback subjects teaches us something not just about the 1920s, but also about the inherent antinomy of the celebrity phenomenon. The same publicity machine that promoted the Divo and the Duce as icons of individualism was also popularizing a consumeristic and a political ethos based on the opposite feature of individualism — imitation and adulation. While conveying Latin firmness, their forceful public personalities conveniently facilitated a cosmopolitan and authoritarian reimagining of US male leadership and a charismatic model of mass governance at a time of expanded mass access to consumer goods and political rights. The resonances between their carefully crafted public personae underscored the paradox that a public with expanded civic and consumer opportunities was also a public primed to embrace a celebrity's iconic authority.

Gangsters as Modern Primitives

The theme of leadership brings us to the third aesthetic phase, associated with 1930s gangster films and featuring the representation of Italian Americans as charming heads of criminal organizations. For a brief, but intense period, at least until the censoring scissors fell on the genre, Italian gangsters embodied a unique combination of contrasting impulses — the all-American drive to succeed and the unapologetic rejection of the precepts of a law-abiding life. This was the result of a decade-long process.[20]

Ever since the advent of Prohibition in 1919, US culture had developed a fascination for the bootlegging criminal, evident among others in Dashiell Hammett's hard-boiled detective stories. These narratives aligned the reader with the viewpoint of the admittedly dark and ambivalent investigator, and not with the daring activities of the criminal. Similarly, before the Depression, gangster film narratives were largely framed as an exposé of how immigrants were threatening the Anglo-Saxon Protestant order and US civic idealism. 'Pre-Crash (1929) silent-era gangster films', as Jonathan Munby has written, operated as 'a space of cultural containment', embodying a 'middle-class crusade to both redeem and stigmatize the ethnic ghetto'.[21]

In 1926, something began to change. A musical about the Prohibition underworld entitled *Broadway* gave tough-talking racketeers a voice, at least to sing and banter.[22] In 1927 and 1928, the arrival of synchronized sound brought a flurry of gangster films, including *Underworld* (1927) and *Dressed to Kill* (1928), which in their glamorization of the criminal figure showed their debt to *Broadway* (not released on film until 1929).[23] Their main characters may have not yet been Italians, but they inspired the same novel form of spectatorial sympathy that novelist W. R. Burnett was adopting in those months while writing the character of Caesar 'Rico' Bandello. Entitled *Little Caesar*, his novel appeared in print a few weeks before the Wall Street crash of October 1929.

By benefiting from the genre's shift of spectatorial alignment and from the introduction of synchronized sound, post-Crash gangster films gave criminals not just a voice, but one 'with an accent, vernacular color, and soon-to-be-adopted idiolect'.[24] The genre's ensuing popularity revealed that gangster films were no longer sites of ideological correction, but of moral challenge.[25] This shift coincided with the emergence of the cinematic Italian gangster who, more than the nationally undefined criminal of 1920s films, derived a surplus of colourful and vicious authenticity from the intertwining of the century-old paragon of the picturesque bandit with recent eugenic prejudices.

While displaying primitive emotional and behavioural trappings, including a decadent penchant for gaudy attires, the Italian gangster nonetheless translated the all-American drive to success into an unquenchable thirst for absolute, business-like leadership. As a man of the city, the gangster made strenuous efforts 'to make his life and impose it on others', as Robert Warshow noted.[26] Moulded on the national popularity of the real-life gangster Al Capone, *Little Caesar* (1931) and *Scarface* (1932) codified the figure of the ruthless leader and showed not only how pointless hard work and honesty were, but also how 'the quality of irrational brutality and the quality of rational enterprise [could] become one'.[27] Caesar Enrico Bandello (*Little Caesar*) and Tony Camonte (*Scarface*) were not picturesque outsiders to be watched with delectation, or foreign celebrities subject to manufactured admiration, but heavily accented outlaws attracting thrilling identification. They 'speak for us', as Warshow noted in a famous passage, 'expressing that part of the US psyche which rejects the qualities and the demands of modern life, which rejects "Americanism" itself'.[28]

Historically speaking, the value and function of the gangster for US film culture and the US public at large was cathartic. First vexed by Prohibition's repressive measures and then devastated by Black Tuesday's shattering crash, in fact, Americans looked at the Italian gangster's primitive brutality as a liberating and even modern departure from the deceiving and anachronistic national idealism associated with traditional screen heroes.[29] In terms of critical impact on the historiography of US cinema, the study of Italian gangster figures can teach us a useful lesson. They reveal the extent to which the polyglot lower-class cultural constituents of the USA resented nativist ideas of naturalization, demanded inclusion against hegemonic formulations of Americanness, and pressed for a disruption of 'Hollywood's obligation to the aesthetics of reform'.[30] These were not easily repressible urges. Just a few years after 1968, when the ratings system replaced the Production Code, the thrilling identification with the ruthless Italian gangster came back into full force. Mario Puzo's bestselling 1969 novel *The Godfather* preceded by just three years its filmic adaptation that he and Coppola signed off on. In a decade that had started with skyrocketing rates of inflation and that was showing disturbing signs of economic crisis and malaise, the film became Hollywood's first modern blockbuster, grossing over 100 million dollars in the USA alone.

Neorealist Characters as Functioning Paupers

The last moment that I wish to focus on relates to the reception of neorealist films within post-Second World War US film culture. Reviews of the time appeared to appreciate these films' alleged authenticity of representation as a refreshing deviation both from fascist cinema and from Hollywood's formulaic rendering of US life. The Academy awarded its first-ever Oscar for a non-English-language film to *Sciuscià* (*Shoeshine*, 1946), followed two years later by the same recognition for *Ladri di biciclette* (1948), incongruously distributed in the singular as *Bicycle Thief*. By the early 1950s, neorealism was a familiar term within film critical circles, amounting to what Robert Sklar defined as 'a template of filmmaking practices' (i.e. non-professional actors, on-location shooting, and narratives centred on lower-class struggles).[31]

The tempting assumption is that in the USA neorealism constituted something new, an unprecedented cinematic correlative that matched the institutional novelty of the Italian republic. Italian screenwriters and authors contributed to this view. In an interview with the Rome-based US poet and playwright Harvey Breit, Cesare Zavattini stressed exactly this point:

> Our movement, which we call neo-realism, is simply what we are doing to keep up, step by step, with the Italian people. So long as there is democracy, there will be this art movement. [. . .] Neorealism was born in democracy and it needs the air of democracy to flourish.[32]

Unfortunately, the underdeveloped scholarship on neorealism's US reception does not yet allow scholars to appreciate any detailed hypothesis about its US reception. There are a few short essays on the topic, one important book-length intervention, which appears to have more theoretical than historical ambitions, but no systematic study.[33] For instance, it is not at all clear which neorealist films were actually distributed and when, and how they were received throughout the country. More broadly, the impact and function of Italian neorealism within US film culture remain unclear. Indeed, statements about the radical novelty of the Italian movement appear historically hasty and unhelpful, as film historian Robert Sklar wisely suggested. Sklar argued that the notion of realism that impressed US critics did not necessarily coincide with the ways the writings of André Bazin and Siegfried Kracauer — both appearing in 1960 — were celebrating it.[34] Instead, he claimed, one ought to place neorealism in a dialectical relationship with the context of US film culture in which critics and screenwriters like James Agee and Manny Farber operated.[35] Agee, for instance, correlated his appreciation for 'the exalted spirit of the actual experience' of *Open City* with the all-too-sentimental, but still comparable, cinematic endeavours of the photographers and filmmakers employed by New Deal institutions, including the Work Progress Administration and the Farm Security Administration.[36] The missing link between US and Italian photographic cultures of the late 1930s and early 1940s, as well as their ostensible impact on neorealist filmmaking, has been the research subject of various recent endeavours, particularly from Italy. These works led us to appreciate neorealism's transnational genealogy and its debt to a notion of photography as a most revealing source of political documentation.[37]

From an historical standpoint, neorealism's apparent popularity raises many questions: why did *these* films, *and not others*, catalyse such an appreciative, humanistic response? The mode of address of *Paisà* and *Ladri di biciclette*, unfolding as a sympathetic stance before destitute and unfortunate characters surrounded by ruin-dotted landscapes, seems to represent, I would argue, an update to the safe viewing experience of the picturesque aesthetics that informed countless paintings, illustrations, and films. This is certainly a hypothesis to test and expand. Still, a few visual cues seems to support it, whether in relationship to the Cyclopean rocks off Aci Trezza, featured in centuries-old illustrations, Giovanni Verga's *I Malavoglia* (1881), and Visconti's *La Terra Trema* (1948); or the postcard-like view of Saint Peter's cupola at the very beginning and end of Rossellini's *Open City*. After all, neorealism's suffering figures ostensibly recall the heart-breaking tragedies experienced by Beban's immigrant characters — icons of picturesqueness and unhappy endings.

In terms of the significance for film studies, a compelling view is offered by Karl Schoonover's insights on neorealism's US reception as something that unfolded in dialogue with both Hollywood's well-honed tradition of mode of address and the new one of art film.[38] Even though his argument does not stem from a wide corpus of archival evidence, he persuasively identifies in US film culture the simultaneous convergence of ethical solicitation and prurience into a single viewing practice.[39] Specifically, Schoonover recognizes a key implication in neorealist films' display of brutalized human bodies — the catalyst for the emergence of a new visual politics of international liberal compassion. As in Hannah Arendt's 'politics of pity', this new visual politics relies on the clear separation between those who suffer and those who do not (but look). Grounding neorealist films of global empathy in a cinematic corporeality of pain, Schoonover pointedly adds, was functionally aligned with the USA's new post-war humanism in that it provided the rationale for a US politics of geopolitical assistance that often undermined national sovereignty and self-determination. Neorealism, therefore, fuelled an aesthetic of sympathetic bystanding that ended up enabling the USA's novel geopolitical prominence.[40]

As I have argued in this chapter, the study of the repeated aestheticization of Italians in US film culture ought to challenge the tempting celebration of US film culture's modernity. Throughout the first fifty years, the reception of images about Italy in US film culture often depended on the perceived historical and anthropological unmodernity of Italians. Their representation, initially translated into charmingly primitive humanity and authoritarian leadership, was functional to early US cinema's modern representational and communicative challenges — how to account for the country's striking national and cultural diversity, particularly in times of crisis, and how to manage it. The aestheticizing imprinting of the picturesque mode tamed the diversity of Italian immigrants from the Anglo-Saxon core of US hegemonic culture and turned them into a source of entertainment. As such, the picturesque form can expose one of the most consistent ways in which the film industry achieved social inclusion and commercial success. Similarly, the study of the popularity in the USA of the Divo and the Duce can reveal how post-First World War US cinema sought to transform itself from mere entertainment into a cultural force by practising a delicate balance promoting culture and soliciting mass compliance. The study of the subtly admired Italian gangster reveals how cinema helped manage the post-1929 Wall Street trauma, when the master tenet of the American Dream could not inspire the reform and moralistic commitments of motion pictures. Finally, neorealist films, in their possible re-staging of picturesque views and modes of consumption, helped domesticate war memories of violence and victory in favour of an agreeable aesthetic of global humanism and solidarity.

After the 1950s, the throwback status of Italians remained serviceable to US film culture. What one registers, however, is a growing cleavage between the representation of Italians and that of Italian Americans. Unmodernity remained a source of modernist appreciation and supercilious delectation. It could originate two distinct and unassimilable ethnographies, either through a tourist mode that from exotic Roman holidays continued into Tuscan sunsets, or through a continuum of charmingly vulgar gangsters and suburban dancers, showing off in some distant Brooklyn neighbourhoods on Saturday nights or over long summers along the New Jersey shores.

Notes to Chapter 4

1. Robert Warshow, 'The Gangster as Tragic Hero', in *The Immediate Experience* (Garden City, NY: Doubleday, 1962), pp. 127–33 (p. 130). The essay originally appeared in 1948 in *The Partisan Review*.
2. Ben Singer, 'The Ambimodernity of Early Cinema: Problems and Paradoxes in the Film-and-Modernity Discourse', in *Film 1900: Technology, Perception, Culture*, ed. by Klaus Kreimeier and Annemone Ligensa (New Barnet: John Libbey, 2009), pp. 37–51 (pp. 38–39; italics mine).
3. Ibid., p. 39.
4. See the contribution to the key anthology exemplifying this approach, *The Cinema and the Invention of Modern Life*, ed. by Leo Charney and Vanessa Schwartz (Berkeley: University of California Press, 1995).
5. I discussed such shortcomings in Giorgio Bertellini, *Italy in Early American Cinema: Race, Landscape, and the Picturesque* (Bloomington: Indiana University Press, 2010), especially pp. 276–92.
6. Further, the utopian modernist paradigm, coupled with the rather arbitrary distinction between early and silent cinema, has excluded a systematic treatment of the Great War as an equally modern phenomenon. I explored this blind spot in Giorgio Bertellini, 'Going Silent on Modernity: Periodization, Geopolitics, and Public Opinion', in *Oxford Handbook of Silent Cinema*, ed. by Rob King and Charlie Keil (New York: Oxford University Press, forthcoming).
7. On Italian early cinema and historical epics, see Giuliana Muscio, '*In Hoc Signo Vinces*: Historical Films', in *Italian Silent Cinema: A Reader*, ed. by Giorgio Bertellini (New Barnet: John Libbey, 2013), pp. 161–70.
8. William Gilpin, *Observations Relative Chiefly to Picturesque Beauty. . .*, 2 vols (London: Blamire, 1792), II, 44–45.
9. Jacob Riis, 'The Italian in New York', in *How the Other Half Lives* (New York: Dover, 1971 [1890]), p. 43.
10. Carl Sadakichi Hartmann, 'Picturesque New York in Four Papers: The Esthetic Side of Jewtown', *Camera Notes*, 6.3 (1903), 145. As in Salvator Rosa's paintings, the picturesque had

also a dark side, most visible in the allegedly timeless figure of the Southern bandit which US journalistic and film culture transferred onto the Italian criminal organizations of the Lower East Side known as the 'Black Hand'. Cf. Bertellini, *Italy*, pp. 165–204.
11. George Beban, *Photoplay Characterization* (Los Angeles: Palmer Photoplay Corp., 1921), p. 19 (italics in the original). On Beban, see Bertellini, *Italy*, pp. 204–35.
12. This was already acknowledged in an early, popular account — Frederick Lewis Allen's *Only Yesterday: An Informal History of the 1920s* (New York: Harper & Row, 1931).
13. Herbert Croly, Walter Lippmann, and John Dewey reflected on the surprising efficiency with which unscrupulous individuals managed national public opinion on behalf of the political leaders. The ensuing debates on the potential and pitfalls of public opinion management, which in some cases dealt with cinema as a paragon of visual suggestiveness, moved beyond the idealized domains of liberalism and democracy (i.e. Lippmann and Dewey) into the utilitarian ones of advertisement and consumer economy (i.e. Edward Bernays).
14. On the fabric of their popularity, see Giorgio Bertellini, *The Divo and the Duce: Film Stardom and Political Leadership in 1920s America* (Oakland, CA: University of California Press, 2019), especially chapters 6-9.
15. Herbert Howe, 'Hitting the Hookah with Rudie', *Motion Picture Classic*, 13.4 (1921), 19 and 72 (p. 72 italics mine).
16. Willis Goldbeck, 'The Perfect Lover', *Motion Picture Magazine*, 4 (1922), 41–41, 94 (p. 40).
17. Howe, 'Hitting', p. 72; and Goldbeck, 'The Perfect Lover', pp. 41 and 94.
18. On the Duce's political and cultural reception in the USA, see John Patrick Diggins, *Mussolini and Fascism: The View from America* (Princeton: Princeton University Press, 1972).
19. Charles E. Merriam, *The Making of Citizens: A Comparative Study of Methods of Civic Training* (Chicago: Chicago University Press, 1931), pp. ix and 223.
20. In 1931, the Motion Picture Producers and Distributors of America (MPPDA) agreed to abide by a series of moral guidelines known as the Production Code in order to avoid government interventions. In 1934, the enforcement of the code determined the end of the daring gangster genre.
21. Jonathan Munby, *Public Enemies, Public Heroes: Screening the Gangster from Little Caesar to Touch of Evil* (Chicago: University of Chicago Press, 2009), p. 4.
22. Gerald Peary, 'Introduction', in *Little Caesar*, ed. by G. Peary (Madison, WI: The University of Wisconsin Press, 1981), p. 9.
23. Ibid.
24. Munby, *Public Enemies*, p. 4.
25. 'What had once been a way to manage the crisis features of America's entry into modernity was transformed into a way to produce crisis'. Ibid., p. 5.
26. Warshow, 'The Gangster', pp. 131–32.
27. Ibid., p. 132.
28. Ibid., p. 130; and Munby, *Public Enemies*, p. 2.
29. Peary, 'Introduction', pp. 25–26.
30. Munby, *Public Enemies*, p. 34.
31. Robert Sklar, '"The Exalted Spirit of the Actual", James Agee, Critic and Filmmaker, and the US Response to Neorealism', in *Global Neorealism: The Transnational History of a Film Style*, ed. by Saverio Giovacchini and Robert Sklar (Jackson, MS: University of Mississippi, 2012), pp. 71–102 (p. 71).
32. Harvey Breit, 'Focus on Italy's Top Scenarists', *NYT* (9 November 1952), S2, 5.
33. In addition to Sklar's aforementioned essay, see Antonio Napolitano, 'Neorealism in Anglo-Saxon Cinema', in *Italian Neorealism and Global Cinema*, ed. by Laura E. Ruberto and Kristi M. Wilson (Detroit: Wayne State University Press, 2007), pp. 111–27; and Karl Schoonover, *Brutal Vision: The Neorealist Body in Postwar Italian Cinema* (Minneapolis: University of Minnesota Press, 2012). For a broader context see *Hollywood in Europa. Industria, politica, pubblico del cinema 1945–1960*, ed. by David Ellwood and Gian Piero Brunetta (Florence: La Casa Usher, 1991; Stephen Gundle, *Between Hollywood and Moscow: The Italian Communists and the Challenge of Mass Culture, 1943–91* (Durham, N.C.: Duke University Press, 2000); and David Forgacs and Stephen Gundle,

Mass Culture and Italian Society from Fascism to the Cold War (Bloomington: Indiana University Press, 2007).

34. In 1960 Bazin published 'The Ontology of the Photographic Image', in *Film Quarterly* and Kracauer published his *Theory of Film: The Redemption of Physical Reality*. Cf. Sklar, 'The Exalted Spirit', p. 81.
35. Agee worked as the film critic for *The Nation* from 1942 to 1948 and for *Time Magazine* from 1941 to 1948. Farber began his career as a film critic in 1942 for *The New Republic*, before moving to *Time Magazine* in 1949 and writing for *The Nation* from 1949 to 1954.
36. James Agee, *James Agee: Film Writing and Selected Journalism*, ed. by Michael Sragow (New York: Library of America, 2005), pp. 223 and 225–26.
37. The most important contributions in this regard have been by Ennery Taramelli, *Viaggio nell'Italia del neorealismo: La fotografia tra letteratura e cinema* (Rome: Società editrice internazionale, 1995); Barbara Crespi, 'Italian Neo-Realism Between Cinema and Photography', in *Stillness in Motion: Italy, Photography, and the Meanings of Modernity*, ed. by Sarah Patricia Hill and Giuliana Minghelli (Toronto: University of Toronto Press, 2014), pp. 183–216; Martina Caruso, *Italian Humanist Photography from Fascism to the Cold War* (New York: Bloomsbury, 2016); Laura Gasparini, *Walker Evans. Italia* (Cinisello Balsamo: Silvana, 2016); and Laura Gasparini and Alberto Ferraboschi, eds, *Paul Strand e Cesare Zavattini. Un Paese: la storia e l'eredità* (Cinisello Balsamo: Silvana, 2017).
38. Karl Schoonover, 'The Comfort of Carnage: Neorealism and America's World Understanding', in *Convergence Media History*, ed. by Janet Staiger and Sabine Hake (New York: Routledge, 2009), pp. 127–38. He expanded this argument in the monograph, *Brutal Vision: The Neorealist Body in Postwar Italian Cinema*, especially ch. 2. See also his 'Neorealism at a Distance', in *European Film Theory* (AFI Film Readers), ed. by Temenuga Trifonova (New York: Routledge, 2009), pp. 301–18.
39. Schoonover, 'Comfort of Carnage', p. 130.
40. Ibid., pp. xiv–xv, 131, and 136. The author makes his compelling argument by mainly referring to English-speaking studies of neorealism and Italian cinema. His decision not to engage with the past or recent literature on neorealism published in Italian paradoxically seems to restage exactly the sort of US-centric liberal compassion he so eloquently writes against.

CHAPTER 5

Narrating New Italianness in the USA in the Early Twenty-First Century

Teresa Fiore

The exodus of Italians from Italy — long considered concluded — has instead grown in size and complexity since the 1990s with an acceleration within the period 2011–16.¹ The USA continues to feature prominently among the overseas destinations for these Italians on the move. 'New Italians' in the USA are young (25–45 years of age), much more educated than in the past (more than half of them hold a BA), and active in a wide variety of professional sectors; they originate from different parts of Italy (with a rapidly growing number from the North), and are equally distributed in terms of gender.² As the latest instantiation of a century-long phenomenon that brought over 5 million people across the Atlantic Ocean and effectively shaped the American Dream that still attracts Italians, this recent flow with its specific contemporary features, and yet also commonalities with the past, has garnered much interest among journalists and scholars. Keen on exploring the sociological, economic, and cultural aspects of this phenomenon, these researchers have for the most part relied on statistical data and the compilation of personal stories. Overall, they have produced non-fiction reportages of the experience of these new Italians in the USA, often literally organized as albums of individual portraits.³

Little to no attention has been devoted to the narrativization of this experience, i.e. the figuration of these new Italians in novels, films, plays, etc., as the result of a blending of reality and fantasy. In other words, the obsession with the quantification of the phenomenon, so typical of migratory flows, has obscured the equally important conversation about the ability to imagine this experience and to share it through different cultural texts across space and time.⁴ The goal of this chapter is to focus specifically on fiction writers who have woven the experience of Italians transplanted in the USA into novels. I am referring, in chronological order, to Elena Attala-Perazzini's *Tre stop a New York* (Three Stops in New York, 2009); Chiara Marchelli's *Le mie parole per te* (My Words for you, 2015), and in part both *L'amore involontario* (Involuntary Love, 2014) and *Le notti blu* (Blue Nights, 2017); and Tiziana Rinaldi Castro's *Come della rosa* (As of the Rose, 2017).⁵ Published in the early decades of the twenty-first century, these books embrace stories of mobility with roots in the late twentieth century.

The novels will be approached as examples of contact points. The term is somewhat reminiscent of the 'contact zones' introduced by Mary Louise Pratt in the early 1990s with reference to 'social spaces where two cultures meet, clash and grapple with each other, often in contexts of highly asymmetrical relations of power'.[6] Instead, the concept of the contact point applies to texts that connect two cultures through individual experiences, in which the relation of power between them is not by definition asymmetrical: it changes depending on the different, and shifting, positionality of the individual. Unlike entire social zones, like those sketched by Pratt, in which individuals speak for large communities, or entire civilizations, and claim new forms of agency and power definition, the contact point revolves around single people who prompt the contact through their relocation, and are the focal points of the bi-cultural encounter. More specifically the texts analysed in this chapter design and thus embody contact points between two places (Italy and the USA), and the sub-cultures that they contain in terms of regional and ethnic variety respectively through the experience of people whose Italian-ness in the USA is defined by macro-structures (immigration bureaus) as well as individual discoveries (sexual and religious encounters).

Marchelli's narrative world reflects one of the most common perceptions of contemporary Italians in the USA: her characters are highly educated professionals who have smoothly and successfully entered glamorous work sectors situated in the New York metropolitan area. Yet, as much as their professional lives unfold smoothly, their internal sphere is shaken at some point, and cracks. Along a somewhat similar but ultimately divergent line, Castro's Italian protagonist has a solid cultural and social background but adventurously steps into US environments ranging from African American religious groups to the network of Latin American fighters and drug dealers that are as fascinating as the subjects of the American literature classics she devoured before crossing the Atlantic. By contrast, Attala-Perazzini's book depicts a restaurant-centred bustling *milieu* that includes an unusual Italian character — Mickey, the head of a graffiti gang — whose vicissitudes expose a lesser-known Italian way of being in the USA, away from established circles and in the shadow of the law. Seen as a whole, these texts are an exemplary snapshot of the plurality of Italian migration experiences in the USA: as I maintain, this flow — despite the main characteristics described at the beginning of the chapter — reveals an internal variety that media representations tend to erase, focused as they are on the Made in Italy-inflected image of a 'prestigious group' (Mucci).[7] Far from being part of the brain drain only, as the phenomenon is often reductively portrayed, these new Italians in the USA come with different educational backgrounds and different expectations about 'America' and thus set in motion different opportunities, or lack thereof — and consequently existential experiences — once on this side of the Atlantic.

This array of writings will not be analysed in terms of content only, since the affabulation of a human experience in literature is by definition conveyed through formal tools ranging from genres to language and inter- and intra-textual layering. The authors under discussion here are not strictly linked to a traditional label, and if anything comfortably sit on the border between several labels. Rinaldi Castro leverages the memoir since her story is partially autobiographical but also relies on intricate dialogues that make the writing resemble a screenplay rather than fiction in numerous sections of the book. Marchelli's prose is terse and dry, painstakingly attentive to detailed descriptions of environments, people, objects, and emotions but ultimately intent on reaching lightness of expression through a realist writing. Attala-Perazzini's training as a journalist is reflected in a fast-paced and nimble narrative style that leaves a recognizable narrator as the lens of the story, in turn taking shape as a literary reportage of the lives of people on the move. While in general little formal experimentation can be identified among these writers — perhaps with the exception of Rinaldi Castro whose narrative proceeds by linguistic and literary accumulation — it is their fresh take on the experience of new Italians in the USA that makes them worth exploring, as it adds a diasporic component to contemporary Italian literature.

These works are mainly centred in New York, which continues to be a captivating city for new Italians in the USA; yet, by no means is the phenomenon of immigration to the USA confined to this metropolis, although clearly its cultural vibrancy keeps on inspiring the creativity of Italian immigrants, which thus enters — even unbeknownst to itself — into a dialogue with a long tradition of Italian writers who have documented the Italian diaspora to the country in the past. The history of Italian American literature is too long, rich and complex to be summarized in a few words.[8] The purpose in connecting these recent works to such an established tradition is threefold: first of all, the definition of a linkage between what we call historical immigration and the contemporary arrivals, in what I contend is a continuum. Despite the specific differences prompted by changing contexts and individual experiences, literature written by Italians in the USA has inevitably represented a space in which conceptualizations of Italy and the USA, and even more markedly of the contact between the two countries and cultures, have found a home. The texts under discussion, even when they do not embrace references to historical migration flows and the literature they produced, will then be interrogated with reference to this topic in the awareness that they belong to both Italian literature abroad and American literature in Italian, so to speak, and thus challenge the traditional canon(s). Secondly, the reference to the established tradition allows for the recognition of internal variations due to the fact that, in the past as well as today, the Italian community is so large that its diversity needs to be addressed in order to avoid flattening it to a generic ethnic label. From regional provenance to selection of themes, the texts analysed in this chapter speak to a variety of interests that simultaneously embody and transcend the central *topos* of the relocation from Italy to the USA. Thirdly, as was the case in the long century from the late 1800s to the late 1900s, these writers rely on the Italian language (in some cases sprinkled with dialect and foreign words) to narrate the Italian experience in the USA, which is a choice ironically comparable to the early stages of Italian literature in the USA.[9]

What we may call a 'new wave' of Italian writing in the USA is thus an interesting blend of echoes from the past and specific utterances emanating from the present. On the one hand, questions concerning one's identity in a new environment as well as readings of the US spaces in which Italians live, work, and create continue to be recognizable constants in the works of the authors under discussion, whether Marchelli's professionally successful protagonists, Rinaldi Castro's cultural wanderers, or Attala-Perazzini's undocumented character. On the other hand, the juggling between two cultures is not necessarily a central drive or at least not a source of angst among people who are part of a modern high-tech globalized world in which travelling and communication are much easier than in the past, and in which higher levels of education allow for — at least on the surface — a smoother adaptation to US culture, coupled with the-not-too secondary fact that these Italians have often chosen to come to the USA, to a degree.

The Unpredictable Routes of Italian Mobility in the USA: *Le mie parole per te* by Chiara Marchelli

> La questione delle radici, delle fughe: cose che ormai la annoiano [The question of roots and escapes: she finds these things boring by now].[10]

The most obvious incarnation of this aspect of the contemporary flow can be found in Marchelli's novels.[11] Accomplished professionals in the educational, research, cultural, or international affairs sectors, her protagonists reflect the double image of Italy. The fact that the country 'exports brains', to put it crudely, is at once the sign of an advanced status in the global scene but also a reminder of a structural economic and political instability that does not allow it to retain the well-educated and managerial class within the national borders as effectively as it could. Marchelli's literary works are hardly sociological investigations, though; through a piercingly stark style, Marchelli obsessively probes her characters' domestic and intimate lives to reveal personal worlds whose fragility contrasts with their solid professional worlds, and opens vast spaces in a quest for existential meaning. The protagonists of Marchelli's books are usually displaced by an encounter in the present or by a past wound that reopens: the encounter derails them in increasing ways since it affects ties ranging from relationships with siblings, children or spouses to sexual identity. What is interesting for the purpose of this chapter is that the crises that ensue involve a process of remembering and/or re-living that is also tied to geography. Marchelli's characters find themselves lingering between Italy and the USA much more than their apparent stability would suggest. As much as they seem to transcend the common existential *angst* of the transplanted Italians that compare this US society to the one they came from, highlight pros and cons in their relocation choices, and undergo ups and downs in accepting their new place of residence, these characters are different, yet they find themselves at the centre of an unstable transnational geography, which divides them internally.

In her novel, *L'amore involontario*, Marchelli digs deeply into the rift between a brother, Riccardo, and a sister, Nina, who live cushioned separate lives in New York and Princeton respectively, until a brutal accident brings them together again, in a sense. The Italianness in the USA of these characters is barely discussed, to the point that there is no reference to the reasons why the siblings' parents moved or how they as children adjusted to the new environment. As Riccardo puts it, 'Ma lui l'Italia l'ha lasciata un sacco di tempo fa, senza nostalgie' [He left Italy a long time ago, with no nostalgia].[12] Yet, in *Le mie parole per te*, the novel published after *L'amore*, Marchelli embraces more references, albeit still scattered, to the exploration of the transplanted status of her characters. The fact that these new Italians in the USA engage with this exploration in a circumscribed way is of relevance in itself. It speaks to a desire to be either cosmopolitan or still Italian away from Italy that betrays some forms of repression as the emotional crises that her protagonists go through indirectly expose. As in *L'amore*, Marchelli's Italians in *Le mie parole* are highly accomplished: they perceive their relocations as a natural development of their skills and achievements. This novel tells the story of Claudia, a woman from Genoa who has moved to New York many years before the time of the plot to work at the UN at 'un lavoro che in Italia nemmeno esiste' [a job that does not even exist in Italy],[13] and has relocated her family as well. In New York she lives in a sort of bubble, absorbed by work and family commitments, and active in social circles where others are a mirror to herself. As the narrator specifies:

> Non si dice più emigrati. Una parola che non serve a definire quelli come loro, tutti all'incirca simili. Partiti per scelta o per opportunità, non per fame. Claudia si annoia a parlarne: quelli come loro sono senza urgenza.
>
> [They are not called emigrants anymore. The word is not able to describe those like them, more or less all alike. Choice or opportunity prompted their departure, not hunger. Claudia finds it boring to talk about them: they are people with no urgency.][14]

Yet, it is the encounter with Alessandra, another woman from Liguria, that offers her a deeper look at the life of these cosmopolitan expats. As Alessandra puts it, 'Si finisce per costruirsi una piccola comunità di esuli privilegiati che mangiano parmigiano e bevono prosecco' [One ends up building a small community of privileged exiled people who eat parmesan cheese and drink prosecco], and this, according to her, is a 'gabbia splendida e fatale' [fatal gilded cage] that promises no happiness.[15] Claudia's initial warm reaction to what feels like an unresolved sense of displacement for Alessandra — who appears to be running away from Italy to forget the loss of a female lover due to a tragic accident — develops into an intellectual interest towards her. From an intense email-based exchange of words (those of the title), the interest morphs eventually into a relationship that is as unexpected as it is dislocating since it entails Claudia's self-questioning in terms of sexuality and geographical belonging. Her parallel story with Alessandra arrives as an earthquake in the life of an Italian family whose self-perceived identity had never been challenged so deeply until that point, despite various trials within the couple and as a family unit. Claudia's intense story with Alessandra will result in a return migration to Liguria, interestingly not just for herself, but also for her daughter Giulia and her husband Roberto: yet, they will be independent entities maintaining intermittent contact. But the most surprising return is that of Alessandra, by now cured of her scar, who searches for and finds Claudia at home, although at this point nobody is at home anymore. As Claudia remarks:

> Tornando ho capito una cosa che prima di andare via uno non sa mai [che] una volta partiti, si è andati per sempre. Non si apparterrà mai completamente al luogo dove si va, e non si sarà mai più della terra che lasciamo. Non si sanno queste cose, prima.
>
> [Coming back I have realized that before leaving you never know [that], once you take off, you are gone forever. You will never belong to the place where you go and you will never be again what you have left behind. But you do not know this in advance.][16]

Interestingly, in this novel it is not the encounter with the 'other' that prompts the awareness of this permanent uprooting, but with the 'familiar' in cultural terms. Claudia meets another way of being Italian — lesbian, seeking internal healing in a foreign space — that explodes her world and makes her aware that her self-contained Italianness was in a way manufactured. At the same time, Alessandra, who looks for a new opportunity in the USA, finds there a manifestation of Italy that ultimately gives her a real other chance. In creating a contact point between themselves, Claudia and Alessandra redesign being from/in Italy, as well as a value that Italian culture interestingly claims as defining of itself: the normative Italian family.

Marchelli has continued to explore the splintering of Italian families along transnational routes in her more recent novel *Le notti blu* (nominated for the prestigious Strega Award in 2017). In it, a middle-aged couple from Liguria that has lived in New York for decades experiences the dreadful loss of their son from suicide, and fashions a form of survival imbued with a highly regimented routine. Michele, a reputable NYU professor, and Larissa, his stay-at-home wife, are yet another instantiation of the brain drain flow of cosmopolitan Italians at the centre of Marchelli's novels. Their contrasting reactions to an unpredictable development in their lives years after their son's death, which is as unsettling as potentially regenerating, lies at the core of a novel in which again a set of Italians does not fully process the experience of migration and yet exists on that fine line between Italy and the USA.[17] Interestingly, in a flashback scene, when Michele and Mirko, his son, are in Liguria, they act like locals, yet the locals see them as foreigners: 'Pagéi doî americhén in vacànsa/Sembrate due americani in vacanza [You look like two Americans on vacation]',[18] the owner of a beach shack tells them, highlighting their inevitable fate as dwellers of the contact point.

Marchelli plays with this trope of shifting identities in all her novels, but it is in *Le mie parole* that this element becomes pivotal: whether in terms of sexuality or geo-cultural belonging, the protagonists accept change, and Claudia in particular embraces forms of liminality previously unimaginable. Through an expert weaving of narration from Claudia's perspective, on the one hand, and of the email messages she and Alessandra obsessively exchange, on the other, Marchelli creates two alternative spaces in the novel as well as in the actual world; yet in the novel, they are both spun with words. Chosen with engrossing precision, accumulating with the rhythm of passion, and eventually dissolving in the silence of glances, these words are a reminder of the power of the act of 'telling' cultural contact points through fiction. The words written by Marchelli are ultimately for 'you', the reader(s) open to experience Italy outside Italy in unexpected directions.

The Unconventional Routes of Italian Mobility in the USA: *Come della rosa* by Tiziana Rinaldi Castro

> C'è però anche un modo di restare senza perdere la libertà e ce n'è uno di andarsene, preservando la fiducia. [Yet there is also a way to stay without losing one's freedom, and a way of leaving that preserves trust.][19]

Come della rosa by Tiziana Rinaldi Castro inserts itself into this 'new wave' of literature about the Italy–USA contact point in an entirely original manner. Disrupting the conventional history of the tension between 'home' and 'new world', Castro proposes a novel of many homes and syncretic worlds that develop around a collective identity, composed of encounters, exploration, and inner search. Bruna di Michele, nicknamed Lupo (wolf), leaves the south of Italy for the Big Apple during the 1980s: her trajectory as a freelance photographer and a woman fighting against alcoholism is intertwined with that of Emiliano Westwood, a Cuban drug smuggler and arms dealer for the Salvadorian guerrilla groups. Interestingly, their relationship unfolds in the midst of the Yoruba-based rituals led by Mama Adebambo, priestess of the Harlem temple. Their journey, full of pain and healing, as well as of revelations and secrets, is also a physical journey, not only through the rough streets of the South Bronx and Brooklyn of that era, but also through the boundless spaces of the south-western United States and even Mexico. But, *Come della rosa* is above all a journey through myths, literature, art, and music that produces a language of quotations through which the protagonists find themselves and discover each other.

In this sense, Rinaldi Castro's book is a rhizome, i.e. the underground extension of the stem of a plant that develops in many directions, above all horizontally, and germinates new plants. The concept of the rhizome,[20] as fashioned by Deleuze and Guattari, represents a continual flow of creative energy active underground, which follows neither hierarchical laws nor antithetical paradigms, but moves, prospers, and creates in a plural sense. In the hands of Rinaldi Castro, the rhizome creates a vast network of resonances and intersections, or rather a creole novel characterized by a 'curdled' writing, to borrow Leonardo Sciascia's term. The valleys of Cilento cross the streets of the New York metropolis; Grandma Angiolina's phrases in Campanian dialect echo the jokes in the Cuban Spanish of Emiliano; and Yoruba therapeutic potions coexist with the memory of the Catholic–pagan traditions of southern Italy. Equally dense is the web of artistic and mythical references that energetically blend Edgar Allan Poe, Antonio Machado, and José Martí, pass through Parsifal and Dionysus to embrace Miles Davis, and range from the poems of Garcia Lorca to those of the grandmother in Italy. Throughout the text, the maxims of Mama, who asks Bruna and Emiliano to talk and talk about themselves in order to recover, are like the congas of the narration, as they articulate an internal deep rhythm.

Many critics have looked for parallels between the content of the novel and the personal experience of the author, who carries a story of uprooting and religious quest herself.[21] But it is precisely in the narrative transposition of a real experience that the intrinsic literary meaning of *Come della rosa* lies. The book relies on an implicit library of Borgesian and Babel-like nature, in which a special place is held by texts from the US literary tradition, which is so dear to the author/protagonist that in many ways it functioned as the engine of her voyage across the ocean, along with her love for jazz. While ironically the Italian literary tradition remains practically absent in this novel written abroad in Italian and published in Italy, it activates interesting linkages to the corpus of literature of the Italians in the USA — such as the turn-of-the-century poet Emanuel Carnevali, 'I am again a vagabond, spilling words from a hole in my pocket',[22] to cite one of his famous lines. It also enters into a dialogue with the rich tradition of Italian American writers like Kym Ragusa, author of *The Skin between Us*,[23] which focuses on the search for the Sicilian past in order to understand the present of an Italian African American woman. Like Rinaldi Castro's novel, Ragusa's memoir hinges on the relation with and between grandmothers, key figures in the quest for roots on the move. Sensibly avoiding the risk of those (sometimes unproductive) searches for one's ethnic-cultural identity in the linear link between the country of departure and the country of arrival, *Come della rosa* nonetheless addresses the question of Italian identity abroad. When Emiliano encourages Bruna to become a Yoruba priest she reveals her hesitation: 'forse ti dimentichi che appartengo ad un'altra cultura' [perhaps you forget that I belong to another culture].[24] And, in another more indicative moment, Bruna, having arrived from Italy only a few years before, identifies with the Italian Americans — a phenomenon rarely found among recent Italian immigrants. When the artist Jean Michel Basquiat makes Emiliano burst out laughing by imitating Don Vito Genovese, Bruna confesses 'Li guardavo un po' scucita, incerta se ridere con loro... perplessa nel vedere la mia gente insultata' [I was looking at him a bit unstitched, uncertain whether to laugh with them... perplexed at seeing my people insulted].[25] But the hesitation with respect to the sense of distance from a culture is precisely not a search for purism in Rinaldi Castro's book; it is, if anything, a cautious and reverent coming together of traditions and places, because a true return to one's roots for those who leave is in reality impossible.

By the same token, a true stay, in the sense of permanence, is unattainable. New York, a creole multi-layered city by definition, and as such a veritable theatre of the tortuous spiritual road of the protagonists, is a character in itself and not just the container of stories. New York never sleeps and constantly evolves. As the novel's narrator puts it,

> È una prerogativa di questa città vedersi demolire davanti agli occhi il fondale di stagioni della vita: ospedali, chiese, scuole, cosa che altrove accadrebbe soltanto in ragione di una guerra o una calamità naturale e che qui fa dire al ventenne: 'Ai miei tempi lì c'era...'
>
> [It is a prerogative of this city to see in front of one's eyes the backdrop to entire seasons of life demolished: hospitals, churches, schools, something that would

occur elsewhere only due to wars or natural disasters and that allows a mere twenty-year-old to say: 'Over there back in my days there was. . .']²⁶

Perhaps to remember it or to forget it, Bruna relentlessly walks the city *à la* de Certeau, defying its safety restrictions. In some of the most lyrical pages of the novel, these walks are simultaneously an occasion to document places with her camera, to discover herself, and to cure her alcoholism. Among the many paths of a city that Bruna defines as generous,²⁷ but that also generates a love/hate relationship with its inhabitants, bridges play a unique role as symbolic places of connection. Bruna crosses them, even at night despite police warnings, in order to feel them vibrate, to vibrate within herself, and to capture new points of view on the city as a photographer. It is on these bridges that she finds the meaning of travelling and of intellectual, emotional, spiritual — ultimately human — searching. In this sense, *Come della rosa* is a bridge that in order to be built destroys something, that creates the future in the present, linking the past that already exists, and that invites us to look for delicate balances between lands and oceans, as occasions of contact.

The Undocumented Routes of Italian Mobility in the USA: Attala-Perazzini's *Tre stop a New York*

> La perdizione . . . costringe a definire chi vogliamo diventare e come desideriamo ridisegnarci sulla pagina bianca e sradicata del nostro futuro ambulante.
>
> [Getting lost . . . forces you to find yourself again, to decide what to become, and to desire how to redraw yourself on the blank and uprooted page of your wandering future.]²⁸

In her work, Attala-Perazzini²⁹ is interested in following the trajectories of characters that are hardly linked to the glitzy Made in Italy label or the established circles of the brain drain. As a writer, she is intent on listening to uncommon stories,³⁰ those out of the comfort zone, where life begins, to paraphrase one of the epigraphs in her 2009 novel.³¹ The Italian protagonist of her *Tre stop a New York* — a book comprising three unexpectedly interlocked stories — is an atypical immigrant, a multiple immigrant to be more precise, whose adventures plunge the reader into social situations that are never automatically associated with Italians on the move. Born in Italy to Sicilian parents, Micky was taken to the USA by his family when he was only five and grew up learning the American way of life until his father, an alcoholic with a penchant for losing jobs, suddenly disappeared. Out of desperation, after one year with no news about him, the mother decides to return to Italy and seek the help of her parents who had moved from Sicily to Turin along a historically established route of internal migration in Italy. Readapting to Italy, from the language to the school system, was not easy for Micky, a reversed immigrant at the age of ten, but he makes it. Yet, all his successful efforts are dissolved by another tragic realization in his life seven years after the move to Italy. Micky learns that his father had not really disappeared but actually returned to Italy himself and rebuilt a life there with another woman and created a new family. Devastated by the news,

Micky waits until his eighteenth birthday to flee Italy, and becomes an immigrant to the USA for a second time, as a way out of his unbearable pain. Once back in the USA, Micky attempts to rebuild a life for himself. He obtains a student visa to earn a degree in computer programming at the New School, which he pays for by working as a bartender, and eventually secures a part-time job for a company. But, meanwhile, his visa expires. While he continues to work for another three years, not only is he in a risky position as an undocumented person, but he is also trapped socially and professionally.

This is Micky's background story as told by the narrator. In the present of the novel, with a brilliant narrative solution, Attala-Perazzini makes Micky resort to a fake marriage in order to fix his frail immigration status; and, to add to the thrill, she makes his wife of convenience into a con woman. After verbally accepting the terms of the agreement, she pockets the not-too-trivial compensation for it, and then disappears, leaving Micky and his lawyer speechless when they find out that she has stolen somebody else's identity. Micky is then an illegal who has committed an illegal action with a woman involved in an illegal operation, so that he can be. . . legal, or as he puts it, so that he can 'esistere ufficialmente in America' [officially exist in America].[32]

Set a short time before the Twin Towers attacks in 2001, Micky's story in the present of the novel is less in tune with the glamorous image of the successful Italian in New York than with the complex immigrant story in a country that forces people to resort to acrobatic solutions to make it. As the narrator remarks:

> Perché ci si ostina a rimanere in un paese che sembra non desiderare stranieri, che rende tanto difficile costruirsi una vita, che chiede di svenarsi per raggiungere la legalità, ma che allo stesso tempo, grazie ad astruse incongruenze, consente in qualche modo di sopravvivere, ancora Micky non lo sa.
>
> [Why one stubbornly stays in a country that does not seem to want foreigners, that makes it so difficult to build a life, that makes you spill blood to be legal, but that also allows you to survive somehow, thanks to mysterious contrasts, Micky does not know why yet.][33]

Unable to secure a regular job due to the lack of papers, Micky joins a graffiti gang and engages in petty crimes such as robbery, while at the same time remaining a charming and sensitive young man with a deep internal wound, whom the narrator has a weakness for, and whose tragic ending in the Twin Towers attack will make him even more unforgettable.

There are scattered instances of undocumented Italian stories in the literature of the Italian diaspora,[34] but they are never as nuanced in their description of the pragmatics of this status, nor as attentive to the emotional and psychic labour entailed in it as in Attala-Perazzini's book. With a clean style smoothly alternating quick and incisive dialogue, more cerebral reflections, and stark descriptions, in the vein of US minimalist writers, Attala-Perazzini offers a penetrating portrayal of the Italian experience in the USA, which is much attuned to the experience of struggling Italian immigrants in the late 1800s and early 1900s. The memory of those times is often erased in the common parlance, subsumed as it is by narratives of success that occlude the nightmares intrinsic to the American Dream. Yet, for Micky, as is the case for many new Italians in the USA, this Dream is still entrancing, perhaps because it forces people into an oddly liberating anonymity. As the narrator of *Tre stop* puts it:

> Per ognuno, la lotta contro questo mostro che chiede di dimostrare chi sei e di cosa sei capace, ha un significato e uno scopo diverso. Le complicazioni fanno intestardire, è vero, oltre a far parte della scelta di allontanarsi dal proprio habitat e avventurarsi in una giungla sconosciuta, dove niente è dovuto e tutto va conquistato. Nessuno status, qui, ti è più riconosciuto. Ed essere nessuno, da un momento all'altro, è una sfida strana, una sensazione che scombussola, a dir poco, che fa sorgere domande nuove, che non solo fa sparire i punti di riferimento, ma può anche far smarrire se stessi. E mi chiedo se non sia questo, in fondo, quello che si cerca.
>
> [For each individual, this fight against a monster that expects evidence of one's identity and worth has a different meaning and goal. Complications make one stubborn, indeed, besides being part of the choice of leaving one's environment behind and venturing into an unknown jungle where nobody is entitled to anything, and everything is achieved with sweat. No previous status receives recognition here. And becoming nobody, all of sudden, is an odd challenge, a discombobulating sensation, to say the least: new questions ensue, points of reference disappear, a sense of loss takes over. And I wonder if this is ultimately what one is after.][35]

There is a sense of un-anchorage that exudes postmodernism here rather than just the sense of displacement experienced by historical immigrants. And yet, the simultaneous sense of loss and liberation and the consequent sense of reinvention have characterized the migration of Italians of today as well as yesterday. Attala-Perazzini captures these dynamics, and perhaps not too surprisingly makes Micky into a graffiti artist. Precisely because his place of origin, Sicily, is identified as a place of non-return due to the devastating pain it contains, and his living space of migration is made up of nightly Blitzkriegs, illegal activities, shifting jobs, and quick sexual encounters, he comes to represent the incarnation of an original contact point between Italy and the USA replete with creative energy but also ridden with tension.

Conclusion: Italian Literature on the Move

While the US book market seems to be primarily captivated by the Italy narrated by Elena Ferrante, whose quadrilogy was still on top of bestseller lists as recently as 2016, and in Italy, US authors such as Dan Brown, Ken Follett, and Wilbur Smith continue to grab the local readership's attention in substantial ways, a less visible literary production in Italian about Italians abroad has palpably grown with writers such as Marchelli, Rinaldi Castro, and Attala-Perazzini. Their books' availability only in Italian at the moment effectively locks them out of the US market, and thus restricts their ability to reach audiences on both sides of the Atlantic. Even if reception *per se* is not fully quantifiable, except in terms of reviews — and indeed these books have received the attention of critics and journalists and, in the case of Marchelli, a certain spotlight for the Strega Award nomination — their contribution to new directions in USA–Italy relations in terms of cultural production is undeniable. They do not simply sketch and probe the contact point between the two countries but effectively embody it and confirm the pliability of the concept of national literature, since they were conceived and developed outside the national borders, in one of the most iconic places of the Italian diaspora, New York, and by extension the USA. They speak to Italy from afar while also speaking to the Italy that resides outside the country; in this sense, the stories have a potential audience in the vast transnational space of the Italian–speaking diaspora from London to Buenos Aires, a community of readers that can give new meaning to this literature on the move, which prompts and enriches the rethinking of the very definition of Italian literature.[36]

Each of the three writers analysed here places more or less emphasis on the closeness to one of the places (the USA versus Italy), although it is the tension between the two places that remains strongly in place, whether out of rejection, distancing, or nostalgia. And that very tension continues to inform their work in some form. Marchelli has developed a guide to New York for joggers, which has allowed her to relate the city that always runs to those who always run. Her perspective will be that of an Italian living in New York speaking mainly to Italians in Italy. In the same transnational and transcultural vein of previous novels, Rinaldi Castro is editing a novel tentatively called *Clara Schumann's Secret* about a Greek Italian woman living in New York and reminiscing about dictatorships and wars across continents. Interestingly, it has been written in English, her first novel in the language of her beloved USA: a choice that was made possible by the recent death of her mother, which further freed her in terms of linguistic expression.[37] Attala-Perazzini has recently finished a documentary adapted and expanded from her book *Far From Us*, which, in linking interviews with Italians living in the USA, interrogates the choice to leave and return.

As the Italian exodus continues to grow, while remaining a smaller-scale phenomenon compared to the gigantic diaspora of the past, the works of fiction discussed above vitally complicate the notion of national identity and transnational movement. Even though a sense of this broader context of mobility remains quite absent in these novels which ultimately look at these Italians as isolated individuals unhooked from Italian groups with similar experiences, their contribution to the rethinking of the composition of the contemporary Italian community in the USA is undeniable. The variety of narrative threads and character definitions in these works certainly challenges the concept of the trendy 'Made in Italy' brand and, if anything, functions as a powerful indicator that the country's emigration, over 150 years after unification, constitute an unspoken Made in Italy trend, and as such one that will continue to create forms of contact between Italy and the USA.

Notes to Chapter 5

1. The latest report on the subject — *Rapporto Italiani nel mondo 2017* — has actually registered a further 15% increase since last year, the expansion of new categories of emigrants, and the growth in the number of Italians born abroad, to list some of the major novelties in the study of the phenomenon. For more details see Niccolò D'Aquino, 'La grande fuga dall'Italia continua: la "patria" è sempre di più all'estero', *La Voce di New York*, 17 October 2017, <http://www.lavocedinewyork.com/people/nuovo-mondo/2017/10/17/la-grande-fuga-dallitalia-continua-la-patria-e-sempre-di-piu-allestero> [accessed 27 October 2019].
2. For more details, see Teresa Fiore, 'Immigration from Italy since 1990', in *The Routledge History of Italian Americans*, ed. by Stanislao Pugliese and William J. Connell (New York: Routledge, 2018), pp. 582–95.
3. For a comprehensive analysis of these publications, see Teresa Fiore, 'Migration Italian Style: Charting The Contemporary US-Bound Exodus (1990–2012)', in *New Italian Migrations to the United States*, II: *Art and Culture since 1945*, ed. by Laura E. Ruberto and Joseph Sciorra (Champaign, IL: University of Illinois Press, 2017), pp. 167–92. Since the completion of that essay, another publication of the same nature has appeared; see Umberto Mucci, *We the Italians: Two Flags One Heart — One hundred interviews about Italy and the US* (North Charleston, SC: CreateSpace Independent Publishing Platform, 2016).
4. In the area of film production, an early work on the subject is Emanuele Crialese's 1997 *Once We Were Strangers* (for a reading of it, see Teresa Fiore, 'Migration Italian Style'). As for theatre, the 2013 play *Neighbors (An Anti-romantic Comedy)* by and with Francesco Meola and Irene Turri is a depiction of the life of recent Italian immigrants in New York, including young struggling and dreaming artists relying on O-1 visas (the latter work is in English with a few lines in Italian). <http://www.ireneturri.com/neighbors> [accessed 27 October 2019].
5. The chapter will not address them in chronological order: the sequence will be primarily thematic and interpretative.
6. Mary Louise Pratt, 'Arts of the Contact Zone', *Profession* (1991), 33–40 (p. 34).
7. The words used by Umberto Mucci, the author of the book *We the Italians*, to describe the community are quite telling:

   The Italian community in the US, comprehending either the Italian American one and that of the Italians born in Italy and just recently arrived in the US, is a prestigious group made by several millions of positive people linked by a wonderful Italian heritage and an American dream. (Mucci, *We the Italians*; originally published in Italian by Armando Editore, Rome, 2016)

   This homogenizing upbeat image can be further identified in his claim that 'when Italy and the US meet and work together, the outcome is wonderful'. The works of the writers analysed in this chapter clearly complicate this notion.
8. For critical texts about the evolution and complexity of this body of literature, and fiction in particular, see Rosa Basile-Green, *The Italian American Novel: A Document of the Interaction of Two Cultures* (Rutherford, NJ: Farleigh Dickinson University Press, 1974); Fred Gardaphé, *Italian Signs, American Streets: The Evolution of Italian American Narrative* (Durham, NC: Duke University Press, 1996); and Robert Viscusi, *Buried Caesars and Other Secrets of Italian American Writing* (Albany, NY: SUNY Press, 2006).
9. For comprehensive volumes on the sizeable and multi-faceted literary contributions of the diaspora in Italian see Francesco Durante, *Italoamericana: The Literature of the Great Migration, 1880–1943*, ed. by Robert Viscusi, Anthony Julian Tamburri, and James J. Periconi (New York: Fordham University Press, 2014); and Martino Marazzi, *Voices of Italian America: A History of Early Italian American Literature with a Critical Anthology* (New York: Fordham University Press, 2011).
10. Chiara Marchelli, *Le mie parole per te* (Segrate: Piemme, 2015), p. 11. The books analysed in this chapter are not available in English, at least at the moment. The translations of the quotations from these books are all mine.
11. Chiara Marchelli was born in Aosta, Italy and obtained her MA in Oriental Languages in Venice,

Italy. She lived in Belgium and Egypt before moving to New York in 1999. She has worked as a Creative Writing Professor at Pavia University and at John Cabot University in Rome. Since 2004, she has taught Italian, Translation and Creative Writing at New York University. She also consults with US and Italian companies and translation agencies as a copywriter, editor, and translator. In 2003 she published her first novel, *Angeli e Cani* (Marsilio), which was awarded the Premio Rapallo Carige Opera Prima. She also published a short story collection in 2007, *Sotto i tuoi occhi* (Fazi), that came out before the novels addressed in this chapter. Marchelli spends extended periods of time in Italy every year.

12. Chiara Marchelli, *L'amore involontario* (Segrate: Piemme, 2014), p. 218. Interestingly, the novel includes a whole section about a Polish man who lives undocumented in New York and writes a story about his painful immigration experience. This shifting operation, heightened by the inclusion of the story within a story, i.e. a *New York Times* article interpolated in the novel (pp. 62–64), remarks on the distancing of the protagonists from the actual migration experience.
13. Marchelli, *Le mie parole per te*, p. 13.
14. Ibid., p. 12.
15. Ibid., pp. 12–13.
16. Ibid., p. 221.
17. Quite tellingly, Michele seems to be simultaneously fascinated and bothered by the fact that working-class immigrants from Latin America in the USA do not necessarily learn the language. Larissa more sensitively explains to him, 'privilegiato ignorante' [the privileged ignorant] (Chiara Marchelli, *Le notti blu* (Rome: Giulio Perrone, 2017), p. 42), that they do not have the time. This brief insertion of an immigration reference emphasizes the rarefied self-perception of some relocated Italians, who despite their own ways of being alien to the USA (pace of life, customs, etc.), prefer to consider themselves as well integrated while still remaining profoundly Italian. It is Larissa, born in Italy of Croatian immigrants, who interestingly brings a more sensitive reading to the challenges brought about by relocation in terms of class.
18. Marchelli, *Le notti blu*, p. 29. In this novel, Marchelli resorts to some expressions in Ligurian dialect. They are included in italics in the main text and are also translated into Italian.
19. Tiziana Rinaldi Castro, *Come della rosa* (Pavia: Effigie, 2017), p. 39.
20. This botanical concept is very much in keeping with a book that wants to be a rose garden, as the similitude of the title suggests in its uncommon syntax: the rose — symbol of love, friendship, death, therapy, beginning — here offers as much scent as thorns.
21. Originally from Calabria, Tiziana Rinaldi Castro has lived in the USA since 1984. She earned degrees in Film (NYU) and African Religions (she is a priestess in the Lucumì community of the Yoruba religion). A journalist for *Alias*, *Il Manifesto*, *Il Reportage* and *Il Venerdì di Repubblica*, she has published two novels before *Come della rosa* (*Il lungo ritorno*, 2001, and *Due cose amare e una dolce*, 2007, both for Edizioni E/O); short fiction in *Embroidered Stories* (Jackson, MS: Mississippi University Press, 2014) and in *Buon Natale e Felice Anno Nuovo* (Rome: Edizioni Castelvecchio, 2013), and poetry. She divides her time between New York and Colorado. See also <www.tizianarinaldicastro.com> [accessed 27 October 2019].
22. Emanuele Carnevali, 'Chicago', in *The Autobiography of Emanuel Carnevali*, compiled by Kay Boyle (New York: Horizon Press, 1967), pp. 155–62 (p. 162).
23. Kym Ragusa, *The Skin Between Us: A Memoir of Race, Beauty and Belonging* (New York: Norton, 2006).
24. Castro, *Come della rosa*, p. 165.
25. Ibid., p. 81.
26. Ibid., p. 65.
27. Ibid., p. 161.
28. Elena Attala-Perazzini, *Tre stop a New York* (Siena: Barbera Editore, 2009), p. 186.
29. Originally from Rimini, Italy, Attala-Perazzini came to New York in the late 1990s to attend a dance course but soon embraced the various exhilarating opportunities offered by New York, and worked in journalism (RAI TV), publishing (Rizzoli), as well as the restaurant business (Cipriani and her own restaurants). Her novel *I miei giorni con Oriana Fallaci* (2014) recounts the period when she worked for the famous Italian reporter who inspired her to write in turn. *Tre*

Stop a New York is in part based on real stories that she heard at her restaurant's bar. Struck by the trust random people would afford her in sharing very intimate secrets, she decided to weave them into a book that is as harshly critical as it is celebratory of New York, the city where people never stop, and never stop looking out for others even when they are looking to their own success. For more details, see Letizia Airos Soria, 'Stop! Let's Talk With Elena', *i-Italy*, 25 August 2009, <http://www.iitaly.org/magazine/focus/life-people/article/stop-lets-talk-elena> [accessed 27 October 2019].

30. This sensitivity is evident even in her gallery of recent Italians in the USA. Her collection *Far from Us: Personal Journey of Those Who Left* (New York: Equilibrium Publishing, 2016), Trans. *Via da noi: Italiani ma in America* (Siena: Barbera Editore, 2013) embraces brain-drain stories next to less explored stories linked to sexual orientation which prompt flight from an Italy still unable to fully accept other forms of love and family. For a look at this topic as an under-considered aspect of the current Italian diaspora, see also Fiore, 'Immigration from Italy' pp. 584–87.
31. Attala-Perazzini, *Tre stop a New York*, p. 160.
32. Ibid., p. 200.
33. Ibid., p. 185.
34. For a look at the issue of undocumentedness in the contemporary Italian diaspora, see Fiore, 'Migration Italian Style', pp. 177–78, and Fiore, 'Immigration from Italy', pp. 587–89.
35. Attala-Perazzini, *Tre stop a New York*, pp. 185–86.
36. For a discussion of the history of this redefinition, including the various terms applied over time (Italian American, Italian/American, Italian-American, Italian in the USA, Italian expat, Italian exile, etc.), see Anthony J. Tamburri, 'Un bi-culturalismo negato. Riflessioni su letteratura e identità "italiana" negli Stati Uniti', *Studi italiani*, 27.1 (2015), 149–61. The piece critiques normative perspectives on the idea of the Italian canon and, in embracing the texts of migrants in Italy as well, calls for a more 'ecumenical' discourse (p. 150).
37. During a lecture at the Calandra Institute in New York (28 October 28, 2017), Rinaldi Castro explained the mechanism by which she felt free to write a book in a language from which her mother would have felt estranged.

PART II

From the Late Nineteenth Century to the Second World War

CHAPTER 6

Buffalo Bill and the Italian Myth of the American West

Luca Cottini

The American West constitutes a privileged terrain of cultural encounter between Italy and the United States of America. In the aftermath of the Second World War, the Old West or Far West becomes a recurring theme in Italian society, through cultural import as well as through a plethora of Italian reinventions. In a way, imported Western movies from Hollywood, such as *High Noon* (*Mezzogiorno di fuoco*, 1952), starring Gary Cooper, *The Alamo* (*La battaglia di Alamo*, 1960), directed by and starring John Wayne, or *The Man who shot Liberty Valance* (*L'uomo che uccise Liberty Valance*, 1962), directed by John Ford, met with incredible success with Italian audiences, engendering a collective fascination for the American West.[1] In another way, Italian reinventions of the Old West theme would also find expression through television, as confirmed by the extraordinary success throughout the 1960s and 1970s of the US TV show *Fury* (1955–60, also known as *Brave Stallion*), broadcast in Italy as *Furia cavallo del West*.[2] While US versions of the Old West were spreading across Italy, the Western theme also prompted an independent Italian production during these same years. Italian-made stories of the American West soon reached a worldwide distribution, as documented by the popularity of Sergio Bonelli and Aurelio Galleppini's character of *Tex Willer* (protagonist of a comic series published since 1948), or by the rapid success of Western movies *all'italiana*, starting with Sergio Leone's *Dollars Trilogy* (*For a Fistful of Dollars*, 1964; *For a Few Dollars More*, 1965; and *The Good, the Bad, and the Ugly*, 1966).[3] In the case of Leone's movies, the Wild West was reconfigured as a new hybrid genre, which was later called the 'Spaghetti Western'. This genre bypassed the perceived lack of genuineness of the Italian production through the Americanization of the Italian cast (and the inclusion of the young actor Clint Eastwood).[4] Similarly, the new hybrid genre overcame the temptation of mere Hollywood imitation, through the Italianization of US themes, for example, the deliberate exaggeration of violence and cynicism (in a reflection of contemporary Italy's increasing social turmoil).[5]

Whether imported from the United States of America or reinvented in new Italian forms, the imagery of the Old West certainly represented a space of fiction, imagination, and myth in the post-war years, allowing the critical observation of the present from a safe distance. In the wake of the Cold War, Kennedy's election, the space race, post-colonialism, and growing social unrest, the Old West then mirrored the primacy of law over the unruly forces of nature and society, the duelling of opposite views, the quest for new frontiers, the pioneering exploration of space, and the latent tensions of post-war societies. Against this background, however, the narration of the Old West also fashioned (or perpetuated) a double-edged imagination of Western civilization, related, on the one hand, to adventure, freedom, and childish imagination, and, on the other, to conflict, conquest, and violence. In the mindset of Americans (exported on a global scale), the 'wild' West projected a nostalgic idealization of a pristine relationship to nature (vis-à-vis the age's rapid technological advancements), yet also, at the same time, the self-confident, relentless, and even brutal march of progress over primitiveness. Likewise, in the Italian milieu, the Old West epitomized, in comics, an island of marvel, epic, and children's imagination (vis-à-vis the industrial boom of the 1960s), and, in relation to cinema, a ruthless mirror of the nation's social divisions (later emblematized by the silent 'gazing duels' of Leone's characters).

This ambivalent imagery — of marvel and violence, myth and history, wilderness and civilizing conquest — traces its origins and cultural template back to the extraordinary success of Buffalo Bill, whose *Wild West* show received international acclaim at the turn of the twentieth century. As for the post-war era, Buffalo Bill's fiction of the Old West had rapidly won over Italian audiences (offering a privileged tool of cultural exchange and the first mass-scale product of US import), and had elicited a similar process of Italianization and reinvention, which coincided with the subsequent elaboration around it of new languages and imaginary spaces. In the similar context of an age of rapid industrialization, the magnetizing figure of Buffalo Bill constituted the ultimate origins of Italy's attraction for the Old West, which would have its golden age after the Second World War. What did the *Wild West* represent in the late nineteenth and early twentieth centuries? What impact did Buffalo Bill have on the formation of the Italian myth of the American West?

In this chapter I reconstruct the historical origin of the Italian fascination with the American West by observing the unprecedented reception of Buffalo Bill's show in Italy and its subsequent re-elaborations. After an initial overview of the spectacle itself (its evolution, core concepts, and production system), I consider the impact of the *Wild West* on Italian society by documenting the collective frenzy (or hysteria) for the United States of America surrounding the show's two tours of Italy in 1890 and 1906. I then trace its influence on three contemporary Italian intellectuals — Filippo Tommaso Marinetti, Emilio Salgari, and Giacomo Puccini, who were also spectators and admirers of Buffalo Bill — relating elements of the show to their contemporary works and analysing their Italian reinventions of the American West.

The *Wild West* from the USA to Italy

The *Wild West* developed in the early 1880s out of the acclaimed fame of William Cody: pioneer, buffalo hunter, and war hero. After a decade of incubation — starting with Cody's widely publicized hunting demonstration to Russia's Grand Duke Alexis in 1872 and continuing with a series of frontier melodramas enacted by Cody's troupe of travelling actors[6] — the show premiered in Omaha in 1883 as a narrated exhibit and, in New York in 1886 (in a grandiose opening night at the Madison Square Garden), as a 'sensational drama' based on the play written by Major A. S. Burt.

The show's success was mainly a result of two factors: Cody's capacity to retell and dramatize 'the sometimes glorious, often bloody, and occasionally heroic Wild West story',[7] and his theatrical intuition of mingling circus and drama (in so-called 'combinations'). Cody's adventures as a scout and a pioneer provided him with an ideal platform for reshaping the conquest of the West into a legendary epic; likewise, his fame as a war hero and his celebrated feat (namely, the scalping of the young Cheyenne chief Yellow Hair as vengeance for the defeat at Little Big Horn and the death of general Custer[8]) also offered a privileged podium for reframing a shameful military defeat into a glorious victory. As a corollary to this, Cody skilfully transformed the aura surrounding his persona into a favourable point of departure for developing a new form of spectacle, which could formulate a viable synthesis between the innovations of Phineas Barnum's circus (simultaneously involving animals, clowns, and acrobats on multiple stages in the 1871 spectacle *The Greatest Show on Earth*), and the need to restructure his own biography coherently around a theatrical plot, a 'sensational drama', or ultimately, a saga.

Built around a core set of standard scenes about the life of cowboys, soldiers, or Native Americans (robberies, unexpected attacks on coaches, slaughters, etc.), the show acquired over the years a distinct and multilayered character as a circus of attractions, an exhibition of wild animals, a drama on the Western frontier, and a live re-enactment of contemporary events (e.g. the US loss to the Sioux of Sitting Bull in the 1876 battle of Little Big Horn, and Cody's scalping of Yellow Hair). Along with the rising success made possible by Cody's stardom (as both a hero and an actor starring himself), the show constantly evolved over the years that followed by virtue of its capacity to maintain its core structure (around the early format of a five-act *Drama of Civilization*),[9] to include, from time to time, elements of surprise, and to incorporate aspects from contemporary life or local cultures. It is worth remembering several of these surprising add-ons: the introduction of electrical illumination to the show (in collaboration with Thomas Edison), as a way to enhance its staged contrast between wilderness and progress; the inclusion of the bandit's queen Annie Oakley, as a way to give voice to the growing phenomenon of the emancipation of women;[10] and even the extraordinary presence on stage of Sitting Bull in 1885, as a way to enact a form of political reconciliation with Native American tribes and to compensate a growing sense of guilt towards them in US society. In addition to Cody's entrepreneurial ability to promote his own legend, the systematic rationalization of production and the construction of a complex marketing machine around the show turned it into a serialized industrial product, able to reach audiences nationwide and to become an international sensation. Therefore, thanks to its intrinsic predictability and malleability, the *Wild West* rapidly moved beyond its original set of themes and fashioned itself as a universal tale, capable, first, of capturing the core values of modernity and, second, of absorbing into its plot elements coming from all the traditions of the world.

In a way, the show subsumed the essence of modernity by way of its capacity to adapt Cody's biography to an elaborate set of universal themes and to connect its elements to a clear ideological subtext. For instance, the symbol of the *frontier*, which constituted the site of Cody's adventures, became a visual metaphor for staging the border between wilderness and civilization, triggering the stereotypical contrast between the natives' primitive genuineness (along the myth of the noble savage) and their 'barbaric' underdevelopment (subsequently leading to the counter-affirmation of Western progress). The *prairies*, which hosted the performances of Cody's hunting records, offered an implicit background to his own personification of Western civilization's relentless exploration of space (at the very end of the age of discoveries, after the completion of the earth's mapping).[11] *Buffalos* and *wild horses* invigorated this association between the conquest of the West and a romanticized rediscovery of a pure state of nature (as implied in their wild force and thoroughbred race). At the same time, they fortified its narrative framework of wilderness and domestication and established a parallel between the taming of animal force and the Westerner's subjugation/'civilization' of indigenous populations. Within this context, the symbol of the *stagecoach* ultimately embodied the connection between the conquest of the West and the imperialist expansion of the United States of America, defining the US appropriation of space as a celebration of progress. The figures of pioneers and bank agents in the show reflect the proud financing by Wells Fargo of commercial stage lines connecting the nation to the West. The scene of the Deadwood stage or the figure of Buffalo Bill exacting justice for the dead soldiers of Little Big Horn mirror the need to protect the stagecoach lines from the dangers of 'Indian' or buffalo attacks. The added figures of immigrants, completing the work through their underpaid labour, also allude to their later replacement with new railroad lines.

In another way, the universalistic tension of Cody's circus/play was also realized by its capacity to complement a serialized pattern with an ever-distinct local flair, as it kept adding elements from multifarious sources and cultural traditions, depending on the location of each performance. By virtue of such all-encompassing inclusiveness, Cody transformed his enterprise into a global phenomenon, and the *Wild West*, first exported to Europe in 1887 following a recommendation by Mark Twain, was reconfigured, over the years, into a universal story of all the nations of the world. In the first European performance, in London (1887), on the occasion of Queen Victoria's Golden Jubilee, the show provided the circumstances for the first rapprochement with Britain a century after the Revolutionary War and contributed to a climate of political détente between the two nations as the Queen (who was among the spectators) bowed in front of the US flag raised by Cody and

Cody then, in reply, lowered it in front of her as a sign of respect.[12] With similar cultural significance, in 1889, in the context of the Paris World's Fair, the *Wild West* offered a magnetizing attraction for the French people, by way of its well-studied marketing expedients (e.g. the climbing of the Eiffel Tower by a group of Native Americans, or the inclusion of the Marseillaise as a piece of the show).[13] At the same time, the show also reached a wider international audience because of the global appeal of the exhibition[14] and because of the intrinsic ties relating its plot to the event itself (in its celebration of the victory of progress and civilization over darkness and barbarism). The link between the spectacle and nineteenth-century universalism became even more explicit at the Columbian Exposition of Chicago in 1893. On that occasion, Cody reconfigured the show as the *Buffalo Bill's Wild West and Congress of Rough Riders of the World* and reinvented it as a global platform, staging the history of Western civilization and adding scenes related to other non-US cultures (e.g. Mexican, Japanese, Arab, Cossack, etc.).[15] Throughout the early twentieth century, Buffalo Bill's *Wild West* show would continue to offer a gathering point for the world's different ethnicities, traditions, and folklore and, at the same time, a mirror for a universal history, as confirmed by the later inclusions of contemporary events like the Boxer Rebellion in China or the Anglo-Boer War in South Africa.

While touring in Europe, the *Wild West* touched Italy on two occasions, in 1890 and 1906, leaving a deep imprint on the nation's urban masses as well as on its broad cultural imagination.

In 1890, the show represented for Italians a 'display of American exoticism'.[16] Along with an unusual attraction, Buffalo Bill and his troupe offered a live taste of the USA during a period of early emigration towards the Americas (made legal in 1888), a growing social critique of the US factory management system, and a fervent ecclesial debate gathering modern doctrinal heresies under the umbrella of *americanismo* (later turned into *modernismo*).[17] Against this widespread scepticism toward the USA (which would be fully voiced in 1898, at the time of the Spanish–American War), Cody's tour (of only five cities) contributed to creating a positive attitude towards the USA, thanks to Buffalo Bill's opportunism and capacity for self-promotion, but also thanks to implicit ties relating the show's rhetoric (the conquest of the West marred by Custer's defeat) to Italian contemporary colonialism (similarly looking for expansion in Eastern Africa and similarly tainted by the shameful loss of Dogali in 1887). After the disappointment of its first date in Naples (trumped by a scandal of false tickets), the *Wild West* event in Rome was an overwhelming success, and even turned into a historical event as Cody (like a new Columbus) brought his 'Indians' to receive Pope Leo XIII's blessing in Saint Peter's Square, and as some local peasants (*butteri*) even managed to defeat him in a wild horse-taming race at Cisterna di Latina. In Florence and Bologna, the show once again captivated both spectators and the general public, by virtue of Cody's entrepreneurial capacity to adapt it to Italian audiences, advertise it in local newspapers (as in the case of the *ad hoc* interview on *La nazione* preceding the Florentine performance),[18] and surround it with galvanizing attractions (as confirmed by the enthusiastic reaction of the people of Bologna to the first appearance of popcorn).[19] With regard to the Milan date, a letter written by the composer Giacomo Puccini to his brother after the performance provides a lively testimony of the favourable reception as well as the thrill surrounding the show:

> c'è stato qui Buffalo Bill che mi piacque. Buffalo Bill è accompagnato da una compagnia di americani del Nord, con una quantità di indiani pellirosse e di bufali, che fanno dei giuochi di tiro splendidi e riproducono al vero delle scene successe alla Frontiera.
>
> [Buffalo Bill was here, and I liked him. Buffalo Bill is accompanied by a company of Northern Americans, together with a number of redskin Indians and buffalos, who perform marvellous games of target shooting and reproduce live scenes that happened on the Frontier][20]

In 1906, the *Wild West* increased its presence to around 100 showings, conveying a real excitement for the USA in conjunction, on the one hand, with Italy's industrial push (while Milan was hosting the Esposizione del Sempione the same year), and, on the other, with emigration — both from Italy to the USA (in a stream which would reach its peak in 1913), and, within the USA, from the East to the West Coast (as Italian emigrants became the new labour force building railway lines). Buffalo Bill once again captured the public imagination, by way of his capacity for cultural mediation and his extraordinary showmanship. In Rome, a year after the foundation of the first Italian cinematographic factory Cines, its founder, the cinema pioneer Filoteo Alberini, documented the arrival of Buffalo Bill in the city. In Parma, a legend was created about the Italian or local origins of William Cody along the lines of his shrewd phrase on stage 'io sono di qui: sono italiano' [I am from here. I am Italian].[21] In Verona, the journalist Emilio Salgari, reporting the show for the local newspaper *L'Arena*, received an ovation as he offered himself as a volunteer for the scene where a group of 'Indians' robbed the Deadwood coach. In Milan, Buffalo Bill paired the show with a race, pitting himself (riding on his wild horses) against a cyclist (riding on a bicycle). Set up as an epic challenge between mechanical and animal power, Buffalo Bill won the race through an ad hoc ruling which prevented the cyclist from changing bicycles, but which still allowed Buffalo Bill to jump from one horse to another in the middle of the contest. A testimony of the actual show can be found in the programme of the Milan performance, held in the archives of the *Buffalo Bill Center of the West* (*Buffalo Bill's Wild West 1906 Program Milano*). Its opening page fashioned it as an advertising platform and a melting pot of cultures, as documented by the overlapping of local advertisements and Cody's own image and as demonstrated by the deliberate intersection of the US and Italian flags over his portrait (Figure 1).

The programme's introductory description bestowed upon the spectacle the aura of a once-in-a-lifetime representation:

> la *mostra* del colonnello Cody universalmente stimata, non è solamente d'un aspetto interessante, ma uno *spettacolo istruttivo* che dà un'*impressione reale* delle guerre, delle guerriglie e dei pericoli delle medesime. Insomma, Buffalo Bill non è un impresario banale, ma bensí il più originale direttore di scena della storia vera di fatti d'armi audaci ed eroici.

Fig. 6.1. Front cover of the *Wild West* programme
(Milan, 1906; *Buffalo Bill Center of the West*).

[the *exhibit* of colonel Cody, universally esteemed, has not only an interesting appearance, but is also an *instructive show* which gives a *real impression* of the wars, guerrilla warfare, and their inherent dangers. Hence, Buffalo Bill is not a mere producer, but rather the most original stage director in the true history of the bold and heroic deeds of warfare.][22]

As evidenced by the variety of its definitions as 'mostra' [exhibit], 'spettacolo' [show], or 'impressione reale' [real impression] and by its clichéd scenes (the robbery or Custer's death), the show maintained its core structure as a multidimensional circus of animals, spectacle of attractions, one-man show, itinerant museum, and impressionistic live painting of the American West. Nonetheless, the performance also aimed at getting the Italian audience involved through the purposeful inclusion of episodes related to other ethnic groups (Mexicans, Russians, Arabs, Japanese), which alluded to the international exhibition of Sempione taking place in Milan. At the same time, the addition of scenes portraying emigrants deliberately tied the show to the nation's contemporary debate on emigration, which similarly attempted to reframe the issue from a form of poverty into an exploration of the world, or rather from a social shame into a colonial form of territorial acquisition.

The Intellectual Reception and Reinvention of the *Wild West*

In its two Italian tours, the *Wild West* captured the attention (both positive and negative) of large crowds, capitalizing on the desire to know more about the USA. At the same time, it also captured the interest of renowned intellectuals/spectators like Marinetti, Salgari, and Puccini, influencing the composition of their contemporary works.

Although indirectly, some elements of the *Wild West* surface in the rhetoric of Marinetti's Futurism, as attested in the first section of the founding 'Manifesto' (1909) and in the theory of 'Teatro di Varietà' [Variety Theatre] (1913). The deliberate display and taming of animal energy in the *Wild West* finds an echo in the narrative part of the 'Manifesto of Futurism'. In the text, the pairing of the beastly and mechanical elements (mirroring Cody's own horse-bicycle challenge of 1906) reinforces the connection between the rhetoric of primitiveness or wilderness (inevitably related to the metaphor of conquest) and the identification of industrial modernity or Futurism itself with the radical takeover of the past and the subsequent dawn (or prehistory) of a new age. Marinetti deliberately compares the new vital energy and speed of automobiles to that of the wild force of the 'belve sbuffanti'[23] [snorting beasts][24] and openly associates cars with a narration of danger and domestication, as evidenced in the following passage: 'la Morte, *addomesticata*, mi sorpassava ad ogni svolto, porgendomi la *zampa* con grazia, e a quando a quando si stendeva a terra con un rumore di *mascelle* stridenti'[25] [Death, *domesticated*, met me at every turn, gracefully holding out a *paw*, or once in a while hunkering down].[26] In a different way, in the 1913 'Manifesto del teatro di varietà', Marinetti identifies in animals a key component of the Futurist spectacle, explicitly relating them either to stage performance (as indicated in the wished for 'massimo sviluppo dell'intelligenza degli animali (cavalli, elefanti, foche, cani, uccelli ammaestrati'[27] [the greatest development of animal intelligence (horses, elephants, seals, dogs, trained birds],[28] or to the circus, hinting at US extravaganza as his model ('il genere degli eccentrici americani, i loro effetti di grottesco esaltante, di dinamismo spaventevole, le loro grossolane trovate, le loro enormi brutalità'[29] [the type of the eccentric American, the impression he gives of exciting grotesquerie, of frightening dynamism; his crude jokes, his enormous brutalities][30]). Along the lines of Buffalo Bill's multifaceted show, Marinetti thus constructs his *serate futuriste* around a similar mix of concomitant elements: as a circus of animals, as a simultaneous movement 'di giocolieri, ballerine, ginnasti, cavallerizzi multicolori, cicloni spiralici di danzatori trottolanti sulle punte dei piedi'[31] [of jugglers, ballerinas, gymnasts, colorful riding masters, spiral cyclones of dancers spinning on the points of their feet],[32] as an art exhibit, as a live enactment of poetry, music, and the visual arts, and, lastly, as an improvised show. Along the model of Cody's cultural entrepreneurship, Marinetti equally grounded his *serate*, like the *Wild West*, on a serial structure (allowing the possibility of free improvisation), promoting them through a deliberate marketing strategy (similarly revolving around provocation, scandals, histrionic feats, and cultural opportunism). While Marinetti found in Cody a viable model of cultural entrepreneurship, a source of the Futurist variety theatre, and ultimately an influential archetype for his own persona, Salgari and Puccini found instead in his show a rich repository of narrative material, which deeply influenced their successive Italian re-elaborations of the American West.

In 1908, two years after reporting on Cody's performance in Verona for *L'arena*, Salgari published the novel *Sulle frontiere del West* (*On the Far West Frontiers*), which would inaugurate his trilogy or *Ciclo del Far West*, later including *La scotennatrice* (*The Scalping Lady*, 1909), explicitly focusing on the episode of Little Big Horn, and *Le selve ardenti* (*The Burning Woods*, 1910).[33] *Sulle frontiere del West* revolves around the story of an 'Indian' girl, Yalla, forcibly married to the US colonel Duvandel, who leaves her after the birth of their daughter, and Yalla chases him for revenge.

The novel frames the clash of US settlers and 'Indian' tribes against the backdrop of their relationship, which ends with Yalla's final scalping of Duvandel, and with the subsequent slaughtering of the Sioux (mirroring the US narrative of loss and revenge implied in Buffalo Bill's vengeance for Custer's scalping). Re-elaborating on the themes of the *Wild West*, the novel similarly focuses on the frontier both as a site of exploration and as the watershed of civilization and primitiveness. As he follows the conquests of the pioneers, Salgari indeed traces a mental record of their advancements, mapping their acquisitions for the Italian readership through long geographic and ethnographic digressions. At the same time, in his narrative of encounter, clash, and domestication, Salgari also fictionalizes a common subtext of Italy's racial and colonial stand toward Africa, especially during the years between the Adwa defeat of 1896 and the Libya campaign of 1911–12. This colonial reference finds expression through the climactic progression of taming acts: of a white stallion, of Mexicans, of 'Indian' tribes, and lastly of the 'thoroughbred' 'Indian' woman Yalla, seen as an attractive wild soul to subdue and as a sexual trophy to conquer. The clichéd juxtaposition of the seemingly animal primitiveness of the 'Indian' tribes (whose assaults are equated to those of wolves, coyotes, or bears) and the laboriousness of the US pioneers (whose *haciendas* are instead symbols of civilization and opulence in the desert lands of the West) finds further expression in Salgari in reference to immigrants. In the historical digression on the year 1863, the writer explicitly relates the 'Indian' danger to emigration, defining it both as a threat to the white man's expansion and as an implicit justification for the later acts of US revenge:

> Convogli interi di emigranti, sorpresi nelle sconfinate praterie, erano stati massacrati; le corriere erano state assalite e bruciate insieme ai viaggiatori che le montavano, le fattorie arse, i campi devastati, tutto insomma era stato messo a ferro e fuoco da quei terribili cavalieri rossi che avevano una mobilità fantastica.
>
> [Whole convoys of emigrants, caught off-guard on the boundless prairies, had been slaughtered; stagecoaches had been attacked and burnt along with the travellers riding in them; farms had been set on fire, fields devastated, and everything indeed had been ravaged by those terrible red knights, who were endowed with an amazing mobility.][34]

Against the backdrop of the Italian contemporary debate on emigration and colonialism — epitomized by Giovanni Pascoli, first in the poem 'Italy' (*Primi poemetti*, 1904), staging the return to Italy of a sick US-born Italian girl, and then in his later speech *La grande proletaria si è mossa* (1911),[35] supporting the invasion of Libya — Salgari's reading thus implicitly embraces an 'expansive' connotation of the phenomenon of emigration, no longer seen as a 'dispersion' of national blood (as outlined in the negative view of De Amicis's novel *Sull'oceano*),[36] but rather denoted, along the lines of the *Wild West*, as a necessary mobility, as a civilizing factor against the forces of chaos, and as an implicit form of conquest.

Two years after Salgari, elements of the *Wild West* would also emerge in Puccini's opera *La fanciulla del West* (libretto by Guelfo Civinini and Carlo Zangarini), premiering in New York on 10 December 1910 and starring Caruso as tenor and with Toscanini as director.[37] Even though the opera was most directly drawn from the US play by David Belasco *The Girl of the Golden West* (which is set during the California Gold Rush and was attended by Puccini on one of his trips to the USA),[38] elements of Buffalo Bill's show had a more indirect influence on Puccini's opera, as seen in reference to common themes (bank agents, the saloon, the sheriff, robberies, the chasing, etc.), scenes (e.g. Minnie and Rance's bet, echoing Cody's public bravados), and leading figures (a woman and the emigrants). The protagonist of the opera, Minnie, is the owner of a saloon on the Western frontier. Like a modern-day *Locandiera* (as in Carlo Goldoni's famous play[39]), she presents herself as an emancipated woman, capable of eschewing the advances of the local sheriff, Jack Rance, and choosing her own lover in the Mexican bandit, Ramerrez, disguised as Dick Johnson in order to evade the law. Like Salgari's Yalla, she is an independent woman, able to defend herself and take action, and like Annie Oakley of the *Wild West*, she asserts her authority by silencing the male audience by way of her sharp-shooting verbal ability. In addition, Puccini's Minnie also acts as a 'domesticating' woman, who straightens out first the saloon patrons and, eventually, the bandit Ramerrez, by way of her beauty and her faith (as she reads the Bible to her clients and calls Dick Johnson to a final conversion). Minnie thus embodies both a trophy to be conquered, as the sheriff Rance and the criminal Ramerrez vie for her affection, and a civilizing figure, taming the raw instincts of the pioneers and the fears of the emigrant workers with a maternal attitude. In a similar way, Puccini's opera relates the imagery of the frontier to an imagery of conquest and exploration, yet also to a nostalgic dimension, thus turning it into a site of instability, melancholy, and need for assurance. *La fanciulla del West* surely retrieves the typical motive of protecting West-bound train lines (along the same lines of Salgari's justification note, and Cody's own personal life), through the evocation of the threat of robberies (associated this time with the Mexican bandits) and the reassuring figures of Ashby (the Wells Fargo agent) and Rance (the sheriff). At the same time, however, it also shifts its narrative focus from the daring and forward-looking figures of the pioneers, to the melancholic characterization of emigrants, who seemed to be mentally moving back to their homelands as they moved West in search of new opportunities. Emigrants indeed are presented in the first act of the opera in connection to risk, adventure, and discovery (as hinted at by their portrayal during a game of poker), yet also appear torn by nostalgia as exemplified by Larkens who suffers the 'mal di terra natia' [homesickness][40] while thinking 'alla madre lontana che l'aspetta' [about his mother waiting for him].[41] Some of them openly mourn the distance from their families ('che faranno i vecchi miei là lontano' [what could my old folks be doing over there, far away][42]) and even curse their fever of gold ('la malaria gialla' [the yellow fever][43]) while they blame the 'terra maledetta, quest'occidente d'oro' [the golden west is a cursed land].[44] The theme of the frontier is thus tinged with epic, but also, at the same time, with sadness and melancholy, as the element of migration emerges both in the prolonged displacement of the customers of the saloon and in their search for a guiding light (emblematized by the attractive/educating figure of Minnie). In light of these observations, the paradoxical setting of Puccini's opera — drawing from the imagery of the Old West (first brought to Milan by Buffalo Bill) and reinventing it in an Italianized version — can be read as an instance of cultural exoticism (along the lines of Puccini's interest toward other cultures as manifested in *Madama Butterfly* of 1903), as a significant episode of encounter and cross-pollination of cultures, or as an implicit reflection on the contemporary issue of emigration. The staged elements of the gold rush, the frontier, and the conquest of the West turn into universal themes, as they migrate from one culture to another. At the same time, they also mirror the similar phases of the immigrant story, from the search for new opportunities (motivated by the promise of future wealth) to the risk of entering a new culture, from the crossing of the border (customs) to the collaboration in the expansion of the new nation (as many workers were moving from the East to the West Coast as a new labour force).

In conclusion, this investigation of the US genesis of the *Wild West* and its Italian reception aims not only to document the first case of global stardom in the age of mass communications[45] or to bring to light a latent source of inspiration for Marinetti's, Salgari's, and Puccini's works, but also to identify the deep origins and cultural template of Italy's post-war fascination with the West. Along these lines, the privileged case of this show then allows four different contributions in the observation of the reciprocal influence of US and Italian cultures over the twentieth century. First, by documenting its evolution, the show offers an example of the transformation of a cultural product into a successful business in its capacity to embody the 'triumph of American mass culture'[46] and in its reconfiguration of a national set of stories into a global narrative of Western civilization. Secondly, by turning spectatorship into authorship (as seen in Marinetti, Salgari, and Puccini), the show, perhaps unwillingly, informs the evolution of new aesthetic idioms like the Futurist theatre, comics (out of the visual illustrations of Salgari's *Ciclo del West*), or the American Musical (as many critics suggest in reference to *La fanciulla del West*[47]). Thirdly, by providing an iconographic pattern and a set of standard themes to the Italian representation of the Old West, the *Wild West* not only constitutes an unavoidable reference, but also defines a clear cultural background to Italy's later West-related productions (movies, comics, and literature). Lastly, by following the makeover of Buffalo Bill from a real historical figure into a fictional character, the show allows the possibility of identifying the archetypal traits of a lively modern myth, whose independent re-editions continue to flourish, from archival rediscovery (through the creation of *The Buffalo Bill Center of the West*, a library and museum dedicated to him in the city of Cody, Wyoming) to the unceasing Italian remakes of Bufalo Bill (sic) as a protagonist of Carlo Cossio's comics series of *L'intrepido* ('The Intrepid Man' published from 1951 to 1964) or as a legendary hero in a 1976 song by the songwriter Francesco De Gregori.

Notes to Chapter 6

1. *High Noon*, dir. by Fred Zinnemann (Stanley Kramer Productions, 1952); *The Alamo*, dir. by John Wayne (The Alamo Company United Artists, 1960); *The Man who shot Liberty Valance*, dir. by John Ford (Paramount Pictures, 1962).

2. *Fury* (also known as *The Brave Stallion*), dir. by Ray Nazarro, Sidney Salkow, and Lesley Selander (NBC, 1955–60). The Italian fascination for the Old West had already been anticipated in Steno's 1954 movie *Un Americano a Roma* (Titanus, Minerva Film), as documented in the scene where the protagonist, Nando Moriconi (Alberto Sordi), returns home filled with excitement after watching the latest Hopalong Cassidy Western. For an extensive commentary on the scene see Austin Fisher, *Radical Frontiers in the Spaghetti Western: Politics, Violence, and Popular Italian Cinema* (London: Tauris, 2011), pp. 11–12.
3. *For a Fistful of Dollars*, dir. by Sergio Leone (Jolly Film, Constantin Film, Ocean Films, 1964); *For a Few Dollars More*, dir. by Sergio Leone (PEA, 1965); *The Good, the Bad, and the Ugly*, dir. by Sergio Leone (PEA, Constantin Film, United Artists, 1966). The production of the spaghetti Western — a genre at first discarded for its supposed lack of genuineness and excessive violence and later rediscovered as an intriguing object of study — reached its peak between the 1960s and 1970s. In 1967, sixty-six Western movies were produced in Italy (27.7% of the 238 produced in the year). In 1968, in a significant coincidence with the start of the student protest in Italian universities, Italian cinema released seventy-one Western movies, accounting for 29.6% of the yearly production. Bert Fridlund, *The Spaghetti Western: A Thematic Analysis* (Jefferson, NC and London: McFarland, 2006), p. 8.
4. Sergio Leone discovered the young actor Clint Eastwood, since he did not have the budget to hire more renowned actors like Henry Fonda or James Coburn for his *A Fistful of Dollars*. In addition, 'so that Italian audiences would not think that *Fistful* was home-made, the distributors made most of the cast and crew hide behind pseudonyms. Leone became "Bob Robertson" [. . .] Volontè became "John Wells," and the Conservatory-trained composer Ennio Morricone [. . .] became "Ben Savio"'. Christopher Frayling, *Spaghetti Westerns: Cowboys and Europeans from Karl May to Sergio Leone* (London: Tauris, 1998), p. 147.
5. As Robert Cumbow points out:

    the Italian Western is an extension of the Hollywood Western layered over a reaction against it. The films are lush with references to the Hollywood classics and the directors to whom the Italians acknowledge a debt [. . .] Even the most outrageous turns of plot, characters, and ethic in Italian Westerns are basically variations on — or inversions of — Hollywood Western conventions.

    However, the critic continues, 'the Italian overhaul of American myth is characterized by a more cynical view of people, of their motivations, and of their capabilities. Violence and cruelty are emphasized — particularly the abuse of innocents'. Robert Cumbow, *The Films of Sergio Leone* (Toronto: The Scarecrow Press, 2008), p. 13.
6. 'From 1872 until 1886 Cody led a troupe of travelling actors (familiarly known as a "combination") around the country playing in frontier melodramas' which 'were mediocre at best' and often caused 'theatre critics to shake their heads in wonder at the unreserved enthusiasm Cody incited in audiences'. Sandra Sagala, *Buffalo Bill on Stage* (Albuquerque: University of New Mexico Press, 2008), pp. 2–3.
7. Ibid., pp. 7–8.
8. A detailed reconstruction and critique of Buffalo Bill's 'first scalp for Custer' (as a historical fact and a theatrical scene) is contained in Candace Fleming's volume *Presenting Buffalo Bill: The Man Who Invented the Far West* (New York: Roaring Brook Press, 2016), pp. 129–40.
9. The five acts of the show (retitled *The Drama of Civilization*) were: 'The primeval forest', 'The prairie', 'The cattle ranch', 'The mining camp', and 'The Battle of Little Big Horn'.
10. For a detailed account of Cody's relationship with Annie Oakley, see Isabelle Sayers's volume *Annie Oakley and Buffalo Bill's Wild West* (New York: Dover, 1981).
11. At the end of the age of exploration, Cody presents himself as a new Columbus, as a legendary discoverer of the prairies of the West. In parallel with his epic narratives, the new technology of photography constituted another way in which this impulse to chart the unknown was manifested. The new phenomenon of the photographic exploration of the earth's geography indeed coincided with the beginning of a 'new age of discovery, comparable to that of the explorers who charted the globe from the fifteenth to seventeenth centuries'. Mary Warner Marien, *Photography: a Cultural History* (Upper Saddle River, NJ: Pearson Prentice Hall, 2011), p. 159.

12. See Mario Bussoni, *Buffalo Bill in Italia. L'epopea del Wild West Show* (Fidenza: Mattioli 1885, 2011), p. 62.
13. See Charles Eldridge Griffin, *Four Years in Europe with Buffalo Bill* (Lincoln, NB and London: University of Nebraska Press, 2010), p. xx.
14. Audiences in Paris were themselves culturally and linguistically diverse, reflecting not only the cosmopolitan nature of the city but also the fact that trains from various parts of the continent were bringing eager spectators from all over Europe to see the recently inaugurated Eiffel Tower, the industrial advances on show at the Exhibition, the Pavilions of the participating nations, the anthropological exhibition on human evolution, and, of course, Buffalo Bill and company. (ibid.)
15. 'Cody and his managers were inspired to bring their show to the gates of the Columbian Exposition for many of the same reasons that had brought it to Rome, Paris, and London. The series of performances in Roman amphitheaters, on the grounds of Windsor Castle, and at the foot of Mount Vesuvius had given Cody and his publicists ample occasion to reflect on the course of Western history' (Joy Kasson, *Buffalo Bill's Wild West. Celebrity, Memory, and Popular History* (New York: Hill and Wang, 2000), p. 98). In particular, on the occasion of the celebration of Columbus, Cody not only introduced in his 'colorful, polyglot, high-energy performance' (ibid.) of the *Wild West* the episode titled 'Pilot of the Ocean, 15th Century — the First Pioneer', but also presented himself in a parallel scene as the 'Guide of the Prairie, 19th century — the Last Pioneer'.
16. Robert Rydell, and Rob Kroes, eds, *Buffalo Bill in Bologna: The Americanization of the World, 1869–1922* (Chicago and London: University of Chicago Press, 2005), p. 111.
17. After the passing of a law that made emigration legal in Italy, Edmondo De Amicis wrote the novel *Sull'oceano* (*On Blue Waters*) (Milan: Garzanti, 1888; repr. 2009), which takes the form of a travel diary of a voyage from Italy to Argentina, offering Italian readers a glimpse of the situation of Italian emigrants to the Americas for the first time. Davide Fiorentino's book *Gli Stati Uniti e l'Italia alla fine del XIX secolo* (Rome: Gangemi Editore, 2010) documents how the concept of *americanismo* applied to both ecclesial ecclesiastical and social spheres. It referred to the modern religious trends coming from the USA, later condemned as heresies in Pope Leo XIII's encyclical letter *Testem benevolentiae nostrae* (1899). *Testem Benevolentiae nostrae: Concerning New Opinions, Virtue, Nature and Grace, with Regard to Americanism*, <http://www.papalencyclicals.net/Leo13/l13teste.htm> [accessed 16 May 2017]. In the context of a widespread cultural bias towards the USA, it also related to the broader European concerns about the growing international and industrial power of the United States of America (overtly manifested in the Spanish–American War of 1898).
18. The interview given by Cody for the Florentine newspaper *La nazione* on 13 March 1890 further confirms the cultural opportunism of the U.S. pioneer as he presented himself to the journalist *Sigaretta*, in a room filled with religious icons and canvases of Garibaldi, Mazzini, Umberto I, and Leo XIII.
19. In Bologna, the Wild West played for eight days, made a huge profit, and left the Bolognese with stirring impressions of the American West and vivid memories of congested streets and oversold arenas. In Bologna and elsewhere, Wild West concessionaires introduced audiences to popcorn, giving them a lasting taste of American mass culture. (Rydell and Kroes, *Buffalo Bill in Bologna*, p. 110.)
20. 24 April 1890; quoted in Bussoni, *Buffalo Bill in Italia*, p. 90. Although not directed at an academic audience, Bussoni's volume nonetheless provides a rich depository of valuable information and material on Buffalo Bill's tours in Italy.
21. See Bussoni, *Buffalo Bill in Italia*, p. 96.
22. *Buffalo Bill's Wild West 1906 Program Milano, Italy* (1906), <http://library.centerofthewest.org/cdm/ref/collection/BBOA/id/1635> [accessed 16 May 2017], p. 11 (emphasis added).
23. Filippo Tommaso Marinetti, *Teoria e invenzione futurista*, ed. by Luciano De Maria (Milano: Mondadori, 1968), p. 8. In the 'Manifesto', Marinetti also characterizes the automobiles as horses in his reference to their sniff: 'il fiuto, il fiuto solo basta alle belve' (p. 8) [the scent, the scent alone is enough for our beasts]. *Futurist Manifestos*, ed. by Apollonio Umbro (Boston: MFA publications, 2001), p. 20.

24. Apollonio Umbro, ed., *Futurist Manifestos* (Boston: MFA publications, 2001), p. 20.
25. Marinetti, *Teoria e invenzione futurista*, p. 8.
26. Umbro, *Futurist Manifestos*, p. 20, emphasis added.
27. Marinetti, *Teoria e invenzione futurista*, p. 87.
28. Umbro, *Futurist Manifestos*, p. 129.
29. Marinetti, *Teoria e invenzione futurista*, p. 89.
30. Umbro, *Futurist Manifestos*, p. 130.
31. Marinetti, *Teoria e invenzione futurista*, p. 83.
32. Umbro, *Futurist Manifestos*, p. 127.
33. Emilio Salgari, *La scotennatrice* (Milano: Sonzogno, 1909); idem, *Le selve ardenti* (Milano: Sonzogno, 1910).
34. Emilio Salgari, *Sulle frontiere del West* (Milano: Fabbri, 1908; repr. 2002), p. 33.
35. Giovanni Pascoli, *La grande proletaria si è mossa* (Bologna: Zanichelli, 1911); *Primi poemetti*, 3rd edn (Bologna: Zanichelli, 1904).
36. In the opening scene of De Amicis's novel *Sull'oceano* (*On Blue Waters*), while depicting the boarding of Italian emigrants on the liner travelling from Genoa to Buenos Aires, the writer presents the ship as a whale sucking Italian blood: 'due ore dopo che era cominciato l'imbarco, il grande piroscafo, sempre immobile, come un cetaceo enorme che addentasse la riva, succhiava ancora sangue italiano' [two hours after boarding started, the great liner, still immobile, continued to draw Italian blood, like a huge whale biting the shore] (p. 6).
37. Giacomo Puccini, *Giacomo Puccini's La Fanciulla del West*, ed. by Burton Fisher (Boca Raton, FL: Opera Journeys Publishing, 2013).
38. For more information about the relationship between Belasco's *Girl* and Puccini's *La Fanciulla*, see Randall and Davis's edited volume *Puccini and the Girl: History and Reception of the Girl of the Golden West* (Chicago and London: University of Chicago Press, 2005).
39. Carlo Goldoni, *La locandiera* (Venice: Marsilio, 2007).
40. Salgari, *Sulle frontiere del West*, p. 8.
41. Ibid.
42. Ibid., p. 10.
43. Ibid., p. 8.
44. Ibid.
45. 'In assenza di televisione, cinema o di altri mezzi di comunicazione di massa, il circo di Buffalo Bill svolse in modo eccellente un ruolo che potremmo oggi definire di mediazione culturale' [In the absence of television, cinema, or other mass media, Buffalo Bill's circus was excellent in playing a role of cultural mediation, as we would define it today]. Federico Cioni, 'Postfazione', in *Buffalo Bill in Italia. L'epopea del Wild West Show,* ed. by Mario Bussoni (Fidenza: Mattioli 1885, 2011), pp. 117–24 (p. 117).
46. Rydell and Kroes, *Buffalo Bill in Bologna*, p. 120.
47. Davis argues that *La fanciulla del West* constitutes the archetype of the American musical not only because of Puccini's accomplished synthesis of operatic language and the successful Broadway play *The Girl of the Golden West* (New York: Grosset & Dunlap, 1905; repr. 1911) by David Belasco, but also because of its innovative elements: its theme ('it was the first grand opera set in America'), its melodies (integrating 'bits of American music'), and its experimental composition techniques ('the opera has no memorable arias because they are integrated into the surrounding music'. Shelby Davis, 'David Belasco and Giacomo Puccini: Their Collaborations', in *Opera in the Golden West: The Past, Present, and Future of Opera in the U.S.A.*, ed. by John DiGaetani and Josef Sirefman (Rutherford: Farleigh Dickinson University Press, 1994), pp. 129–39 (p. 136).

CHAPTER 7

Turin between French and US Culture: The Film and Car Industries in 1904–1914*

Guido Bonsaver

The French Model

Throughout the age of the Enlightenment, Paris had established itself as the cultural capital of Europe: French had replaced Latin as the language of diplomacy, and the educated elites of all Europe — from the British isles, to Western Russia, down to the Mediterranean coasts of Sicily and Greece — all looked at the fashions and lifestyle of the Parisian upper classes as a model of modernity. The French revolution imposed France as a most ground-breaking political experiment, whose repercussions shook continental Europe to its very foundations. The ideals of Liberty, Equality, and Fraternity, however interpreted, glorified or betrayed throughout the first decades of the nineteenth century, travelled throughout continental Europe. In Italy they arrived sewn to the flags of the French republican army, providing Italian nationalists with the inspiration and much-needed military help in their struggle towards unification. And when unification eventually arrived, in 1861, it was thanks to an alliance between the Piedmontese and the France of Napoleon III.

During the second half of the nineteenth century, in iconic terms, the most accomplished attempt to confirm Paris as the cultural capital of Europe was the construction of the Eiffel Tower as the gate and giant beacon to the Universal Exposition of 1889. Whilst glorifying the centennial of the French revolution, it proved even more successful as a symbol of the cutting-edge modernity of contemporary Parisian culture. As for Italy, one only has to look at the fields of literature and the figurative arts. French Naturalism provided the most influential literary expression of the positivistic turn in Western culture. The manifesto-like

---

* This chapter was made possible thanks to research funding provided by both the John Fell Fund of the University of Oxford and the Damon Wells Fund of Pembroke College. I am also particularly grateful to the staff of the archival institutions I visited in Italy (Turin) and in the USA (New York and Washington). Finally, I am grateful for the comments and suggestions from colleagues following the presentation of a first draft of this chapter at the conference 'Cultures on the Move: Italy and the USA' on 24 September 2016, in Oxford. Particular thanks go to Giorgio Bertellini for his expert and wise help.

prefaces of the novels by the Goncourt Brothers, by Émile Zola and others became guidelines which in Italy were entirely absorbed and turned into the foundations of the *verista* school led by Giovanni Verga. Equally, French symbolist poetry had a clear influence on contemporary Italian authors such as Gabriele d'Annunzio (who lived in France for about four years). In the art world, French impressionism and more importantly the role of Paris as a potent magnet for every aspiring artist had a more indirect but equally paradigm-shifting impact. A 'Paris period' was a recurrent feature in the biography of most Italian artists at the time, and many settled there for good, from Giovanni Boldini, Italy's most famous portrait painter who moved there in 1872, to Amedeo Modigliani who made Paris his home in 1906 and who metamorphosed into a ground-breaking artist. Italy's most prominent avant-garde movement was also Paris-born: Futurism. Its founder, Filippo Tommaso Marinetti, had studied there, and from the pages of *Le Figaro* he launched the movement's manifesto, on 20 February 1909. Not surprisingly, Walter Benjamin entitled his influential chapter on culture and modernity 'Paris, Capital of the 19th century'. And more prosaically, but with specific regard to Italy, Antonio Gramsci condensed his thoughts on pre-twentieth century Italian culture with this epigrammatic remark: 'Se non si studia la cultura italiana fino al 1900 come un fenomeno di provincialismo francese, se ne comprende ben poco' [Unless one studies nineteenth-century Italian culture as a phenomenon of French provincialism, very little of it can be understood].[1]

At the turn of the twentieth century, there is little doubt that France and particularly Parisian culture was considered a model and a yardstick. Italian intellectuals and socialites were inevitably attracted by Paris. Although Italy did not develop a Grand Tour tradition, if we were tempted to imagine a parallel, then by far the most important foreign city in the cultural journey of a young Italian intellectual in the nineteenth century would have been Paris. This was also linked to education and foreign-language learning. In the late nineteenth century, French was the one and only foreign language taught in the Ginnasio-Liceo, the secondary school attended by Italy's ruling classes-to-be, and it was only taught for two years. The study of classical languages entirely dominated the curriculum and hence the learning of modern foreign languages, even French, was left mainly to family-led experiences, that is, the presence of foreign private tutors and/or childminders, and the occasional stay abroad. The British Isles and the USA remained distant, linguistically and geographically. This debatable situation was only addressed in 1911 when Luigi Credaro, then minister for education, introduced the Liceo Moderno, in which English could be studied for four years. However, it was to remain an unsuccessful and short-lived experiment: it was introduced in only eight Italian provinces, and was eventually abolished by the Fascist reform of education in 1923. Italy's establishment was destined to remain stuck with a foreign-language education based on Ancient Greek, Latin, and a smattering of French, well into the second half of the twentieth century.[2]

Beyond — and hopefully helped by — these introductory remarks, this chapter's main research question can be spelled out in simple terms: when did the Italian elite begin to shift their attention away from France and look instead across the Atlantic? In other words, when did the United States of America begin to emerge on the cultural horizon of educated Italians?

Such a wide question needs then to be better defined and narrowed down to the aims of this chapter. Firstly, why 'educated Italians' and not the entire population of the then Italian Kingdom? If Benjamin Disraeli's expression — 'two nations' — aptly described the huge divide between rich and poor in Victorian England, it can easily be adopted for this chapter since the situation was very similar, and in fact worse, in post-unification Italy. The economic divide was accompanied by a cultural divide, greater in Italy due to its poorer record of school attendance and literacy. In 1861 only about 27% of Italians could read, a figure far below that of Britain which was closer to 70%. In her influential book on the Italian diaspora around the world, Donna Gabaccia addresses the question of Italy's social make-up and makes the bold suggestion that this divide created 'two peoples who often seemed as different as two races'.[3] For this reason, instead of making generic claims about 'Italians', this chapter will concentrate on the educated elite. The choice of this minority group is due to the fact that their social milieu is the one from which came the leaders in the fields on which we will concentrate.

The second issue is one of a geographical nature: why Turin? A first reason behind this choice is linked to the city's role in the history of silent cinema. As is well known, during the first decade of the twentieth century, when cinema took its first steps, Turin could lay claim to being the Italian capital of this new culture industry. Film historian Gianni Rondolino went as far as calling it the 'Hollywood' of that decade.[4] At the same time, Turin can also easily be considered as the most Francophile of Italy's main cities. This is for obvious historical and geographical reasons. The combination of these two factors makes it an interesting case for the study of the way in which US culture entered Italian society in a field like cinema, which was dominated by France in its very first stages.

Thirdly, the decision to extend this study to the car industry is also linked to Turin's dominant status in this other nascent industry. But not only. Other, interesting parallels between the film and car industries can be drawn. The car industry too, as we will see, came to Italy mainly through France and at the same time had to face the growing importance of its equivalent across the Atlantic. Moreover, both industries were an expression of new technologies which brought a fundamental and soul-defining contribution to twentieth-century culture. I would argue that even from an aesthetic viewpoint the two can be easily connected. One of the earliest Italian films, shot in 1904 by the pioneers of Turin's film industry, Roberto Omegna and Arturo Ambrosio, documented a car race, the *Prima corsa automobilistica Susa Moncenisio*. Here, a new form of representation, cinema, was used in order to immortalize another newly born phenomenon: the automobile. This is coincidental but at the same time it signals the impact of the car as a cultural object and, as such, an object of beauty and art too. In Futurism's 1909 Manifesto, it is a car that provides the rebirth of the artist in the narrative preface. Point four of the manifesto then famously continues with a glorification of the car which peaks in the provocative statement that 'un automobile ruggente, che sembra correre sulla mitraglia, è più bello della *Vittoria di Samotracia*' [a roaring car that seems to ride on grapeshot is more beautiful than the Victory of Samothrace].[5] Note the masculine gender of 'un automobile': Marinetti saw the car as a male, virile expression of power. He was not alone in his glorifying tones. The car played a central role not just as a revolutionary mode of transport, but also as the ultimate symbol of modernity, and of a new idea of beauty, made out of scientific precision and industrial labour.

Finally, together with cinema, the car was to become a symbol of another marker of twentieth-century culture: mass production and mass consumption. In the conclusions to this chapter, I shall return to this common trait to discuss its implications in the perception of the USA on the part of Turinese film and car makers.

Early Cinema in Turin

One of the most authoritative experts of early Italian cinema, Paolo Cherchi Usai, warns us against the study of influence. Given that in the first years of the motion picture so much was taking place at the same time, and therefore it is difficult to know for certain whether a certain filmmaker or producer was aware of what was being done by their competitors in their country as much as in other corners of the world, Cherchi Usai rightly suggests a cautious use of the term 'influence', which is close to the concept of *contact* in art history.[6] In our case, it is important to attain a sense of how the fledgling Turinese film industry placed itself among the two emerging giants which the French and US film industries had quickly become.

In the first decade of the new century, Paris-based Pathé-Frères managed to impose themselves as the most entrepreneurial company in the field and one with clear global ambitions. France's great start was also due to the simple fact that their hardware — that is the Lumière Brothers' *Cinématographe* — quickly proved far superior to the US equivalent — Thomas Edison's Kinetoscope — which was cumbersome and did not allow for collective screening. France dominated not just in terms of production and distribution. Pathé also led the move of film screening from fairground entertainment to venues which could compete with theatre and opera: by 1908, Paris had more than one hundred permanent cinemas, twenty of which were managed by Pathé. This also meant elevating the artistic status of cinema in order to attract the interest of the cultured elites: the Société du Film d'Art, founded by Paul Lafitte (with Pathé's financial help) in 1908, began the trend, making ample use of literary adaptations. Two years later Pathé followed suit with its own *Séries d'Art*, and at the same time one other emerging French giant, Gaumont, launched its *Le Film Esthétique*.[7]

The US film industry, in these early years, very much found itself on the back foot. If Pathé dominated the European market, it equally managed to enter the US one with enormous weight: in 1906 Pathé was distributing about six films a week, each prepared in seventy-five copies. By 1908 the figure had risen to ten films a week, distributed in about 200 copies in the USA: this made it the largest single source of films in the American market. Only protectionist policies could shield the US industry from French competition, and this was achieved thanks to the relentless efforts of Thomas Edison. In 1908 he led the creation of a trust, the Motion Pictures Patents Company (also known as Edison Trust), in order to streamline film distribution in the USA, but more than anything else it established a system of near-monopoly which kept foreign competitors at bay.[8]

In those same years, the Italian film industry was taking its first steps. In Turin, the two leading companies, Ambrosio and Itala Film, were founded respectively in 1906 and 1907. Although the very first film showing took place in Turin on 21 April 1895 using an Edison Kinetoscope, once Italians began to manufacture and screen their own films, their hardware, modes of production and distribution were undoubtedly imported from France.[9] And so was some of their staff. Itala Film, in particular, in its first year, when still called Carlo Rossi & Co., poached personnel directly from Pathé. Their artistic director, Charles Lucien Lépine, had been general director of Pathé's factory outside Paris (and was successfully sued by his old company for breach of confidential industrial knowledge), and when the young Giuseppe Pastrone became the driving force of the company, the following year, France was still the model. Suffice it to say that, consistent with his decision to compete in the niche market of comical films, he went across the Alps and hired one of the then most popular French actors at the time, André Deed, who had been working with Georges Méliès and Pathé. With Itala Film, Deed started the popular series based around the comical character of *Cretinetti*, which ensured international fame to both actor and film company. Others followed suit, with Ambrosio in 1910 hiring another comedian active in France, Marcel Fabre, to appear in their popular comic series as Robinet.[10]

These few details already give a sense of the entrepreneurial boldness of this first generation of Italian filmmakers. There was no fear in taking the fight to the most powerful of Europe's film industries. At the same time, everything in the world of early cinema was changing very rapidly. The already mentioned protectionist near-embargo on French imports in the USA — fought on the grounds of morality as much as of financial interest — allowed the US industry to develop quickly and, by the time its internal market had expanded to thousands of cinemas, it had become a clear leader in terms of both production and international competitiveness.

So, how could the fledgling Italian film industry stand up to such an ever-growing giant? In its initial steps, it very much followed the example of its French neighbour and developed its production in the four main markets which were already turning into fairly coded *genres*: (i) documentary footage on contemporary life (so-called *actualités*); (ii) the description of extraordinary places or events; (iii) narratives based on historical or literary/biblical material; and (iv) comedies. Of these four, it was the production of films set in ancient times, whether historically or literary based, which began to give Italian companies prestige and international success. Italy's association with Ancient Rome and classical culture was a factor but only to some extent: after all, when Pastrone began to work on the production of *Cabiria*, in 1912, he went to the Louvre in Paris in order to study examples of classical antiquity. Equally important was Italy's established excellence in the staging of operas, a practice which was not so distant from building monumental, static sets in which dozens of extras were made to move. Italians were also quick to grab the opportunities for longer and more complex narratives allowed by the growing length of reels available. The first international success was Ambrosio's *Gli ultimi giorni di Pompei* [The Last Days of Pompei] (co-directed by Arturo Ambrosio and Luigi Maggi), the first of a series of films based on the eponymous 1834 historical novel by Edward Bulwer-Lytton. Produced in 1908 with a length of approximately 360 metres (lasting about sixteen minutes), the film was received enthusiastically, being much praised for its attention to the reconstruction of an ancient Roman city and for its dramatic effects in the eruption scene.[11] The distribution of Italian films in US cinemas began to grow. If only eight Italian films were screened in the USA in 1906, figures increased massively: two years later there were 105 (83 of which were Turinese); and that rose to 255 films in 1910 (194 Turinese). In that year, Itala had established two releases a week in New York, while Ambrosio and Cines contented themselves with one.[12]

By 1910, technological advance and screening practices allowed the full development of the production of long feature films. Being set over four or more reels, narratives could last more than an hour. Now individual films could compete with theatre and opera productions, and Italy contributed substantially to the elevation and prestige of cinema as an art. The first Italian long feature film which achieved international success was a four-reel adaptation of Dante Alighieri's work *L'Inferno*, directed by Francesco Bartolini and Adolfo Padoan, and distributed in 1911 by Milano Film. In the same year, Itala Film successfully produced *La caduta di Troia*, directed by Pastrone and Luigi Romano Borgnetto. Of a shorter length — two reels for a duration of about thirty minutes — the film was lauded abroad for its *mise-en-scène* deploying a realistic set, moving beyond the still traditional use of canvas backdrops. In the same period, the leading film company in Rome, Cines, achieved fame on the international scene with historical epics such as the three-reeler *Gerusalemme liberata* [Jerusalem Delivered] (Enrico Guazzoni, dir., 1911), inspired by Torquato Tasso's eponymous literary masterpiece. These were the films which sparked interest in the Italian industry and particularly so on the part of one of the most entrepreneurial distributors in the USA, George Kleine.

Chicago-based George Kleine (1864–1931) had started to import and distribute foreign films in 1903 and had tried to resist Thomas Edison's drive towards a total regimentation of the US film market. He eventually became a member of the Edison Trust but still continued to pursue his interest in the foreign market as an independent distributor, concentrating in particular on Italian productions. In 1913, he masterminded the arrival of Italian historical epics, not just in US cinemas around the country, but in the heart of New York's theatre land: Broadway. It was a project aimed at raising interest in the screening of a film in order to achieve the prestige normally accredited to theatre and opera premières. A full orchestra was hired to accompany the screening. Ticket prices rose accordingly in an attempt to lure the wealthy, educated crowds who would normally spurn cinema as an inferior art form. The subject of this operation was Cines's *Quo Vadis?*, directed by Guazzoni and based on Henryk Sienkiewicz's eponymous bestseller of 1909. The gamble paid off and the film was hailed as an example of the artistic heights reached by Italian cinema.[13] On the Turinese front, other blockbusters followed in its wake, with Ambrosio's *Spartaco* (based on an eponymous Italian novel published in 1874) and a much longer remake of *Gli ultimi giorni di Pompei*. For his part, Giovanni Pastrone at Itala Film had been working on his own blockbuster since the year before: once finished in 1914, its *première* around the world was soon to turn it into an icon of the historical epic. I am naturally referring to the almost two-hour-long *Cabiria*. Set during Rome's Carthaginian wars and vaguely inspired by the novel *Cartagine in fiamme* [Carthage in Flames] (1908) by Turin-based popular novelist Emilio Salgari (Pastrone always denied this connection), the plot of *Cabiria* tells the story of the rescue of a Roman aristocratic girl by her servant and a duo of Roman spies while around them the historical figures of Scipio, Hannibal, Massinissa, and Queen Sophonisba open the film to a massive reconstruction of luxurious interiors and epic battles. Pastrone was relentless in his eye for detail as much as in his intention to create 'art'. Italy's most famous literary figure at the time, Gabriele D'Annunzio, was hired to add his prestigious touch to the film's intertitles (drafted by Pastrone himself). And for the music score Pastrone gave another prestigious figure, Ildebrando Pizzetti, the task of composing an *ad hoc* piece for the most spectacular scene of the sacrifice of children at the monumental temple of Moloch. In the USA, *Cabiria* was distributed by Itala Film Company of America, which made the most of this grand film, managing a considerable profit despite the enormous expenses related to the advertising campaign and the cost of a live orchestra.[14]

By then, George Kleine had already decided that his links with the Italian film industry had to be nurtured and taken to new heights. His correspondence with Italian producers shows the extent to which he became so eager to exploit Italy's newly achieved fame that he would suggest topics and themes around which films should be made. In other words, the US distributor of Italian films was keen to become a producer himself, and he proceeded to do so.

The correspondence related to Kleine's relationship with Cines suggests that his attempt to exploit the sensational success of *Quo Vadis?* had been hampered by Cines's limitations in producing films both at the agreed rate (600 metres per week) and of sufficient quality. The latter was the object of a number of complaints by Kleine: the film used by Cines (which produced its own film material) was not chemically stable, and the perforation adopted was of insufficient precision, often ending up with reels being damaged during projection. The Turinese companies were more reliable on that front, hence Kleine's decision to invest there and at the same time aim to retain as much control as possible.[15]

The first move was to sign an exclusive contract with Ambrosio, in April 1913, in which the latter was contracted to produce the already mentioned remake of *Gli ultimi giorni di Pompei*. The contract specified that the film was to be of similar length and spectacular value of *Quo Vadis?* and that Kleine's company would retain full ownership. Another four films were to follow on similar conditions.[16] A few months later, Ambrosio offered Kleine the opportunity to enter into co-production with his firm but Kleine declined: he wanted executive control. After a long negotiation and a number of meetings (Ambrosio and Kleine had first met in New York, in 1911, after which the latter visited Italy twice during his European tours, in 1911 and 1913), a deal was struck between him, Alfredo Gandolfi (Ambrosio's then financial director), and Mario Alberto Stevani. The latter was a partner of Kleine, since 1912, in exporting European films to the USA. The result was the creation of a film production company based in Turin and the immediate acquisition of the land necessary to build a fully functional studio on the outskirts of the city, in Brugliasco. The Photo Drama Producing Company was legally founded only in March 1914, but by then the construction of the new studios was already in full swing and, indeed, by the summer of the same year they were functional.

In the long telegram in which, from Italy, Kleine announced to his Chicago associates that Photo Drama was now a reality, on 12 December 1913, he described it as follows:

> You are now at liberty to announce formation of Photodrama production company of Italy by myself and two associates stop have bought beautiful estate permitting staging of fifty scene [sic] simultaneously in varied natural and artificial setting stop policy is to combine artistic perfection of italian with virility of american method taking the best out of best schools stop big features only stop [. . .] Important features being made for me by other plants are nearly ready.[17]

The following January, Kleine was in Turin to follow the construction of the studios. Given the reciprocal lack of knowledge of the other's language, all communications between Kleine and Gandolfi took place in French. Together they planned the first round of productions which the Photo Drama studios were supposed to give birth to. Spanish director Segundo de Chomòn, a famous name in French silent cinema who, for Pathé, had rivalled Georges Méliès as a master in special effects, had been hired by Ambrosio since 1912: he was contracted to be the director of Photo Drama's early films. The first to go into production, in the summer of 1915, was a film adaptation of Arrigo Boito's opera *Mefistofele* (1868). Other films equally based on opera works were supposed to follow.

By then, however, Italy had entered the First World War (23 May 1915) and the financial prospects of the new company quickly became catastrophic. In a series of telegrams, Gandolfi tried to convince Kleine to inject more money, but by then the US entrepreneur had decided that the radical stall suffered by the European film industry asked for a cautious approach. As a consequence, Gandolfi stopped production and instead rented the studios out to Ambrosio's main competitor, Itala Film. Personal tragedy was soon to follow: one of the three partners, Stevani, turned out to have accumulated so much debt that he eventually committed suicide, in July 1915. Stevani's widow asked for the company to go into liquidation so that she could rescue some money and, unable to convince Kleine to intervene, Gandolfi was forced to follow that path. Photo Drama ceased to exist in 1919 (company liquidations were frozen during the war years) and its Brugliasco studios were taken over by the city council and converted to other purposes.

Fig. 7.1. The headed paper of Photo Drama in a letter sent by Gandolfi to Kleine on 25 June 1914 (courtesy of Manuscript Division, Library of Congress, Washington DC).

As already evidenced in the footnotes, this important episode in Turin's early cinema history has been studied by more than one film historian. However, one aspect which, in my view, still remains unclear relates to the role of Arturo Ambrosio. Judging from Kleine's correspondence, Ambrosio was initially keen to collaborate with Kleine. However, since the latter decided to create his own company, there must have been inevitable competition between Ambrosio Film and Photo Drama. Moreover, Gandolfi's resignation from Ambrosio Film in order to become an associate of Kleine should not necessarily be considered an act of collaboration. Indeed, in his own correspondence, once he moved to Photo Drama, Gandolfi never mentioned Ambrosio, either as a collaborator or as a possible source of help during the company's final crisis. The fact that the studios were eventually rented out to Ambrosio's main rival, Itala Film, is another sign that the creation of Photo Drama had perhaps taken place at the expense of the relationship of Ambrosio with Kleine as much as with his former financial director, Gandolfi. Two other details emerging from the correspondence seem to point in that direction. First, when Stevani, on 27 May 1914, wrote to Kleine from Paris to report on the disappointing results of the first films produced by Ambrosio on Photo Drama's account (*The Lion of Venice*, *Othello*, and *Madame du Barry*), he made mention of the fact that at the same time Ambrosio had launched on the market his own historical epic — *The Destruction of Carthage* — and was selling it at a much lower price. Stefani also found it to be of a better quality than the Photo Drama ones, hence in order to try to stem its competition, he was forced to buy the distribution world rights to Ambrosio's film at a very high price. The implicit comment of Stevani's long report was that the films produced by Ambrosio for Photo Drama were of inferior quality to the ones that the firm produced under its own aegis. When replying to Stevani from Chicago, Kleine also dropped two comments related to Ambrosio which appear slightly derogatory. Firstly, he warned Stevani, who at the time was Ambrosio's agent for the distribution of its films in the USA, that he knew for certain that Ambrosio was trying to replace him. Secondly he mentioned having read in the *Moving Picture World* that Ambrosio had employed an American as its new Commercial Director General and that the firm 'had begun to install American push into the business by engaging numerous high salaried people in all departments'. He accompanied this piece of information with a dry comment: 'It is to laugh'.[18]

The First World War provided a watershed in the history of early cinema since it created enormous difficulties for the European film industries. The Italian industry spiralled into a crisis from which it did not recover until the Fascist state came to its rescue in the mid-1930s. The demise of Photo Drama is part of this process as much as the demise of the Turinese film industry. Rome was to impose itself in the interwar years as the new capital of the Italian film industry. However, with regard to the topic of this chapter, these few pages should have provided a sense of the way in which Turinese filmmakers developed their business while negotiating their relations with the leading industries of France and the USA. What emerges is the picture of a generation of filmmakers who had few fears in facing international competition and the world markets. The success of Italian historical/literary films certainly emboldened this attitude. At the same time, there is a clear sense that if France was, in the early years, the model from which to import ideas, hardware, and human know-how, by the 1910s, the pendulum was swinging towards the USA. No doubt this was the result of the enormous prospects for export, given the size of the US cinema market. Equally, there is the perception that the Italian film industry had by then emancipated itself from its dependence on France. Despite Kleine's sarcasm, it is true that Ambrosio in 1914 was attempting to 'Americanize' its staff, starting from the appointment of Frank Joseph Goldsoll as its new Commercial Director General.[19] As for Photo Drama, apart from Kleine's explicit intention to hire US actors to make their productions more attractive to the American market, it is interesting to note that when the company's staff was hired, the traditional French brain-drain and head-hunting which characterized the early years of Italian cinema had disappeared: in the list of all staff employed by Photo Drama on 28 February 1915, there is not a single surname of French origin among the technical personnel.[20]

Finally, the popularity in the USA of Italy's 'kolossals' such as *L'Inferno* and *Cabiria* marked a short but intense period — 1911–14 — during which the relationship between the Italian and US film industries spoke of reciprocal influence in different areas. As Kleine had envisaged, the capacity of US entrepreneurs to organize and deliver entertainment on a large, industrial scale could merge with the Italian tradition of artistic refinement and artisanal skills. Film historians constantly remind us that the father figure of US cinema, D. W. Griffith, was deeply influenced by the spectacular settings of Italian epic films. Equally telling, though, is the fact that Griffith admired other, although similar, Italian skills when he visited Italy's pavilion at San Francisco's Panama-Atlantic International Exposition of 1915. He was impressed by the reconstruction of historical buildings (The Doge's Palace was the main one), and that was the quality he had in mind when he planned to build a film set for the Babylonian episode of *Intolerance* (1916) inspired by Pastrone's *Cabiria*.

As his young assistant director at the time, Joseph Henabery, remembers, Griffith sent him all the way to San Francisco to try to find the artisans who had been working at the Italian pavilion so that they could be hired for his film production. Henabery found that the art and building restoration business in San Francisco was in the hands of the Italians and he managed to track down and employ some of the artisans and artists who had been working on the Italian pavilion. Irony dictates that one of them turned out to be French.[21]

Griffith's passion for expensive, spectacular historical reconstructions was to be his Achilles's heel which eventually made him an outdated figure in the commercially savvy world of post-First World War Hollywood. The Italian film industry was equally showing strengths as much as weaknesses: its attention to epic historical landscapes creating an obsession with *mise-en-scène* and scenography at the expense of the development of coherent, well-paced narratives might have brought a crisis even if the Great War had not taken place.[22] Despite all this, in the early 1910s the Turinese film industry seemed fully set towards developing its relations with the USA, perceiving it as both a profitable market and a land where filmmaking was being brought to a new level.

I should finally add that there was in those years one more reason behind this meeting of Italian and US cultures. For both countries, ancient history was raw material on which to build a sense of national identity; it was a heritage providing the reassurance of a prestigious past. Since its separation from their colonial motherland, a separate identity of the USA was achieved also through a cultural shift which privileged the classical roots of western culture as against the northern European gothic tradition celebrated in nineteenth-century England. The choice of neoclassical architecture in the USA made Italy's ancient past a shared heritage: and the arrival of cinema nurtured this through the monumental reconstructions of cities such as Pompeii and Rome. It is not surprising that in the post-First World War years, once the fever for epic films seemed to be over, George Kleine's activity should move towards the distribution of Italian historical films in schools and universities, where they were consumed as illustrative reconstructions rather than as entertaining narratives.[23]

The Turinese Car Industry

As with film technology, France's contribution to the birth of the automobile was vital. Once again, however, it would be problematic and ultimately of little use to try to put together a timeline of 'who-invented-what' at a time when internal combustion engines and their application to vehicles were being developed in many corners of Europe and across the Atlantic. Nevertheless, all car historians would agree on two facts: firstly, that the forefather of the automobile is Nicholas-Joseph Cugnot, a French military engineer who in 1770 tested a steam-propelled cart. Secondly, that if Germany managed to produce the most reliable and paradigm-setting engines in the second half of the nineteenth century, it was France which dominated the market of car production in its early years. Panhard et Levassor produced in 1891 their four-wheeled vehicle which was to set the standard for the years to come (front engine, sliding gearbox, rear wheel-drive). The historic names of Peugeot and Renault added their capacity to blend technological innovation and industrial production, and by the end of the century the French car industry dominated the world market. By 1903, France was still producing nearly half the total number of cars in the entire world, almost three times more than the USA.[24]

France's leading edge left its mark on the industry's lexis too. The French neologism 'automobile' defeated the competition of 'horseless carriage' (USA), 'motor car' (GB) and 'Selbstfahrer' (Germany) and became the model for many European languages, Italian included. The same for other key expressions such as 'carburateur', 'chassis', 'volant' and 'garage'. Similarly, in the newly born world of motor racing, the expression 'grand prix' was to dominate despite the resistance from the US motoring press which, until 1908, tried to replace it with the anglicized version 'grand prize'.[25]

As far as Italy is concerned, beyond various prototypes which were developed in different parts of Italy, the fledgling Italian car industry rose to a new level with the 1899 foundation of an anonymous company led by a group of motor enthusiasts in Turin: the Fabbrica Italiana Automobili Torino. Among them was Giovanni Agnelli, who became FIAT's managing director in 1901, attached control of the company to his family, and led it personally until the end of the Second World War. Agnelli and his other associates involved in the creation of FIAT were a group of Turinese aristocrats and rich bourgeois (Giovanni's father had been a successful entrepreneur in the silk industry) whose interest in car manufacturing derived from neighbouring France. The first edition of the pioneering Paris–Rouen motor race, in 1894 (won by two cars, a Panhard et Levassor and a Peugeot Frères) fired the imagination of many, eager to enter the competition with an Italian-made vehicle. We also know that Giovanni Agnelli's first contacts with the motoring world came partly from his contacts with Luigi Storero, a mechanic who imported French tricycle cars in Turin. One of the first decisions taken by the newly formed company was to acquire the latest Panhard et Levassor model in order to study it in detail.[26]

The first years saw the company move from one financial crisis to another. Giovanni Agnelli was the most vocal about the need to step away from an artisanal approach, producing unique models in a constant state of development and adjustment, and move instead towards a well-structured and financially viable industrial production. This only became a reality in 1908, with the production of the Fiat Tipo 1, which, particularly in its taxi version (aptly named 'Fiacre'), became Fiat's first commercial success, with a total of about 1,600 vehicles being produced, many of which were exported to the main cities of Europe and the USA. The relatively underdeveloped stage of the circulation of cars in Italy made export a necessity: in 1908, out of 1,215 cars being produced by FIAT, 747 were sold abroad.[27]

By then, Giovanni Agnelli had already set his sights on a new paradigm: the US car industry and its enormous internal market. Agnelli's first visit to the USA dates

FIG. 7.2. The newly built FIAT factory in Poughkeepsie NY, 1909 (photo courtesy of Centro Storico FIAT, Turin).

to the autumn of 1905, when he travelled to New York together with the firm's President, Lodovico Scarfiotti, in order to discuss sales in the USA and consider the possibility of building a factory there.[28] Protectionist tariffs hindered car exports to the USA, hence Agnelli's idea of creating a US subsidiary. Four years later, in the autumn of 1909, FIAT built its own factory in Poughkeepsie, north of New York City, and production of luxury and racing cars began the following year. About 700 vehicles were built in the first two years.[29]

How did FIAT's development and its early access to the US market fit with the development of the car industry in the USA at the time? As in Europe, a plethora of small, artisanal companies had been born in the last years of the nineteenth century. From these emerged the future giants of the industry, and among them was Henry Ford who, after leading a number of pioneering attempts, managed to secure the funding for the creation of the Ford Motor Company, in 1903. Thanks to his efforts and those of other established firms such as Oldsmobile and Rambler, the following year the USA's car industry began to overtake France in overall production figures and their leadership increased exponentially: by 1907 US car production was almost double that of France (c. 44,000 units vs. 25,000).[30]

The first to develop car production to an advanced industrial level was Henry Ford, with his Model T, whose production in Detroit started in 1908. It was a car designed to be simply built, reliable, easily maintained, and, more than anything else, affordable. Its success spoke for itself: in 1909 production rose to 10,666 vehicles; in 1910 it reached 19,050. The much-mentioned assembly line method was only introduced in the new Ford factory in 1912, but by then Henry Ford had already made a name for himself as a careful practitioner of the approach to the scientific management of industrial production theorized by Frederick W. Taylor. Every stage of assemblage was studied in detail and organized so as to streamline production and reduce costs. The net result was the sale price of the Ford Model T which, at $680 in 1911, was a fraction of the cost of any other vehicle of similar size and class. By making cars affordable to the lower middle classes and later on even to his own workers, Ford led the car industry to a much wider market: in 1913, production of the Model T rose to 170,211 units and surpassed 200,000 vehicles the following year. The European car industry, by then, was a very distant second.[31]

During one of his visits to the USA, in 1911, Giovanni Agnelli made sure to meet Henry Ford and was taken on a tour of his factory. Agnelli came to a firm opinion about the need to move towards a similar, standardized, low-cost production structure. He arranged for his engineers to visit Ford's factories in order to study and compare the reciprocal organization of labour and assemblage.³² FIAT's ultimate aim was to produce a similarly economical car to Ford's Model T. The first attempt was the FIAT Zero, a four-seater of which about 2,000 units were produced between 1912 and 1915 (after which the factory was converted for war production). It was, however, a far cry from its US rival, in terms of both production levels and price. An entirely new factory was needed in order to radically move forward. The path was set in 1914 when Agnelli commissioned architect Giacomo Matté Trucco to plan a cutting-edge factory adopting Ford's moving assembly line and sporting a futuristic flat roof to provide a test track for the newly built vehicles. The 'Lingotto', as the factory was called from the toponym of the Turinese district where it was built, was inaugurated in 1923. In the same year, the inspiring figure of modern architecture, Le Corbusier, referred to the 'Lingotto' in his manifesto-book *Vers une architecture* as an example of the achievements of contemporary industrial culture.³³

From the assembly line of the Lingotto was to emerge in 1936 FIAT's first real *utilitaria*: the Fiat 500. Thanks to this little, relatively inexpensive vehicle, Italy's lower middle class could finally afford to buy their first car. More than half a million were sold between 1936 and 1955. Today everybody remembers it as the Fiat 'Topolino', a nickname it received because its protruding main lamps reminded people of Mickey Mouse's ears. However, this homage to US popular culture was never intentional: it does not appear in the company's paperwork nor was it ever used when advertising the car. A journalist used it first, after which it was quickly adopted by the public.³⁴

In actual fact, Giovanni Agnelli's relationship with the USA was not exactly one of grateful admiration. As he knew well, the extraordinary growth of the US car industry posed a serious threat to European car manufacturers. We have already seen how Giovanni Agnelli had no deferential fears. The creation of a factory on US soil was a clear move to bring the war into the enemy's territory. Giovanni Agnelli was also particularly active in making use of the prestige deriving from the success of FIAT racing cars. Since the early years of car racing in the USA, FIAT cars were present, and successfully so. On the occasion of the first Grand Prix in the USA, the American Grand Prize which took place in Savannah, Georgia, on Thanksgiving Day, 26 November 1908, Agnelli sent an official FIAT racing team which fielded three cars, driven respectively by a French, Italian, and US driver. Only eleven of the twenty cars on the starting line finished the race but all three FIATs completed it and secured two podium places (first and third) and ninth position. French, German, and another Italian car manufacturer (Itala; no relation to Itala Film) occupied the other places, with the first US-built car clocking an embarrassing eleventh position and finishing 41 minutes later. Given that this was happening during the same year in which Henry Ford was beginning to produce his Model T by the tens of thousands, it is clear that Agnelli's initial strategy was to concentrate on the market of luxury and sport cars. This, after all, had been the profile of European manufacturers from their very beginning. Indeed, that is what the US factory in Poughkeepsie was set up to do.³⁵

Back in Italy, however, it was a different matter. As we said, Agnelli's ultimate aim was to emulate Ford in the field of mass-produced, inexpensive cars. It took

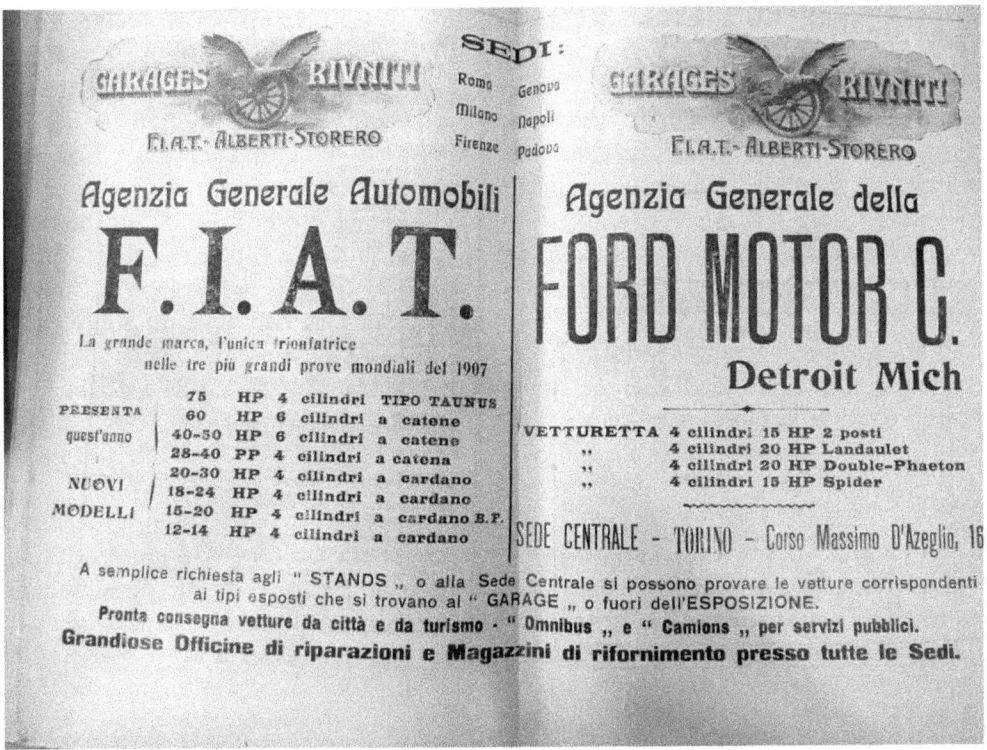

Fig. 7.3. From the official catalogue of the Esposizione internazionale di automobili, Turin, 18 January–2 February 1908 (courtesy of Centro Documentazione — Museo Nazionale dell'Automobile, Turin).

FIAT more than twenty years to achieve that. In the meantime, competition had to be kept at bay. Initially this seemed to take the shape of collaboration. Ford arrived in Italy in 1905: this is the first year in which the US company appeared at the Esposizione internazionale di automobile in Turin, Italy's principal motor show. It was present with a single stand, represented by its European distributor, H. B. White, based in Paris. The Ford Motor Company was absent in the following two years, until in 1908 it came back to the Esposizione internazionale in a big way. This time it shared an imposing set of stands with Italy's leading car factory, FIAT. What happened is that in that year the official distributor and repairer of FIAT cars — Garages Riuniti — had acquired sales and maintenance services of Ford cars too. This surprising 'marriage' lasted only for two years, after which Ford returned to being independently represented. On the part of Agnelli, this seems the result of an attempt to keep Ford under FIAT's roof with two obvious advantages: acquiring a detailed knowledge of Ford's cars and being able to influence its distribution in Italy.

It must be added, however, that Henry Ford did not think of the Italian market as of sufficient size to deserve particular interest. In the pre-First World War years, the circulation of cars in Italy was greatly inferior to that of more developed European countries. In 1910, for example, there were fewer than 8,000 registered vehicles on the road in Italy, compared to about 100,000 in Great Britain.[36] It was only in the years following the Great War that Ford and the other US giant, General Motors, began a more aggressive campaign towards securing their presence in Europe, Italy included. Protectionist tariffs were already exceedingly high: in 1920, imported US cars paid a 36% tariff plus another 35% *ad valorem*, complete with a road tax which was three times more expensive than that of an Italian car. In 1926, taxation was still at 62%. Crunch time came two years later when Ford decided to buy the Italian company Isotta Fraschini, as a sort of Trojan horse, and planned the creation of a new factory in Trieste. At that point Giovanni Agnelli used all his influence to try to convince Mussolini to stop the process. The two had been on good terms following Agnelli's early support of Fascism. Mussolini eventually relented and in November 1929 declared that the Italian car industry was vital to the nation and therefore had to be protected.[37]

Conclusion

Looking at Turin in the early years of the twentieth century and concentrating on the film and car industries provided an opportunity to study the development of two fields which very much defined the twentieth century at a time when the USA was beginning to rival French culture. In both cases, it is clear that a shift from France to the USA took place in a matter of a few years, well before the First World War. Another common factor is the degree of self-assuredness demonstrated by Turinese entrepreneurs. The recognition of the dominance of a certain foreign industry did not imply a sense of inferiority, nor did it create adulation towards its model. Arturo Ambrosio and Giovanni Agnelli were representatives of an entrepreneurial class which boldly developed their businesses and simply looked at what the international market had to offer. Both were protagonists in developing new trends, although in this case the two industries moved in opposite directions. As a cultural object, film was taken out of the niche market of cheap, popular entertainment and was elevated to the realm of artistic production. The automobile, on the other hand, went from being an elitist object of luxury to a mass-produced one for the enjoyment of huge numbers of people.

A central and final question related to the move from French to US culture remains to be answered: why did it happen so early in comparison with other facets of Italian culture? Indeed, the traditional understanding of Italy's Americanization is that it is a phenomenon which took off in the interwar years and exploded in the 1950s. This study points towards two probable causes. First, both films and automobiles are commodities which are highly dependent on technology. This is an area in which the US economy was capable of competing with its European rivals at the turn of the century and — with regard to mass production and distribution — was already showing its supremacy against the old continent. In both fields, France had been a leading country but within a few years a number of factors — including the huge potential of the US internal market (the world's largest at the time) — allowed the USA to gain the upper hand. The First World War certainly gave an enormous advantage to the US film industry (no disruption to either its production or national market), but it is doubtful whether the process would have been much different without it. FIAT and the car industry in general benefitted from the war (FIAT's army truck 18BL became, after all, FIAT's first mass-produced vehicle) but once it was over, they would have suffered the same fate as Italy's film industry if it had not been for the protectionist policies which kept the USA outside the national borders. If 'Hollywood on the Tiber' was to become a reality in later years, it was political and economic interests which ensured that the USA were never allowed a 'Detroit on the Po river'.

The second point concerns the fact that cinema and automobiles were entirely new products. In both cases, the USA did not have to face a European, sedimented tradition which somehow gave it an initial advantage. In fact, the weight of the past came to function as a hindrance. Intellectual snobbery towards the medium of film persisted in European intellectual circles for decades: one of its consequences is the US birth of Film Studies as an academic subject, something which European universities were slower to turn towards. As for the car industry, a classic example is the 'horse-friendly', self-harming Locomotive Act of the British parliament which in 1865 stated that self-propelled vehicles on public roads had to be preceded by a man on foot armed with a red flag. By the time the law was repealed, in 1898, the British car industry had lost precious ground.[38]

Finally, given that the years which have been considered here coincide with one of the most intense periods of Italian migration to the USA, one could reasonably ask whether this fact was indeed a factor. With regard to the film industry, there is no doubt that the presence of hundreds of thousands of Italian migrants in the big cities of the USA formed a specific market which film distributors took into account.[39] Beyond that, however, it is difficult to see other instances, in the film as much as in the car industry. In those years, Turin had a very limited rate of migration to the USA as much as to any other part of the world. The local economy, as we have seen, was strong, and therefore there is a sense that this is a particular case in which a national phenomenon — that of Italian migration — does not fit the local reality of a particular area. But even in more general terms, generations had to pass before a substantial influence of Italian migration on US culture could be detected. There is no doubt this happened, with chapters of US film history being written by Italian American actors and directors. Whether this had any influence on how Italians saw the USA is a different matter, totally outside the chronological frame of this chapter. In the car industry, one cannot even talk of a similar phenomenon taking place. The only example is rather symbolic, however. The leader of FIAT who, after the acquisition of the limping US giant Chrysler, turned the company into a multinational corporation in 2014 (FCA: Fiat Chrysler Automobiles), was an Italian migrant. Sergio Marchionne's family had migrated to Canada when he was thirteen. There Marchionne built his managerial career, later re-crossed the Atlantic, and eventually wrote the most important chapter of FIAT's recent history. If the early years of the twentieth century had seen the emergence of the USA as a world economic power, a century later, Giovanni Agnelli's descendant found himself able to rescue a US company and create a new, transnational entity. It would be naïve, however, to interpret this as a paradigm-shifting change in the relationship between Italy and the USA. This recent alliance between an Italian and a US company has probably more to do with the need to face competition in a global market in which non-Western countries are now the emerging giants.

Notes to Chapter 7

1. Walter Benjamin, 'Paris, Capital of the 19th Century' [originally entitled 'Paris, Hauptstadt des XIX. Jahrhunderts', 1955], *Perspecta*, 12 (1969), 163–72; Antonio Gramsci, *Quaderni del carcere*, ed. by Valentino Gerratana (Turin: Einaudi, 1975), p. 1694. On the cultural influence of nineteenth-century Paris see Christopher Prendergast, *Paris and the Nineteenth Century* (Oxford: Blackwell, 1992).
2. On linguistic policies in modern Italy see Schirru's chapter in this book and Paolo E. Balboni, *Storia dell'educazione linguistica in Italia. Dalla legge Casati alla riforma Gelmini* (Turin: UTET, 2009).
3. Donna Gabaccia, *Italy's Many Diasporas* (London: UCL Press, 2000), p. 19. Regional variations were also substantial, moving between above 50% of literacy in Piedmont down to 10% in various southern provinces of the former Kingdom of the Two Sicilies. On education in post-Unification Italy see for example Giovanni Vecchi, *Measuring Wellbeing: A History of Italian Living Standards* (Oxford: Oxford University Press, 2017).
4. Gianni Rondolino, *Torino come Hollywood* (Bologna: Capelli, 1980).
5. Filippo Tommaso Marinetti, *Fondazione e Manifesto del futurismo*, first published in French in *Le Figaro*, on 20 February 1909; then in *I manifesti del futurismo* (Florence: Edizioni di 'Lacerba', 1914). English translation from Umbro Apollonio, ed., *Documents of 20th Century Art: Futurist Manifestos* (New York: Viking Press, 1973), p. 23. On Futurism and cars, see Samuele Pardini, 'The Automobile', in *Futurism: A Microhistory*, ed. by Sascha Bru, Luca Somigli and Bart Van den Bossche (Oxford: Legenda, 2017), pp. 48–58.
6. Paolo Cherchi Usai, 'On the Concept of "Influence" in Early Cinema', in *Cinéma sans frontières 1896–1918: Images across Borders*, ed. by Roland Cosandey and François Albera (Payot, Québec: Nuit Blanche Editeur, 1995), pp. 275–86.
7. Richard Abel, *The Ciné Goes to Town: French Cinema, 1896–1914* (Berkeley, CA: University of California Press, 1994), pp. 9–58. See also, by the same author: 'The Perils of Pathé, or the Americanization of American Cinema', in *Cinema and the Invention of Modern Life*, ed. by Leo Charney and Vanessa R. Schwartz (Berkeley, CA: University of California Press, 1995), pp. 183–223.
8. Kristin Thompson, *Exporting Entertainment: America in the World Film Market 1907–34* (London: BFI Publishing, 1985), pp. 4–19. See also Abel, *The Ciné Goes to Town*, p. 185.
9. See Aldo Bernardini, *Cinema muto italiano*, I: *Ambiente, spettacoli e spettatori 1896–1904* (Rome and Bari: Laterza, 1980), pp. 9–64.
10. Silvio Alovisio, '"The Pastrone System": Itala Film from its Origins to World War I', *Film History*, 12.3 (2000), 250–61. See also Maria Adriana Prolo, 'Francesi nel cinema italiano muto', *Bianco & Nero*, 14.8–9 (1953), 69–74. On André Deed see Jean Antoine Gili, *André Deed: Boireau, Cretinetti, Gribouille* (Bologna: Cineteca Bologna, 2005).
11. Davide Turconi, 'I film storici italiani e la critica americana dal 1910 alla fine del muto', *Bianco e Nero*, 1.2 (1963), 40–54 (p. 41).
12. Paolo Cherchi Usai, 'Maciste all'Hell's Kitchen: Il cinema muto torinese negli Stati Uniti', in *Cabiria e il suo tempo*, ed. by P. Bertetto and G. Rondolino (Milan: Il Castoro, 1998), pp. 132–48. See also Aldo Bernardini, *Cinema muto italiano*, III: *Arte, divismo e mercato 1910–1914* (Bari and Rome: Laterza, 1982), p. 145; and Giorgio Bertellini, 'Epica spettacolare e splendore del vero. L'influenza del cinema storico italiano in America (1908–1915)', in *Storia del cinema mondiale*, ed. by G. P. Brunetta, 5 vols (Turin: Einaudi, 1999), II, 227–65.
13. See Turconi, 'I film storici italiani e la critica americana', pp. 40–54.

14. On the making of *Cabiria* see *Giovanni Pastrone: Gli anni d'oro del cinema a Torino*, ed. by Paolo Cherchi Usai (Turin: UTET, 1985).
15. Documents in Box 7 'Cines', in The George Kleine Papers, Washington: Library of Congress [henceforth GKP]. Paolo Cherchi-Usai comes to the same conclusion in his ground-breaking essay on George Kleine: 'Un americain à Turin à la conquete de l'Italie. George Kleine à Grugliasco 1913–1914', *Archives*, 22–23 (1989), 1–20 (p. 5). A following issue of *Archives*, 26–27 (1989), contained a selection of documents from the Kleine Papers. For a more comprehensive study on George Kleine, see Joel Frykholm, *George Kleine and American Cinema: The Movie Business and Film Culture in the Silent Era* (London: Palgrave Macmillan, 2015).
16. They were 'Othello', 'The Lion of Venice', 'Madame du Barry', and 'Delenda Carthago!'. Only the first three were completed. Confusingly, the company which Kleine had created in 1913, together with Stevani, for this purpose was named 'Photo Drama Company'. It was, however, based in Illinois and had nothing to do with the Italian Photo Drama created the following year by Kleine, Stevani, and Gandolfi. Indeed, the bankruptcy of the latter did not the affect the former.
17. Telegram by George Kleine to Led Sterokinet, 12 December 1913, in GKP, Box 30 'Kleine European Trips', file 'European Trip 1913–14'.
18. Letter from George Kleine to Alfredo Gandolfi, dated 21 July 1914; in GKP, Box 54, File 'Mario Stevani 1913–1914'.
19. The appointment was announced in an anonymous short article entitled 'F. J. Goldsoll's New Post', which appeared in the *New York Times* on 1 July 1914 (p. 3).
20. The document containing the full list of personnel working at the Brugliasco studios of Photo Drama is in GKP, Box 44, File 'Photo Drama Producing Co. General 1913–1917'.
21. See the long interview with Joseph Henabery in Kevin Brownlow's *The Parade's Gone By...* (New York: Alfred Kopf, 1968), pp. 43–52. The story of Italian migrants helping to build the sets of D. W. Griffith films was liberally used by the Brothers Taviani in their 1987 film *Good Morning Babylon*.
22. Arturo Ambrosio himself seemed to be very aware of the dead end which Italian cinema faced. In an interview after his return from a trip to the USA, he admitted that the 'stile italiano' in cinema was no longer sought after in the USA. See Veritas [pseudonym], 'Il cavaliere Ambrosio di ritorno dall'America', *La vita cinematografica*, 7–15 February 1916, p. 74.
23. On the role of classical culture in shaping U.S. national identity, and on the combined role of U.S. and Italian cinema, see the work of Maria Wyke, in particular her *Projecting the Past: Ancient Rome, Cinema and History* (London: Routledge, 1997).
24. Serge Bellu, *Histoire mondiale de l'automobile* (Paris: Flammarion, 1998), p. 18. See also James Laux, *In First Gear: The French Automobile Industry to 1914* (Liverpool: Liverpool University Press, 1976); and Gijs Mon, *Atlantic Automobilism: The Emergence and Persistence of the Car: 1890–1940* (New York: Berghahn, 2014).
25. Charles Bishop, *La France et l'automobile* (Paris: Génin, 1971), p. 7.
26. Valerio Castronovo, *Giovanni Agnelli: La FIAT dal 1899 al 1945* (Turin: Einaudi, 1977), pp. 9–10. Valerio Castronovo, *FIAT 1899–1999: Un secolo di storia italiana* (Milan: Rizzoli, 1999), pp. 7, 12. See also Progetto Archivio Storico FIAT, *FIAT 1899–1930. Storia e documenti* (Milan: Fabbri, 1991).
27. Precise production data can be found in Archivio Storico FIAT, *FIAT: Le fasi della crescita: Le cifre dello sviluppo aziendale* (Turin: Scriptorium, 1996) (copy held at Archivio Storico Fiat: from now on abbreviated as ASF).
28. Historians disagree on the exact timing of this first visit. According to Castronovo (*Agnelli*, p. 48), Agnelli travelled to New York in April 1906, on the occasion of the opening of FIAT's commercial offices. Castronovo's assertion is doubted by Giorgio Mori in his *Il capitalismo industriale in Italia* (Rome: Riuniti, 1977, p. 123), in which he suggests that the only trip of which we have clear evidence is that of 1912. However, the minutes of FIAT's administrative board meetings present incontrovertible evidence: the meeting of 13 November 1905 contains a report on the visit to the USA by FIAT's President and its Director ('Amministratore delegato'), Giovanni Agnelli. No firm dates are mentioned but the timing and content of the report makes

it clear that the two visited the USA in the weeks preceding November 1905. See Progetto Archivio Storico FIAT, *I primi quindici anni della FIAT: Verbali dei Consigli di amministrazione 1899–1915* (Milan: Franco Angeli, 1987), pp. 347–48; copy held at ASF.
29. On FIAT's activity in the USA see: Giuseppe Capirone, 'Fiat "compra" in America, storia di cent'anni', *Il Registro*, 28.4 (2014), 12–17; and A. Amadelli, 'La Fiat in USA: le origini', *La manovella*, 1983. See also Giuseppe Volpato, 'L'internazionalizzazione dell'industria autumobilistica italiana', in Archivio Storico Fiat, *L'industria italiana nel mercato mondiale: Dalla fine dell'800 alla metà del 900* (Turin: Fiat, 1993), pp. 157–216; copy held at ASF. See also various documentation in ASF, f. 'La Fiat all'estero', sc. 10, f. VII.
30. James Flink, *The Automobile Age* (Cambridge, MA: M.I.T. Press, 1988), p. 25.
31. In 1913, the USA produced 485,000 out of the 606,124 vehicles produced in the whole world (Flink, *The Automobile Age*, p. 25). Although car historians fully agree on Henry Ford's Model T as being the first mass-produced car, some suggest more due should be given to the invention of the monocoque (a structural metal body which fulfils all structural functions) by Edward G. Budd and his engineer Joe Ledwinka: developed in Philadelphia between 1910 and 1914, this technique was to be adopted by the global car industry and is still dominant today. See Paul Nieuwenhuis, 'Car Manufacturing', in *The Global Automotive Industry*, ed. by Paul Nieuwenhuis and Peter Wells (Hoboken, NJ: Wiley, 2015), pp. 41–51.
32. The full report of the 1918 visit is held at ASF, sc. 1, f. 'Relazione Tecnica, Ing. Maraini'. In 1918, the differential between Ford's and FIAT's assemblage times was still huge: assembling the doors, for instance, varied from 2 minutes in a Ford factory against 15 at FIAT; painting a vehicle differed from 2h 40m in a Ford factory against 17h 25m at FIAT (pp. 16, 18). See also: Pier Luigi Bassignana, 'Tayloristi loro malgrado', in *Taylorismo e fordismo alla Fiat nelle relazioni di viaggio di tecnici e ingegneri (1919–1955)*, ed. by P. L. Bassignana (Turin: AMMA, 1998), pp. 7–36.
33. Le Corbusier, *Vers une architeture* (1923); English trans.: *Towards a New Architecture* (London: The Architectural Press, 1987), p. 287.
34. On the history of the Fiat 500 see Valerio Castronuovo, *Fiat 1899–1999: Un secolo di storia italiana* (Milan: Rizzoli, 1999), pp. 236–64; see also Marco Bossi, *Fiat 500 Topolino* (Milan: Nada, 1989).
35. See Bruno Bottiglieri, 'Strategie di sviluppo, assetti organizzativi e scelte finanziarie nel primo trentennio di vita della Fiat', in Progetto Archivio Storico FIAT, *FIAT 1899–1930*, pp. 13–40.
36. See Sara Moscatelli, 'Il veicolo della modernità: l'automobile', in *La capitale dell'automobile: imprenditori, cultura e società a Torino*, ed. by Paride Rugafiori (Venice: Marsilio, 1999), pp. 65–138 (pp. 78–80).
37. Castronovo, *FIAT*, pp. 278, 339–45, 401.
38. On the early history of Film Studies as an academic subject see Dana Polan, *Scenes of Instruction: The Beginnings of the U.S. Study of Film* (Berkeley, CA: University of California Press, 2007). For the text of the 1865 Locomotive Act, see *A Table Containing the Titles of All the Statutes Passed in the Seventh Session of the 18th Parliament*, ed. by G. K. Rickards (London: Eyre & Spottiswoode, 1865), p. 183; see also Brian Ladd, *Autophobia: Love and Hate in the Automotive Age* (Chicago: University of Chicago Press, 2008), pp. 14–28.
39. On this see, for example, Giorgio Bertellini, 'Shipwrecked Spectators: Italy's Immigrants at the Movies in New York, 1906–1916', *The Velvet LightTrap*, 44 (1999) [Special Issue on 'Beyond the Image: Race and Ethnicity in the Media'], 39–53.

CHAPTER 8

US Culture and Fascist Italy: The Case of *Omnibus* (1937–1939)

Manuela Di Franco

Throughout the years of Fascist rule, the attitude of the Italian government towards the USA was characterized by ambivalence. From the admiration of American power to harsh critiques of its reckless capitalism, from parallelisms with Roosevelt's New Deal and the exaltation of Hollywood's superiority to condemnation of American modernity and its society, the Fascist regime's relationship with the USA reflected its ambivalent attitude to modernity. As Emilio Gentile put it, 'Americanism was, for fascist culture, one of the main metaphors of modernity [. . .] perceived ambivalently, as [. . .] both terrifying and fascinating.'[1] However, after 1936 and the League of Nations sanctions against Italy for its aggressive colonial policies in Africa, the Fascist regime adopted a consistent and increasingly anti-US position. Sanctions resulted not only in a strident anti-US rhetoric, but also in a campaign for the cultural autarchy that aimed to decontaminate Italian culture from foreign influence, particularly US influence. Yet the USA remained a powerful and widespread presence and cultural model in late 1930s Italy.[2]

The Fascist campaign for creating a national culture purified from any foreign pollution was reflected in the periodical press. In particular, illustrated weeklies, whose popularity had been increasing since the end of the 1920s, are a privileged source for the study of the ambivalent relationship between the Fascist regime, the Italians, and the USA, as they reflected with particular sensitivity the political and cultural climate of the time.[3] As popular commercial products, illustrated magazines of the time mirrored the demands of readerships, processes of modernization, and foreign influences on the one hand; and, as products subjected to Fascist regulations, they reflected the impact of Fascist censorship and monitoring, on the other. The aim of this chapter is to show the complex and contradictory attitude to the USA and US culture reflected in a pioneering popular illustrated magazine, *Omnibus*. Founded and edited by Leo Longanesi in 1937 and published by Rizzoli, *Omnibus* reached a circulation record of around 100,000 copies per week before being shut down in 1939.[4] By focusing on *Omnibus*'s cultural content, and especially the film and literary sections, the chapter argues that the USA and US models were not only a constant presence, but also a source that influenced the entire magazine's layout and style. In other words, *Omnibus* offers a clear example of how US models functioned as part of Italian culture in the second half of the 1930s. More importantly, it mirrored both the ambivalence of the relationship the Fascist regime had to the USA, and the parallel fascination Italians had with US culture, therefore also reflecting a certain discrepancy between Italians and the Fascist regime, and a contradictory attitude among Italian intellectuals which would shape Italy's attitude to the USA also after the end of the war.[5]

The political attitude of *Omnibus* towards the USA has been widely addressed by both Michael Beynet in one of the most influential studies of the image of the USA in Fascist Italy, and recently again by Ivano Granata.[6] Both Granata and Beynet define *Omnibus* as an anti-US magazine aligned with the Fascist regime, pointing out how US society and culture were consistently depicted as barbaric and immoral; whereas Indro Montanelli and Marcello Staglieno, in their biography of Longanesi, with whom they collaborated, suggested that the magazine was an expression of anti-conformism and dissent.[7] However, the aim of this chapter is not to assess the attitude of *Omnibus* or Longanesi towards the Fascist regime nor to label its 'Fascist' or 'anti-Fascist' alleged traits, but rather to bring to light the ambivalence towards the USA that characterized *Omnibus*, and to suggest how, in the 1930s, US culture was a significant element of the emerging Italian mass culture, characterized by the spreading of popular entertaining products made available to a wide audience, such as films, radio broadcasts, and print media products, particularly illustrated magazines.[8] Whether negative or positive, a great deal of the magazine's space was dedicated to the USA or echoed US models, suggesting the depth of interest shared by *Omnibus*'s readers in US values and culture.

Before analyzing the presence of the USA in *Omnibus* in detail, it is worth dwelling on the function of magazines in the 1930s as both shapers and mirrors of their readers' demands. Cesare Zavattini, one of the protagonists of the Italian publishing industry, recalled in many testimonies about his career the effects of the publication of Hollywood stars' photos on the number of copies sold of a women's magazine, *Novella* (Milan: Rizzoli, 1919–44): 'bastava pubblicare la faccia di una certa diva che *Novella* saliva. Era una delle chiavi di successo dei rotocalchi di Rizzoli' [We only needed to publish a film star's photograph to increase *Novella*'s sales. It was one of the key reasons for Rizzoli's *rotocalchi*'s success].[9] The magazines, in other words, developed by responding to market and readers' demands: as Zavattini declared in 1937, 'Oggi il pubblico non si accontenta di leggere. Vuole la fotografia. Lo stadio e il cine gli hanno insegnato a vedere' [Today the audience does not settle for reading. They want photography. The stadium and movie theater taught them to see].[10] Rizzoli stated bluntly 'il mercato ha sempre ragione' [the market is always right]:[11] the main aim of a magazine was to sell as many copies as possible, and thus the content of a magazine was not only shaped by editors and publishers, but also by the 'Americanized' tastes of its readers. *Omnibus*, in particular, as we shall see, offered its readers insights into Hollywood stars' private and professional lives — not without criticism — attracting readers with exclusive interviews and an extensive use of photos.

US Influence in *Omnibus*

In the twenty-one months during which *Omnibus* was published, between April 1937 and January 1939, every single issue communicated an image of the USA. Whether through articles, translations of novels, photos, comic strips or advertisements, the USA was a regular presence in *Omnibus*. Praising reviews of US cultural products coexisted with harsh judgements on US society, while translated novels were published next to King Feature Syndicate comic strips.[12] In its literary sections, in particular, *Omnibus* is drawn to US culture, disseminating the work of US authors and giving space to emerging Italian writers who often showed strong connections with US culture. Moreover, the presence of many crime novels, the main genre to be published in *Omnibus* and one with deep US roots, not only suggests Italian readers' interest in the genre, but also offers evidence of the emergence of an Italian crime fiction based on the Anglo-Saxon model, challenging the Fascist regime and reflecting the cultural dialogue with the USA.

The presence of the USA was not limited to *Omnibus*'s content, but is also noticeable in the magazine's structure and layout. 'Se gli americani fanno la guerra come fanno *Life*, vinceranno di certo' [If the Americans make war as they make *Life*, they will definitely win], said Longanesi.[13] Indeed, according to former collaborator Indro Montanelli, Longanesi shaped his magazine following the examples set by popular US weeklies such as *Life* and *The New Yorker*. The layout of the page, the mix of text and images, and particularly the quality of the writing were in fact imitating the style of *The New Yorker*, while the use of images and photos was inspired by *Life*.[14] However, an even clearer influence of other European magazines can be traced. Looking at the French weekly *Marianne* (Paris: [n.pub.], 1934–40), for example, it can be noted how the cover and structure of the two periodicals, the style of their titles and even the subtitle and description of the magazines were very similar: *Marianne* defined itself as a 'Grand hebdomadaire politique et littéraire illustré' [An important political and literary illustrated weekly], while *Omnibus* was a 'settimanale di attualità politica e letteraria' [political and literary news weekly]. *Marianne* was not the only European magazine that shared similarities with *Omnibus*: similar layout, use of photographs, and the balance between images and text can be also found in *Vu* (Paris, [n.pub.], 1928–40) and the *Berliner Illustrierte Zeitung* (Berlin: Ullstein, 1892–1945), possibly the most influential European models of illustrated magazines.[15] Like other Italian weeklies of the 1930s, *Omnibus* was not only influenced by American illustrated periodicals, but also by European magazines, and specifically French and German ones.[16] However, although from a formal point of view the European model clearly played a part, as far as the content was concerned US culture was clearly dominant among foreign cultural references in the pages of *Omnibus*.

Omnibus first appeared at the end of March 1937 in a large format, the so-called *formato lenzuolo*, and its first issue sold up to 42,000 copies. The first element that captured the readers' attention was the dimension and the visual aspect: *Omnibus* was the same size as a daily newspaper, but the space was mainly occupied by pictures. Thanks to the size and the production method of the periodical, printed using the rotogravure process, Longanesi was able to combine the modern use of photographs with traditional articles. The use of photography was central to the success of the magazine and was one of its main points of originality. This reflected Longanesi's idea of a new form of journalism that used images as a means of information:

> È l'ora dell'attualità. È l'ora delle immagini. Il nostro nuovo Plutarco è l'obiettivo Kodak, che uccide la realtà con un processo ottico e la fissa come lo spillo fissa la farfalla sul cartoncino. Oggetti e persone, fuori del tempo, dello spazio e delle leggi di casualità divengono una visione. La fotografia coglie il mondo in flagrante. Diamo tante immagini accanto a testi ben fatti: ecco un nuovo genere di giornalismo.
>
> [It's time for modernity. It's time for images. Our new Plutarch is the Kodak lens, which kills reality with an optical process and fixes it as the needle fixes the butterfly on the cardboard. Objects and people, out of time, space and laws of randomness, become a vision. Photography captures the world *in flagrante*. Let's give many images next to well-written texts: here's a new genre of journalism.][17]

Photos added meaning and provided support to articles but, at the same time, they could be absolutely independent. Longanesi played with pictures, assembling the magazine as a film, reflecting the printing industry's technological innovations but also the change in habits of Italian readers, who as a result of the popularity of cinema got more interested in and used to images than words.[18] By delivering implicit messages, as will be seen below, photographs were used not only to attract readers, but also to communicate as much as words. Nonetheless, the text, or content, remained a key feature of *Omnibus*, and particular attention was paid to the quality of the writing. Longanesi's aim was to make a quality popular magazine, that is to say that serious attention was paid to the writing style, but without losing sight of the ordinary readers. 'High' and 'popular' culture coexisted in *Omnibus* as much as traditional and modern features, making it appealing to a wide range of readers. This dualism, and the smart and ironic use of photography in support of or alongside articles, made *Omnibus* a popular magazine whose structure became a model for other publications in the following years.[19]

A certain dualism can also be found in the way *Omnibus* addressed the USA. The USA was often depicted as a barbarian and materialistic society — such as in an article written by Alberto Moravia on the habits of American women, 'Le americane', published on 28 August 1937 — while in the film section Hollywood was praised and its superiority acknowledged. Further, the majority of novels published in instalments in *Omnibus*'s literary columns were translations of US authors, such as James Cain, Dashiell Hammett and William Saroyan. This interest in US culture clearly challenged the Fascist regime's censorship of foreign imports and its promotion of an 'autarchic' culture.

A range of Italian writers, both young and already well-known, such as Elio Vittorini, Mario Praz, Alberto Moravia, Giaime Pintor, Mario Soldati and Emilio Cecchi (Il Tarlo), collaborated with Longanesi on *Omnibus*, as translators from English and/or writers of original pieces with links to the USA, bringing to light another dualism of *Omnibus*: the coexistence of two different generations with different attitudes. On the one hand, there were authors such as Mario Praz and Emilio Cecchi who were sceptical of prevalent myths of the USA. On the other hand, figures such as Elio Vittorini, Giaime Pintor and Mario Soldati perceived the USA as a new, inspiring world, a myth that conditioned their work.[20] These two different attitudes influenced the way *Omnibus* wrote about the USA, fostering the conflicting attitude the Fascist regime had towards the USA.

The ambivalence towards US culture is clearly shown by the attraction to Hollywood and the repulsion felt for US society, as interpreted through the lens of Fascist propaganda, which condemned US civilization variously as decadent, dominated by machines, or characterized by a lack of history.[21] From this point of view, *Omnibus* offered a form of compromise between the Fascist regime's anti-Americanism of the 1930s and Italian readers' fascination with the USA. The strong presence of Hollywood and its stars in *Omnibus*, in particular, illustrates how US cinema had become part of Italian culture and readers' lives. This found particular expression in the regular column 'Giorno e notte' [Day and Night], which focused mainly on the latest news from Hollywood, and which is the section that, more than any other, paid attention to the USA, influenced by the US model of the fan magazine. Moreover, 'Giorno e notte' also embodies *Omnibus*'s dual nature of a cultured popular magazine, as the following brief analysis of its content indicates.

'Giorno e notte': Images from Hollywood

'Giorno e notte' appeared weekly and was usually divided into three different columns, dealing with gossip, film reviews and analysis of the film industry, respectively, with a particular focus on US films. Of the thirty-nine 'Giorno e notte' sections published in 1937, for example, only one issue did not deal with Hollywood, while nine were exclusively dedicated to the US film industry.

The articles on film stars were the most distinctive feature of 'Giorno e notte' and were largely focused on Hollywood. They contained biographies or interviews that revealed details on film stars' private lives or commented on particular situations of the filmmaking process. The key feature of these articles was that they were fake reports, allegedly written exclusively for *Omnibus* by a US correspondent. These articles, written as alleged correspondences from Hollywood, were in fact concocted by *Omnibus*'s editorial staff, including pieces presented as autobiographies of film stars, which even quoted the name of the Italian translator. Longanesi's collaborator Gino Visentini recalls how they used to spend nights in the newsroom 'a fare interviste, finte, a Greta Garbo nella casa di Hollywood, oppure a Joan Crawford in studio, creando interviste all'americana, ma inventate di sana pianta da noi, con lo stile americano che deducevamo leggendo *Life*, altre riviste americane o francesi' [making fake interviews with Greta Garbo in her Hollywood home, or with Joan Crawford in studio, creating American-like interviews, but completely made up by us, with the style we learnt reading *Life*, other American or French magazines].[22] There is no clarity about who was behind these articles, or if and what elements of truth they might have had. The articles were signed by names like James W. Bell, Allen Alien or F. James Smith, fake correspondents created by the editorial staff mentioned by Visentini. This much is clear even from the fact that the articles all have the same writing style. In particular, the articles on film stars read as if the author were part of the scene, and the impression the reader gets is that the author is a friend of the star and is sharing his/her privileged point of view. In May 1937, for example, James W. Bell shares the memory of a winter spent in Dallas in 1935, when he met Jean Harlow's grandfather, whom the film star recommended to visit: 'Se andate nel West, fategli una visita; è un uomo ruvido mio nonno, ma se gli parlate di me, ve ne farete un amico' [If you go to the West, go visit him; my grandfather is a gruff man, but if you talk to him about me, you will make him a friend].[23] These articles were not only designed to bring Hollywood stars closer to the audience, but also to reveal how, out of the spotlight, they were not as glamorous as they appeared on the screen. As we shall see, although generally praising Hollywood, *Omnibus* also focused on exposing the differences between Hollywood and reality. An article on Greta Garbo, for example, reveals the flaws of the popular actress, highlighting the differences between the actress and the woman: Allen Alien discloses how Garbo is in real life, describing how she spends most of her free time at home, reading books, and seems to be a lunatic lonely woman who would benefit from the presence of a man, although, reflects the writer, 'chi delle due amerebbe il suo uomo, l'attrice che lo schermo rende tanto bella e affascinante [. . .] o la donna che essa è veramente, dal fisico sgraziato?' [which one would her man love, the actress made so beautiful and appealing by the screen [. . .] or the woman she really is, with an ungraceful body?].[24] This attitude characterized the pieces on Hollywood's everyday life, which read like a gossip column and recall the style of a US fan magazine.

Film stars and details on their lives were not the only element of 'Giorno e notte'. As already anticipated, two other columns characterized the page dedicated to the film industry: 'Nuovi film' [New Films] and 'Celluloide' [Celluloid]. 'Nuovi film' was dedicated to new releases, and was written by Mario Pannunzio, *Omnibus*'s film critic and a member of the editorial team who became one of the most influential journalists in post-war Italy. The peculiarity of this column was the fact that Pannunzio did not limit himself to a mere critical review of the latest films; writing about a new release was in fact an excuse to make remarks on other matters. In his pieces, Pannunzio analyzes films as a form of artistic expression, paying attention at the same time to the context of their screening, or to the impact of a specific genre. On 26 June 1937, for example, reviewing *The Lady of Secrets* — directed by Marion Gering in 1936 and released in Italy with the Italian title *Il peccato di Lilian Day* in 1937 — Pannunzio harshly criticizes the director, and her alleged incompetence is a cause for reflection on the (negative) role of women in the arts.[25] The critiques of Pannunzio were also directed to Italian national productions, as demonstrated by his condemnation of the *telefoni bianchi* comedy films, a popular genre in Italy which he describes as a failed product.[26] The Italian audiences were also the object of Pannunzio's disapproval, and his review of the US film *They Won't Forget* — directed by Mervyn LeRoy and released in Italy with the Italian title *Vendetta* in 1938 — highlights the ignorance and superficiality of Italian audiences, who received the film as a *giallo* failing to understand the deeper meaning of a film that he sees as condemning the racist, cruel reality of the USA.[27]

Generally, Pannunzio's reviews were focused on Hollywood, even if his comments ranged beyond the films themselves. The number of US films reviewed in 'Nuovi film' is higher than all other national productions, and in most of Pannunzio's articles Hollywood emerges as a model to follow. The review of an Italian film, *Luciano Serra pilota* [*Luciano Serra, pilot*] — directed by Goffredo Alessandrini in 1938 — clearly confirms his view. *Luciano Serra pilota* was a major film supported by the regime and supervised by Mussolini's son Vittorio,[28] and, for Pannunzio, it finally showed the direction the Italian film industry should take:

> un film come *Luciano Serra pilota* può insegnare molte cose, essendo un'opera ch'è riuscita non solo a scordare le vecchie strade piene di polvere seguite dai più, ma a segnarne di nuove, che si confanno all'indole del nostro pubblico, annoiato di tante nostre commedie sentimentali e insensate, di tanti capricci in dialetto, di tante avventure modeste di tranquilli eroi. E gli applausi con cui è stato accolto il film stanno a testimoniare come non sia difficile dare un indirizzo diverso al nostro cinema.
>
> [A film such as *Luciano Serra pilot* can teach many things, as it is a work which not only forgot the old dusty paths followed by the majority, but also created new ones, which are suitable to the nature of our audience, bored by many of our romantic and meaningless comedies, of many whims in dialect, of modest adventures of bland heroes. And the applauses the film received testify how it is not hard to give our cinema a different direction.][29]

Pannunzio praised an Italian film that, as stated by Vittorio Mussolini himself, was not aimed at generating propaganda, but was rather an attempt to imitate Hollywood: 'airplanes correspond to the 7th cavalry, the Ethiopians to the Indians. Errol Flynn could be substituted for Amedeo Nazzari without changing anything.'[30] In other words, according to Pannunzio, the Italian film industry should have followed the model set by Hollywood, in contrast to the Fascist regime's attempts of contrasting the popularity of US films.

The third section of 'Giorno e notte', 'Celluloide', was written by Antonietta Drago and also made the US film industry the main subject of its attention. It put together foreign newspaper cuttings that showed readers what was behind a film's production, from funding to all the workers needed for one film.[31] The subject was cinema in general, not only US, but also European and Soviet, although the main focus remained on Hollywood. The main characteristic of 'Celluloide' is the attention it paid to practical aspects of the industrial organization of film production, such as the problems posed worldwide by censorship. On 10 July 1937, for example, the article explained the problem Hollywood companies had to face because of their own country's censorship and the nationalistic policies adopted by importing countries that protected their national film industries from the massive US production, highlighting specific features of international film industries, from Singapore to Scandinavia, and anticipating the Fascist regime's restriction on US imports to Italy approved shortly thereafter.[32] While the Fascist regime was working towards the control of film distribution and screening, which led to the approval of the so-called *legge Alfieri* and the institution of the state monopoly on the import of foreign film, *Omnibus* kept focusing on Hollywood, in contrast to the regime's promotion of Italian productions.[33]

The attention paid by Drago to specific and technical aspects of film production worldwide contributes to making 'Celluloide' a column comparable to material in specialist cinematographic magazines, such as *Cinema* (Milan: Hoepli, 1936–56). However, the tone of Drago's articles is consistent with the general sharp tone of *Omnibus*, differentiating it from any other film magazine, and in line with Pannunzio's criticisms. Some pieces are used to highlight what is seen as ridiculous or negative aspects of film production, such as the system of US censorship created by Will H. Hays, which led to a controversy between the Hays office and Warner Bros about a short film on 'l'arte di indossare le calze [the art of wearing stockings]', or the failures of Soviet film production to emulate Hollywood.[34] In other words, *Omnibus*'s ambivalent attitude to the USA also found expression in 'Celluloide': Hollywood is praised and considered a model for film production, therefore challenging Fascist censorship, but at the same time it is also ridiculed, echoing the Fascist anti-US rhetoric which, as noted above, depicted US society as barbarian.

Overall, 'Giorno e Notte' provides a clear example of *Omnibus*'s sustained fascination with the USA. The articles dedicated to film stars were inspired by US magazines, and some of them were even translations of original US articles, and contributed to the spreading of the Hollywood star system in Italy.[35] Moreover, 'Giorno e Notte' also demonstrates the complexity of *Omnibus*: the critical film reviews by Pannunzio and the comment pieces by Drago were consistent with the cultured tone of the magazine, but the strong presence of articles on film stars that read like a gossip column made 'Giorno e Notte' also a popular culture section. Together, they created a mixture of a low and high culture where the US model of the fan magazine coexisted with sophisticated or expert critique, making these two 'cultures' available to everyone. Moreover, in 'Giorno e notte' US culture can be found not only as the main subject of the articles, but also as a model for the column's layout, with film stars' photographs and big, catchy titles attracting the readers' attention, such as 'Marlene Dietrich in casa' [Marlene Dietrich at home] (17 April 1937), 'Il nonno di Jean Harlow' [Jean Harlow's grandfather] (8 May 1937), and 'Fame a Hollywood' [Craving in Hollywood] (11 June 1937).

Hollywood vs US Society: *Omnibus*'s View on the USA

Omnibus's fascination with Hollywood was certainly shared by its broad Italian readership. However, the attention paid to Hollywood and its products could be also interpreted as a means to highlight the differences between the real United States of America, violent and ignorant, and the fake, sparkling world of Hollywood. Through photos and cinematographic reviews, *Omnibus* confirmed the dream world embodied by the US film industry, but the fascination with Hollywood was counterbalanced with images and articles that aimed to reveal the other side of the USA, made of violence and even absurd habits (see Fig. 8.1).

In this context, photographs once again play a crucial role in the way *Omnibus* addressed the USA, delivering implicit messages. Beyond the photos of film stars, portrayed in flattering poses, the more common aim of the pictures and photocollages about the USA found in *Omnibus* was to ridicule US society. This

Fig. 8.1. William Saroyan, 'L'uomo col cuore negli altipiani' [The man with his heart in the mountains], trans. by Elio Vittorini, and 'Documenti americani', *Omnibus*, 15 January 1938. Next to Saroyan's novel a photograph of a young woman kissing the lover whom she is accused of murdering. [Courtesy of Centro APICE, Milan]

is the case with a photo of notorious American women, from the first American policewoman to theater actress Minnie Maddern Fiske, all depicted in denigrating and unflattering poses. These images aimed to show what real American women looked like, highlighting the difference with Hollywood actresses, whose beauty was fake (see Fig. 8.2).[36]

Although infrequently, photos of film stars were also used to highlight the artificial look of Hollywood actresses, as is the case of a photograph of Marlene Dietrich, in which she is portrayed while smoking, or two pictures of Mae West which, under the captions 'Mae West com'è' and 'Mae West come appare' respectively, reveal the difference between the woman and the glamorous actress, as was the case with the piece on Greta Garbo described above (see Fig. 8.3).[37]

Even president Roosevelt was a victim of *Omnibus*'s mockery: a series of pictures taken on various occasions portrayed the president in grotesque and denigrating poses that undermined his credibility (see Fig. 8.4).[38]

FIG. 8.2. Contrasting images: on the left, the Hollywood beauty, *Omnibus*, 17 April 1937; on the right, the real look of American women, 'Donne americane', *Omnibus*, 16 October 1937. [Courtesy of Centro APICE, Milan]

Photographs were not only used to ridicule US society, but also to highlight its violence. In the third issue of 1938, for example, a photo under the title 'documenti americani' [American documents] accompanies a translation of a William Saroyan short story, and portrays a woman kissing a dead man in a coffin; the caption says: 'Elena Wills Love, di anni 31 accusata di avere ucciso il suo amante, mentre bacia la vittima nella bara' [Elena Wills Love, 31 years old, accused of killing her lover, kissing the victim in his coffin].[39] Not only did the photo implicitly highlight the violence and hypocrisy of American women, but it accompanied a short story that had no connection with violence, the negative photograph counterbalancing the attention paid to American literature.[40]

In the use of photographs lay the deepest ambivalence in the way *Omnibus* depicted the USA. On the one hand, there was the sparkling world of Hollywood and its stars, a world made of life-changing opportunities that can turn a simple secretary into a wealthy wife; on the other hand, there was the real face of the USA, greedy and violent. This dual face of US society, and *Omnibus*'s ambivalent feelings towards the United States of America, can be traced even in positive reviews of films such as *Gold Diggers*, in which Pannunzio praised the US actors — 'Gli attori

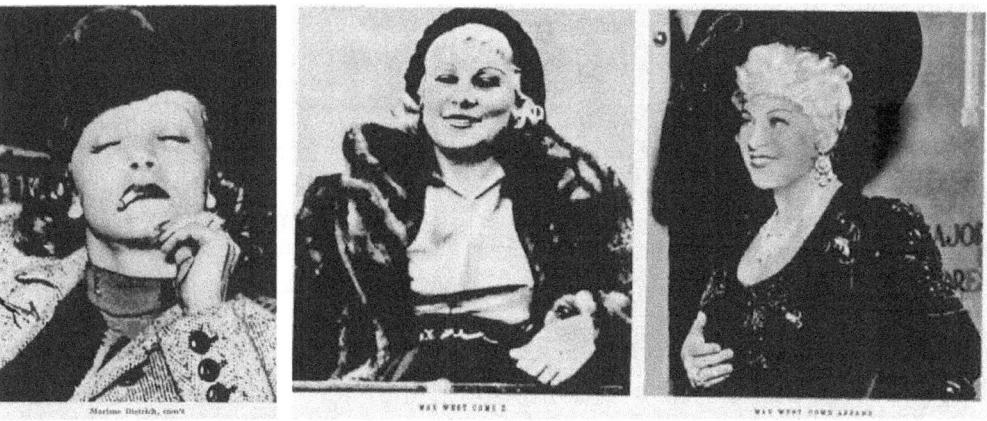

Fig. 8.3. Marlene Dietrich portrayed while smoking, 3 April 1937; 'Mae West com'è/Mae West come appare' [Mae West as she is/Mae West as she appears], 4 December 1937. [Courtesy of Centro APICE, Milan]

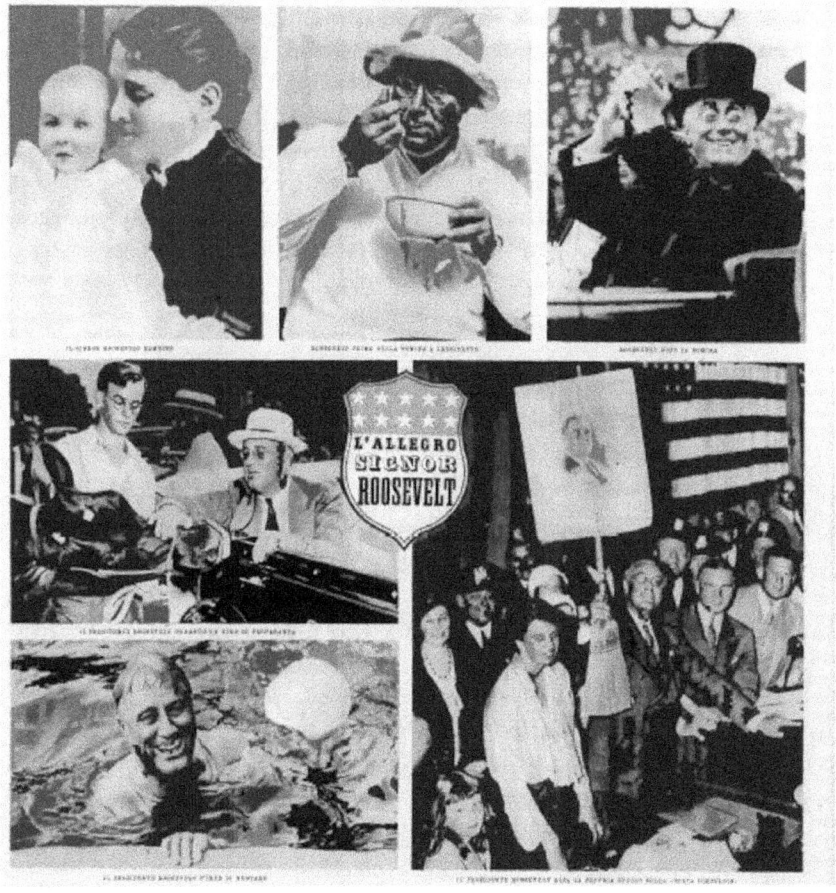

Fig. 8.4. 'L'allegro Signor Roosevelt' [The happy Mr Roosevelt], *Omnibus*, 8 January 1938. [Courtesy of Centro APICE, Milan]

[. . .] giocano su una recitazione esatta, precisa, realistica' [The actors [. . .] play on an exact, precise and realistic recitation] — but depicted American women — and US society in general — as immoral: 'traspare anzi qua e là quella frenetica, angosciosa, brutale sete di danaro, ch'è propria degli americani, e che a malapena è velata da un candore e un'ingenuità superficiali' [it shows through that frantic, anxious, brutal thirst for money, typical of the Americans, which is barely hidden behind superficial candour and innocence].[41] Negative aspects of US society can be traced even in the gossip column. An article signed by James W. Bell highlights how the majority of Hollywood stars claim to come from poor families and disadvantaged backgrounds — 'ogni attrice è una Becky Sharp e ogni attore un Oliviero [sic] Twist [. . .] i genitori, le madri, i padri e gli zii degli attori, sembrano uscire tutti dalla penna di Zola' [Every actress is a Becky Sharp and every actor an Oliver Twist [. . .] the parents, mothers, fathers and uncles of actors all seem to come from Zola's pen] — because the Americans liked 'gli eroi che salgono alla gloria dalla strada' [the heroes who rise to fame from the street], as it suggested that anyone could become famous.[42] Bell explains that 'ciò ha la sua ragione sociale, il suo segreto commerciale: ed è che agli americani [. . .] piacciono gli eroi *self-made* [. . .] [ed] è un'ambizione postuma di tutti i ricchi, quella di essere stati poveri' [it has its social reason, its commercial secret: which is that the Americans [. . .] like self-made heroes [. . .] [and] it is a posthumous ambition for all the rich, to have been poor]; accordingly, 'la Crawford era una dattilografa e viveva in una soffitta' [Crawford used to be a typist and lived in a loft], and Marlene Dietrich had to sell her precious violin, a gift from her father who had died in the Great War, in order to save her ill mother.[43] In other words, Hollywood was praised but US society condemned.

* * * * *

On 2 February 1939, Dino Alfieri, the minister of the Ministero della Cultura Popolare, sent a telegram to the prefect of Milan to stop the publication of *Omnibus*: 'Prego V. E. disporre che settimanale "Omnibus" edito Rizzoli-Milano sospenda sue pubblicazioni per revoca riconoscimento del gerente responsabile Leo Longanesi causa atteggiamento tenuto dal periodico in questi ultimi tempi' [I request His Excellency to order the interruption of the publication of the weekly 'Omnibus' published by Rizzoli (Milan) due to the suspension of the managing editor Leo Longanesi because of the recent attitude of the journal].[44] Allegedly, it was an article written by the drama critic Alberto Savinio on 28 January 1939 which caused the intervention of the Fascist censors and the closure of the magazine, as clearly emerges in a letter Longanesi sent to Alfieri on 2 February 1939: 'mi è stato comunicato l'ordine di sospensione di *Omnibus* per un articolo a firma Alberto Savinio riguardante Leopardi a Napoli' [I received the order to suspend *Omnibus* for an article signed by Alberto Savinio on Leopardi in Naples].[45] However, there are three different theories as to why *Omnibus* was closed down by the Fascist regime.

The first theory maintains that *Omnibus* was closed because Savinio offended one of Italy's greatest poets, Giacomo Leopardi; using unflattering words, Savinio stated that Leopardi died of indigestion caused by ice-cream: 'una leggera colite che i napoletani chiamano "'*a cacarella*"' [A mild colitis which the Neapolitans call "'*a cacarella*" (the trots)].⁴⁶ The second theory, the most corroborated, argues that Savinio offended the *prefetto* of Naples and his wife by calling them 'donkeys': Savinio criticized the closure of the famous *bar Gambrinus* not knowing it was decided by the prefect himself, who expressed his indignation to Mussolini ('Duce, questo gazzettiere mi dà del somaro [Duce, this hack reporter calls me a donkey]'), who in turn ordered the closure of *Omnibus*.⁴⁷ Finally, the last interpretation is given by Francesco Bolzoni, who in his study on *Omnibus* suggests that it was an allusion to 'uno sbrindellato reparto di soldati in partenza per la Macedonia [. . .] che, al modo di una dispettosa fotografia, fermava la voracità e la sconsolata miseria di fantaccini che ci si preparava a inviare di nuovo al fronte' [a tattered unit leaving for Macedonia [. . .] who, like a mischievous photograph, stopped the voracity and disconsolate misery of infantrymen we were about to send back to the front] that caused the intervention of the censors.⁴⁸ According to this version, then, the derision by Savinio of the Italian navy was the real reason behind the forced closure of *Omnibus*: 'La maggior divoratrice di gelati è la marina da guerra' [the main devourer of ice-cream is the navy].⁴⁹

After being notified of the government's measure against *Omnibus*, Longanesi appealed to Mussolini and asked to 'poter dimostrare al Capo del Governo che *Omnibus* non ha nessun indirizzo discordante dalle direttive del Regime' [be able to demonstrate to the Head of the Government that *Omnibus* has no different orientation from the regime's directives].⁵⁰ Even Angelo Rizzoli tried to intercede to save *Omnibus*: 'L'Editore Rizzoli, che deve rientrare a Milano, insiste per essere ricevuto oggi da Sua Eccellenza Alfieri, cui vorrebbe parlare del cambio della gerenza di "Omnibus", onde evitare a tutti un danno generale' [The publisher Rizzoli, who has to go back to Milan, insists on being received today by His Excellency Alfieri, to whom he would like to talk about the change of *Omnibus*'s management, to avoid damaging everyone].⁵¹ In spite of these attempts, Mussolini's decision was final and *Omnibus* was never published again.

In spite of its brief life, *Omnibus* represents a turning point in the history of the Italian popular press as it evolved into a modern mass medium, and its attention to US culture reveals how much Italian society was looking overseas for models and inspiration, even if with ambivalent feelings. The sheer amount of space dedicated to the USA was part of Longanesi's aim to make *Omnibus* a periodical that would target the largest possible readership by satisfying the fascination with the USA that many Italians had, at all levels of society.

Already writers from the period, such as Cesare Pavese, Elio Vittorini and the Americanist Fernanda Pivano, created in their work a self-conscious myth of America, which has been much studied as a literary phenomenon. Historians such as Emilio Gentile, Stephen Gundle, David Forgacs and Victoria de Grazia have developed a complex picture of the Americanization of Italian culture both during and after Fascism, both in the Italian popular imagination and for the new cultural elite. The analysis of *Omnibus* illustrates this complexity, through its production values, format, and cultural content. What is more, the ambivalence and contradictory nature of the articles on the USA, and the heavy presence of US cultural products, make *Omnibus* a mirror of the ambivalent feelings the Fascist regime displayed towards the USA. In other words, *Omnibus* reveals how, in spite of the Fascist campaign for cultural autarchy and the adoption of an anti-US rhetoric, in the interwar years Italy kept in intense dialogue with US culture, laying the foundation for post-war Italian culture, which would be profoundly influenced by US models.

Notes to Chapter 8

1. Emilio Gentile, *The Struggle for Modernity: Nationalism, Futurism, and Fascism* (Westport: Praeger, 2003), p. 40.
2. On Fascist Italy's anti-Americanism and ambivalence, see Anna Maria Martellone, '"Blood against Gold": Anti-American Propaganda in Fascist Italy', *Storia Nordamericana*, 3.2 (1986), 55–56; Michela Nacci, *L'antiamericanismo in Italia negli anni trenta* (Turin: Bollati Boringhieri, 1989); Emilio Gentile, 'Impending Modernity: Fascism and the Ambivalent Image of the United States', *Journal of Contemporary History*, 28 (1993), 7–29; Michel Beynet, *L'Image de l'Amérique dans la culture italienne de l'entre-deux-guerres* (Aix en Provence : Publications de l'Université de Provence, 1990); Ruth Ben-Ghiat, *Fascist Modernities: Italy, 1922–1945* (Berkeley: University of California Press, 2001), particularly pp. 40–53.
3. Since 1925, Italian illustrated magazines began to be printed using the rotogravure printing machine, which allowed the printing of more copies at a lower cost and the reproduction of higher-quality images, launching a product known as *rotocalco*. The *rotocalco* made possible a wider dissemination and expanded readership for magazines, making them available and appealing also to readers from different classes and of different levels of education. For the development of the periodical press in Italy in the nineteenth and twentieth centuries, see Mario Lombardo, Fabrizio Pignatel, *La stampa periodica in Italia. Mezzo secolo di riviste illustrate* (Rome: Editori Riuniti, 1985). On *rotocalchi*, see *Forme e modelli del rotocalco italiano tra fascismo e guerra*, ed. by Raffaele De Berti and Irene Piazzoni (Milan: Monduzzi, 2009).
4. There is no official documentation on circulation records. According to *Storia degli editori italiani*, ed. by Nicola Tranfaglia and Albertina Vittoria (Rome and Bari: Laterza, 2007), p. 322, *Omnibus* had a weekly circulation of 42,000 copies and reached 70,000 in 1939 when it was suppressed; however, Indro Montanelli and Marcello Staglieno, in *Leo Longanesi* (Milan: Rizzoli, 1984) p. 239, state that it reached 100,000 copies. In both cases, no sources are quoted in support of the statements.
5. Ben-Ghiat, *Fascist Modernities*, p. 40.
6. Beynet, *L'image de l'Amérique dans la culture italienne de l'entre-deux guerres*, pp. 119–67; Ivano Granata, *L'Omnibus di Leo Longanesi. Politica e cultura: aprile 1937–gennaio 1939* (Milan: Franco Angeli, 2016).
7. Montanelli and Staglieno, *Leo Longanesi*, pp. 231–53.
8. Key studies on the topic include: *Cultural Transmissions and Receptions: American Mass Culture in Europe*, ed. by Rob Kroes, R. W. Rydell, and Doeko F. J. Bosscher (Amsterdam: VU University Press, 1993); Rob Kroes, *If You've Seen One, You've Seen the Mall: Europeans and American Mass Culture* (Urbana: University of Illinois Press, 1996); and David Forgacs, Stephen Gundle, *Mass Culture and Italian Society from Fascism to the Cold War* (Bloomington: Indiana University Press, 2007).
9. Cesare Zavattini, *Io: un'autobiografia* (Turin: Einaudi, 2002), p. 68; see also Franco Bechis and Sergio Rizzo, *In nome della rosa* (Rome: Newton Compton, 1991), pp. 31–33.
10. *Le Grandi Firme*, 22 April 1937, nr. 308, quoted in *Bibliografia dei periodici femminili lombardi, 1786–1945*, ed. by Rita Carrarini and Michele Giordano (Milan: Lampi di stampa, 2003), p. 182.
11. Alberto Mazzuca, *La erre verde. Ascesa e declino dell'impero Rizzoli* (Milan: Longanesi, 1991), p. 76.

12. Among the American comic strips published in *Omnibus* it is worth highlighting its introduction to Italian readers of Otto Soglow's *Little King*, a comic strip that made its first appearance in 1931 in the *New Yorker*.
13. Quoted in Annamaria Andreoli, *Leo Longanesi. La fabbrica del dissenso* (Rome: De Luca, 2006), p. 12.
14. Arrigo Benedetti, 'Diario italiano. Omnibus', *L'Espresso*, 6 October 1957, quoted in Ivano Granata, 'L'"Omnibus" di Leo Longanesi', *Forme e modelli del rotocalco italiano tra fascismo e guerra*, ed. by Raffele De Berti and Irene Piazzoni (Milan: Monduzzi, 2009), pp. 131–32.
15. On the transformation of periodical press in Europe between 1880 and 1920, see Evanghélia Stead and Hélène Védrine, *L'Europe des revues (1880–1920): estampes, photographies, illustrations* (Paris: Press de l'Université Paris-Sorbonne, 2008). On the German periodical press and photojournalism see Karl Christian Fuhrer and Corey Ross, *Mass Media, Culture and Society in Twentieth Century Germany* (Basingstoke: Palgrave, 2009); and Daniel H. Magilow, *The Photography of Crisis: The Photo Essays of Weimar Germany* (University Park, PA: Penn State University Press, 2012). On the French popular press see Rosemary Chapman and Nicholas Hewitt, *Popular Culture and Mass Communication in Twentieth-Century France* (New York: Mellen, 1992), and Michel Frizot, Cédric de Veigy, *Vu: The Story of a Magazine That Made an Era* (London: Thames & Hudson, 2009).
16. Illustrated magazines began to circulate in Europe from the first half of the 1840s. Key early examples included the English *Illustrated London News* (London: William Little, 1842–2003), the French *L'Illustration: Journal Universel* (Paris: [n.pub.], 1844–1944), the German *Illustrierte Zeitung* (Leipzig: Weber, 1843–1944), and the Italian *Illustrazione italiana* (Milan: Treves, 1875–1962). The interwar years were characterized by the emergence in Europe of illustrated magazines that used photographs not only as a form of entertainment but also as a means of information. They first developed in Germany, with illustrated magazines such as the *Berliner Illustrierte Zeitung* (Berlin: Ullstein, 1892–1945), *Uhu* (Berlin: Ullstein, 1924–34) and *Das Magazin* (Leipzig: Giesecke & Devrient GmbH, then Berlin: Dr. Eysler & Co. Verlag GmbH, 1924–41); followed by the French *L'Illustration*, *Vu* and *Marianne*. In Italy, the first magazine based on the use of photographs was *Novella* (Milan: Rizzoli, 1927–44), but it was only with the publication of *Omnibus* that the *rotocalco* formula was applied to a weekly aimed not only at entertaining but also at informing the readership, commenting on current events and foreign affairs.
17. *Leo Longanesi: 1905–1957. Editore, scrittore, artista*, ed. by Giuseppe Appella, Paolo Longanesi, and Marco Vallora (Milan: Longanesi, 1996), p. 267. This definition of the role of photography in journalism is consistent with photojournalism as a practice to deliver the news launched in Germany in the 1920s by illustrated magazines such as the *Berliner Illustrierte Zeitung* (Berlin: Ullstein, 1892–1945), *Uhu* (Berlin: Ullstein, 1924–34) and *Das Magazin* (Leipzig: Giesecke & Devrient GmbH, then Berlin: Dr. Eysler & Co. Verlag GmbH, 1924–41), which further confirms the influence of European models in the shaping of *Omnibus*.
18. Italian illustrated magazines of the 1930s had many references to cinema, from the focus on film stars to the use of photomontage. Recent works on the topic include: Raffaele De Berti, *Dallo schermo alla carta. Romanzi, fotoromanzi, rotocalchi cinematografici: il film e i suoi paratesti* (Milan: Vita e Pensiero, 2000); Anna Cellinese, 'Le riviste fotografiche: "Life", "Look" e l'importazione di uno stile americano', in *Italiamerica. L'editoria*, ed. by Emanuela Scarpellini and Jeffrey T. Schnapp (Milan: Il Saggiatore, 2008), pp. 125–55; and Gian Piero Brunetta, *Il cinema italiano di regime: da 'La canzone dell'amore' a 'Ossessione'* (Rome and Bari: Laterza, 2014).
19. According to Nello Ajello all the key features of Italian post-war magazines can be found already in *Omnibus*. Nello Ajello, 'Il settimanale di attualità', in *La stampa del neocapitalismo*, ed. by Paolo Murialdi, Valerio Castronovo and Nicola Tranfaglia (Rome and Bari: Laterza, 1976), pp. 173–249 (p. 185).
20. *Chi stramalediva gli inglesi*, ed. by Arturo Cattaneo (Milan: Vita e Pensiero, 2007), pp. 39ff.; on the relationship of Italian intellectuals and the USA in the Fascist era see also Francesca Billiani, *Culture nazionali e narrazioni straniere. Italia, 1903–1943* (Florence: Le Lettere, 2007); Claudio Antonelli, *Pavese, Vittorini e gli americanisti* (Florence: Edarc edizioni, 2008); Christopher Rundle, *Publishing Translations in Fascist Italy* (Oxford: Peter Lang, 2010); and Jane Dunnett, *The 'Mito Americano' and Italian Literary Culture under Fascism* (Rome: Aracne, 2015).

21. On Fascist Italy's anti-Americanism see Anna Maria Martellone, ' "Blood against Gold": Anti-American Propaganda in Fascist Italy', *Storia nordamericana*, 3.2 (1986), 55–56; Michela Nacci, *L'antiamericanismo in Italia negli anni trenta* (Turin: Bollati Boringhieri, 1989); and Emilio Gentile 'Impending Modernity: Fascism and the Ambivalent Image of the United States', *Journal of Contemporary History*, 28 (1993), 7–29.
22. Gino Visentini, in *Parliamo di Longanesi*, ed. by Corrado Pizzinelli (Rome: Grafica San Giovanni, 1988, p. 79.
23. James W. Bell, 'Il nonno di Jean Harlow', *Omnibus*, 8 May 1937.
24. Allen Alien, 'Greta Garbo in casa', *Omnibus*, 10 April 1937.
25. Mario Pannunzio, 'Il peccato di Lilian Day', *Omnibus*, 26 June 1937.
26. Mario Pannunzio, 'I volontari della noia', *Omnibus*, 21 January 1939.
27. Mario Pannunzio, 'Vendetta', *Omnibus*, 14 May 1938.
28. Vittorio Mussolini co-authored the story with Fulvio Palmieri, and was co-director of Aquila Film, the company which produced *Luciano Serra pilota*. On Vittorio Mussolini's role in Italian cinema see Dario Zanelli, 'Quando Vittorio Mussolini dirigeva "Cinema"', in *Il neorealismo nel fascismo. Giuseppe De Santis e la critica cinematografica 1941–1943*, ed. by Marcella Furno and Renzo Renzi (Bologna: Compositori, 1984); Giovanni Sedita, 'Vittorio Mussolini, Hollywood and Neorealism', *Journal of Modern Italian studies*, 15.3 (2010), 431–57; and Ruth Ben-Ghiat, 'Narrating War in Fascist Empire Cinema', in *Narrating War: Early Modern and Contemporary Perspectives*, ed. by Marco Mondini and Massimo Rospocher (Bologna: Il Mulino, 2013), pp. 249–47.
29. Mario Pannunzio, 'Luciano Serra pilota', *Omnibus*, 1 January 1939.
30. Vittorio Mussolini quoted in Tag Gallagher, *The Adventures of Roberto Rossellini* (New York: Da Capo, 1998), p. 49. See also Pannunzio, 'Luciano Serra pilota', *Omnibus*, 5 November 1938.
31. Detailed research on Antonietta Drago has not been carried out; there is even confusion over her real name. Some authors, such as Granata, consider Nenè Centonze her real name and Antonietta Drago her pseudonym. Other authors, instead, claim the opposite. Her novels are signed with the name Antonietta Drago, as well as her articles written for *Omnibus*. See Patrizia Guida, *Scrittrici di Puglia* (Lecce: Congedo, 2008), pp. 128–33.
32. Antonietta Drago, 'Proibito', *Omnibus*, 10 July 1937.
33. See Regio decreto-legge, 16 June 1938, no. 1061, and Regio decreto-legge, 4 September 1938, no. 1389.
34. Antonietta Drago, 'Parole tabù' and 'L'arte di infilarsi le calze', *Omnibus*, 1 May 1938; 'Guai Sovietici', *Omnibus*, 25 September 1937.
35. In *Omnibus* in general a significant number of articles were translated from American magazines. In 'Giorno e notte' examples include: Eustis Morton, 'Intermezzo con Fred Astaire', Omnibus, 29 May 1937, probably a translation and a reduction of original articles and interviews with Fred Astaire originally published in Morton Eustis, *Players at Work* (New York: Theatre Arts, Inc., 1937), see especially pp. 100 ff.; and Jim Tully, 'Charlot segreto', Omnibus, 4 September 1937, a translation of Jim Tully, 'The Unknown Chaplin', *The New Movie Magazine*, July–December 1930.
36. 'Donne americane', *Omnibus*, 16 October 1937.
37. See 'Giorno e Notte', *Omnibus*, 3 April 1937 and 4 December 1937.
38. 'L'allegro Signor Roosevelt', *Omnibus*, 21 August 1937.
39. 'Documenti americani', *Omnibus*, 15 January 1938.
40. William Saroyan, 'L'uomo col cuore negli altopiani', trans. by Elio Vittorini, *Omnibus*, 15 January 1938.
41. Pannunzio, 'Cercatrici d'oro', *Omnibus*, 22 May 1937.
42. James W. Bell, 'La rettorica di Hollywood', *Omnibus*, 30 October 1937.
43. Ibid.
44. *Telegramma N. 16 indirizzato a Prefetto Milano, 2 February 1939*, Archivo Centrale di Stato, Roma, Ministero Cultura Popolare, b. 119, fasc. 735 'Leo Longanesi'.
45. Letter written by Leo Longanesi addressed to Alfieri, ACS, MCP, b. 119, fasc. 735 'Leo Longanesi'.
46. Alberto Savinio, 'Il sorbetto di Leopardi', *Omnibus*, 28 January 1939, p. 3.

47. Massimo Alberini, '"Omnibus" la vita e la morte del famoso settimanale di Longanesi', *La Gazzetta di Parma*, 15 September 1982, reproduced in Granata, 'L'"Omnibus" di Leo Longanesi', pp. 205–06.
48. Francesco Bolzoni, *Sull'Omnibus di Longanesi* (Rome: C.S.C., 1996), pp. 109–10.
49. Savinio, 'Il sorbetto di Leopardi', p. 3.
50. Letter written by Leo Longanesi addressed to Mussolini, ACS, MCP, b. 119, fasc. 735 'Leo Longanesi'.
51. *Appunto* for Alfieri, author unknown, ACS, MCP, b. 119, fasc. 735 'Leo Longanesi'.

PART III

From the Second World War to the Twenty-First Century

CHAPTER 9

The Forbidden City: Tombolo between American Occupation and Italian Imagination

Charles L. Leavitt IV

Silvio Micheli was awarded the 1946 Premio Viareggio for *Pane duro* [Hard Bread], a novel whose moving account of the iniquities of Italian society under Fascism attracted stellar reviews, elevating Micheli, for a brief time, to the ranks of the great Italian writers of his generation. In a subsequent novel, *Paradiso maligno* [Evil Paradise, 1948], Micheli sought once again to diagnose the ills of Italy, focusing this time not on the inter-war years, as he had done in *Pane duro*, but instead on a post-war society struggling under US occupation. *Paradiso maligno* depicts the challenges that followed from Italy's liberation — the destruction of Italian cities, the desolation of Italian families, the deprivation of Italian society — not only with devastating realism but also with remarkable concision. Indeed, Micheli sums up the challenges of post-Fascist Italy in a single word, which recurs throughout the novel, punctuating its narrative and reinforcing its critique. That word is 'Tombolo'.

When Nunzia, the novel's protagonist, stumbles upon her best friend flirting with the US soldiers who occupy her town, she recalls that '[m]i dette una rabbia vederla così [. . .]. Tombolo? mi veniva da dire' [it made me so angry seeing her like that [. . .]. Tombolo? I wanted to say].[1] The others in the town express a similar disappointment, a shared disgust at such behaviour: 'Tombolo? dicono alle ragazze che la sera stanno all'incrocio della Via Aurelia' [Tombolo? they say to the girls who stand at the intersection of the Via Aurelia at night].[2] When Nunzia is forced to join her friend in working at a local hotel that caters to US clientele, she is similarly assailed: 'il personale ce l'ha con me. Mi guardano infatti. E non so a chi dicevano, ma è già la terza volta che sento mentovare Tombolo quando passo nei corridoi' [all of the employees are angry with me. In fact, they watch me. And I don't know who they were saying it to, but it's already the third time that I've heard Tombolo when I pass by in the hallway].[3] When Nunzia becomes the lover of one of the hotel's clients, a US Captain, who takes her on an extended holiday across the Italian peninsula, she is thus relieved to be free of her fellow townspeople and their incessant mockery: 'A Firenze non mi vergogno più per le strade con lui abbraccetto.

Nessuno mi conosce né dicono: Tombolo?' [In Florence I'm not ashamed to walk the streets with him, arm-in-arm. No one knows me and no one says: Tombolo?].[4] She is surprised, therefore, when even in Florence, even in Rome, even in Naples the accusatory word seems to be on everyone's lips: 'da un negozio escono davanti a noi due signorine con un moro, e un ragazzo fa dalla strada: Tombolo?' [two women and a black man leave a shop in front of us, and a boy from the road says: Tombolo?].[5] Startled as she is to hear this rebuke so far from home, Nunzia is entirely resigned to hearing it once her holiday ends and she has to return to her town: 'ho idea che qualcuno si metta a gridare: Tombolo? Anche se non lo dicono, l'hanno nel cuore, lo so' [I have this idea that someone will shout: Tombolo? Even if they don't say it, they have it in their hearts, I know].[6] Indeed, this result is so thoroughly predictable, this fate so clearly assured, that Nunzia has internalized the critique, pre-empting it by berating herself before anyone else even has the chance: 'mi prende da piangere, col cuore che batte negli orecchi come a dire: Tom-bo-lo' [I want to cry, with my heart ringing in my ears as if it were saying: Tom-bo-lo].[7] The refrain of Nunzia's conscience, this single word encapsulates the humiliation and corruption that Silvio Micheli's novel identifies in the miasma of post-war Italy, and that it dramatizes in the demise of its female protagonist.

In order to achieve this effect, *Paradiso maligno*'s characteristic metonymy requires historical and cultural knowledge that is no longer as commonplace as it was when the novel was first published. Addressing an audience who could be expected to know what he meant, Micheli needed neither to gloss his terms nor to decode his message. Tombolo was so central to Italian culture and politics that even allusive references to the term could conjure the doubt, anxiety, and indignation of a society working to recover after the war. As one reporter put it at the time, 'Tombolo [. . .] è l'esempio più espressivo e sintomatico di quello che ci ha lasciato il dopoguerra' [Tombolo [. . .] is the most expressive and symptomatic example of what the post-war period has left us].[8] Others declared that Tombolo offered a 'fiera campionaria dei nostri malanni postbellici' [trade fair of our post-war misfortunes], that the very word 'significò una delle brutture italiane nel dopo guerra recente' [signified one of the ugly features of the recent post-war period].[9] While the post-war period continues to attract substantial scholarly interest, however, Tombolo has been largely forgotten. This chapter, which presents the preliminary findings of a research project still in its early stages, is an attempt to begin to reconsider Tombolo's significance in Italian cultural history.[10]

A pine forest located between Pisa and Livorno, Tombolo was the site of a US military encampment and a key staging site for the Allied invasion of Italy, due to its close proximity to Livorno's port. After the war, it became the site of a flourishing black market, attracting large numbers of Italian prostitutes, the so-called *segnorine*, who were drawn to the camp by the free flow of US dollars.[11] Because many of the soldiers served by these *segnorine* were African American, Italian fascination with and opposition to the prostitution and black marketeering in Tombolo were framed in overtly racial and often racist terms. The resulting mix of prurience and prejudice made Tombolo a kind of Italian obsession after the war.

This obsession was continually fed by the Italian media, who sold the public on lurid tales of white slavery, murder, kidnapping, money laundering, and thefts totalling billions of *lire*.[12] Virtually every Italian newspaper sent reporters to provide exposés of the squalid and sensational goings-on in the pine forest. Indro Montanelli filed a series of reports from Tombolo for the *Corriere della Sera*.[13] So did Milziade Torelli.[14] Gustavo D'Arpe stopped off there as part of his tour of Italy, commissioned by *La Gazzetta del Mezzogiorno*.[15] *L'Unità* similarly commissioned several investigative series on Tombolo, with multiple articles by both Davide Lajolo and Riccardo Longone, who looked to Tombolo in order to explain to his readers, as the title of his series intoned, 'Quanto ci costa l'occupazione alleata' [What the Allied occupation costs us].[16] 'Tutta una letteratura giornalistica è sorta in merito alla "città proibita" del Tombolo' [An entire corpus of journalistic literature has arisen as a result of the "Forbidden City" of Tombolo], explained a contemporary account.[17] Thanks to the pervasiveness of this journalistic literature, brimming with scandalous detail, Tombolo began to figure as a symbol for all of the depredations of the post-war period, achieving the emblematic status that Silvio Micheli drew on in his 1948 novel.

Micheli was far from alone in assigning to Tombolo this symbolic role. Cesare Pavese's *Tra donne sole* [Among Women Only, 1949], for instance, relates a conversation on the subject between two characters at a party: one of them '[p]arlava dei negri del Tombolo' [was talking about the Negroes in Tombolo]. 'Erano sempre ubriachi di liquori e di droghe. Di notte facevano orge e si tiravano coltellate. Quando una ragazza era morta, la sotterravano nella pineta e ci appendevano alla croce le mutandine e il reggiseno. Giravano nudi' [They were always drunk or on drugs. At night they had orgies and pulled knives. When a girl died they would bury her among the pines and hang her pants and brassiere on the cross. They went around naked], he says. 'Erano primitivi autentici' [They were authentic primitives]. 'Dopo nessuna guerra sono mai successe cose simili' [Nothing like that has ever happened after any other war]. The other responds glibly: 'Peccato che sia finita [. . .]. Sarebbe stata una bella villeggiatura' [Shame it's all over [. . .]. It would have made for a fine holiday resort].[18] Tombolo, and the salacious tenor of the conversation it inspired, does much of the work of characterisation here. It plays a similar role in Carlo Cassola's *Un matrimonio del dopoguerra* [A Post-War Wedding, 1957], where a fascination with Tombolo marks a character as both amoral and apolitical, more devoted to crime than to any political conviction.[19] In Leonida Répaci's play *La madre incatenata* [The Enchained Mother], Tombolo stands in for Italy's post-war transformation. First performed in 1925, the play was revived in 1948, with the addition of a fourth act in which, playing the role of author, Répaci discusses the play's shifting meaning over time, noting that '[n]oi non siamo più quelli di ieri, ecco la verità. Ci pesa addosso tutto quel che è accaduto nell'arco di due guerre' [we are no longer the same as we used to be, that's the truth. Everything that happened across the two wars weighs upon us], he says, listing among the heaviest of those weights, along with the atomic bomb and the Nazi death camps, 'l'epopea delle "segnorine" culminata nella repubblica di Tombolo' [the ordeal of the "segnorine" that culminated in the Republic of Tombolo].[20] In Alba De Céspedes's epistolary novel *Il rimorso* [Regret, 1963], Tombolo similarly serves to mark out distance in time, but now it is the distance from the post-war moment, which has been replaced by the conservative cultural and political climate of the early 1960s. 'Sono passati vent'anni dalla Resistenza. I mulatti nati dai soldati negri e dalle prostitute di Napoli e di Tombolo, tra un anno o due saranno chiamati loro sotto le armi' [Twenty years have passed since the Resistance. In a year or two the mulattoes born from the Negro soldiers and the prostitutes of Naples and Tombolo will themselves be called to arms].[21] In each instance, the same word is invoked suggestively to conjure a cultural moment.

Tombolo could serve this function because it had become a virtual commonplace of Italian literature after 1945. 'Tombolo ghermisce e più non rende, | Tombolo stronca, sbriciola, avvelena, | cupo crogiolo di tragedie orrende, | d'insana gioia, d'assillante pena' [Tombolo grasps and doesn't let go, | Tombolo obliterates, crumbles, poisons, | dark crucible of horrendous tragedies, | of senseless joy, of unbearable suffering]', wrote Carlotta Mandel in 'La città proibita' [The Forbidden City], a 1947 poem.[22] 'Tombolo, oggi è sinonimo di perdizione, di depravazione, di sovvertimento morale' [Tombolo is today synonymous with perdition, depravation, moral subversion], Mandel explained.[23] In the pages dedicated to 1947 in *Quasi una vita* [Almost a Life, 1950], Corrado Alvaro's diary of the post-war years, Tombolo is similarly symptomatic of the iniquities, the 'abietta miseria' [abject misery], that followed Italy's liberation from Fascism.[24] For the protagonist of Giorgio Caproni's 1948 short story 'Il bagno di Luce' [The Bath of Light], Tombolo is a sign of the desolation of life in post-war Rome, appearing on the tarnished visage of his housekeeper, prematurely aged by her time as a *segnorina* in Tombolo and by the memory of the black baby she aborted there.[25] In the poems that make up Luciano Luisi's *Piazza Grande* (1949), a collection carrying a dedication to Caproni, Tombolo is little more than a tissue of clichés — 'le mani dei negri' [the hands of the Negroes], 'una bianca prostituta' [a white prostitute], a 'Segnorina livornese' [*Segnorina* from Livorno], and a 'Lamento del soldato negro' [Lament for the Negro Soldier] — formulaic references to cultural commonplaces.[26] No less clichéd are the portraits offered in Enrico Pea's *Zitina* (1949), where Tombolo, that 'boscaglia nera e maledetta' [black and cursed wood], is identified as the source for the paltry luxuries that manage to enter the Pisan marketplace, and in Silvano Ceccherini's semi-autobiographical *Dopo l'ira* [After the Anger, 1965], wherein a US soldier named Joe Sharpe — 'il negro [. . .] enorme, mostruoso' [the enormous, monstrous [. . .] Negro] — steals the narrator's girlfriend the first night they all find themselves under the same roof.[27] Fear of African-American virility similarly structures Alberto Moravia's short story 'Il negro e il vecchio dalla roncola' [The Negro and the Old Man with the Scythe, 1948], which recounts the sexual humiliation of a nineteen-year-old Italian at the hands of an African-American soldier. Moravia never once names Tombolo, but he suggestively sets his story in a 'pineta', a pine forest: 'Dapperttutto, addossate ai tronchi dei pini o ai cespugli, macchine militari, verdi con la stella bianca dell'esercito americano' [Everywhere, leaning against the trunks of the pine trees or the bushes, were military vehicles, green with the white star of the US Army], the narrator relates in preparing the scene.[28] From this description alone, Moravia's contemporaries could have been expected to grasp the source of the social, political, and sexual anxieties that drive his narrative.

After all, the cultural discourse of the time was suffused with references to Tombolo. On the stage, the most anticipated play of the 1946 season at Milan's Teatro delle Arti was Enzo Mancini's *Città proibita* [The Forbidden City], a show, set in the infamous Tuscan *pineta*, which dramatized an illicit affair between an African-American soldier and an Italian woman.[29] At the cinema, two prominent neorealist films were similarly set in the much-discussed US encampment: Giorgio Ferroni's *Tombolo, paradiso nero* [Tombolo, the Black Paradise, 1947], and Alberto Lattuada's *Senza pietà* [Without Pity, 1948]; a third, Luigi Zampa's *Campane a martello* [Alarm Bells, 1949], begins there. This setting was so familiar, in fact, that Tombolo became a kind of neorealist convention, such that the dance sequence in Giuseppe De Santis's *Riso amaro* [Bitter Rice, 1949] — a film set not in Tuscany but in Piedmont — was dismissed as a 'scena da Tombolo' [scene from Tombolo], a cynical and sensational attempt to recall 'la famigerata pineta livornese. Tanto che c'eravamo, perché non farci entrare anche un robusto negro?' [the infamous Livornese pine forest. As long as we were going there, why not include a strapping Negro?], sarcastically asked a critic in *L'Unità*.[30] Little wonder, then, that Micheli believed he could refer repeatedly to Tombolo without ever explaining the term, or that Moravia felt he could count on his audience to recognize his story's setting without ever pronouncing the name: even when narratives took up seemingly unrelated events, even when they took place in quite distant locales, Tombolo seemed to occupy everyone's attention.

If that situation no longer obtains, it is due in no small part to the concerted effort made by Italian political and cultural authorities to remove Tombolo from public consciousness through deliberate acts of obfuscation, suppression, and censorship. Ferroni's *Tombolo, paradiso nero*, for instance, was pulled from theatres after its first showing and only returned in a heavily edited form.[31] After just one performance, Mancini's *Città proibita* was shut down completely at the behest of Italy's theatrical censorship board, and was never again staged.[32] The Italian press, too, was similarly censored. The editor of *Crimen*, a tabloid devoted to stories of true crime, was charged with public indecency and faced eight months in prison for the exposé of Tombolo's *segnorine* his paper published in 1946.[33] Such censorship did not go unopposed: Luigi Russo was among those to speak out against the hypocrisy inherent in banning such cultural expressions while ignoring what he called 'il fenomeno della città verde del Tombolo o di Migliarino, a cui approdano le ragazze anche di buona famiglia' [the phenomenon of the green city of Tombolo or of Migliarino, which attract even girls from good families].[34] Russo, like many of his contemporaries, recognized that Italian authorities were more interested in hiding the problem from view than they were in remedying it. That may have been true, but they do seem to have succeeded eventually in hiding it. Perhaps as a result, Tombolo cannot be said to figure in histories of post-war Italy to the same extent to which it figured in accounts written at the time.

To understand the motivation both for this censorship and for the cultural discourse it sought to silence, I propose approaching Tombolo as an instance of what Mary Louise Pratt has termed the 'contact zone': 'the space in which peoples geographically and historically separated come into contact with each other and establish ongoing relations, usually involving conditions of coercion, radical inequality, and intractable conflict'.[35] Borrowing Pratt's term and approaching Tombolo as a 'contact zone', I mean to indicate that this space figured so prominently in the Italian imagination at the time because it represented both literally and symbolically the fraught confrontation with the US. But I mean to say something more than this as well. When we consider the 'radical inequality' of the social relations in Tombolo, it is important to recognise that this inequality existed not only between the American occupiers and their Italian hosts, but also within each camp. Put differently, in Tombolo, what Pratt calls the 'conditions of coercion' and 'intractable conflict' characteristic of the 'contact zone' not only pitted American against Italian but also white against black, northern against southern, man against woman, right against left. If the conflicts in Tombolo were inflamed by the occupation, therefore, they were fuelled by conditions that pre-existed the arrival of the US armed forces on Italian soil. In particular, Tombolo became the 'contact zone' for the competing racial regimes of Jim Crow and Fascism, and for the resistance against those regimes: the nascent US Civil Rights movement and Italian anti-Fascism.[36]

The multi-dimensional conflicts exacerbated by Tombolo deserve to be explored in detail. For reasons of space, however, in this chapter I can only sketch out some of the contours of this complex and over-determined historical phenomenon. In the first instance, the experience in Tombolo was shaped, in part, by the African-American struggle for equality, and by the racist backlash that rose up in opposition. Fighting in a racially segregated military and on behalf of a racially segregated country, black soldiers sought to link the battle against European fascism to the battle against American racism, launching what came to be called the 'Double V' campaign: 'Victory over our enemies at home and victory over our enemies on the battlefields abroad', in the words of the editor of the *Pittsburgh Courier*.[37] Explicitly paralleling the racist violence in the USA to its counterpart in Nazi Germany and Fascist Italy, they decried the hypocrisy of those who called the Second World War 'a crusade for freedom', as Richard Wright put it, while demonstrating through their treatment of racial minorities that they would still 'categorically reject the very concept of freedom and democracy'.[38] That the African-American troops who liberated and subsequently occupied Italy reported better treatment from the Italians than from their white US compatriots was an unmistakable sign of such hypocrisy.[39] This point was articulated with particular clarity by the black soldier who sent to Mississippi Senator Theodore Bilbo, a virulent segregationist, a picture of himself kissing an Italian woman, including with it a note that read 'I am sending you this picture because I know that it will be making you happy [. . .] since you are strictly for democracy.'[40] The free exercise of such sexual democracy appears to have inflamed still further white American racial hatred, which found its outlet in the frequent round-ups, in reality violent incursions into Tombolo, whose ostensible purpose was to capture black deserters, traffickers, and bandits, along with the prostitutes they frequented. Each roundup led not only to hundreds of arrests but also to increasingly ferocious clashes between the military police and the inhabitants of Tombolo.[41] The nature of these round-ups, as revealed by their coverage in the Italian press, makes evident that they were a form of racial violence, a targeted assault on African-American soldiers. Thus, for instance, recounting what it called a 'Sanguinoso conflitto' [Bloody conflict], 'una vera battaglia' [a real battle], which took place in August 1946, one Italian newspaper reported that

> sono intervenuti i carabinieri contro i quali i negri si sono ribellati cominciando a sparare. È allora entrata in azione in forze la 'celere', che ha fatto uso dei mitra, mentre i negri, sistematisi a difesa fra le macerie del Duomo, continuavano a sparare accanitamente. La battaglia si è prolungata nell'oscurità per un paio di ore ed anche vari civili hanno riportato ferite di arma da fuoco. Cinque di essi sono stati ricoverati mentre quattro negri sono rimasti uccisi.
>
> [the Carabinieri got involved, and the Negroes rebelled against them, starting to shoot. At that point the Military Police got involved, using machine guns, while the Negroes, taking shelter in the ruins of the Cathedral, continued to fire furiously. The battle continued in the darkness for a few hours and a few civilians reported gunshot wounds. Five of them were hospitalised and four Negroes were killed.][42]

Events such as this, a kind of intermittent civil warfare, can only be explained in the context of the racial segregation — and race hatred — that predominated in this period. Indeed, John A. Williams, whose 1972 novel *Captain Blackman* contains a lengthy chapter on Tombolo, claimed that these raids were merely a pretext for an extended clandestine assault on African-American soldiers, in which hundreds of men were murdered by the US Army. Evidence for a massacre on this scale is scarce, even if reports of casualties in the round-ups were not infrequent.[43] Yet '[t]he black grapevine says it happened', Williams told an interviewer at the time, and suppression and censorship might help to explain the lack of verification.[44] Even if they did not reach the level of casualties alleged by Williams, the deadly confrontations in the 'contact zone' of Tombolo served to demonstrate the US racial regime's encroachment onto Italian soil.

They also demonstrate the lasting effects of the racial regimes of Fascist Italy and Nazi Germany. The area around Tombolo housed several US camps for prisoners of war, and for the German and Italian detainees held there, the presence of African-American troops, some of them entrusted to stand guard, seemed an intolerable offence. That these black soldiers were often found sleeping with Italian women was an even greater affront. One of the prisoners, describing his transfer to Coltano, the largest of the camps, with over 33,000 detainees, recalled seeing Tombolo as he neared the gates: 'Nessuno di noi immagina che il folto della pineta è impenetrabile anche per gli MP e che negli anfratti, in mostruosi abbracci, negri disertori e "segnorine" danno l'ultimo colpo alla "difesa della razza"' [None of us imagined that the dense pine forest was impenetrable even to the MPs, and that in its nooks and crannies, Negro deserters and *segnorine*, with their monstrous embraces, gave the final blow to the 'defense of the race'].[45] In his memoir of a

Fascist youth, *Un ragazzo di Salò*, Benito Bollati, future Deputy of the far-right Movimento Sociale Italiano, recalled encountering Tombolo as a result of his own post-war imprisonment by the Allies: 'Vedevo gruppi di donne in compagnia di soldati d'ogni razza. Attorno a quei campi si consumava la vergogna di una sconfitta che si era voluto contrabbandare in vittoria' [I saw groups of young women in the company of soldiers of every race. Around these encampments there lay the shame of a defeat that they wanted to smuggle into victory], he wrote; 'sembrava dimenticato tutto il passato e la dignità di un popolo, la sua civiltà e la cultura che gli italiani avevano offerto al mondo' [they seemed to have forgotten all the history and the dignity of our people, the civilisation and the culture Italians had offered to the world].[46] A similarly bitter patriotism, and a similar sense of wounded pride, may have precipitated the deadly brawls that broke out between Italian locals and the US soldiers in and around Tombolo. It may also have inspired the fear of brown babies — 'fanciulli reduci da Tombolo' [the young veterans of Tombolo], 'i bambini mulatti con padre a Kansas City' [the mulatto children with fathers from Kansas City], 'bambini che facevano pensare più all'Africa che al paese della madre' [children who made you think more of Africa than of the country of their mothers] — that permeated press accounts of the time.[47]

If African-American soldiers and their offspring were the targets of Italian bigotry, so too were the *segnorine*, and the round-ups in Tombolo were frequently accompanied by vigilante assaults on these women as they fled the police. From the numerous and disturbing accounts of these assaults in the Italian newspapers, it emerges that the women were despised not only for sleeping with African Americans but also because, in the eyes of their assailants if not always in reality, 'la maggioranza delle *segnorine* provengono da fuori, principalmente dal Sud' [the majority of the *segnorine* come from outside, primarily from the South], as one commentator put it.[48] It was precisely for this reason, another claimed, that Tombolo gave rise to a 'campagna contro gli "indesiderabili" [. . .] identificati *tout court* con i meridionali' [campaign against the 'undesirables' [. . .] identified *tout court* with the Southerners] — a campaign that seemed to parallel Fascist Italy's 'altra persecuzione razziale' [other racial persecution], that against the Jews.[49] The *segnorine* were victims, in other words, of the anti-southern prejudice that has endured in some quarters of Italian society since unification. 'Non ancora spenta è l'eco nella cittadinanza, a proposito della violenta lotta sostenuta ieri sera contro le "segnorine"' [After the violent battle waged yesterday against the *segnorine*, the echoes still reverberate among the citizenry], reported *La Provincia del Po* following an August 1947 attack.

> Chi sente ancora un senso di dignità nazionale [. . .] non può che schierarsi dalla parte del popolo di Livorno che ieri sera ha vissuto una grande ora. [. . .] [I]n diversi punti della città alcuni gruppi di giovanotti si sono sfogati contro le malcapitate 'segnorine' che incontravano per strada. Essi hanno iniziato una vera e propria caccia alle ragazze, affrontandole e denudandole dovunque; nei bar, nei ritrovi, per le vie e per le piazze. Una decina di esse, completamente nude, sono state accompagnate in giro per il centro da una turba di gente che gridava loro: 'Tombolo, Tombolo!'. Un clamore indescrivibile in tutta Livorno; urla, fischi, invettive accompagnavano le 'segnorine' sequestrate, molte delle quali, completamente nude erano accompagnate ai posti della polizia.

> [Whoever still feels any sense of national dignity [. . .] must take the side of the people of Livorno, who lived it up last night. [. . .] At several points throughout the city groups of youth unloaded on some of the *segnorine* they met in the street. Launching a real hunt for the girls, they confronted them and stripped them naked wherever they found them: in the bars, the hangouts, the streets and the piazzas. A dozen or so of the girls, completely naked, were marched through the city centre by a crowd screaming 'Tombolo, Tombolo!'. An indescribable commotion ran throughout Livorno: screams, whistles, and invectives accompanied the captured *segnorine*, many of whom were brought, completely nude, to the police station.][50]

Once captured, the *segnorine* were driven out of Tuscany and forcibly shipped back to their native regions.[51] This was done with such cruelty that a petition was prepared by 168 fathers of arrested girls, in which the US authorities were asked to intervene to prevent treatment described as 'disgusting, brutal and inhuman'.[52] Despite these protests, however, the mob violence continued, as did the process of involuntary resettlement. As one newspaper recounted at the time,

> [o]gni mese la polizia rastrella la città quattro, cinque, dieci volte. Ogni mese impacchetta dalle 600 alle 1000 ragazze provenienti da tutte le parti d'Italia. Le esamina, le cura, le munisce di un foglio di via obbligatorio e di regolare diffida, rispedendole al paese d'origine.
>
> [every month there are four, five, ten police round-ups. Every month they put away between 600 and 1000 girls from all over Italy. They are examined, cured, given an expulsion and a cease and desist order, and sent to their cities of origin.][53]

If Tombolo's anti-black violence is evidence of the extension into Italy of the US racial regime, the violent removal of the *segnorine* is evidence that the tensions of this 'contact zone' exacerbated Italian prejudices as well. Tombolo compelled the social conflicts of two continents to intersect, reinforcing — indeed, intensifying — local and national hatreds through the collision not only of conflicting cultures but also of competing racial regimes.

Traces of this collision can be found in all of the many literary, cinematic, dramatic, and artistic representations that Tombolo inspired in the years after the war, and not only in Italy. After Curzio Malaparte's exploration of what he called 'la forêt du Tombolo, où les nègres avaient créé une espèce d'horrible casbah, une jungle habitée par des fauves à l'aspect humain' [the forest of Tombolo, where the Negroes had created a kind of horrible Kasbah, a jungle inhabited by wild beasts with a human appearance], countless lurid accounts would follow in the French popular press, as would novels like Jacques Strezza's *Avec les filles de Tombolo* [Among the Girls of Tombolo, 1950], Piero Lucetti's *Les Déserteurs* [The Deserters, 1954], and Jacqueline Dana's *L'Été du diable* [The Devil's Summer, 1985].[54] There were likewise a number of English-language publications exploring this theme, including John A. Schillace's *The Tragic Forest* (1951), and Nicholas Fersen's *Tombolo* (1954) and *The Hideout* (1965), in addition to the aforementioned *Captain Blackman*. Tales of Tombolo, Italy's 'città proibita', its Forbidden City — the name made popular by Gino Serfogli and adopted as the title for Mandel's poem and Mancini's banned play — once captivated audiences worldwide.[55] Then they were forgotten.

They are worth recollecting and reconsidering today, in order better to understand why, at a fateful historical juncture, Tombolo appears to have dominated the Italian imagination. My explanation is that this so-called Forbidden City represented for post-war Italians a contact zone, a locus of cultural change and thus of social instability. That is certainly how it functions in Micheli's *Paradiso maligno*, where Tombolo, a transformative space, facilitates the kinds of cross-cultural encounters that can both improve one's fortunes and seal one's fate. Nunzia, Micheli's protagonist, comes from a poor family, and is drawn to Tombolo in the hopes of supporting her elderly father and her four young brothers. Even as the money begins to come in, she recognizes the risks she is running. She is afraid of winding up like the ageing prostitutes who line the Via Aurelia, ridiculed by the Italians and ignored by the GIs. She is likewise afraid of those same GIs, and particularly the African-American soldiers. At the same time, however, she sympathizes with the soldiers, and identifies with them. 'A me fanno pena e anche paura' [I feel bad for them and I'm afraid of them], Nunzia says.

> Sono pericolosi. Dopo la liberazione, mica si poteva uscire, con quei mori che appena scuriva t'assalivano anche fra la gente. [. . .] Ma anche sono come bimbetti a saperli pigliare e ce l'hanno coi bianchi per colpa degli americani. Infatti tutti quelli di Tombolo sono mori che non vogliono più tornare fra gli americani che li trattano come schiavi, specie ora che in Italia han trovato da far bene e possono avere donne bianche che in America guai se azzardano alzarci gli occhi soltanto!
>
> [They're dangerous. After the liberation, you couldn't even go out, with those blacks who would assault you as soon as it got dark, even with other people around. [. . .] But at the same time they're like little children if you know how to handle them, and they hate white people because of what the Americans have done to them. Indeed, Tombolo is filled with blacks who don't want to go back to live with the Americans who treat them like slaves, especially now that they've found that they can do well for themselves in Italy and they can have white women who in America they couldn't even look at!][56]

Despite the retrograde racial attitudes, the substance of Nunzia's sentiments here is apparent. Tombolo is a land of opportunity for the African-American soldiers, as it is for Nunzia herself. Yet, in light of the racial regimes there enforced, the opportunities made possible in Tombolo carry with them grave risks as well. *Paradiso maligno* thus dramatizes how, by bringing into contact — and into conflict — the social hierarchies and racial prejudices of Italian and US culture, Tombolo challenged the structural norms of two societies. My hope is that further study will help to reveal how the contact and conflict of Tombolo reshaped those societies in the years that followed the conclusion of the Second World War.

Notes to Chapter 9

1. Silvio Micheli, *Paradiso maligno* (Turin: Einaudi, 1948), p. 112. All translations are my own unless otherwise indicated.
2. Ibid., p. 101.
3. Ibid., p. 150.
4. Ibid., p. 166.
5. Ibid., p. 174.
6. Ibid., p. 227.
7. Ibid., p. 259.
8. Antonio Meucci, 'La guarigione di Tombolo. Una spina nel cuore dell'Italia', *L'Unità*, 3 April 1947, p. 3.
9. lan. [Arturo Lanocita], 'Rassegna cinematografica. *Senza pietà*', *Corriere della Sera*, 3 Oct. 1948, 2; Ettore Allodoli, Preface, *Profili di vita italiana nelle parole nuove*, by Alberto Menarini (Florence: Felice Le Monnier, 1951), pp. v–xvi (p. xvi).
10. Several books have explored the topic, including Aldo Santini's novelistic *Tombolo* (Milan: Rizzoli, 1990) and Tiziana Noce's exacting *Nella città degli uomini. Donne e pratica della politica a Livorno fra guerra e ricostruzione* (Soveria Mannelli: Rubbettino, 2004). My work seeks to build on these significant predecessors in order to situate the Tombolo case within both the Italian and U.S. contexts from which it emerged.
11. On the etymology of this term, including its connection to Tombolo, see Menarini, pp. 185–87.
12. See, for instance, 'La "città proibita" ingoia un'illusa milanese. Una sorella la ritrova morta e descrive gli orrori delle boscaglie di Tombolo', *Corriere d'informazione*, 21–22 May 1946, p. 2; 'Un uomo ucciso nei pressi di Tombolo. Rapina consumata da frequentatori della malfamata pineta?', *Corriere d'informazione*, 7–8 Dec. 1946, p. 1; 'Un bestiale delitto. Giovane massacrata da un negro suo ex-amante', *La Stampa*, 18 Dec. 1946, p. 1; 'Storia triste di una quattordicenne. Le tre sciagurate tappe: Livorno, Tombolo, Firenze', *Corriere d'informazione*, 5–6 June 1946, p. 2; 'Militare americano autore di vari omicidi arrestato con la sua amante', *La Gazzetta del Mezzogiorno*, 4 Feb. 1947, p. 1; 'Negro tradito dall'amente rapisce il figlio e fugge', *La Nuova Stampa*, 9 March 1947, p. 1; N., 'Negli intrighi segreti di Tombolo. È stato il negro "pazzo" a rapire la bimba mulatta', *Corriere d'informazione*, 7–8 April, 1947, p. 1; 'Ingenue ragazze condotte alla perdizio', *La Nuova Stampa*, 24–25 June, 1947, p. 2; 'A Tombolo un miliardo di merci asportate', *L'Unità* 1 Nov. 1947, p. 1; Gino Serfogli, 'Miliardi sepolti tra i pini di Tombolo. I tedeschi tornano a ricuperare i tesori', *L'Unità*, 28 Aug. 1947, p. 1.
13. Indro Montanelli, 'C'è un negro pazzo che urla nella pineta', *Corriere della Sera*, 30 March 1947, p. 3; Indro Montanelli, 'Inchiesta sulla villeggiatura, *Corriere d'informazione*, 1–2 April 1947, p. 1; Indro Montanelli, 'Vive a Tombolo un uomo che si fa ricco con l'onestà', *Il Nuovo Corriere della Sera*, 10 April 1947, p. 1; Indro Montanelli, 'Più della Casbah la pineta di Tombolo, *Corriere d'informazione* 26–27 May 1947, p. 1.
14. Milziade Torelli, 'Montagne di merci comperate a prezzi irrisorî rivendute a dieci volte tanto', *Corriere d'informazione*, 27–28 March 1947, p. 1; Milziade Torelli, 'Alla fortuna si va per mare', *Corriere d'informazione*, 9–10 April 1947, p. 3; Milziade Torelli, 'C'è un''armata' a Viareggio ma è di placidissimi bagnanti', *Corriere d'informazione*, 3–4 June 1947, p. 1; Milziade Torelli, 'San Rossore non è più tabù ora vi regnano le "segnorine"', *Corriere d'informazione*, 23–24 June 1947, p. 3; Milziade Torelli, 'Sbarcano a Livorno truppe per la Germania', *Corriere d'informazione*, 17–18 Oct. 1947, p. 1.
15. Gustavo D'Arpe, 'Conclusione di un'inchiesta. Sorge una città carceraria civile consorzio di redenzione', *La Gazzetta del Mezzogiorno*, 6 Dec. 1949, p. 3.
16. Riccardo Longone, 'Quanto ci costa l'occupazione alleata. Il gran parco dei divertimenti', *L'Unità*, 11 Sept. 1946, p. 1; Riccardo Longone, 'Quanto ci costa l'occupazione alleata. I negri sulla giostra', *L'Unità*, 14 Sept. 1946, p. 1; Riccardo Longone, 'Quanto ci costa l'occupazione alleata. Alla "Metallurgica" si balla', *L'Unità*, 15 Sept. 1946, p. 1; Riccardo Longone, 'Quanto ci costa l'occupazione alleata. Glynn Ross ha trovato l'America', *L'Unità*, 24 Sept. 1946, p.

1; Riccardo Longone, 'Quanto ci costa l'occupazione alleata. Ora che arriva la IV Armata', *L'Unità*, 27 Sept. 1946, p. 1; Riccardo Longone, 'Quanto ci costa l'occupazione alleata. L'ostinata difesa delle nostre officine', *L'Unità*, 3 Oct. 1946, p. 1; Riccardo Longone, 'Quanto ci costa l'occupazione alleata. Borsa nera sotto le tende di Anders', *L'Unità*, 6 Oct. 1946, p. 1; Riccardo Longone, 'Quanto ci costa l'occupazione alleata. Un lungo treno per pochi soldati', *L'Unità*, 13 Oct. 1946, p. 4.

17. Maurizio Ferrara, 'La guerra in Grecia incomincia a Livorno', *L'Unità*, 28 May 1947, p. 3.
18. Cesare Pavese, *Tra donne sole*, in *Tutti i romanzi*, ed. by Marziano Guglielminetti (Turin: Einaudi, 2000), pp. 676–778 (p. 770).
19. Carlo Cassola, *Un matrimonio del dopoguerra* (Turin: Einaudi, 1957), p. 159.
20. Leonida Répaci, 'La madre incatenata', in *Omaggio al Teatro*, ed. by Giampaolo Rugarli (Soveria Mannelli: Rubbettino Editore, 2003), pp. 109–75 (p. 163).
21. Alba De Céspedes, *Il rimorso* (Milan: Mondadori, 1963), p. 667.
22. Carlotta Mandel, 'La città proibita [Livorno, 1947]', in *La città proibita*, 8th edn (Milan: Relations Latines, 1960 [1947]), pp. 90–100 (p. 98, vv. 131–34).
23. Carlotta Mandel, 'Tombolo [Livorno, aprile 1947]', in *La città proibita*, pp. 9–37 (p. 36).
24. Corrado Alvaro, *Quasi una vita*, in *Romanzi e racconti*, ed. by Libero Bigiaretti (Milan: Mondadori, 1974), pp. 873–1392 (pp. 1364–65) [First published by Bompiani, 1950].
25. Giorgio Caproni, 'Il bagno di Luce', in *Racconti scritti per forza*, ed. by Adele Dei (Milan: Garzanti, 2008), pp. 295–98 (p. 297) [first published in *L'Italia socialista*, 11 Dec. 1948].
26. Luciano Luisi, *Un pugno di tempo* (Parma: Guanda, 1967), pp. 33–47.
27. Enrico Pea, *Zitina* (Florence: Vallecchi Editore, 1949), p. 212; Silvano Ceccherini, *Dopo l'ira* (Milan: Rizzoli, 1965), pp. 63, 67.
28. Alberto Moravia, 'Il negro e il vecchio dalla roncola', in *Opere*, II, *Romanzi e racconti 1941–1949*, ed. by Simone Casini (Milan: Classici Bompiani, 2000), pp. 1381–91 (p. 1381) [first published in 1948].
29. R. S., 'Corriere degli spettacoli. La città proibita di Enzo Mancini', *Corriere della Sera*, 22 Dec. 1946, p. 2; 'Stagione teatrale', *Il Dramma*, 23.29 (15 Jan. 1947), p. 52.
30. Francesco Leone, 'Una lettera su "Riso amaro". Mondine in celluloide', *L'Unità*, 2 Oct. 1949, p. 3.
31. For contemporary accounts of this censorship, see salg., 'Prime sullo schermo. *Tombolo* di G. Ferroni', *L'Unità*, 9 Dec. 1947; Marco Cesarini, 'Anche in Italia censura contro i films antifascisti', *L'Unità*, 17 Dec. 1947, p. 1; 'Foggia. Vicende di Tombolo', *La Gazzeta del Lunedì*, 1 March 1948, p. 2.
32. For contemporary accounts of this censorship, see Vito Pandolfi, 'Perché la censura?', *Il Dramma*, 23.34 (1 April 1947), p. 63; X., 'Non rivedremo al Parco ciò che avvenne a Tombolo', *Corriere d'informazione*, 27–28 Dec. 1946, p. 2.
33. 'Gerente di una rivista assolto dell'accusa di oltraggio al pudore', *Il Nuovo Corriere della Sera*, 26 Jan. 1947, p. 1.
34. Luigi Russo, 'Cavatemi dalla testa questo Bruto', in *De vera religione. Noterelle e schermaglie, 1943–1948* (Turin: Einaudi, 1949), pp. 259–69 (p. 268).
35. Mary Louise Pratt, *Imperial Eyes: Travel Writing and Transculturation* (London and New York: Routledge, 1992), p. 6.
36. I borrow the notion of racial regimes from Cedric Robinson, who defines them as 'constructed social systems in which race is proposed as a justification for the relations of power'. Cedric J. Robinson, *Forgeries of Memory and Meaning: Blacks and the Regimes of Race in American Theater and Film before World War II* (Chapel Hill: University of North Carolina Press, 2012), p. xii.
37. *Pittsburgh Courier*, 13 Dec. 1941, reported in Christine Knauer, *Let Us Fight as Free Men: Black Soldiers and Civil Rights* (Philadelphia: University of Pennsylvania Press, 2014), p. 16.
38. Wright speech to the Fourth American Writer's Conference in June 1941, reported in Dan Shiffman, '"12 Million Black Voices" and World War II-era Civic Nationalism', *African American Review*, 41.3 (2007), 443–58 (p. 443).
39. See Silvia Cassamagnaghi, *Operazione Spose di guerra. Storia d'amore e di emigrazione* (Milan: Feltrinelli, 2014), p. 130; as well as the accounts of African-American soldiers in Carolyn Ross

Johnston, *My Father's War: Fighting with the Buffalo Soldiers in World War II* (Tuscaloosa: The University of Alabama Press, 2012), pp. 95, 106.
40. The letter is quoted in Jason Morgan Ward, *Defending White Democracy: The Making of a Segregationist Movement and the Remaking of Racial Politics, 1936–1965* (Chapel Hill: The University of North Carolina Press, 2011), p. 49.
41. 'Nella 'città proibita' la battuta alleata dà buoni frutti. Retata di negri, Tedeschi e "segnorine"', *Corriere d'informazione*, 20–21 Aug. 1946, p. 1; 'Rastrellati soldati negri, prigionieri tedeschi, donne di malaffare', *La voce del Po*, 2 Jan. 1947, p. 1.
42. 'Sanguinoso conflitto a Livorno provocato da soldati negri. Incidenti a Mestre fra alleati e civili', *La Gazzetta del Mezzogiorno*, 26 Aug. 1946, p. 1.
43. After a raid in May 1947, *La Gazzetta del Lunedì* noted ominously that 'the Commander of the Military Police has decided to rid the area of numerous undesirable elements once and for all'. 'La zona di Tombolo sarà ripulita', *La Gazzetta del Lunedì*, 19 May 1947, p. 1. The next week, a morning raid conducted jointly by 90 members of the U.S. Military Police and 100 Carabinieri led to over 300 arrests, and further round-ups would follow until the encampment of Tombolo was destroyed and its inhabitants scattered, imprisoned, or killed. G.S. [Gino Serfogli], 'Nella pineta di Tombolo è passata la scopa del colonnello Meely', *Corriere d'informazione*, 14–15 May 1947, p. 1.
44. John Williams and Dan Georgakas, 'John Williams at 49: An Interview', *Minnesota Review*, 7 (1976), 51–65.
45. Pietro Ciabattini, *Coltano 1945. Un campo di concentramento dimenticato* (Milan: Mursia Editore, 1995), pp. 48–49.
46. Benito Bollati, *Un ragazzo di Salò* (Milan: Mursia, 1998), pp. 235–37.
47. Quoting, respectively, 'Una città dei ragazzi in un vecchio convento', *La Provincia* 31 Dec. 1948, p. 1; Indro Montanelli, 'Non se l'aspettava la morigerata Marina di Pisa', *Corriere d'informazione*, 19–20 March 1947, p. 1; 'Siamo partiti da zero. Ci arrangiavamo così. È proprio vero?', *L'Europeo*, 9.23 (1953), 30–33. See, on this point, Silvana Patriarca, 'Fear of Small Numbers: "Brown Babies" in Postwar Italy', *Contemporanea*, 4 (2015), 537–68.
48. Luis Piazzano, *Leghorn: Decimo Porto. Cronaca di un dopoguerra 1944–1947* (Livorno: Brunello De Batte Editore, 1979), p. 121.
49. Arrigo Petacco, *Livorno in guerra. Come eravamo negli anni di guerra* (Livorno: Editoriale Il Telegrafo, 1988), p. 382. On the hatred engendered by the *segnorine*, see also Chiara Fantozzi, 'L'onore violato: stupri, prostituzione e occupazione alleata (Livorno 1944–47)', *Passato e presente*, 99 (2016), 87–111 (pp. 94–107).
50. 'Nude le segnorine cacciate dalla folla', *La Provincia del Po*, 5 Aug. 1947, p. 1.
51. See, for instance, 'Le rastrellate di Tombolo transitano per Bari', *La Gazzetta del Mezzogiorno*, 14 Jan. 1947, p. 1.
52. Franco Ferrarotti, 'Le "segnorine" contro la Military Police. L'ultima da Tombolo la raccontiamo noi', *L'Unità*, 12 June 1947, p. 1; '22 "segnorine" di Tombolo sono giunte ieri a Roma', *L'Unità*, 4 July 1947, p. 2; 'Arrivo da Tombolo di trentotto "segnorine"', *L'Unità*, 12 Aug. 1947, p. 2; 'Le recluse di Alberobello. 102 straniere sparse dalla guerra per le vie del mondo attendono di essere rimpatriate', *La Gazzetta del Mezzogiorno*, 22 Jan. 1947, p. 1.
53. F. B., 'Tormentata Livorno dopoguerra. Nessuno può sgominare l'esercito delle "segnorine"', *Corriere d'informazione*, 19–20 Aug. 1947, p. 1.
54. Curzio Malaparte, *Deux chapeaux de paille d'Italie* (Paris: Les Éditions Denoël, 1948), p. 54. Preceding even this account was W. F., 'La pinède en folie', *L'Impartial*, 23 Nov. 1946, p. 3.
55. See, for instance, G. S., 'La "città proibita" di Tombolo calamita delle ragazze smarrite', *Corriere d'informazione*, 14–15 May 1946, p. 1.
56. Micheli, *Paradiso maligno*, pp. 176–77.

CHAPTER 10

The Other America: Contact and Exchange in the Italian Folk Revival

Rachel E. Love

Nel mese di gennaio 1969 due ricercatori italiani, Sandro Portelli e Ferdinando Pellegrini, muniti di registratore e macchina fotografica, hanno incontrato e documentato L'AMERICA DELLA CONTESTAZIONE.

[In January 1969 two Italian researchers, Sandro Portelli and Ferdinando Pellegrini, armed with a tape recorder and a camera, found and documented the AMERICA OF PROTEST.][1]

These words — which accompany an image of a Black Panther and the silhouette of a fist gripping a rifle — appear on the cover of an LP that includes recordings of a protest of Nixon's inauguration, school children in Harlem, sermons by minister Frederick Douglass Kirkpatrick, and songs by Harlem teacher Mable Hillery and folk singer Barbara Dane. The Dischi del Sole, the label that published the album, touted it as evidence of a 'nuova America del dissenso' [new America of dissent], proof of the endurance of class struggle in the USA.[2] That same year, Alessandro Portelli also published an anthology of Black Power songs, *Veleno di piombo sul muro* [*Lead Poison on the Wall*], with a lengthy introduction examining song lyrics and orienting Italian readers within the larger context of African American culture and race relations in the USA. Both the album and the anthology were the product of Portelli's passion for US political culture and the civil rights movement. Moved by the integration of schools in Little Rock, Arkansas, and a year spent as an exchange student in Los Angeles, in January of 1969 he had travelled to New York City with Pellegrini, read *The Autobiography of Malcom X*, and set out to document radical America. He would later claim that only after this encounter with US politics did he begin to connect with Italy's own tradition of class struggle: 'I owe my first political and moral motivations to Little Rock, to Martin Luther King, to [civil rights activist] Fannie Lou Hamer.'[3]

Although the evidence he brought back of a new USA might have seemed fresh, it continued a process that some Italian intellectuals had begun three decades earlier: the search for and documentation of 'l'America "altra"', an alternative, more radical America. This chapter seeks to add to our understanding of cultural exchange between the USA and Italy by examining this search and the role that US culture played in the Italian 'folk revival'. Like other revivals in the USA in the 1940s and Great Britain in the immediate post-war period, this period of intellectual and artistic interest in oral musical traditions stirred in Italy in the 1950s, developed into a political movement in the 1960s, and exploded onto television screens and mainstream recorded albums in the 1970s.[4] However, as I explore the role of US influence on this movement, I must also underscore the complex intersection of cultural theories, musical and theatrical production, and field research that contributed to it, including Antonio Gramsci's writings on folklore, the radical anthropology of Ernesto de Martino, the ethnomusicology of Diego Carpitella and Alberto Mario Cirese, and the experimental songwriting and reworking of Resistance songs by the Cantacronache musical group, among other factors.[5] Indeed, the Italian movement was not a simple imitation of its US and British predecessors, nor was the influence of US culture its only catalyst.

In addition to the loci of linguistic and cultural exchange explored in this volume, scholars have investigated many facets of US influence on Italian culture and society, from the 'Americanization' of television and consumer practices to rock music and youth culture.[6] Post-Second World War US intervention in Italian politics and governance has also been well documented, from the Marshall Plan to decades of tacit support of the centre-right Democrazia Cristiana party.[7] The role of this influence on the mid-century Italian folk revival — and on the renewed Italian interest in and political use of oral traditions in general — remains understudied, yet it offers a unique opportunity to examine the complexity of contact and exchange between the USA and Italy and how this exchange impacted various leftist cultural productions there.

In this chapter, I survey how contact with American people and culture informed the early iterations of the Italian folk revival movement. US popular culture and especially music provided a rich yet problematic source of inspiration for several leftist Italian intellectuals and artists of the folk revival, as by turns they embraced American music and rejected US capitalism and militarism. This relationship arose not only from the indirect influences of US cultural products in Italy — in this case, recorded albums — but also from direct contact between Italians and Americans. We can divide this exchange into roughly two phases: an initial openness of Italian intellectuals to the music and culture of 'another' America in the 1950s and, in the 1960s, a shift towards a sceptical cycle of adaptation and rejection of cultural models as new forms of militancy arose in both countries.

To explore the evolution of this relationship, I take as case studies five particular moments involving both contact between people and the exchange of cultural productions. In the immediate aftermath of the Second World War, as leftist intellectuals embraced US realist literature and jazz music, Alan Lomax arrived in Italy to record oral traditions in every region of Italy. During his time abroad, he met Roberto Leydi, who already had a passion for US culture. Leydi's relationship with Lomax and his own interaction with US culture would impact the early phase of the folk revival. With the escalation of the Cold War in the 1960s, however, the artists of the leftist musical collective, the Nuovo Canzoniere Italiano (NCI), could no longer simply find inspiration in US culture without critique. Giovanna Marini's use of the talking blues to reject US capitalist society and Rudi Assuntino's translation of US protest songs exemplify how Italian musicians adapted US forms for new political purposes.[8] I conclude with a consideration of how Portelli's album helped usher in new collaborations between US and Italian radical folk figures. Tracing these relationships reveals how US musical and cultural models remained viable sources of inspiration throughout the 1960s even for musicians within a sphere — the militant Italian left — that would otherwise seem hostile towards US influence. I situate each case within larger trends of US influence in Italy, from the embrace of US literature and music after the Second World War to the role of rock and roll in Italian youth culture. In addition to previous scholarship on US influence in Italy, I rely on unpublished archival materials at the Istituto Ernesto De Martino in Sesto Fiorentino (FI) and original interviews with Marini and Assuntino.

Alan Lomax's eight-month journey to Italy in 1954 and 1955 offers an early, seminal example of how contact with an American contributed to later efforts to document and promote Italian folk culture. By 1954, Lomax had already worked extensively as a folklorist in the USA, making field recordings and exposing a wide audience to commercially overlooked genres through his work for the Library of Congress, anthologies of folk music, and various radio series for CBS. Leaving behind the hostile political environment of McCarthyism in the USA, Lomax travelled to Italy with the goal of recording oral traditions in every region for a series of long-playing discs for Columbia Records.[9] In 1953, he arrived in Rome and consulted with Giorgio Nataletti, the director of the Centro Nazionale di Studi sulla Musica Popolare (CNSMP), and Diego Carpitella, the assistant director who would become an influential ethnomusicologist in his own right. As he explored the archives at the CNSP, Lomax determined that a trip to record Italian popular music throughout the country would be necessary for a complete survey of regional traditions.

Lomax began the expedition in Sicily in July 1954 before moving on to Calabria, Puglia and the northern regions, accompanied for the majority of the trip by Carpitella. He considered himself a 'kind of musical Columbus in reverse', an outsider uncovering practices that had always been present but not documented.[10] Despite the colonial implications of an American 'discovering' Italian traditions, influential Italian scholars corroborate the significance of Lomax's project. Carpitella acknowledges its shortcomings, such as a lack of correlative data about the performers and an uneven understanding of social context, yet also emphasizes the importance this trip held for later research:

> Many of the regions that were barely explored at that time have never been re-examined. It is also necessary to consider the fact that during the period 1952–1954, the situation, particularly in southern Italy and on the Italian islands, was still quite favourable for the conservation of traditional heritage, while from 1954 on, the processes of urbanization, of emigration, both internal and external, have created many lacerations in the traditions.[11]

Not only the scope of the project, then, but also the timing — on the cusp of modernization and social shifts that would in turn alter the practice of these traditions — made it of great worth to work that came after it. Leydi also claims that Lomax's presence in Italy proved 'decisiva per lo sviluppo di una ricerca etnomusicologica moderna e culturalmente aperta nel nostro Paese' [decisive for the development of modern and culturally open ethnomusicological research in our country].[12] Lomax did not discover these traditions, he documented them, but the breadth and timing of the project ensured that it would achieve a lasting impact.

While Columbia Records released two LPs of Lomax's field recordings in 1957 — *Northern and Central Italy and the Albanians of Calabria* and *Southern Italy and the Islands* — Italian audiences would have to wait until 1973 for a release of these recordings in Italy.[13] It thus seems that Lomax's journey itself and the relationships he fostered proved more influential in Italy than the recordings he produced. Nonetheless, some Italians heard Lomax's recordings in the soundtrack to various films set in southern Italy, like Vittorio De Seta's documentaries *Lu tempu di li pisci spata* [The Age of the Swordfish] (1954) and *Surfarara* [Sulphur Mine] (1955) and Pier Paolo Pasolini's *Il Decameron* (1971). Within the circle of the folk revival, Lomax's work was also present. Leydi and Filippo Crivelli's *Bella ciao* — the original performance at the Spoleto Festival dei Due Mondi in 1964, the performances that followed, and the 1965 LP — opened and closed with 'La lizza delle Apuane' ['The Challenge of the Apuans'] a song of the marble quarry workers at Carrara that Lomax had recorded in December 1954. In 1966, Dario Fo's fantastical interpretation of folk culture, *Ci ragiono e canto* [I Think and I Sing], relied on various Lomax and Carpitella recordings, although only two lullabies were included on the LP. This repeated usage suggests that Lomax's work provided the NCI with a valuable resource to access and to reproduce oral traditions.

If Lomax's impact extends beyond the legacy of his research, it may be explained by how his work exposing an international audience to American folk and blues fits into the Italian leftist search for 'another' America. In a 1974 interview, Leydi explained that urban intellectuals understood the culture of marginalized Americans differently from the dominant vision of the USA in 1950s Italy. Their focus on the cultural products of those excluded from the fabled riches of US society — as he says, 'l'America dei negri, dei poveri del Sud, dei mandriani del West, dei boscaioli del Nord' [the America of negroes, of poor southerners, of the cowboys of the West, of the lumberjacks of the North] — was 'la disperata ricerca di una patria da parte di una generazione senza patria' [the desperate search for a homeland [*patria*] by a generation without one], a 'patria popolare' [homeland of the people].[14] Before the fall of Fascism, US culture had offered to left-leaning intellectuals, in the words of Cesare Pavese, 'il primo spiraglio di libertà, il primo sospetto che non tutto nella cultura del mondo finisse coi fasci' [the first glimmer of liberty, the first suspicion that not everything in the world's culture ended with fascism].[15] Indeed, both Pavese and Elio Vittorini used their love of this literature as a legitimization of their anti-Fascist credentials, equating their Americanism with a latent resistance to the ideology of the regime.[16] This idealization of the American downtrodden smoothens out conflicts of race and class into a unified vision, one intrinsically marked by leftist politics for its early Italian consumers.

After the fall of Fascism and the end of the Second World War, many Italian *americanisti* felt that their cultural world had opened up, as American books, films, and records, in Leydi's words, 'ci arrivò addosso quasi di colpo' [fell upon us almost like a blow].[17] This impression may have increased in retrospect, as the Fascist regime had a conflicted relationship with jazz. Even as Fascist critics attacked the music for its ties with race and its perceived licentiousness, the music enjoyed prominence on Italian radio and watered-down Italian interpretations of jazz rhythms weathered the regime's cultural autarchy and demonstrated popularity through record sales even into the 1940s.[18] Nonetheless, after the war US music — and especially jazz and the blues — found an audience eager for new cultural forms. Given Lomax's role in documenting and promoting these genres, we can consider him an ambassador of US folk culture in Italy. Indeed, when in 1974 Leydi deemed Lomax 'il punto di riferimento di tutto il revival' [the point of reference for the whole revival], he was probably referring not just to Lomax's project but also to his mythic place in this vision of the USA.[19] Lomax's position as someone who defied, in Leydi's words, 'la cultura ufficiale' [the official culture] of McCarthyism and mass-produced music thereby participates in a longer narrative of the search for alternative cultural models.[20]

While in Milan, Alan Lomax met Leydi, and their interaction, combined with Leydi's pre-existing passion for US culture, would help shape the early years of the folk revival in Italy. Leydi's omnivorous interest manifested itself in various projects for print, radio, and television during the 1950s: essays on Westerns and comics as well as concerts and television and radio programmes devoted to jazz and folk. As he developed his friendship with Lomax, Leydi published a collection of American protest songs, *Ascolta, Mr. Bilbo!* (1954), named after a 1946 song condemning the anti-immigrant stance of Theodore Bilbo, the Mississippi senator and governor and symbol of white supremacy in the USA. For the materials of the book, it seems likely Lomax put Leydi in touch with People's Songs, a New York organization that Lomax had founded with Pete Seeger and that possessed many of the copyrights.[21] The small volume included an introduction followed by six chapters devoted to song lyrics, musical notation, and Italian translations among various themes, including anti-war and labour union songs, 'Russian propaganda' songs, and songs of the civil rights movement. The volume — with its presentation and analysis of American protest culture and its musical accompaniment — offers an important precedent to Portelli's *Veleno di piombo sul muro*, albeit without the focus on African American culture of the later volume. In the 1974 interview, Leydi celebrates the positive reception of the volume on the left, which had surprised him 'perché si era ormai accentuato, con la stalinizzazione del Partito comunista, il rifiuto di questa America' [because with the Stalinization of the Italian Communist Party, the rejection of this America had become by this point emphatic].[22]

Yet with the publication of *Ascolta, Mister Bilbo!* critics questioned the necessity of looking to protest culture in the USA when political songs already existed in Italy. In his review of the book, Alberto Mario Cirese noted the abundance of Italian 'canti di carcerati, canti di operai, canti di perseguitati' [prison songs, workers' songs, songs of the persecuted], constituting 'un tipo di espressione dell'anima popolare' [a form of expression of the popular soul], that deserved better study.[23] Diego Carpitella, while praising the new perspective on the 'movimento democratico americano' [American democratic movement], also points out that Italian protest songs appeared during the Resistance and factory strikes.[24] Leydi, too, soon turned towards the study of Italian folk culture, a shift that he would later describe as a personal epiphany:

> Noi ci siamo attaccati ai cow boy perché ignoravamo che in Maremma c'erano i butteri, ci siamo attaccati ai poveri che vivevano nelle baracche in Louisiana o nel Tennessee perché ignoravamo che c'erano i poveri che vivevano nelle baracche anche qui. Ecco, questo era forse al fondo di tutto. Il mio passaggio a interessarmi di mondo popolare è stato semplicemente il punto in cui io ho incominciato a rendermi conto che questa patria americana era un mito, un'astrazione, e che era possibile trovarla qui.
>
> [We grew attached to cowboys because we didn't know that in Maremma there were the *butteri*. We were attached to the poor who lived in shacks in Louisiana or in Tennessee because we didn't know that there were poor people who lived in shacks here too. So this was perhaps at the root of everything. My interest in the popular world simply began when I started to realize that this American *patria* was a myth, an abstraction, and it was possible to find it here.][25]

For Leydi, Italian folk culture offered a productive alternative to the abstraction of US popular culture, yet — in a parallel to Portelli's political awakening through the US civil rights movement — his early Americanism catalysed his interest in researching Italian oral traditions. While in the same interview he implies that his passion for US culture was naïve, Leydi's repeated emphasis on the significance of Lomax and US music, literature, and film underscores his belief in the centrality of contact with the USA to the formation of a new field of interest in Italy as well as his own professional trajectory.

In 1962, Leydi and Gianni Bosio — a socialist intellectual and editor of *Movimento operaio*, the Edizioni Avanti!, and later the Edizioni del Gallo — founded the Nuovo Canzoniere Italiano (NCI), a leftist group of intellectuals and musicians that would lead the political phase of the folk revival in the 1960s.[26] They believed that the documentation, analysis, and performance of folk culture amplify the voices of marginalized people and aid the class struggle, which at the time was manifested in worker and student movements. By 1969, the NCI had produced 569 performances across Italy, collaborating with artists like poet Franco Fortini and playwright Dario Fo.[27] By late 1966, the NCI's record label, the Dischi del Sole, had already released over 100,000 copies of eighty-two albums, and by 1973, they had built a formidable collection of over 160 distinct records.[28] The NCI also brought together artists who had found varying degrees of inspiration in US culture and especially American music. However, at this historical moment, these models could no longer be embraced without significant criticism of capitalism and the actions of the USA.

Given the prominence of US popular culture in Leydi's development and his central role in the creation of the NCI, it follows that the early activities of the group would reflect its influence. Cesare Bermani, NCI member and the group's *de facto* historian, notes that Woody Guthrie and Seeger's magazine *Sing Out!* inspired the style of printing of the first issue of the NCI.[29] He also highlights the early Americanism of diverse NCI members in addition to Marini and Assuntino: Bruno Pianta, who played American folk music; Paolo Ciarchi, devoted to jazz-like improvisation; Riccardo Schwamenthal, a photographer of jazz musicians; and Bermani himself, a jazz enthusiast and founding member of the Hot Club Novara. In spring 1964, the NCI hosted a series, 'L'altra Italia' [The Other Italy], that included an event devoted to the US work of Lomax and his ethnomusicologist father, John Lomax, 'I Lomax e la scoperta della musica popolare americana' [The Lomaxes and the Discovery of American Folk Music], organized by Leydi and featuring original Lomax recordings.[30] Performances like *Chitarre contro la guerra* [*Guitars against the War*] (1967) and *Il Vietnam è qui* [*Vietnam is Here*] (1967), even as they condemned US imperialism and the war in Vietnam, also utilized pieces from US militant movements, including the hymn-turned-protest anthem 'We Shall Overcome' and a documentary featuring a speech by Malcolm X. From the beginning, the adaptation of US influences and the rejection of US capitalism and militarism characterized an important part of the NCI's artistic production. In order to best understand the shifting effects of contact with US culture, we should examine the early artistic production of two NCI members in particular: Giovanna Marini's 1966 album, *Vi parlo dell'America* [*I Speak to You of America*] and Rudi Assuntino's translations of American protest songs and his 1965 original, 'La rossa provvidenza (Le basi americane)' ['Red Providence (The American Bases)]. In creating these works, Marini and Assuntino reckoned with the significant role that American musical styles played in their own artistic development and used these styles to deliver scathing critiques of the US state and society.

Vi parlo dell'America, Marini's first album and a relatively early release from the Dischi del Sole, is the complex product of contact with both people and cultural productions: first in Rome and then in Cambridge, Massachusetts. As Marini's first published exercise in songwriting, it holds a seminal place in her career. Archival documentation of sales suggests that, alongside original albums by Ivan Della Mea and Paolo Pietrangeli, it was one of the more popular solo albums released by the Dischi del Sole, outperforming her 1967 anti-clerical ballad *Chiesa chiesa* [*Church Church*].[31] It allows us to observe how Marini processed her US experiences into a sweeping musical criticism of US society and the capitalist system it represents. The album would not have been possible without contact with US culture in Rome and in Cambridge, Massachusetts. By examining its genesis, we understand how a leftist Italian artist could negotiate diverse US influences in the context of the mid-1960s, absorbing musical traditions in order to reject US society.

Before ever travelling to the USA, Marini interacted with American music at the Folkstudio, a Roman locale founded by Harold Bradley and Giancarlo Cesaroni in 1959. Bradley — a former professional American football player (for the Cleveland Browns and the Philadelphia Eagles), a gospel singer, and a painter — acted as a kind of ambassador for American folk music in Rome. Interestingly, he claims that he began performing American music only after arriving in Italy: 'I started singing because I was hearing all this folk music from the States. I would be up all night listening to this American music on Italian radio stations and it was very inspiring.'[32] His words testify to the ubiquity of American music on the radio and offer an inverse complement to the trajectory of the Italian artists and intellectuals discussed in this chapter: being in a foreign place prompted his reclamation of a black American musical tradition. He soon transformed his apartment into a gathering place for artists and folk musicians, and, with the help of Cesaroni, eventually designated the locale a 'non-political private cultural club'.[33] The venue blossomed into a very popular destination for folk music — drawing comparisons to the folk scene bars in Greenwich Village — and it became an important centre of activity for committed leftist singers and songwriters, despite Bradley's determined apolitical stance.[34]

The Folkstudio acted as the locus for the meeting between Pete Seeger, Roberto Leydi, and Giovanna Marini, an encounter that serves as Marini's origin story for her interest in both American and Italian folk music. Seeger, in Italy by invitation of the Teatro Club, had decided to hold a press conference at the venue.[35] Both Marini's archival biography and Bermani's account suggest that she had already been performing folk material before Seeger arrived in the winter of 1963. In her memory, however, her discovery of both Italian and American folk traditions blend, and she cites the night Roberto Leydi summoned her to translate for Seeger as her true introduction to the genre:

> Ho scoperto tutto a un tratto il canto popolare quando è venuto Roberto Leydi perché era arrivato Pete Seeger a Roma. Io ero l'unica che parlasse inglese, allora ho tradotto Pete Seeger ad un concerto che lui ha dato a Roma senza capire una parola perché io parlavo l'inglese, lui parlava americano. [. . .] Anche Pete Seeger, poveretto, si ricordava, mi ha difeso di fronte al pubblico, diceva, 'Basta, smettila!' E quando sono andata a Boston abbiamo cantato insieme, è stato molto bello. Sì, è stato molto gentile.
>
> [I discovered folk songs all at once when Roberto Leydi arrived since Pete Seeger was in Rome. I was the only one who spoke English, so Leydi asked me to translate for Pete Seeger at a concert that he put on in Rome, even though I didn't understand a word because I spoke English, but he spoke American. [. . .] Even Pete Seeger, poor thing, he recollected, he defended me from the audience, saying, 'Enough! Stop it!' And when I went to Boston, we sang together, and it was wonderful. Yes, he was very kind.][36]

This evening also precipitated Leydi's suggestion that she join the NCI, which probably contributed to her sense of discovering both Italian and American folk music in one evening through Leydi and Seeger. She would perform with the NCI for the first time at *Bella ciao* at the 1964 Spoleto Festival.[37] Her narrative of Leydi and Seeger's appearance in her life, ushering in her passion for diverse forms of popular culture, signals the catalytic importance both had in her career.

Shortly after this fateful meeting, Marini accompanied her husband, who had been hired as a physicist at MIT, to Cambridge, Massachusetts, where she lived until 1966. She recorded her experiences there in letters to friends in the NCI and, years later, in interviews. As she told Alessandro Portelli in a 2012 interview, she developed her interest in Italian folk music once she was in the USA, in a parallel to Leydi's trajectory from US to Italian oral culture: 'La cosa strana è che l'America mi ha fatto scoprire le cose italiane' [The strange thing is that America helped me discover Italian traditions].[38] Marini arrived in the USA at a time of heightened social tension, and her accounts suggest that she and her husband soon became involved in Boston's political scene: 'Una volta arrivata là poi abbiamo cominciato a partecipare — lui andava all'università e io andavo alle manifestazioni del Vietnam' [As soon as we arrived we started participating — my husband went to the university and I went to Vietnam protests].[39] She frequented a group of progressive intellectuals, both US and European, alienated by the climate of McCarthyism and energized by the civil rights and anti-war movements. She also remembers tracking down Pete Seeger at Club 47 in Boston, where she met his sister Peggy and her husband, the British folksinger and activist Ewan MacColl. Also at Club 47, she heard Almeda Riddle, an Arkansas folk singer born in 1898 who had been recorded by Lomax: 'Era la prima volta che sentivo una autentica' [It was the first time I heard someone authentic].[40] She purchased records, including LPs of Woody Guthrie and Lead Belly. She further developed contacts with prominent figures of the American folk movement, writing in a February 1965 letter of meetings with Seeger, Joan Baez, and Irwin Silber — the co-founder and editor of the journal *Sing Out!* and organizer of the Newport Folk Festival — who even proposed that they organize an appearance of the NCI at the festival in 1966, an opportunity that never materialized.[41] She also performed popular material on her own, with varying responses from her US public. A March 1965 letter mentions singing 'all'Unicorn', probably referencing the Unicorn Coffee House located in Boston's Back Bay that was host to an array of folk and blues performers during the 1960s.[42] All in all, she embraced opportunities to engage not just with US culture but also with the people who produced it.

Marini's connections with the folk revival scene in Boston may have proved productive, but in her letters' accounts of protests and the mainstream responses to them she begins to express disillusionment with US society. In a March 1965 letter, she describes the intersection of civil rights, anti-Lyndon Johnson, and anti-Vietnam war protests: 'Grandi cortei dignitosi e silenziosi, ma ho tanto la sensazione che all'americano in genere basti sentirsi la coscienza apposto avendo fatto un corteo o due e poi si ritira nella sua beata stupidità e del resto se ne frega' [Great dignified and silent processions, but I very much feel that the average American feels his conscience is clear after participating in a procession or two, and then he retreats into his blessed stupidity and doesn't care about the rest].[43] She also mentions that she and her husband — who had signed several petitions against Johnson — had been summoned to the Italian consulate, where they were discouraged from attending further demonstrations. While they may have withdrawn temporarily, her letters from November 1965 recounted further protests in Cambridge, where the police presence was growing increasingly threatening: 'Vi penso particolarmente oggi, giorno di marce, la nostra qui ad Harvard Square, è stata interrotta dalla polizia [. . .] Insomma stanno diventando particolarmente feroci per quanto riguarda i contrari alla guerra in Vietnam' [I'm thinking about you today in particular, a day of marches, ours here in Harvard Square was interrupted by the police. [. . .] Anyway, they are getting particularly ferocious towards the people against the war in Vietnam].[44] The frustrated protests of her letters and her criticism of an alienated and apathetic 'average *americano*' reappear with vehemence in *Vi parlo dell'America*. These letters impart Marini's growing disappointment with US political and social systems and also suggest how her direct involvement in protest movements shaped her understanding of the USA.

In 1966, Marini returned permanently to Italy and began writing *Vi parlo dell'America*, which she has referred to as 'il mio ricordo dell'America' [my souvenir of America].[45] As she tells her biographer, she conceived the album as a kind of report on her experiences, one that would satisfy friends eager for a first-hand account of what the USA was really like:

> Tornai dall'America. Tutti mi chiedevano come fosse quest'America. Me l'avevano chiesto anche prima, quando stavo lì. E allora ho deciso di fare un disco di talking blues inframmezzato da melodie compiute: qualcuna era americana e l'avevo imparata lì; le altre erano da me inventate. *Vi parlo dell'America* è stata la mia prima ballata. Il modello a cui mi sono ispirata era certamente Lead Belly di cui conoscevo i dischi. Avevo anche ascoltato diversi bluesman e vari artisti popolari americani. E poi c'era l'influenza di Pete Seeger e degli altri cantanti folk che andavano per la maggiore già allora.
>
> [I returned from America. Everyone asked me how this America was, and they had asked me before, when I was still there. And so I decided to make an album of talking blues interspersed with complete melodies. Some were American and I learned them there, and others I invented myself. *Vi parlo dell'America* was my first ballad. The model that inspired me most was certainly Lead Belly, whose albums I knew. I had also listened to various bluesmen and American popular artists. And then there was the influence of Pete Seeger and American folk singers who were fashionable even then.][46]

We can understand the album as the product of different processes of cultural contact and exchange. Marini's deliberate use of the talking blues reflects the profound influence of American folk performers — especially Guthrie and Seeger, in addition to Lead Belly — on her own performance style. She mines her US experiences to create a reportage in ballad form on the state of the USA, a place much imagined by her Italian audiences. The resulting album proves to be a complex engagement with US culture, as rather than solely consuming it, she absorbs it and incorporates in into her own artistic production alongside Italian melodies and those of her own invention. Her US prototypes act as what Umberto Eco referred to as a 'luogo di simulazione' [site of simulation] to be adapted to new contexts.[47]

Through this profound engagement with talking blues and American folk traditions, she delivers a scathing critique of the USA. Rather than solely an unproductive abstraction, the USA has come to represent a violent force in the world and in Italy, and an avowed leftist singer needed to respond to this intensification of associations. She addresses what she perceives as the numbing capacity of television and mass culture, racism, classism, the hypocrisy of leftist intellectuals, and organized religion. Throughout the ballad, she integrates her own personal experiences as an Italian there — protests against the war, noise complaints from neighbours, conformist teachers of her young children, interactions with Italian-American 'gangsters' — into her wider examination of US society. She also provides linguistic examples for her audience, explaining concepts like a 'date', 'bad section' or bad neighbourhoods, '[keeping] up coi Johnses next door' [sic], 'privacy', and even the 'Unitarian Church'. The use of personal experiences and these vocabulary lessons adds to her authority as a privileged informant returned from abroad, and they form an introduction to Marini's vision of the layered aspects of US society. As the ballad progresses, Marini's critique of mass culture and working-class alienation seems to delocalize, and her closing section 'Se avessi cento figli (O padrone non lo fare)' ['If I Had a Hundred Sons (O Don't Be a Boss)] extends beyond the borders of the USA to condemn the capitalist system as a whole. In this way, Marini's speaking about the USA becomes her speaking about capitalism at large. Her time in the USA proves fundamental for the development of this analysis, and her ballad, by moving between autobiography and critique, creates a narrative of political formation.

Rudi Assuntino's formation through rock and roll and folk music presents an alternative trajectory to Marini's without extended time spent in the USA: having arrived at musical protest through US cultural products, he used the artistic style he developed to critique US power and influence in Italy. Born in 1941, Assuntino performed frequently with the NCI during the 1960s and released one record with the Dischi del Sole, *Uccidi e capirai* [*Kill and You Will Understand*] (1965). Like Leydi and Marini, he closely links his experience in the NCI with American music: 'Io arrivo al Nuovo Canzoniere Italiano perché mi piaceva molto la musica, quella leggera, ma quella leggera americana soprattutto' [I came to the Nuovo Canzoniere Italiano because I liked music, pop music, and American pop music above all].[48] His affinity as a young adult for rock and roll, Elvis Presley, and Bob Dylan influenced his political development, and he soon began writing his own songs. These included 'La rossa provvidenza (Le basi americane)' (1965), directed against US militarism and Italian support for it. His trajectory reflects both the influence of US popular culture on Italian activism in the 1960s and the need for the protagonists of these movements to distance themselves from these compromised influences.

Unlike Leydi and Marini, who were a little older, Assuntino's first passion was for rock and roll, Elvis Presley in particular. He remembers its influence as a physical force: 'Sono stato colpito e affondato dal rock and roll' [I was struck and sunk by rock and roll].[49] Paolo Ciarchi, another NCI performer, confirms that when they met in the summer of 1959, Assuntino was writing love songs and attempting to put together a rock band.[50] Assuntino's attraction to this music was not particularly political, and his experience parallels that of rock's young Italian audience. For these listeners, rock gave voice to rebellious youth as well as the pleasures of consumption and the US lifestyle.[51] It was marketed to an urban audience — mostly in northern

Italian cities like Assuntino's birthplace, Milan — and young members of the middle class, who had the capability to purchase records.[52] Alessandro Carrera argues that rock served a private rather than political function: it was not sung at protests, though combined with new dance music it did give its listeners a vague sense of corporeal anti-conformity.[53] Nonetheless, Umberto Fiori suggests that it offered possibilities of political and cultural resistance, even when these implications were not articulated or even intended by the artists producing this culture: 'The large majority of young people took the symbols and models, often indirectly, and vested them with extra meaning, translating them in terms of their own culture and experience.'[54]

Elvis Presley did not lead Assuntino to protest songs, however: he discovered the possibilities of political expression in music through Bob Dylan. After hearing a young couple perform 'Blowin' in the Wind' on a trip to Great Britain, he decided to translate into Italian Dylan's 'Masters of War' (1963), a song that condemned the state machinations of the Cold War. While thematically similar, Assuntino's translation — 'L'uomo che sa' [The Man Who Knows] — is a liberal interpretation of the original: only the final two verses resemble Dylan's version in structure and lyrical content. He would later translate two more anti-war American songs: Ann and Marti Cleary's 'Strontium 90' and P. F. Sloan's 'Eve of Destruction' ('L'alba della fine'). In a literal realization of Fiori's statement, Assuntino adapted American songs to fit the Italian political moment and participated in the wider trend of Italians covering American songs.[55]

Assuntino's first record, *Uccidi e capirai* (1965), included this translation as well as new compositions, which shaped the protest song genre to the concerns of the Italian student movement. While Marini's first record used the talking blues to critique US society, this record confronted international injustice and US militarism through protest songs. Alongside songs in translation, including 'L'uomo che sa', the record showcases two original compositions: 'Canzone del mondo nostro' [Song of Our World], a call to build a more just society, and 'Rossa provvidenza (Le basi americane)'. Targeting the presence of US military bases in Italy, Assuntino condemns Italian support for the USA since the start of the Cold War and calls on 'compagni' to return to direct action: 'Buttiamo a mare le basi americane | cessiamo di fare da spalla agli assassini | giriamo una pagina lunga di vent'anni | andiamo a guadagnare la nostra libertà' [Let's throw the American bases into the sea | Let's stop supporting murderers | Let's turn a page twenty years long | Let's go earn our freedom]. The central protest against US militarism thus opens up to a larger critique, one that implicates the Italian government and the established Italian left. 'Rossa provvidenza' quickly became Assuntino's most well-known song, with Bermani affirming that it was widely performed during the 1968 movements and beyond.[56] It was even included in a 1969 collection of international protest songs compiled by Barbara Dane, *The Vietnam Songbook*.[57]

'Le basi americane' may focus on a specific aspect of US influence in Italy and the world, but *Uccidi e capirai* as a whole reflects Assuntino's need to distance himself from his Anglophone sources of inspiration and develop his own Italian voice. Ciarchi, describing the record in 1966 for the NCI's journal, affirmed that Assuntino had absorbed American folk styles but had moved beyond them:

> [A]ccumula nuove esperienze, compone nuove canzoni, si focalizza sempre più in uno stile personale, distaccandosi persino dai suoi modelli folk americani, nel momento in cui divengono cantanti di largo consumo sul mercato ufficiale e vendono i propri dischi a milioni di copie, nel momento in cui si moltiplicano in tutto il mondo gli imitatori di Dylan, Baez, Mc Guire, Sloan, ecc.; l'impegno politico ha avuto in lui il sopravvento ed entra in opposizione col carattere paternalistico e qualunquista dei cantanti folk anglosassoni.
>
> [He collects new experiences, he composes new songs, he focuses more and more on a personal style, detaching himself even from his American folk role models, while at the same time these role models become famous singers in the mainstream market and sell millions of copies of their albums, and at the same time the imitators of Dylan, Baez, Mc Guire [sic], Sloan, etc., proliferate all over the world. In him, his political commitment has the upper hand, opposing the paternalistic and apathetic [*qualunquista*] character of Anglo-Saxon folk singers.][58]

Assuntino's artistic formation may have begun with Elvis and Bob Dylan, but he has now developed a style that is distinct and less commercial than its US prototype. Ciarchi's narrative of how Assuntino shaped his first record underscores the latter's balancing act between these sources of influence and the political imperative to assert his independence from them. As we have seen, Assuntino's relationship with these forms was ambivalent, alternating between their use and rejection.

Assuntino's 1967 arrest in Bologna while protesting against the US escalation of the war in Vietnam further encapsulates the complexity of his relationship with the USA. Indeed, he remembers the students' protest strategy as derived from the US civil rights movement, and even seems to view the USA as more tolerant of dissent: 'Eravamo seduti tutti intorno, come avevamo visto che facevano nei paesi civili, in America, noi mica violenza! *Sit-in*' [We were sitting in a circle, as we had seen that they did in civilized countries, in America. We weren't violent! It was a *sit-in*].[59] After the clash with the police escalated to violence, Assuntino and others were arrested and imprisoned for several months. By the time he was released, he had decided to give up music — seeing it as no longer politically viable — and turned instead to 'politica attiva' [active politics] including various documentary and ethnomusicology projects.[60] The events of May 1967 encapsulate Assuntino's balancing act: he uses a technique learned from Americans to protest against US military operations, much as he had used American protest songs for the same purpose in a continuing cycle of adaptation and resistance.

The album and book that opened this chapter — Portelli and Pellegrini's *L'America della contestazione* and Portelli's *Veleno di piombo sul muro* — epitomized the NCI's enduring interest in radical US culture and ushered in a new phase of collaboration between Italian and American folk militants. Both anthologies recuperate the image of 'another' America, one that recalls the post-war appeal of images of black Americans and the New Deal. Indeed, the book offers a kind of update to Leydi's *Ascolta, Mr. Bilbo!*, providing new material from a more radical source and suggesting that the Italian left need only look deeper to find useful examples of American protest. A Dischi del Sole press release announced the record and emphasized its documentation of 'questa nuova fase della lotta di classe in America' [this new phase of the class struggle in America].[61] *L'America della contestazione* thus offers an example of the cycles within the perception of US culture. The nature of the 'other' America changes — no longer the literature of the Great Depression, now the songs of the Black Power movement — but it nonetheless exists, waiting to be recorded and communicated to an Italian radical audience.

The impact of *L'America della contestazione* would further encourage collaborations between the folksinger and activist Barbara Dane, Irwin Silber, the NCI, and the Italian left at large. In 1968, Irwin Silber had contacted the Edizioni del Gallo, the press that backed the NCI, to announce that he was founding a record label with Dane, Paredon Records, that would document protest music around the world. Gianni Bosio responded to Silber's proposal that they begin an exchange between Paredon and the Dischi del Sole: 'As regards the exportation of our records, or the pressing for your label, we find your proposal extremely interesting.'[62] In 1969, after the release of *L'America della contestazione*, the Partito Comunista Italiano [Italian Communist Party] invited Dane and Mable Hillery to sing at their official Festival de *l'Unità* in Florence, after which Portelli also organized a meeting with Dane and the protagonists of il Manifesto.[63] A year later, Dane wrote a report on the Newport Folk Festival for the second series of the NCI's journal, and Paredon Records would publish an anthology of NCI songs, *Avanti Popolo! Revolutionary Songs of the Italian Working Class*, a realization of the collaboration proposed in Bosio's letter.[64] In the decades to come, Portelli would devote much of his career to different aspects of this 'other' America, from his work on Woody Guthrie in the 1970s to his more recent publications of an oral history of Harlan County, Kentucky, and the working-class dreams of Bruce Springsteen.[65]

Although the lyrics of *Vi parlo dell'America* and 'Le basi americane' reject US models, their use of American musical styles — as well as the biographical experiences of their authors — suggests that the productive possibilities still existed. The cultural exchange fostered by Lomax's project and its legacy in Leydi's work is perhaps expected when oriented in the embrace of US culture after the Second World War. More surprisingly, as US intervention in Italy and around the world escalated and mainstream US culture seemed permanently coloured by its state and capitalist economy, radical US culture continued to offer models to adopt and adapt. The experiences of Marini and Assuntino offer examples of artists who used American musical styles to reject US society and politics. *Vi parlo dell'America* satirizes through the talking blues; 'Rossa provvidenza' follows in the footsteps of Bob Dylan. Only a few years later, Portelli's compilations would return to the documentation of radical culture, providing a new set of models for Italians to adopt and contrast. More aspects of this phenomenon deserve to be studied, most pressingly the Italian left's use of African-American culture as a persistent source of political inspiration. As we have seen, *Veleno di piombo sul muro*'s militant fascination with the Black Power movement follows years of Italian passion for jazz and the blues. Within the limits of this piece, I hope to have added to our understanding of the many facets of cultural shifts through exchange in post-war Italy. Leydi's, Marini's, Assuntino's, and Portelli's experiences are individual examples of a complex phenomenon. American music — blues, jazz, folk, and rock — provided the soundtrack, which was readily consumed, adapted, and contrasted by people who otherwise rejected the core values of mainstream US culture and the actions of the US state. Each time previous American models seemed too compromised, these intellectuals and artists recuperated newer, more radical versions: *Ascolta, Mister Bilbo!* evolved into *Veleno di piombo sul muro* in the enduring search for an 'America della contestazione'.

Notes to Chapter 10

1. Various artists, *L'America della contestazione*, Dischi del Sole, DS 179/81/CL, 1969.
2. Undated press release (but probably from 1969), Archive of the Istituto Ernesto De Martino (AIEdM), Fondo Nuovo Canzoniere Italiano (NCI), Cartellina 34.
3. Alessandro Portelli, 'Between Rome, Harlem, and Harlan', in *White Scholars/African American Texts*, ed. by Lisa Long (New Brunswick: Rutgers University Press, 2005), 145–53 (p. 146).
4. In using this phrase as the best shorthand for a complex movement, I follow Italian ethnomusicologists Diego Carpitella, 'Etnomusicologia', in *Conversazioni sulla musica (1955–1990). Lezioni, conferenze, trasmissioni radiofoniche*, ed. by the Società Italiana di Etnomusicologia (Florence: Ponte alle Grazie, 1992), 52–65; and Roberto Leydi, *Il folk music revival* (Flaccovio: Palermo, 1972), as well as the more recent scholarship of Goffredo Plastino, *La musica folk. Storie, protagonisti e documenti del revival in Italia* (Milan: il Saggiatore, 2016).
5. For further scholarship on the complexity and particularities of the folk revival in Italy, see Alessandro Carrera, 'Italy's Blues: Folk Music and Popular Song from the Nineteenth Century to the 1990s', *The Italianist*, 21.1 (2001), 348–71; Fabio Dei, *Beethoven e le mondine. Ripensare la cultura popolare* (Rome: Meltemi, 2002) and 'Dal popolare al populismo. Ascesa e declino degli studi demologici in Italia', *Meridiana*, 77 (2013), 83–100; Rachel Haworth, *From the Chanson Française to the Canzone D'autore in the 1960s and 1970s: Authenticity, Authority, Influence* (Farnham: Ashgate 2015); Goffredo Plastino, *La musica folk. Storie, protagonisti e documenti del revival in Italia* (Milan: il Saggiatore, 2016); Jacopo Tomatis, 'La "nuova canzone" e il folk revival. Narrazioni, intrecci e scontri di generi musicali negli anni sessanta e settanta', in Plastino, *La musica folk*, pp. 1059–82; and Antonio Fanelli, *Contro canto. Le culture della protesta dal canto sociale al rap* (Rome: Donzelli, 2017).
6. See Alessandro Portelli, 'Elvis Presley è una tigre di carta (ma sempre una tigre)', in *La musica in Italia. L'ideologia, la cultura, le vicende del jazz, del rock, del pop, della canzonetta, della musica popolare dal dopoguerra ad oggi*, ed. by Diego Carpitella (Rome: Savelli, 1978), pp. 9–68; Alessandro Carrera, *Musica e pubblico giovanile. L'evoluzione del gusto musicale dagli anni sessanta ad oggi* (Milan: Feltrinelli economica 1980); Umberto Fiori, 'Rock Music and Politics in Italy', *Popular Music*, 4 (1984), 261–77; Franco Minganti, 'Rock'n'roll in Italy: Was It True Americanization?', in *Cultural Transmissions and Receptions*, ed. by Rob Kroes, Robert W. Rydell, and D. F. J. Bosscher (Amsterdam: VU University Press 1993), pp. 139–51; idem, 'Jukebox Boys: Postwar Italian Music and the Culture of Covering', in *Transactions, Transgressions, Transformations: American Culture in Western Europe and Japan*, ed. by Heide Fehrenbach and Uta G Poiger (New York: Berghahn Books, 2000), pp. 148–65; Stephen Gundle, 'The Americanization of Daily Life: Television and Consumerism in Italy in the 1950s', *Italian History and Culture*, 2 (1996), 11–39; and idem, *Between Hollywood and Moscow: The Italian Communists and the Challenge of Mass Culture, 1943–1991* (Durham, NC: Duke University Press 2000), in particular pp. 31–35.
7. See Alan A. Platt and Robert Leonardi, 'American Foreign Policy and the Postwar Italian Left', *Political Science Quarterly*, 93.2 (1978), 197–215; and John Lamberton Harper, *America and the Reconstruction of Italy, 1945–1948* (Cambridge: Cambridge University Press, 1987).

8. I explore in greater detail Giovanna Marini's adaptation of American musical models for her album *Vi parlo dell'America* in my article, 'Talking Italian Blues: Roberto Leydi, Giovanna Marini, and American Influence in the Italian folk revival, 1954–1966', *Popular Music*, 38.2 (2019), 317–34.
9. For more detailed accounts of Lomax's journey, see Alan Lomax, 'Ascoltate, le colline cantano!', *Santa Cecilia*, 5.4 (1956), 81–87; idem, 'Saga of a Folksong Hunter: A Twenty-Year Odyssey with Cylinder, Disc and Tape', *HiFi Stereo Review*, 4.5 (1960), 38–46; and idem, *L'anno più felice della mia vita. Un viaggio in Italia 1954–1955*, ed. by Goffredo Plastino (Milan: Il Saggiatore, 2008).
10. Lomax, 'Saga of a Folksong Hunter', p. 46.
11. Diego Carpitella, 'Ethnomusicology in Italy', *Journal of the Folklore Institute*, 11.1/2 (1974), 86–87.
12. Roberto Leydi, *L'altra musica. Etnomusicologia. Come abbiamo incontrato e creduto di conoscere le musiche delle tradizioni popolari ed etniche* (Florence: Giunti Ricordi, 1991), p. 272.
13. Goffredo Plastino, 'Introduction: Un sentimento antico', in Lomax, *L'anno più felice della mia vita*, ed. by Plastino, pp. 46–47.
14. Cesare Bermani, 'La preistoria del Nuovo Canzoniere Italiano: un colloquio con Roberto Leydi', *Il de Martino*, 14 (2003), 119–41 (pp. 122–24).
15. Cesare Pavese, 'Ieri e oggi', in *Saggi Letterari* (Turin: Einaudi, 1968), p. 173.
16. For further analysis of the relationship between Italian authors and American literature during Fascism and in the post-war period, see Dominque Fernandez, *Il mito dell'America negli intellettuali italiani dal 1930 al 1950* (Caltanissetta: Sciascia, 1969); Claudio Antonelli, *Pavese, Vittorini e gli americanisti. Il mito dell'America* (Florence: Edarc, 2008); Guido Bonsaver, *Elio Vittorini. Letteratura in tensione* (Florence: F. Cesati, 2008); and Jane Dunnett, *The 'Mito Americano' and Italian Literary Culture under Fascism* (Ariccia: Aracne editrice, 2015).
17. Roberto Leydi, 'Furore. Il film dell'America che abbiamo amato', *L'Europeo*, 2 December 1971, 30, as quoted in Domenico Ferraro, *Roberto Leydi e il 'Sentite buona gente.' Musiche e cultura nel secondo dopoguerra* (Rome: Squilibri, 2014), p. 84.
18. For a history of jazz performance in Italy and more on the complex relationship between the Fascist regime and jazz, see Adriano Mazzoletti, *Il jazz in Italia. Dalle origini alle grandi orchestre* (Turin: EDT, 2004); and Fabio Presutti, 'The Saxophone and the Pastoral: Italian Jazz in the Age of Fascist Modernity', *Italica*, 85.2/3 (2008), 273–94.
19. Bermani, 'La preistoria del Nuovo Canzoniere Italiano', p. 135.
20. Ibid.
21. Chiara Ferrari, *Politica e protesta in musica. Da Cantacronache a Ivano Fossati* (Milan: Unicopli, 2014), p. 90; and Roberto Leydi and Tullio Kezich, *Ascolta, Mister Bilbo! Canzoni di protesta del popolo americano* (Milan: Edizioni Avanti!, 1954), p. 148.
22. Bermani, 'La preistoria del Nuovo Canzoniere Italiano', p. 125.
23. Alberto Mario Cirese, 'Ascolta mister Bilbo!', *La Lapa*, 2.4 (1954), p. 76, as quoted in Ferraro, *Roberto Leydi e il "Sentite buona gente."*, p. 87.
24. Diego Carpitella, 'Mister Bilbo!', *Il Contemporaneo*, 1.31 (1954), p. 11, as quoted in Ferraro, *Roberto Leydi e il 'Sentite buona gente'*, p. 87.
25. Bermani, 'La preistoria del Nuovo Canzoniere Italiano', pp. 122–24.
26. For more on the Nuovo Canzoniere Italiano — in addition to the works on the folk revival previously cited — see the anthology of its 1960s issues, *Il Nuovo Canzoniere Italiano dal 1962 al 1968*, ed. by Cesare Bermani (Milan: Mazzotta 1978); and Cesare Bermani, *Una storia cantata, 1962–1997. Trentacinque anni di attività del Nuovo Canzoniere Italiano-Istituto Ernesto De Martino* (Milan: Jaca Book; Sesto Fiorentino: Istituto Ernesto De Martino, 1997).
27. Cesare Bermani, 'Giovanna Daffini e Il Nuovo Canzoniere Italiano', in *Giovanna Daffini. L'amata genitrice. Atti del convegno: Palazzo Bentivoglio, 30–31 maggio 1992*, ed. by Cesare Bermani (Comune di Gualtieri: Assessirati alla cultura, 1993), pp. 21–45.
28. Unsigned letter to Giuseppe Pedercini, *Argomenti Socialisti*, Rome, 17 November 1966, AIEdM, Fondo Edizioni del Gallo (EDG), C. 35 and catalogue, *I Dischi del Sole* (Milan: Edizioni del Gallo, 1973).
29. Cesare Bermani, 'Dalla cultura contadina alla cultura urbana', in *Il Nuovo Canzoniere Italiano dal 1962 al 1968*, ed. by Bermani, p. 8.

30. 'Il Nuovo Canzoniere Italiano presenta L'altra Italia. Prima rassegna italiana della canzone popolare e di protesta vecchia e nuova', March–May 1964, AIEdM, Fondo NCI, C. 41.
31. Letter Gianni Bosio to Pietro Da Falce, RI-FI Record Company, 'I dischi più venduti', 5 February 1971, AIEdM, Fondo EDG, C. 40.
32. Harold Bradley, *Gridiron Gauntlet: The Story of the Men Who Integrated Pro Football in Their Own Words*, interview by Andy Piascik (Lanham, MD: Taylor Trade Publications, 2009), p. 185.
33. Alessandro Carrera, 'Oh, the Streets of Rome: Dylan in Italy', in *Highway 61 Revisited: Bob Dylan's Road from Minnesota to the World*, ed. by Colleen J. Sheehy and Thomas Swiss (Minneapolis: University of Minnesota Press, 2009), pp. 84–105 (p. 88).
34. Ibid.
35. Dario Salvatori, *Folkstudio Story* (Turin: Studio Forma, 1981), p. 14.
36. In conversation with author, October 2015.
37. Bermani, *Una storia cantata, 1962–1997*, p. 19.
38. Giovanna Marini, 'Una storia di famiglia', interview by Alessandro Portelli, *Lady of Carlisle. Giovanna Marini canta canzoni popolari inglesi e americane* (Block Nota/Circolo Gianni Bosio, 2012) [on CD].
39. Ibid.
40. Ibid.
41. Letter, Giovanna Marini to Nanni Ricordi, 12 February 1965, AIEdM, Fondo NCI, C. 8.
42. Letter, Giovanna Marini to Nanni Ricordi, 25 March 1965, AIEdM, Fondo NCI, C. 5.
43. Ibid.
44. Letter, Giovanna Marini to Nanni Ricordi, 27 November 1965, AIEdM, Fondo NCI, C. 8.
45. In conversation with the author, October 2015.
46. Ignazio Macchiarella, *Il canto necessario. Giovanna Marini compositrice, didatta e interprete* (Udine: Nota, 2005), p. 56.
47. Umberto Eco, 'Il modello Americano', in *La riscoperta dell'America*, ed. by Gian Paolo Ceserani, Umberto Eco, and Beniamino Placido (Bari: Laterza 1984), pp. 3–4.
48. In conversation with author, 20 October 2015.
49. Ibid.
50. Paolo Ciarchi, 'Rudy Assuntino', *Il Nuovo Canzoniere Italiano*, 7–8 (Milan: Edizioni del Gallo, 1966), in *Il Nuovo Canzoniere Italiano dal 1962 al 1968*, ed. by Cesare Bermani (Milan: Mazzotta, 1978), pp. 38–41.
51. For a fuller account of rock and roll in Italy, see Alessandro Carrera, *Musica e pubblico giovanile. L'evoluzione del gusto musicale dagli anni sessanta ad oggi* (Milan: Feltrinelli economica, 1980); Fiori, 'Rock Music and Politics in Italy'; and Alessandro Portelli, 'L'orsacchiotto e la tigre di carta. Il rock and roll arriva in Italia', *Quaderni Storici*, 58.1 (1985), 135–47.
52. Fiori, 'Rock Music and Politics in Italy', pp. 262–63.
53. Carrera, *Musica e pubblico giovanile*, p. 46.
54. Fiori, 'Rock Music and Politics in Italy', p. 264.
55. See also Minganti, 'Jukebox Boys', in *Cultural Transmissions and Receptions*, ed. by Fehrenbach and Poiger.
56. Bermani, *Una storia cantata, 1962–1997*, p. 111.
57. Barbara Dane, *The Vietnam Songbook* (New York: The Guardian, 1969).
58. Ciarchi, 'Rudy Assuntino', p. 41.
59. Bermani, *Una storia cantata, 1962–1997*, p. 107.
60. Ibid. p. 109.
61. Undated press release (but likely from 1969), AIEdM, Fondo NCI, C. 34.
62. Letter, Gianni Bosio to Irwin Silber, 26 June 1968, AIEdM, Fondo EDG, C. 37.
63. Alessandro Portelli, *We Shall Not Be Moved. Musiche dagli Stati Uniti, 1969–2017* (Rome: Squilibri, 2018) (in press).
64. Barbara Dane, 'Il Folk Festival di Newport. Il solito affare', *Il Nuovo Canzoniere Italiano*, Sapere Edizioni/Edizioni del Gallo (November–December 1970), pp. 66–68. Various artists, *Avanti Popolo! Revolutionary Songs of the Italian Working Class*, Paredon Records, PAR01026, 1974.
65. See Alessandro Portelli, *La canzone popolare in America. La rivoluzione musicale di Woody Guthrie* (Bari: De Donato, 1975); idem, *La line del colore. Saggi sulla cultura afroamericana* (Rome:

Manifestolibri, 1994); idem, *America profonda. Due secoli raccontati da Harlan County, Kentucky* (Rome: Donzelli, 2011); and idem, *Badlands. Springsteen e l'America, il lavoro e i sogni* (Rome: Donzelli, 2015).

CHAPTER 11

❖

PC or not PC?
Some Reflections upon Political Correctness and its Influence on the Italian Language

Federico Faloppa

Public Enemy No. 1

In the aftermath of the election of Donald Trump as President of the United States of America, the Italian newspaper 'Il Sole 24 Ore' published an opinion piece entitled *In quel voto liberatorio la Waterloo del politicamente corretto*.[1] In order to explain why Donald Trump had won the election against all odds, its author, Luca Ricolfi, argued that the main reason for Trump's success had probably been the 'insofferenza per gli eccessi del politicamente corretto' [intolerance towards the excesses of the politically correct] which the candidate had clearly embodied in the eyes of his voters:

> [. . .] il secondo, e forse più importante, fattore del successo di Trump è l'insofferenza per gli eccessi del politicamente corretto [. . .] Da questo punto di vista il voto a Trump è stato anche un gesto liberatorio [. . .] Ma liberazione da che cosa? E liberazione di chi? Liberazione dal marchio di infamia che una parte della società americana, la parte bassa, sente sopra di sé. Spiace doverlo ricordare, ma [. . .] il politicamente corretto e i suoi derivati sono straordinarie macchine generatrici di distinzione sociale. Servono a definire un sopra e un sotto, un alto e un basso, un 'noi civili' e 'voi barbari' [. . .] La trasversalità del voto a Trump, forse, ci segnala proprio questo: che la rivolta contro l'establishment [. . .] esprime [. . .] il rifiuto di una parte della società americana, che non aderisce al credo dei benpensanti del nostro tempo, di essere stigmatizzata per le proprie idee, per i propri sentimenti, per il proprio modo di parlare [. . .] Una reazione che mostra che, dietro il voto a Trump, c'è anche una sorta di richiesta di cittadinanza, di riammissione nel consenso delle persone degne di rispetto.

> [[. . .] the second, and perhaps most important, factor of Trump's success is the intolerance towards the excesses of the politically correct [. . .] From this point of view, the vote for Trump was also a liberating gesture [. . .] But liberation from what, and release of whom? Liberation from the brand of infamy that a

part of American society, the lower part, feels is above it. Sorry to mention it, but [. . .] the politically correct and its derivatives are amazing machines for generating social distinction. They serve to define an above and a below, a high and a low, a 'we civilized people' and 'you barbarians' [. . .]. The transversal nature of the vote for Trump, perhaps, means precisely this: that the revolt against the establishment [. . .] also expresses [. . .] the rejection of being stigmatized for its own ideas, its own feelings, its own way of speaking by that part of American society which does not adhere to the conformist beliefs of our time. [. . .] A reaction showing that, behind the vote for Trump, there is also a sort of request for citizenship, for readmission into the assembly of people worthy of respect.]

Far from being eccentric, this explanation has been supported by several analysts both in Europe and in the USA.[2] Donald Trump, they say, has successfully turned his overt aversion to political correctness (from now on also PC) into one of his strongest arguments. While travelling across the USA during his campaign, Trump constantly attacked PC for being one of the country's biggest problems, and one of the enemies of that common sense that should be, instead, the best resource to solve those problems.[3] 'I refuse to be politically correct', said Trump the day after a gunman shot dead forty-nine people in a nightclub in Orlando, 'they have put political correctness above common sense, above your safety, and above all else'.

Despite blaming PC, neither Trump and his supporters nor any commentator managed to define in a clear way what they meant by it. Apparently, they did not need to, since PC had been sufficiently criticized and discredited in the USA and beyond, and had therefore become an easy target. Britain's right-wing tabloid *The Daily Mail* had issued frequent denunciations of political correctness 'gone mad' and railed against the hypocrisy of the 'metropolitan elite'.[4] In Germany, conservative journalists and politicians made similar complaints: after the assaults on women in Cologne on New Year's Eve 2015, for instance, a comment by the chief of police, Rainer Wendt, who claimed that leftists pressuring police officers to be *politisch korrekt* had prevented them from doing their jobs, was echoed by several media outlets.[5] In France, Marine Le Pen has condemned more traditional conservatives as 'paralysed by their fear of confronting political correctness'.[6] In Italy, beside *Il Giornale* and *Libero* — which discredit political correctness on a regular basis — the concept and its articulations are seen as a burden also by left-wing parties and liberal media.[7]

In Italian, this stigmatization is currently spread over different registers and can be found in a variety of discourses. By looking at *politically correct* and *politicamente corretto* (which translates both the US English cognate *political correctness* and the adjectival phrase *politically correct*) in wide corpora of Italian such as Italian Web (*ItWaC*) and Italian Web 2010 (*itTenTen*), it is possible to see that most collocations give the expressions a varied range of negative connotations and evaluations. In *ItWaC*, among the most frequent collocates of *politicamente corretto* (0.71 per million tokens) and *politically correct* (whose frequency looks higher: 1.7 per million tokens) there are, respectively, 'piagnisteo' (whimpering), 'infischia' (does not give a damn about), 'aborre' (to find repulsive), 'conformismo' (conformism) and 'conformista' (conformist), and 'buonismo', 'buonista' (do-goodery).[8] At cluster level, the finding is even more revealing. In *itTenTen*, for instance, left collocations — namely the cluster 'X del PC' — include 'trappole del PC', 'tranelli del PC' (PC traps), 'ipocrisie del PC' (PC two-facedness), 'schiavitù del PC' (PC slavery), 'dittatura' or 'egemonia del PC' (PC dictatorship, PC hegemony), 'dominio del PC' (PC control), 'moda del PC' (PC fashion), 'ossessione del PC' (PC obsession), 'mania del PC' (PC mania), 'follia del PC' (PC madness), 'virus del PC' (PC virus), 'prigione del PC' (PC prison), 'pastoie e moine del PC' (PC red tape), 'briglie del PC' (PC rein), 'vincoli del PC', 'lacci del PC' (PC ties), 'diktat del PC' (PC diktat), 'dogmi e tabù del PC' (PC dogma and taboo), 'aberrazioni linguistiche del PC' (PC linguistic aberrations). The PC mainly appears as a propagandistic tool with its 'retorica' (rhetoric), 'ideologi' (ideologues), 'conformismo ideologico' (ideological conformism), and 'sacerdoti' (priests, responsible for a hegemonic 'religione del PC', with its 'gregge', flock of followers), marked by 'superficialità' and 'ottusità' (superficiality and stupidity).[9]

The Birth of a Troublesome Label

If we move from a synchronic to a diachronic analysis, however, it becomes clear that there is no neat history of, or approach to, PC and PC-related expressions either in US English or in Italian. While in the last thirty years there have been several attempts to define PC, a complete and satisfying definition for American English has barely been achieved, as partially shown by Robin Tolmach Lakoff in *The Language War*.[10] There are of course lexicographic definitions, such as in Merriam-Webster (1993),[11] Christine Ammer's *Random House Dictionary of Idioms* (1997),[12] *The American Heritage Dictionary of the English Language* (fourth edition, 2000),[13] and *The Oxford American Dictionary and Thesaurus* (2003).[14] But all these definitions look formulaic, as if they had been drawn from glossaries rather than from usage. On the other hand, most attempts by non-lexicographers — Lakoff argues — would not constitute definitions in any objective sense, since virtually all of them may be influenced by partial and ideological interpretation. For 'a term on everyone's lips — Lakoff claimed in 2000 — PC remains remarkably elusive'.[15] What clearly does not sound elusive, however, are the campaigns *against* something called *political correctness* and *politically correct*.

In US English the adjectival phrase *politically correct* can already be found in early documents such as a verdict by the Judge of the Supreme Court James Wilson, who in 1793 argued that the use of 'The United States' instead of 'The people of the United States' was not 'politically correct'.[16] Some occurrences appear throughout the nineteenth century, for instance in an address to the Senate in February 1820 by Mr Richard Johnson of Kentucky in 'The Missouri Question' (reprinted in *Teachings of Patriots and Statesmen: Or, The 'Founders of the Republic' on Slavery*, 1860)[17] or a speech by Mr Brent of 17 February 1845, collected in the *Proceedings and Debates of the Convention of Louisiana* (1845).[18] However, in all these examples *politically correct* stands for 'politically wise', 'politically appropriate or advisable', 'politically defensible': a literal meaning that has nowadays disappeared.

In order to trace back the origin of the current expression and connotation we would need to refer back to the communist doctrine of the 1920s, where the phrase implied the idea of doing (and thinking) the right thing by following the party line. According to Geoffrey Hughes, the concept would date back to Mao Tse-Tung, and in particular to his edict *On Correcting Mistaken Ideas in the Party* (1929). By identifying spreaders of non-proletarian ideas with 'peasants and other elements of petty-bourgeois origin', Mao blamed the 'failure of the Party's leading bodies to wage a concerted and determined struggle against these incorrect ideas' and emphasized the importance of educating 'the members in the Party's correct line'.[19]

Although there is no evidence of a direct connection to Mao's thought, the expression appears in US English in 1932, when Harrison George, a leader of the US Communist Party (CPUSA), expressed his concern over the CPUSA while giving support for the United Farmers League regarding the distance between practicable and 'politically correct' doctrines ('We looked over the programme, but are sure that few farmers would ever understand it. Of course, it is "politically correct" to the last letter').[20] George's words reveal a polemical connotation, which in the same period was also stressed by the influential British Marxist John Strachey, who in 1934 claimed that political correctness was deemed to be a valuable criterion to establish whether a writer was good by the measure of the British Communist Party ('We are sometimes a little apt to pretend, to wish, to suggest that such writers [Marxists] are necessarily better writers because they are more politically correct than our fellow travellers'[21]). And Herbert Kohl argues that in the 1940s 'politically correct' was already perceived as a derogative epithet addressed to those too zealous and acritical towards the official line of the Communist Party, which was at the time aligned to a Stalinist position.[22] It was meant to demand political orthodoxy and, at the same time, to make fun of it, jokingly referring to doctrinaire approaches.

Scattered examples of doctrines or people being described as 'politically correct' in American communist publications from the 1930s in a tone of mockery have also been found by the intellectual historian L. D. Burnett.[23] However, these examples were mainly restricted to communist circles. In American English, the circulation of the expression — according to Ruth Perry — increased only with the publication of the sayings by Mao Tse-Tung in 1964, where the concept of 'political correctness' was clearly mentioned again.[24] *Politically correct* spread out within the American New Left in the second half of the 1960s, as recalled by Ruth Perry in *A Short History of the Term Politically Correct*, and it started having a wide circulation also in the feminist movement and eventually in the lesbian movement of the 1970s. In her essay *The Black Woman: An Anthology* (1970), Toni Cade Bambara with some irony claimed that 'a man cannot be politically correct and a [male] chauvinist, too'.[25] As a result, towards the end of the 1970s, the connotations of the expression were already taken mostly as ironic with reference to a standard set of ideas about politics, religion, and other issues, and were used jokingly and good-naturedly by people who sought to poke fun either at views that corresponded with that set (I sound pretty PC, don't I?), or at views that did not (that's not very PC of you).

The New Left, therefore, reinvigorated the expression, but with a different connotation: not to demand political orthodoxy or to be polemical towards the party line, but to make fun of whoever was or pretended to be politically orthodox. As Debra L. Schultz says: 'Throughout the 1970s and 1980s, the New Left, feminists, and progressives used their term politically correct ironically, as a guard against their own orthodoxy in social change efforts.'[26]

One of the most significant intra-Left disputes informing discussions of the 'politically correct' was the emergence of second wave feminism as a separate political force on the Left. As Bambara and other scholars have noted, the rise of the women's liberation movement in the late 1960s grew out of women activists' rejection of the male chauvinism of the New Left. Feminist critics pointed out that, as envisioned by the male leadership of the New Left, the radical politics of liberation was perfectly compatible with a traditional practice of subordinating women to men. As a radical feminist put it a few years later:

> Males in the 1960s tried to turn daughters off to [sic] their mothers' raps about how all men wanted was cunt — they turned this wise old woman knowledge that has been passed down from mother to daughter since the fall of the matriarchies into something that was known as unhip and unpolitical. The hippie chick became politically correct ass.[27]

In feminist statements, 'politically correct' sounded definitely sarcastic and ironic at the beginning of the 1980s, and the expression became very polemic when the feminist debate over sexuality escalated, hitting fever pitch in 1982, when a panel on 'Politically Correct/Politically Incorrect Sexuality' was held at the Bernard College 'Conference on Sexuality'. The conference marked a pivotal point in the debate, L. D. Burnett argues:[28] feminists who opposed pornography and certain sexual behaviours were labelled 'Politically correct' by their 'pro-sex' counterparts in the movement — a term meant as a sneer, suggesting that those women were succumbing to patriarchal influence.

The acronym 'PC' also began to be used with an ironic and derisive connotation in the 1980s.[29] Nevertheless 'political correctness' and 'politically correct' were exclusively used within the left or left-oriented movements until the second half of the 1980s. Then — and this was a turning point — the term was strongly re-launched and rebranded by the American right, which made it a fixed collocation by turning its meaning inside out.

The Right-Wing Appropriation of PC

All of a sudden, instead of being a phrase that left-wing activists used to criticize (and make fun of) dogmatic tendencies within their movements, *political correctness* became an argument for neo-conservatives, who managed to persuade public opinion that PC constituted a left-wing political programme that was seizing control of US universities and cultural institutions — and that they, in the name of freedom and the First Amendment of the US Constitution, were determined to stop it.

However, this was not an abrupt move. Neo-conservatives had been instigating a campaign against liberal academics for more than a decade. Starting in the mid-1970s, a handful of conservative donors had funded the creation of dozens of new think-tanks and 'training institutes'. They had awarded fellowships for conservative graduate students, postdoctoral positions, and professorships at prestigious universities. And their clear aim was to challenge what they saw as the supremacy of liberalism and attack left-leaning tendencies within academia.[30]

Starting in the late 1980s, this well-funded conservative movement entered the mainstream with a series of bestsellers that took aim at US higher education. The first, by the University of Chicago philosophy professor Allan Bloom, came out in 1987.[31] For hundreds of pages, *The Closing of the American Mind* argued that colleges were embracing a shallow 'cultural relativism' and abandoning long-established disciplines and standards in an attempt to appear liberal to their students. Bloom's bestseller sold more than half a million copies and inspired numerous imitations, among them Roger Kimball's *Tenured Radicals: How Politics Has Corrupted our Higher Education* (1990).[32] Like Bloom, Kimball argued that an 'assault on the canon' was taking place and that a politics of 'victimhood' had paralysed universities. As evidence, he cited the existence of departments such as African American Studies and Women's Studies. And he sarcastically quoted the titles of papers he had heard at academic conferences, such as 'Jane Austen and the Masturbating Girl' or 'The Lesbian Phallus: Does Heterosexuality Exist?'.[33]

One of the most influential pieces on (and against) PC, however, was not a book but a newspaper article published on 28 October 1990 in the *New York Times*: 'The Rising Hegemony of the Politically Correct'. Its author, Richard Bernstein, had been to Berkeley to write a report on student activism. But instead of finding student-led subversive initiatives, there he found an 'unofficial ideology of the university', through which 'a cluster of opinions about race, ecology, feminism, culture and foreign policy defines a kind of "correct" attitude toward the problems of the world'.[34] According to Bernstein, US colleges were threatened by 'a growing intolerance, a closing of debate, a pressure to conform'.

Bernstein's article generated a chain-reaction. In November, the *Wall Street Journal* columnist Dorothy Rabinowitz blamed the 'brave new world of ideological zealotry' in American colleges, a cultural as well as physical threat to all its opponents:

> PC-ism, as it has come to be called, reigns on campuses from sea to shining sea. Dissent from politically correct positions on women, minorities, multiculturalism and the like comes at a high cost — a cost that may include threats, vandalism, sit-ins, shout-downs, charges of racism and sexism and, frequently, administrative punishment.[35]

In December, *Newsweek* — which at the time had approximately three million readers — devoted its cover to the 'Thought police', by alerting its readership to the politically correct way to talk about race, sex, and ideas ('Taking Offence: Is This the New Enlightenment or the New McCarthyism?').[36] In January 1991 a similar approach was shared by the *New York Magazine*, which deplored the hands of the

'New Fascists' on US universities. In April a 'new intolerance' would be the object of an article in *Time Magazine*, and in June Dinesh D'Souza echoed Bloom and Kimball with his *Illiberal Education: The Politics of Race and Sex on Campus*.[37] Whereas Bloom had lamented the rise of relativism and Kimball had attacked what he called 'liberal fascism', and what he considered frivolous lines of scholarly inquiry, D'Souza argued that admissions policies that took race into consideration were producing a 'new segregation on campus' and 'an attack on academic standards'. This accusation did not pass unobserved, also because *The Atlantic* printed a 12,000-word excerpt of D'Souza's book as its June cover story.[38] And D'Souza, as much as Bloom and Kimball, came to be regularly cited in the flood of anti-PC articles that kept appearing in publications such as *The New York Times* and *Newsweek*. When they did, the authors were cited as neutral authorities, and further articles uncritically repeated their arguments.

To some extent, these books and articles were responding — from a right-wing perspective — to some genuine changes taking place within academia. First, some colleges had been (and would be) implementing their speech codes to sanction verbal assaults which could threaten 'the security of the university community, the rights of its individual members, or its basic norms of academic integrity'.[39] And this generated controversy and was seen as the imposition of a censorship on freedom of speech, although a 1994 study of speech codes at the twenty largest public universities in the USA would find that only half had policies of any kind regulating 'hostile or harassing speech or conduct' (and even these were rarely enforced),[40] and the 'speech code crisis' would end up being a well-manipulated hysteria rather than a threatening reality.[41] It is true that certain campus activist groups in the late 1980s and early 1990s adopted the slogan 'P.C. and proud' to advocate a non-offensive and more inclusive language. But this was an initiative limited to a handful of colleges (such as the University of Michigan in Detroit).[42] Thirdly, quite a few scholars had become increasingly sceptical in the second half of the 1980s about whether it was possible to talk about universal truths that lay beyond language, representation, and cultural appropriation. And it was also true that many universities were creating new 'studies departments', which started emphasizing the cultural contributions of groups that had previously been excluded from academia and from the canon, such as queer people and ethnic minorities. But far from been eccentric, these departments were just reflecting new social realities. The demographics of college students were undeniably changing: by 1990, only two thirds of Americans under 18 were 'white', and in California, more than 50% of first-year students were already 'non-white'. Changes to undergraduate curricula therefore only reflected changes in the student population. This new awareness aimed at rebalancing the curriculum, not at banning the old one, i.e. 'dumping the [Western] classics', as conservatives were saying.[43]

The responses that the conservative bestsellers offered to these changes were disproportionate and misleading, the most misleading aspect of these books being the way they claimed that their adversaries were too 'political', wanted to smash a well-established canon, and threatened 'the humanistic tradition', which therefore needed to be preserved. Of course, these crusaders against political correctness were as political as their opponents. As Jane Mayer documents in her book *Dark Money: The Hidden History of the Billionaires Behind the Rise of the Radical Right*, Bloom and D'Souza were funded by networks of conservative donors who had spent the 1980s building programmes that they hoped would create a new counter-intelligentsia. The scuffles over syllabuses were indeed part of a broader political programme, and became instrumental in forging a new conservative alliance across the country between intellectuals, corporations, and populist movements. By making fun of professors who spoke in language that most people considered incomprehensible ('The Lesbian Phallus'), wealthy Ivy League graduates could pose as an anti-elite. And by mocking courses on writers such as Alice Walker and Toni Morrison, they made a racial appeal to white people who felt as if they were losing their country. As the 1990s wore on, because multiculturalism was associated with globalization — and the loss of many jobs — attacking it allowed conservatives to displace responsibility for the hardship that many of their constituents were facing. It was not the slashing of social services, lowered taxes, union busting or outsourcing that was the cause of their problems: it was the PC obsession, a winning argument that was and — as the election of Donald Trump shows — still is hard to eradicate.

PC was a useful invention for the Republican right because it helped the movement to drive a wedge between working-class people and the Democrats who claimed to speak for them. 'Political correctness' became a term used to drum into the public imagination the idea that there was a deep divide between the ordinary people and the liberal elite, who sought to control the speech and thoughts of the former. Opposition to political correctness also became a way to rebrand racism in ways that were politically acceptable in the post-civil-rights era. Generally speaking, as Robin Tolmach Lakoff argues in *The Language War*, 'Political correctness' had become an epithet of choice used to discredit a wide array of discursive practices generally thought of as leftist, including the adoption of self-descriptions which originated among minorities and the postmodern doubting of the reality of historical truth and the trustworthiness of authority.[44]

Soon, Republican politicians were echoing on the national stage the message that had been product-tested in the academy. In May 1991, President George Bush gave a commencement speech at the University of Michigan. In it, he identified political correctness as a major danger to the USA. 'Ironically, on the 200th anniversary of our Bill of Rights, we find free speech under assault throughout the United States', Bush said. 'The notion of political correctness has ignited controversy across the land', but, he warned, 'In their own Orwellian way, crusades that demand correct behavior crush diversity in the name of diversity.'[45]

As a result, 'politically correct' became a real mantra in the early 1990s. By querying the Lexis/Nexis News Database, PC (both *political correctness* and *politically correct*) rises from 3 occurrences in 1983 to 30 in 1985 to 450 in 1990.[46] In ProQuest, the digital database of US newspapers and magazines, the cluster 'politically correct' can barely be found before 1990. In 1990, it appears 700 times, while in 1991 and 1992 2,500 and 2,800 times respectively. While no article mentions the cluster in 1985, 6,985 articles contain the expression in 1995.[47]

Close Encounters of a PC Kind

The early 1990s are precisely the time in which the expression, already heavily connoted, enters the Italian language. According to some major monolingual dictionaries, PC entered the Italian language between 1991 and 1992. All dictionaries agree that *politicamente corretto* was adopted as a calque from US English, but — surprisingly — they all provide definitions underlining the supposed positive effects of PC on language and society, by assuming (and overtly suggesting) that there had been a movement calling itself 'politicamente corretto', and by ignoring the semantic negative shift that had already emerged in US English.

The *Grande Dizionario della Lingua Italiana* (Gradit) does not record the entry either under the letter C (*Corretto*) or under the letter P (*Politicamente*): the volume PERF-PO was published in 1986, and the absence of the entry would be evidence that the expression was not common in Italian before that date.[48]

The Devoto-Oli is the only dictionary that lists the expression as an autonomous headword, both in English and Italian:

> *Politically correct*: loc. ingl. in it. agg. e s.m. lo stesso che politicamente corretto.
>
> [Politically correct: Engl. phrase in It. adj. and noun the same as *politicamente corretto*.]
>
> *Politicamente corretto*: loc. usata come agg. e s.m. — espressione di origine nordamericana che indica condotte, comportamenti, modi di dire improntati al pieno rispetto dell'identità politica, etnica, religiosa, sessuale, sociale, ecc. di altri soggetti. Estens. Rispettoso nei confronti di soggetti deboli o minoritari. Traduzione dell'espressione angloamericana politically correct. Sec. XX.
>
> [Politically correct: phrase used as adj. and noun — an expression of North American origin that indicates behaviours and idioms marked by full respect for the political, ethnic, religious, sexual, social identity, etc. of other subjects. Ext. Respectful towards unprivileged people and minorities. Translation of the American English expression politically correct. Twentieth Century.][49]

The Zingarelli lists the English original expression with a cross-reference to the Italian headword *corretto*.

> *Politically correct:* loc. ingl. propr. 'politicamente corretto', movimento politico americano affermatosi alla fine degli anni '80 del Novecento, fautore di una maggiore giustizia sociale e di una effettiva uguaglianza per le minoranze, gli emarginati e sim. 1991 loc. sost.m.inv.e loc. agg. inv. politicamente corretto.
>
> *Corretto*: Politicamente corretto, detto di atteggiamento o linguaggio non offensivo nei confronti dei soggetti deboli o minoritari (trad. dalla loc. ingl. politically correct).
>
> [Politically correct: Engl. phrase 'politically correct', the American political movement that emerged at the end of the 80s of the twentieth century, asking for greater social justice and effective equality for minorities and marginalized people. 1991 noun and adj. phrase politically correct.
>
> Correct: Politically correct, said of non-offensive attitude or language towards marginalised people and minorities (translated from English phrase *politically correct*).][50]

The Sabatini–Coletti only registers the expression in English, while in Gradit the expression can be found under the entry *politicamente*.

> Politically correct: loc. ingl. inv.; in it. loc. agg. sost. loc. agg. politicamente corretto, soprattutto nel l. giornalistico. loc. sost. m. movimento politico che rivendica parità di diritti per le minoranze etniche e sociali. a.1991.
>
> [Politically correct: Engl. phrase; in it. adj. and noun phrase. Politically correct, especially in the language of the press. Noun phrase. Political movement that claims equal rights for ethnic and social minorities. a.1991.][51]

Zingarelli and Sabatini–Coletti are the only dictionaries that give a specific date for the first occurrence in Italian: the other monolingual dictionaries vaguely indicate the twentieth century. However, no examples or etymological clarifications — has the expression first entered the Italian language as a calque or as non-adapted borrowing? What was the first occurrence? — are provided.

Semantic Shifts and Cultural Adaptation

Formally, the expression already existed in Italian as a free collocation. Instances of the phrase *politicamente corretto* can be found towards the end of the nineteenth century in *La Gazzetta Piemontese* ('Dopo la vittoria di un voto, prendere dei ministri fra i vinti del voto non pare al polemista una cosa ruralmente dicevole, ma ciò sarà politicamente corretto, e basta' [After the victory by one vote, to include ministers from those defeated in the vote does not seem, to the polemist, an appropriate thing to say, but this will be politically correct, and that's it]; 'Ma prima un grande fatto era accaduto, e quel mio voto, per quanto politicamente corretto o determinato da circostanze di primo ordine generali, era stato anche la conseguenza di una circostanza non speciale mia, ma comune a tutti noi, pur sempre d'indole particolare però al Collegio che rappresento' [But a great event had happened, and that vote of mine, though politically correct or determined by general circumstances, had also been the consequence of a circumstance common to all of us, although always of a kind peculiar to the College that I represent][52]), in the *Giornale degli economisti e annali di economia* ('Non è indiscreto il chiedere che non indugi troppo, perché non è politicamente corretto lasciare il paese in preda all'agitazione elettorale senza che il governo abbia in modo chiaro e netto affermato il proprio programma' [It is not imprudent to ask that we do not delay too much, because it is not politically correct to leave the country in the grip of electoral agitation until the government has clearly stated its programme]),[53] and in *Il nuovo Rosmini periodico scientifico e letterario* (finding 'politicamente corretto un tale linguaggio' [such a language politically correct]),[54] but as in English these instances stand for 'politically appropriate or advisable'.

Some random examples, with the same connotation, can also be found at a later stage, but the expression does not seem to be very common in Italian until the beginning of the 1990s, as argued by the aforementioned lexicographers. Even in the 1960s, whereas PC seems to flourish in US English, examples are scarce: their meanings seem to be influenced by a vague (ideological) context, in which a sense of belonging to a political orthodoxy and adherence to moral integrity and principles, rather than an ironic detachment from that very orthodoxy, is emphasized.[55] And there is no clear evidence that they are connected to the reprise of the Maoist and communist interpretation or to the Anglo-American left-wing discourse.[56]

At the beginning of the 1990s the frequency suddenly increases, due to the evident influence of the Anglo-American debate on political correctness. The phrase becomes more and more frequent in both its original English form, as a non-adapted lexical borrowing (which therefore often requires inverted commas, italics, or an explicatory gloss), and in translation as a calque which can become morphologically productive.[57]

In the summer of 1991, the lexical borrowing (a case of loan translation, more precisely) is still glossed in order to explain its origin and meaning to the unfamiliar Italian readership:

> Nelle più prestigiose università americane, a Princeton come ad Harvard, a Stanford come nel Michigan o a Berkeley, son numerosi i professori che, pur di sedurre si sottomettono alle nuove regole, e scrivono, dicono, insegnano solo cose 'politicamente corrette' (o pc, come accorciano oltre Oceano). 'Politicamente scorretto' è dire maschilmente 'seminario', invece di 'ovulario'.
>
> [In the most prestigious American universities, at Princeton, Harvard, Stanford, Michigan or Berkeley, there are many professors who, to be popular, submit themselves to the new rules, and write, say and teach only 'politically correct' things (or pc, as they shorten the expression on the other side of the Ocean). 'Politically incorrect' is to say in a masculine way 'seminar' instead of 'ovular'.]
>
> È impossibile prevedere quale forza effettiva avrà l'onda di opposizione alle celebrazioni del cinquecentesimo anniversario della scoperta dell'America, da parte di quanti negano radicalmente che scoperta ci sia stata. Ma qualcosa già sappiamo della forza del discorso politicamente corretto, il severo codice intellettuale e liberale che induce nelle università e nei gruppi giovani a non prendere mai posizione contro le minoranze.
>
> [It is impossible to predict the force of the wave of opposition to the celebrations of the 500th anniversary of the discovery of America, by those who radically deny that there was any discovery. But we already know something about the power of the politically correct discourse, the severe intellectual and liberal code that leads universities and young groups never to take a stand against minorities.]
>
> Boutros Ghali forse si ravvederà, ma nel frattempo se ne è uscito con strane dichiarazioni: molto politically correct, come si dice in America, molto allergiche a quella che ritiene una fissazione dell'Occidente bianco sulla Jugoslavia, all'indifferenza dello stesso Occidente di fronte a sciagure come quella somala.
>
> [Boutros Ghali will perhaps repent, but in the meantime, he has come out with odd statements: very politically correct, as they say in America, very allergic to what he considers a fixation of the white West on Yugoslavia, to the indifference of the West in the face of misfortunes such as those of the Somali people.][58]

PC is mainly seen as a US cultural and linguistic 'trend' whose aim is to impose a new language and cultural conformism, dictated by a blunt interpretation of multiculturalism:

> Perché la diaspora intellettuale innescata dal 'multiculturalismo' non si esaurisce certo nell'African Renaissance. Le università la conoscono sotto la sintetica formula di Politically correct, i cui effetti stanno a cavallo tra il tragico e il ridicolo. In sintesi. Quella della società aperta e multirazziale, dicono i 'movimentisti', è una frode, una panzana. Non esistono una storia e una verità oggettiva (ci risiamo. . .). Mentre evidentissimi sono i presupposti eurocentristi, maschilisti e imperialisti dell'America odierna. Dunque, a mare Shakespeare e Virgilio. E ciascuno sia libero di ricostruire la propria storia etnica, e di genere sessuale. Dunque, pensiero e docenti neri per i neri. Pensiero e docenti lesbiche per le lesbiche. Pensiero e docenti gay per i gay. Altro che Torre di Babele! Davvero l'ideale, per rimettere sui giusti binari un sistema scolastico che per ammissione generale ha toccato il fondo. Non manca, del resto, chi manifesta una certa comprensione; quasi che questo sia un passaggio difficile, eppure necessario.
>
> [Because the intellectual diaspora triggered by 'multiculturalism' certainly does not end with the African Renaissance. Universities know it under the synthetic formula of Politically correct, whose effects lie between the tragic and the ridiculous. Briefly: an open and multiracial society, radicals say, is a fraud, a lie. There is no objective history and truth (here we go again. . .). While the Eurocentric, masculine and imperialist assumptions of today's America are very evident. So, get rid of Shakespeare and Virgil. Anyone should be free to write his/her own ethnic and gendered history. Therefore, black thought and black teachers for blacks. Lesbian thought and lesbian teachers for lesbians. Gay thought and gay teachers for gays. Forget the Tower of Babel! This is really an ideal option in order to put on the right tracks a school system that by general admission has touched the bottom. However, there are people that express a certain understanding; as if this were a difficult, but necessary, stage.][59]

However, as was soon underlined by Alberto Arbasino and other commentators, PC has gone beyond American borders to become a sort of 'intolleranza internazionale' [international intolerance], a widespread 'conformismo terroristico' [a terrorist conformism], an Italian 'perdita di trebisonda' [loss of control].[60] Far from referring only to an American context, political correctness has now become an imported fashion to be sceptical about, if not firmly to reject:

> Il nostro Paese rifiuta la moda del *politically correct*
> Il trionfo dello 'scorretto' L'Italia è una patria di sfacciati?
> [. . .] Non si chiamano più neri ma afroamericani o, ancora più 'correttamente', 'membri della diaspora africana'. Quando si scrive 'human' o 'humanity' si sottolineano in neretto le tre fatidiche lettere 'man', per indicare il perenne occultamento linguistico della donna. Gran parte della popolazione istruita degli Usa trema al solo pensiero di dire 'inabile' in pubblico al posto dell'eufemismo 'differentemente abile'. Una maledizione segna le parole: una spada di Damocle pende sul capo di milioni di persone colte, di intellettuali e giornalisti d'America, pronta ad abbattersi sulla loro ignavia lessicale. Guai a sbagliare su un'espressione, si è irrimediabilmente fottuti nella carriera e nei

> rapporti sociali. E in Italia? Come ci comportiamo, linguisticamente parlando, con le minoranze, con gli immigrati, con le donne, con i gay? Sta per piombare anche da noi, sull'esempio Usa, il ciclone del 'politically correct'? O ci lascia indenni?
>
> [Our country rejects the fashion of *politically correct*
> The triumph of 'incorrect': is Italy a country of shameless people?
> [. . .] They are no longer called blacks but Afro-Americans or, even more 'correctly', 'members of the African diaspora'. When one writes 'human' or 'humanity' the three fatal letters 'man' are written in bold, to indicate the perennial linguistic concealment of the woman. Much of America's educated population trembles at the thought of saying 'unable' in public instead of the 'differently able' euphemism. A curse marks the words: a sword of Damocles hangs over the heads of millions of educated American people, intellectuals and journalists, ready to strike down their lexical ignorance. Woe betide you to make a mistake on an expression: you are hopelessly fucked in career and social relationships. And in Italy? How do we behave, linguistically speaking, with minorities, immigrants, women, gays? Is the cyclone of the 'politically correct' going to fall on us too, following the US example? Or it will leave us unscathed?][61]

This exaggerated scepticism, Flavio Baroncelli suggested in his well-known (and celebrated) 1996 pamphlet *Il razzismo è una gaffe. Vizi e virtù del politicamente corretto* [Racism is a blunder. Vices and Virtues of the Politically Correct], could have been caused by two main factors: in Italy there was 'una sensibilità peculiare perché qualcuno ricorda, e tutti conosciamo, grottesche vicende linguistiche del ventennio fascista' [a peculiar sensitivity because someone remembers, and we all know, grotesque linguistic events of the Fascist period]; Italy does not sees itself as a former colonial power, and therefore does not feel guilty 'nei confronti dell'Altro' [towards the Other]; in Italy the complex American debate has from the beginning been oversimplified and often reduced to a superficial and alien lexical and lexicographic quarrel.[62]

Also, in Italy, PC has been often dismissed and mistaken as an unnecessary variety of euphemism. Its critics claim that PC has introduced above all a euphemistic overflow in the Italian language.[63] But, as argued by Flavio Baroncelli and Michael Minutiello, this assumption is based on an oversimplification.[64] And, as Minutiello reminds us, euphemisms were not a new phenomenon in Italian, but had been widely studied in Italy since the publication of Nora Galli de' Paratesi's *Le brutte parole. Semantica dell'eufemismo* (1964). As we know, euphemism is a mild or indirect word or expression substituted for one considered to be too harsh or blunt when referring to something unpleasant or embarrassing. It serves to avoid linguistic interdictions or taboos, which according to Galli de Paratesi 'dipendono tutti da un'unica causa psicologica' [all result from a single psychological cause], i.e. the speakers feel uncomfortable when, or just before, pronouncing them. The origin of euphemistic phenomena would be then totally extra-linguistic, and the domains more affected by linguistic interdiction are normally sexuality, religion, social labelling, politics, and physical handicaps. As Minutiello correctly points out, however, it would be simplistic to say that a word, or an expression, is a euphemism: whether its use is euphemistic depends on the context. Moreover, PC was not really interested in finding milder words for professions — as the Italian critics argue by using the famous example of *operatore ecologico* instead of *spazzino* [street cleaner], but in promoting a plural society where ethnic, sexual and social minorities were equally represented, also — but not only or exclusively — in language and discourse.

If immediately after 1991 most occurrences referred more or less explicitly to Anglo-American culture, however, references to the original context tend to decrease over time, as clearly shown by Minutiello with regard to media discourse. The expression increasingly loses its original meaning, in order to cover a broader spectrum of contexts and meanings, which have little to do with the Anglo-American PC: the tendency towards stereotyping is clear.[65]

However, less sceptical approaches can be found as well, not only as a reaction to the generally biased interpretation, but — and more importantly — to advocate a better representation of reality and to acknowledge imminent and inevitable social change:

> . . .Nella generale attesa per il 'Malcolm X' di Spike Lee. . . constatiamo che 'politically correct' non è soltanto la formula di una moda cui conformisticamente adeguarsi ma anche, almeno per i migliori, l'obiettivo di un sincero sforzo di non allontanare la fantasia cinematografica dalla realtà.
>
> [. . .Waiting for Spike Lee's 'Malcolm X'. . . we see that 'politically correct' is not only the formula of a fashion to which we need to conform but also, at least for the best directors, the final goal of a sincere effort not to move the cinematographic fantasy away from reality.][66]
>
> Università [. . .]: Molte le adesioni alla linea rosa: Perugia, Palermo, Salerno. Il 'politicamente corretto' avanza: tutti si augurano che sia un passo verso la pace e non l'inasprirsi della guerra.
>
> [University [. . .]: there are many supporting the pink line: Perugia, Palermo, Salerno. The 'politically correct' moves forward: everyone hopes that it is a step towards peace and not an escalation to war.][67]
>
> Nessun americano direbbe: 'Guarda, guarda la cinesina'. Mi hanno spiegato: ma vedi, cinesina non è un insulto, è un vezzeggiativo. Io continuo a pensare che sarebbe meglio dire 'la giovane donna cinese', e non la 'cinesina'. Un'esagerazione? Forse. Ma solo perché non siamo in un ristorante newyorkese in cui potrebbe essere seduta una cinese-americana che alla parola 'cinesina' avrebbe avuto uno scatto di fastidio. Mi rendo conto che il linguaggio non è tutto. Ma è molto. Soprattutto perché spesso è inconscio. Perciò ferisce. . . Bisogna stare molto attenti a non ferire. Allora si dice: 'So che questa barzelletta è politicamente scorretta ma io la racconto comunque perché tutti sanno che io non ho pregiudizi' [. . .]. Bisogna sapere che sta arrivando anche in Italia il politicamente corretto. Arriva per forza. Arriva con la sensibilità degli immigrati, degli stranieri. Arriva con lo scontro preannunciato fra chi sta arrivando nel paese e coloro che sono già qui. Sempre meglio chiedere: 'Tu come vuoi essere chiamato?' e agire di conseguenza.
>
> [No American would say, 'Look, look at the little Chinese woman'. They

explained to me: but you see, 'little Chinese woman' is not an insult, it is a term of endearment. I still think that it would be better to say 'the young Chinese woman', and not 'little Chinese woman'. An exaggeration? Maybe. But just because we are not in a New York restaurant where a Chinese-American customer could be annoyed to hear the word 'little Chinese woman'. I realize that language is not everything. But it is a lot. Above all because it is often unconscious. Therefore it hurts. . . We must be very careful not to hurt. Then people say: 'I know that this joke is politically incorrect but I tell it anyway because everyone knows that I have no prejudice' [. . .]. We need to know that politically correct is also coming to Italy. It will necessarily come. It will come with the sensitivity of immigrants and foreigners. It will come with the predicted clash between those who are arriving and those who are already here. It is always better to ask 'How do you want to be called?', and act accordingly.][68]

Some PC Linguistic Innovations in the Italian Language

Though overtly and predominantly criticized, PC has nonetheless caused the rise of a new awareness on some key issues, i.e. social and gender equal opportunities, dynamic demographics, multiculturalism and multicultural society. And it has to some extent required the alignment of some of these challenges and transformations with a fairly consistent (although disputed) 'mutamento di sensibilità linguistica' [change of linguistic sensitivity].[69] Among the possible examples, one could mention the widely studied and debated sexism in language,[70] the terminology related to disability,[71] and words and expressions referring to ethnic origin and skin colour, such as *nero/negro/di colore* [black, negro, of colour].

PC's impact on this last-mentioned case has been extensively documented,[72] but it is worth mentioning as an emblematic case. Already in the second half of the 1960s — in the post 'Malcolm X' era, as suggested by Marazzi[73] — some established translators (Bruno Cartosio and Franco Fabbri) started using *nero* instead of *negro* not for PC sensitivity, but in order to translate *black* in a more accurate way, which had become a very loaded term in US English because of its political value (*Black power*). For similar reasons, *afro-americano* started appearing as a political term too at the end of the 1960s: in the *Autobiografia di Malcolm X*, written by Alex Haley and translated into Italian in 1967 by Roberto Giammanco, *afro-americano* is frequently seen;[74] in Bruno Cartosio's 1973 translation of *From Sundown to Sunup* [Lo schiavo americano dal tramonto all'alba] by George P. Rawick, *nero* and *afro-americano* are both used.[75]

At the beginning of the 1970s, the expression *di colore* appears too, as a calque of the Anglo-American *colored, person of color*, and as an unmarked option for *negro*. The growing presence of *nero* and *di colore* did not immediately inhibit the use of *negro*, which — especially as an adjective — was totally acceptable in media discourse about the Afro-American community in the USA (*A Hollywood la risata è negra* [In Hollywood, laughing is black], *La Stampa*, 28 August 1983) and the new migrants moving to Italy from Africa between the 1970s and the 1980s ('il 24 per cento degli italiani non vorrebbe avere una relazione sentimentale con un negro' [24%

of Italians would not want to have a romantic relationship with a negro]), *Epoca*, 13 December 1987; 'Negra muore asfissiata, senza un aiuto' [Negro woman dies asphyxiated, without any assistance], *La Stampa*, 3 November 1988, on the death of a Nigerian woman).

This terminology seems to have been inconsistently used for more than a decade. As Leonardo Buonomo has shown, for instance, in the Italian adaptation of the racial terminology of the popular TV series *The Jeffersons* (1974–85; in Italy from 1985), we see 'una deplorevole mancanza di attenzione alle diverse connotazioni e sfumature, oltre che alle implicazioni ideologiche e sociali' [a deplorable lack of attention to the different connotations and nuances, as well as to the ideological and social implications], together with a lack of consistency on the paradigmatic axis, i.e. about the different signifiers which would be syntagmatically legitimate in that context.[76] This 'disinvoltura lessicale' [lexical nonchalance] would be evident, for example, in the use of *negro/a* to translate both the Anglo-American *nigger* and *black*, or arbitrarily to introduce *negro/nero* where the original script does not explicitly mention them ('The day my mother marries is the day your husband changes to the right color' in Italian becomes 'Il giorno in cui mia madre si sposa, sarà il giorno in cui tuo marito diventerà *nero* come te'). According to Buonomo, this adaptation would imply that in Italian 'the right color cannot be the black one, and the black pride of a black person is incomprehensible to the Italian public'.[77]

But this starts to change with the introduction of the PC debate in Italy. The awareness brought about by political correctness and the different connotations and reception of this terminology are gradually — although not peacefully — acknowledged in media discourse and lexicography. Whereas in De Felice-Duro, *Dizionario della lingua e della civiltà italiana contemporanea* (1985), *negro* is still both adjective and noun, and its meaning does not seem to carry any special connotation,[78] in the *Vocabolario Treccani della lingua italiana* (1989), its definition has already slightly changed:

> Frequente l'uso sostantivato per indicare gli individui di razza negra [. . .]. Nell'uso attuale, negro è talvolta avvertito o usato con valore spregiativo, sicché [. . .] in ogni accezione riferibile alle popolazioni di colore e alle loro culture gli si preferisce spesso (analogamente a quanto avvenuto in Paesi in cui la questione razziale era particolarmente viva) l'aggettivo e sostantivo *nero* (corrispondente all'inglese *black* e al francese *noir*).
>
> [The use as a noun to indicate individuals of Negro race is quite frequent [. . .]. In the current use, Negro is sometimes perceived or used with derogatory value, so [. . .] when referring to people of colour and their cultures the adjective/noun *nero* (corresponding to English *black* and French *noir*) is preferable (as happened in countries where racial issues were particularly strong).][79]

Whether accepted or rejected, by 1995–96, the opposition *nero* vs *negro* had been fully acknowledged in public and media discourse:

> Per il 50% degli italiani la parola *negro* è da ritenersi offensiva.
>
> [For 50% of Italians the word *negro* is to be considered offensive.][80]

Mi riferisco al sostantivo e aggettivo 'negro' pressoché bandito dall'uso politicamente corretto a favore di nero su imitazione di quanto avviene in inglese. Non so chi abbia iniziato a parlare di neri anziché di negri o se si sia trattato di un automatismo di traduzione. . . fatto sta che da diversi anni è stata introdotta in italiano l'antinomia *nero negro* che arriva dall'inglese *nigger*.

[I mean the noun and adjective *negro*, almost banished from the politically correct use in favour of *nero*, to imitate what happens in English. I do not know who started talking about *neri* instead of *negri*, or if it was lack of thought. . . the fact is that several years ago the opposition *nero* vs *negro*, which comes from English *nigger*, was definitely introduced in Italian.][81]

'Letture', periodico dei Paolini, difende il diritto di cittadinanza di 'una parola che rischiava (e forse rischia ancora) di essere immolata sull'altare del politicamente corretto'. Se una differenza tra nero e negro è ora avvertita nella lingua italiana lo si deve al confronto con qualcosa di estraneo alla nostra tradizione, nella quale i due continuatori del latino *nigru(m)* sono convissuti pacificamente per secoli, scambiandosi le parti indifferentemente.

[*Letture*, a periodical published by the clerical congregation of the Paulines, defends the right of citizenship of 'a word that risked (and perhaps still risks) being immolated on the altar of the politically correct'. If a difference between *nero* and *negro* is now perceived in the Italian language, this must have been caused by something that does not belong to our tradition, in which the two continuators of the Latin *nigru(m)* have lived peacefully for centuries, exchanging their roles indifferently.][82]

In italiano, la parola negro non è mai stata offensiva [. . .] per gli americani, invece, è offensiva la parola nigger. . . gli americani politicamente corretti non sbagliano quando chiamano black un cittadino afroamericano, perché cosi ritengono di riscattare questo cittadino da una definizione umiliante. . . sbagliano gli italiani, quando dicono (o scrivono) nero, perché, cosi facendo, mostrano complessi di inferiorità [. . .] e atteggiamenti subalterni nei confronti della correttezza politica imposta dagli americani.

[In Italian, the word negro has never been offensive [. . .] To Americans, however, the word nigger is offensive. . . politically correct Americans are not mistaken when they call an African-American citizen black, because they believe they spare this citizen a humiliating definition. . . Italians are wrong when they say (or write) *nero*, because, in doing so, they show an inferiority complex [. . .] and subaltern attitudes towards the political correctness imposed by the Americans.][83]

An Open Conclusion

In mainstream media language, PC has biased connotations, for it has been seen at various levels and from different political points of view as an unnecessary imposition, but it has also managed to introduce and spread across wide audiences a new awareness of the importance of labelling, in relation to linguistic and social change from a diachronic and synchronic perspective. It has definitely pushed further the discussion on *sessismo* in language, which in Italy started in the 1970s and was then fostered by Alma Sabatini's *Il sessismo nella lingua italiana* (1986), and the critical reflection on paradigms (such as skin colour and disability) that previously had never been challenged in a systematic way. Conversely, because of its overextended meaning and usage, PC has acquired the ability to recast old news as once again newsworthy, through its enduring capacity to act as a discursive frame for a wide and diversified range of topics seen as inherently problematic, and to be used against alleged PC stances and supporters to debunk and ridicule them, as had already happened in American English. The feeling is that the more it is attacked, the more evidence emerges of its disturbing influence on the Italian language and culture. After all, the 'Waterloo' to which columnist Luca Ricolfi refers in the article quoted at the very beginning of this chapter could be seen as eponymous not of a random defeat, but of the defeat of an enemy that could not be ignored.

Notes to Chapter 11

1. Luca Ricolfi, 'In quel voto liberatorio la Waterloo del politicamente corretto', *Il Sole 24 Ore*, 13 November 2016, <http://www.ilsole24ore.com/art/commenti-e-idee/2016-11-13/in-quel-voto-liberatorio-waterloo-politicamente-corretto-102134.shtml?uuid=AD2jXWuB> [accessed 16 October 2017]. Cf. also Fiamma Nirenstein, 'La prima grande sconfitta del politicamente corretto', *Il Giornale*, 10 November 2016, <http://www.ilgiornale.it/news/politica/grande-sconfitta-politicamente-corretto-1329857.html> [accessed 16 October 2017].
2. Taki, 'This election was the politically correct vs the politically incorrect', *The Spectator*, 12 November 2016, <https://www.spectator.co.uk/2016/11/this-election-was-the-politically-correct-vs-the-politically-incorrect/> [accessed 16 October 2017]; James Taranto, 'Trump vs. Political Correctness', *The Wall Street Journal*, 15 November 2016, <https://www.wsj.com/articles/trump-vs-political-correctness-1479233123> [accessed on 16 October 2017]; Moira Weigel, 'Political correctness: how the right invented a phantom enemy', *The Guardian*, 30 November 2016, <https://www.theguardian.com/us-news/2016/nov/30/political-correctness-how-the-right-invented-phantom-enemy-donald-trump> [accessed on 16 October 2017]; François Dufour, 'J'avais pronostiqué la victoire de Donald Trump. Les 18 signes qui ne trompaient pas', *L'Obs*, 13 November 2016, <http://leplus.nouvelobs.com/contribution/1590270-j-avais-pronostique-la-victoire-de-donald-trump-les-18-signes-qui-ne-trompaient-pas.html> [accessed on 16 October 2017].
3. In the first debate during the primary elections, Fox News anchor-woman Megyn Kelly asked Trump how he would reply to those accusing him of being a misogynist: 'You've called women you don't like "fat pigs", "dogs", "slobs", and "disgusting animals".' And Trump answered, to the applause of the audience: 'I think the big problem this country has is being politically correct. . . I've been challenged by so many people, and I don't frankly have time for total political correctness. And to be honest with you, this country doesn't have time either' (<http://www.facebook.com/FoxNews/videos/10153545049191336/> [accessed on 16 October 2017].
4. <http://www.dailymail.co.uk>.
5. 'Wendt beklagt: Politiker fordern von Polizisten "politische Korrektheit"', *Epoch Times*, 26 January 2016, <http://www.epochtimes.de/politik/deutschland/wendt-beklagt-politiker-fordern-von-polizisten-politische-korrektheit-a1301033.html> [accessed on 16 October 2017].
6. Emmanuel Galiero, 'Marine Le Pen se voit comme une "exception" de la présidentielle', *Le Figaro*, 3 September 2016, <http://www.lefigaro.fr/politique/2016/09/03/01002-20160903ARTFIG00078-marine-le-pen-se-voit-comme-une-exception-de-la-presidentielle.php> [accessed on 16 October 2017].
7. Cf. Giovanni Orsina, 'La crisi della sinistra nel mondo che si trasforma', *La Stampa*, 22 February 2017, <http://www.lastampa.it/2017/02/22/cultura/opinioni/editoriali/la-crisi-della-sinistran-nel-mondo-che-si-trasforma-w7fvEpZdF2dbzvV8vWHfSI/pagina.html> [accessed on 16 October 2017]. To understand fully the spread of PC and PC-related terms across countries, however, it would be necessary to see when discourses of PC have permeated

different languages, and to what extent they have been inflected by local historical and cultural formations. For example, while PC-related terms (*political correctness, politically correct, PC*, etc.) in British newspapers more or less mirror the rise they have experienced in the USA, the analysis of the German and French newspapers *Die Welt* and *Le Monde* has shown how the appearance of borrowed or integrated variants of 'political correctness' did not really begin to gather momentum until the mid to late 1990s. Cf. Sally Johnson, J. O. Nathan Culpeper, and Stephanie Suhr, 'From "politically correct councillors" to "Blairite nonsense": discourses of "political correctness" in three British news', *Discourse and Society*, 14.1 (2003), 29–47; Sally Johnson and Stephanie Suhr, 'From "Political Correctness" to "Politische Korrektheit": Discourses of "PC" in the German Newspaper *Die Welt*', ibid., 49–68; Michel Toolan, 'Le politiquement correct dans le monde français', ibid., 69–86.

8. On the relation between *politicamente corretto* and *buonismo/buonista* see Federico Faloppa, 'Buonisti o cattivisti? Meglio realisti', *Associazione Carta di Roma*, 28 May 2015, <https://www.cartadiroma.org/news/buonisti-o-cattivisti/> [accessed on 16 October 2017].
9. Cf. <www.sketchengine.co.uk> [accessed on 16 October 2017].
10. Robin Tolmach Lakoff, *The Language War* (Berkeley and Los Angeles: University of California Press, 2000), p. 93.
11. *Merriam-Webster Collegiate Dictionary* (1993), sub voce: 'conforming to a belief that language and practices which could offend political sensibilities (as in matters of sex or race) should be eliminated'.
12. Christine Ammer, *The Random House Dictionary of Idioms* (The Christine Ammer Trust: Boston, 1997):

    politically correct. Also PC or p.c. showing an effort to make broad social and political changes to redress injustices caused by prejudice. It often involves changing or avoiding language that might offend anyone, especially with respect to gender, race, or ethnic background... This expression was born in the late 1900s, and excesses in trying to conform to its philosophy gave rise to humorous parodies.

13. *The American Heritage Dictionary of the English Language* (Boston: Houghton Mifflin, 2000):

    politically correct adj. Abbr. PC 1. Of relating to, or supporting broad social, political, and educational change, especially to redress historical injustices in matters such as race, class, gender, and sexual orientation. 2. Being or perceived as being over-concerned with such change, often to the exclusion of other matters.

14. *The Oxford American Dictionary and Thesaurus* (2003), sub voce *political*: 'political correctness: avoidance of forms of expression and action that exclude or marginalize sexual, racial, and cultural minorities; advocacy of this'.
15. Lakoff, *The Language War*, p. 93.
16. Quoted in John K. Wilson, *The Myth of Political Correctness* (Durham, NC and London: Duke University Press, 1995), p. 3.
17. Ezra B. Chase, *Teachings of Patriots and Statesmen: Or, The 'Founders of the Republic' on Slavery* (Philadelphia: Bradley, 1860), p. 227:

    On reviewing the scope of argument, on both sides, I am satisfied that the one [the anti-slavery faction] cannot be justly charged with advocating the sentiments which their language would seem to indicate; nor the other [the pro-slavery faction], with an attempt to justify the abstract principle of slavery as either religiously, morally, or politically, correct.

18. *Proceedings and Debates of the Convention of Louisiana: Which Assembled at the City of New Orleans January 14, 1844* (New Orleans: Besancon, Ferguson, & Company, 1845), p. 244:

    Instead of our institutions reposing on the broad foundation of the popular sovereignty, it seems to be supposed that its stability can only be secured by a reliance upon the officers and agents of the people — From whence was the doctrine derived that the agent is greater than the principal? Such a doctrine I repudiate; for it is neither legally nor politically correct.

19. Cf. Mao Tse-Tung, *On Correcting Mistaken Ideas in the Party*, in *Selected Works of Mao Tse-Tung* (Peking: Foreign Language Press, 1965), p. 105.

20. Harrison George, 'Causes and Meaning of the Farmers' Strike and Our Tasks as Communists', *The Communist*, October 1932, p. 926.
21. John Strachey, *Literature and Dialectical Materialism* (New York: Covici Friede Publishers, 1934), p. 47.
22. Herbert Kohl, 'Uncommon Differences: On Political Correctness, Core Curriculum and Democracy in Education', *The Lion and the Unicorn*, 16 (1992), 1–16:

> I first heard the phrase 'politically correct' in the late 1940s and early 1950s in reference to the political debates between socialists and members of the United States Communist Party (CP) [. . .] Members of the CP talked about current party doctrine as the 'correct' line for the moment. During World War II the Hitler–Stalin pact caused many CP members considerable pain and often disgrace on my block, which was all Jewish and mostly socialist. The 'correct' position on Stalin's alliance with Hitler was considered to be ridiculous, a betrayal of European Jewry as well as socialist ideas. The term 'politically correct' was used disparagingly to refer to someone whose loyalty to the CP line overrode compassion and led to bad politics. It was used by socialists against Communists, and was meant to separate out socialists, who believed in egalitarian moral ideas, from dogmatic Communists, who would advocate and defend party positions regardless of their moral substance.

23. L. D. Burnett, *'Politically Correct': A History (Part I)*, US Intellectual History Blog, 7 February 2015, <https://archive.is/17VnP#selection-147.0–147.41> [accessed 16 October 2017].
24. Ruth Perry, 'A Short History of the Term Politically Correct', in *Beyond PC: Toward a Politics of Understanding*, ed. by Patricia Aufderheide (Saint Paul: Graywolf, 1992), pp. 71–79.
25. Toni Cade Bambara, *Black Woman* (New York: New American Library, 1970), p. 107.
26. Debra L. Schultz, *To Reclaim a Legacy of Diversity: Analyzing the 'Political Correctness' Debates in Higher Education* (New York: National Council for Research on Women, 1993), p. 7.
27. Marychild, 'Calling all dykes. . . come in place', *Off Our Backs*, 4.8 (1974), 22.
28. L. D. Burnett, *'Politically Correct': A History (Part II)*, <https://s-usih.org/2015/02/politically-correct-a-history-part-ii> [accessed 16 October 2017].
29. Geoffrey Hughes, *Political Correctness: A History of Semantics and Culture* (Chichester: Wiley-Blackwell, 2010), p. 64.
30. Cf. Stuart Hall, 'Some "Politically Incorrect" Pathways through PC', in *The War of the Words: The Political Correctness Debate*, ed. by Sarah Dunant (London: Virago Press, 1995), pp. 164–84 (p. 165):

> the first time I actually encountered the term 'political correctness' was when I was giving a talk at an American university in the mid-1980s. I was warned by the organisers of a conference that I should be careful about what I said because, in the new climate of the times following the Reagan election, the right had established campus committees to monitor speakers and take notes on everything said in lectures which could be interpreted as undermining the American Constitution or sapping the moral fibre of the nation's brightest and best. Here, PC was clearly part and parcel of the 1980s backlash against the 1960s. It was the right and the Moral Majority who were trying to prescribe what could and could not be taught and said in academic classrooms.

Cf. also Favio Baroncelli, *Il razzismo è una gaffe. Vizi e virtù del politicamente corretto* (Rome: Donzelli, 1996), pp. 20–21:

> Ci vuole molta ingenuità per credere che si sprechino tante costose munizioni solo per battere le trincee di pochi politically correct duri e puri. L'obiettivo reale delle polemiche [. . .] erano invece proprio i liberals che formavano il cuore di quell'establishment universitario e intellettuale che aveva votato in massa per Bill Clinton, e che venivano implicitamente ed esplicitamente accusati di essere stati contagiati dai disvalori del politically correct, e di esserne gli alleati e i protettori [...]. Ma dove sono tutti questi individui politically correct? [. . .] La supposta preponderanza dei radicali nella scuola statunitense è, se si guarda alle cifre, una pura e semplice fandonia [. . .] il dominio delle sinistre nelle università non esiste.
>
> [It takes a lot of ingenuity to believe that so much expensive ammunition is wasted only

to defeat a few tough-and-pure politically correct supporters. The real objective of the polemics [...] were instead the liberals that formed the heart of the university and intellectual establishment that had voted *en masse* for Bill Clinton, and that were implicitly and explicitly accused of being infected by the disvalues of the politically correct, and to be its allies and protectors [...]. But where are all these politically correct individuals? [. . .] The alleged radicals' predominance in US colleges is, if we look at the figures, pure and simple nonsense [. . .] the domination of the left in American universities does not exist.]

31. Allan Bloom, *The Closing of the American Mind* (New York: Simon & Schuster, 1987).
32. Roger Kimball, *Tenured Radicals: How Politics Has Corrupted our Higher Education* (New York: HarperCollins, 1990).
33. Cf. Eve Kosofsky Sedgwick, 'Jane Austen and the Masturbating Girl', *Critical Inquiry*, 17.4 (1991), 818–37. At the very beginning of the article, the author explicitly mentions Kimball's sarcastic comment:

    The phrase itself is already evidence. Roger Kimball in Tenured Radicals — a treatise on educational 'corruption' that must have gone to press before the offending paper was so much as written — cites the title 'Jane Austen and the Masturbating Girl' from a Modern Language Association convention program quite as if he were Perry Mason, the six words a smoking gun: the warm gun that, for the journalists who have adopted the phrase as an index of depravity in academia, is happiness-offering the squibby pop (fulmination? prurience? funniness?) that lets absolutely anyone, in the righteously exciting vicinity of the masturbating girl, feel a very pundit.

    Cf. Judith Butler, 'The Lesbian Phallus and the Morphological Imagery', in Butler, *Bodies that Matter: On the Discursive Limits of 'Sex'* (New York: Routledge, 1993), pp. 51–92.
34. Richard Bernstein, 'The Rising Hegemony of the Politically Correct', *The New York Times*, 28 October 1990, <http://www.nytimes.com/1990/10/28/weekinreview/ideas-trends-the-rising-hegemony-of-the-politically-correct.html?pagewanted=all> [accessed on 16 October 2017]:

    The term 'politically correct,' with its suggestion of Stalinist orthodoxy, is spoken more with irony and disapproval than with reverence. But across the country the term p.c., as it is commonly abbreviated, is being heard more and more in debates over what should be taught at the universities. There are even initials — p.c.p. — to designate a politically correct person. And though the terms are not used in utter seriousness, even by the p.c.p.'s themselves, there is a large body of belief in academia and elsewhere that a cluster of opinions about race, ecology, feminism, culture and foreign policy defines a kind of "correct" attitude toward the problems of the world, a sort of unofficial ideology of the university.

35. Dorothy Rabinowitz, 'Vive the Academic Resistance', *The Wall Street Journal*, 13 November 1990.
36. *Newsweek*, 24 December 1990, p. 48.
37. Dinesh D'Souza, *Illiberal Education: The Politics of Race and Sex on Campus* (New York: Free Press, 1991).
38. Dinesh D'Souza, 'Illiberal Education', *The Atlantic*, March 1991, Volume 267, No. 3, pp. 51–79.
39. *University of Chicago Student Information Manual* (Chicago: University of Chicago, 1993), p. 94.
40. Stanley Fish, 'No such Thing as Free Speech and It's a Good Thing, Too', in *Debating P.C.: The Controversy over Political Correctness on College Campuses*, ed. by Paul Berman (New York: Laurel, 1992), pp. 231–45.
41. Wilson, *The Myth of Political Correctness*, pp. 90–108.
42. *Detroit Free Press*, 16 March 1991, p. 40.
43. Wilson, *The Myth of Political Correctness*, pp. 64–89.
44. Lakoff, *The Language War*, p. 91.
45. George Bush, Remarks at the University of Michigan Commencement Ceremony in Ann Arbor, 4 May 1991, <http://www.presidency.ucsb.edu/ws/?pid=19546> [accessed 16 October 2017]:

> ...Ironically, on the 200th anniversary of our Bill of Rights, we find free speech under assault throughout the United States, including on some college campuses. The notion of political correctness has ignited controversy across the land. And although the movement arises from the laudable desire to sweep away the debris of racism and sexism and hatred, it replaces old prejudice with new ones. It declares certain topics off-limits, certain expression [sic] off-limits, even certain gestures off-limits [. . .] We all should be alarmed at the rise of intolerance in our land and by the growing tendency to use intimidation rather than reason in settling disputes. Neighbours who disagree no longer settle matters over a cup of coffee. They hire lawyers, and they go to court. And political extremists roam the land, abusing the privilege of free speech, setting citizens against one another on the basis of their class or race.

It is interesting to note that the pejorative meaning is the only meaning recorded in the 1992 *Oxford Companion to the English Language*:

> The phrase is applied, especially pejoratively by conservative academics and journalists in the US, to the views and attitudes of those who publicly object to: 1) The use of terms that they consider overtly or covertly sexist [. . .] racist [. . .] ableist [. . .] ageist [. . .] etc.; 2) Stereotyping, such as the assumption that women are generally less intelligent than men and blacks less intelligent than whites; 3) inappropriately directed laughter, such as jokes at the expense of the disabled, homosexuals, and ethnic minorities.

46. Lakoff, *The Language War*, p. 94.
47. Most of these articles, however, recycled the same stories and anecdotes collected in a handful of Ivy League colleges, exaggerating their impact and decontextualizing their most controversial aspects. Cf. Wilson, *The Myth of Political Correctness*, pp. 8, 20–23. Cf. also Lakoff, *The Language War*, p. 95.
48. Salvatore Battaglia, *Grande dizionario della lingua italiana*, *Perf-Po* (Turin: Unione tipografico-editrice torinese, 1986).
49. Giacomo Devoto and Gian Carlo Oli, *il Devoto-Oli 2008* (Florence: Le Monnier, 2008).
50. Nicola Zingarelli, *lo Zingarelli: vocabolario della lingua italiana* (Bologna: Zanichelli, 2011).
51. Francesco Sabatini and Vittorio Coletti, *il Sabatini-Coletti: dizionario della lingua italiana* (Milan: Rizzoli-Larousse, 2005).
52. *Gazzetta Piemontese*, 15 July 1879, p. 3; *Gazzetta Piemontese*, 1 November 1880, p. 1.
53. *Giornale degli economisti e annali di economia*, 2 (1892), p. 179.
54. *Il nuovo Rosmini periodico scientifico e letterario* (1889), p. 125.
55. This lack of irony — shown also from other examples from *La Repubblica* — gives the impression that Italian political correctness may have skipped the 'in-group' ironic phase characteristic of pre-1980s Anglo-American usages, immediately taking on board its latter-day pejorative connotations in English.
56. Cf. 'Annuncio economico', *La Stampa*, 1968: 'Quarantenne massima onestà politicamente corretto cerca occupazione come persona assoluta fiducia oppure manutenzione sorveglianza impianti' [Forty-year-old max honesty politically correct seeks employment as an absolutely trustable person or in maintenance facility surveillance].
57. On morphological productivity and creativity in English, cf. Ewa Konieczna, 'Morphological Productivity and Creativity in a Politically Correct Language: A Case Study on Lexical Innovation', *Bulletin of the Transilvania University of Brașov*, Series IV: Philological and Cultural Studies, 54.2 (2012), 9–16.
58. Cf. *La Stampa*, respectively 12 August 1991, 21 September 1991, and 7 August 1992. As one could expect, at the very beginning inverted commas were widely used to signal the borrowing, or to indicate its ironic or *sui generis* use. Around 1992 the acronym 'pc' also makes its first appearances, but at the beginning it requires a gloss and an explanation: 'Invece la curiosità e la voglia di giudicare da solo hanno avuto la meglio sul comportamento pc (che non vuol dire partito comunista ma politically correct). Sono stato non pc e sono andato a vederlo' [Instead, the curiosity and the desire to personally give my evaluation have prevailed over PC (which does not mean communist party but politically correct) behaviour. I was not PC and I went to see it] (*La Stampa*, 19 September 1992).

59. Franco Marcoaldi, 'L'Africa a stelle e strisce', *La Repubblica*, 20 September 1991.
60. Cf. Alberto Arbasino, 'Facciamo un censimento dei tabù', *La Repubblica*, 9 Febrary 1993; idem, 'Signora mia, ah quei pomeriggi a luci rosse', *La Repubblica*, 6 May 1993; idem, 'I barbari e gli snob', *La Repubblica*, 13 June 1993.
61. Mirella Serri, *La Stampa*, 7 February 1996.
62. Baroncelli, *Il razzismo è una gaffe*, pp. 43.
63. This is the main argument in Massimo Arcangeli, *Cercasi Dante disperatamente. L'italiano alla deriva* (Rome: Carocci, 2012), pp. 121–39; and Edoardo Crisafulli, *Igiene verbale. Il politicamente corretto e la libertà linguistica* (Rome: Vallecchi, 2004).
64. Baroncelli, *Il razzismo è una gaffe*, pp. 79–92; Michael Minutiello, 'La ricezione del "politicamente corretto" nella stampa italiana: un sondaggio dal 1992 ad oggi' (Tesi di Laurea Triennale inedita, Università degli Studi di Modena e Reggio Emilia, AA 2013–14), pp. 9–15.
65. Cf. Minutiello, 'La ricezione del "politicamente corretto" nella stampa italiana', p. 50: 'Dinanzi a questi casi di uso del PC, la prima domanda che ci poniamo è: qual è il significato del PC in espressioni come, ad esempio, *supermercato politicamente corretto, caffè politicamente corretto, tram politicamente corretto,* oppure un'*auto... politicamente corretta?* [Looking at these PC cases, the first question we should ask is: what is the meaning of PC in expressions like, for instance, *politically correct supermarket, politically correct coffee, politically correct tram*, or a *car... politically correct?*].
66. 'Quel prete da sempre ribelle', *La Repubblica*, 14 May 1992.
67. Marina Cavalierli, 'Il decalogo anti molestie', *La Repubblica*, 24 February 1994.
68. Alice Oxman, 'Parole e razze', *L'Unità*, 16 February 1997.
69. Cf Rita Fresu, 'Politicamente corretto', in *Enciclopedia dell'italiano Treccani*, <www.treccani.it> [accessed 16 October 2017].
70. Although the literature on this specific topic continues to grow, some of the best reflections on the relation between language, political correctness and 'sessismo' in the Italian language are still to be found in Anna Laura Lepschy, Giulio Lepschy, and Helena Sanson, 'Lingua italiana e femminile', *Quaderns d'Italià*, 9 (2001), 9–18.
71. Cf. Federico Faloppa, 'Handicappato o portatore di handicap? Disabile o persona con disabilità? Diversamente abile o diversabile?', *Accademia della Crusca*, 3 aprile 2013, <http://www.accademiadellacrusca.it/en/italian-language/language-consulting/questions-answers/meglio-handicappato-portatore-handicap-disabi> [accessed 16 October 2017].
72. Cf. Federico Faloppa, 'La linea del colore: appunti per la storia della parola negro', *Quaderni della Sezione di Glottologia e Linguistica dell'Università di Chieti*, 9 (1997), 93–129; idem, *Parole contro. La rappresentazione del diverso in italiano e nei dialetti* (Milan: Garzanti, 2004); idem, 'Negro, nero, di colore', *Accademia della Crusca*, 12 October 2012, <http://www.accademiadellacrusca.it/en/italian-language/language-consulting/questions-answers/nero-negro-colore> [accessed 16 October 2017].
73. Cf. Martino Marazzi, 'Preistoria e storia di "afro-americano"', *Studi di Lessicografia Italiana*, 24 (2007), 249–64.
74. *Autobiografia di Malcolm X. Redatta con la collaborazione di Alex Haley*, intro., trans., and with notes by Roberto Giammarco (Turin: Einaudi, 1967).
75. George P. Rawick, *Lo schiavo americano dal tramonto all'alba: la formazione della comunità nera durante la schiavitù negli Stati Uniti*, trans. by Bruno Cartosio (Milano: Feltrinelli, 1973).
76. Leonardo Buonomo, 'Indovina chi viene a cena? La rappresentazione degli afroamericani nel doppiaggio italiano di The Jeffersons', in *Parlare di razza. La lingua del colore tra Italia e Stati Uniti*, ed. by Tatiana Petrovich Njegosh and Anna Scacchi (Verona: Ombre Corte, 2012), pp. 220–40.
77. Ibid., p. 235.
78. Emilio De Felice and Aldo Duro, *Dizionario della lingua e della civiltà italiana contemporanea* (Palermo: Palumbo, 1985), s.v. *negro*.
79. *Vocabolario della lingua italiana*, 3.1 (M-PD, Rome: Istituto dell'Enciclopedia Italiana, 1988), sv. *Negro*.
80. 'Negro è un insulto per metà degli italiani', *La Repubblica*, 9 December 1995.
81. Mario Barenghi, 'La strana coppia del nero e del negro', *L'Unità*, 27 November 1995.

82. Claudio Marazzini, 'Ma quanto sei razzista?', *Letture*, 51 (1996), p. 79.
83. Giuliano Zincone, 'Contrordine compagni, dire "negro" è politicamente corretto', *Corriere della Sera*, 29 November 1995.

PART IV

Long-Term Influences and Effects

CHAPTER 12

❖

'Little Italy' on the Move: The Birth and Transatlantic Relocation of a Cultural Myth*

Mattia Lento

Introduction

The history of the interactions between the Italian and US cultures during the twentieth century cannot be reduced to only bidirectional processes. The intense and multidirectional mobility of Italian citizens from the Unification of the country onwards produced a worldwide spread of Italian culture. Large Italian communities established in Australia, South America, Africa, and in many European countries created the so-called 'altre italie'.[1]

Donna Gabaccia describes the dispersion of Italian migrants in the world as a 'diaspora';[2] Robert Cohen calls it a case of 'labour diaspora'.[3] This term, whilst often abused, might well be transformed into a useful expression on a heuristic level.[4] The concept of diaspora, in fact, opens up the possibilities for comparative historical analysis in a transnational perspective, and forces us to consider both the links between the dissemination of Italian citizens and their homeland, and the concrete and symbolic connections that exist between different Italian communities around the globe.[5]

The most visible Italian community outside Italy in the realm of popular culture has undoubtedly been that of Italian Americans. Through the representation of Italian migrants and their descendants, US cinema has conveyed a hegemonic image of the Italian diaspora, its cultures, and, more generally, of Italianness all over the world. In other words, US cinema has in different ways influenced the perception (or the self-perception) of other Italian communities outside Italy.[6] The interaction of different Italian communities around the globe and their reciprocal cultural influences has not been adequately investigated.[7] The importance of Hollywood cinema in shaping the worldwide image of Italian migration, for example, has often been taken for granted. In this article, I will analyse in particular the cinematic popularity of *Little Italy*[8] in the USA and its transfer to Swiss cinema.

* This research was supported by a postdoctoral grant from the Swiss National Science Foundation.

First, I will analyse the birth of *Little Italy*, with reference to scholarly works by historians and social scientists; I will then consider the multiple relationships between *Little Italy* and the cinema of the USA. Subsequently, I will investigate the transatlantic relocation of the term, and will focus on the history of the 'Italian' district of Zurich and its filmic representation in *Bäckerei Zürrer* (Kurt Früh CH, 1957). This chapter does not presume to be exhaustive, but opens a new avenue in the study of the Italian diaspora through a multidirectional transnational perspective. Its aim is in fact to analyse a process of indirect cultural influence and exchange, which involves the communities of people with Italian origins in the USA and Switzerland.

The Birth of *Little Italy*

New York's Little Italy became a popular icon, a cultural fact of collective interest, and a space of memory, one that, today, evokes charm, interest, curiosity, and surprise. New York's Little Italy belongs both to cultural history and to the sphere of the myth.[9] The district is no longer populated by a majority of Americans with Italian origins, nor has it been for a long time,[10] but it is still an 'Italian-American ethnic theme park' and remains a monument to Italian immigration in the USA.[11]

From the Unification of Italy onwards, the migration of millions of its inhabitants created many Italian urban clusters worldwide, which provoked often negative reactions among the commentators of the host societies. These neighbourhoods were labelled *Little Italies* exclusively in North America, Australia and in the United Kingdom. Following Robert H. Harney, *Little Italies* were the product of the 'Italophobia' of the English-speaking world.[12] As Donna Gabaccia writes:

> English-speakers' understandings of race and their history of anti-Catholicism helped to create an ideological foundation for fixing foreignness upon urban spaces occupied by immigrants who seemed racially different from the earlier Anglo-Celtic and northern European settlers.[13]

The term *Little Italy*, born in New York, was soon adopted by other metropolitan areas in North America,[14] Great Britain[15] and Australia.[16] It described urban areas of transition between Italy and the host societies, which were formed thanks to chain or serial migration phenomena.[17] Little Italies in the USA and Canada have long been an object of investigation for North American sociologists. The School of Chicago, or better, the sociological tradition of Chicago,[18] in particular, was profoundly interested in the relationships between migration and metropolitan configurations. Little Italies were considered particular forms of residential segregation, landing places for Italian migrants and essential collective agents in the development of North American cities by scholars such as Ernest Burgess, Robert Ezra Park, and Roderick McKenzie.[19] They became a terrain of scholarly experimentation for North American intellectuals: William Foote Whyte's *Street Corner Society: The Social Structure of an Italian Slum* (1943) has become a classic of sociological research thanks to the pioneering methodology of its author, based on participant observation. Following his example, North American historians studied the formations of Little Italies, their spatial articulation, institutions and 'ambiente'.[20]

The study of Italian urban clusters outside Italy also attracted the interest of scholars devoted to the study of cinema and popular culture. The 'racialized topographies of New York City'[21] have been analysed in their role of spreading worldwide stereotypes related to Italian immigrants and Italian Americans; mafia criminals, passionate lovers and uncompromising policemen living in the Italian ghetto soon became widely popular cinematic characters, and Italians became the most represented ethnic group in the history of US silent cinema.[22]

Little Italy in US Popular Culture

The fascination with Little Italy began at the end of the nineteenth century in New York, when people such as Jacob Riis (1849–1914), a Danish American social reformer, evangelist, journalist, magic lantern lecturer, and photographer, started to document both visually and in writing the conditions in the tenements of New York.

His illustrated collection of narrative sketches, *How the Other Half Lives: Studies among the Tenements of New York* (1890), quickly made him famous. In this book, Riis details the squalid living conditions in New York City's tenements, where he focuses on ethnic minorities and, in particular, on Jews and Italians.[23] His description of New York's Italian ghettos showed not only an attention and concern towards the material and spiritual living conditions of its inhabitants, but also a high degree of fascination for their exotic appearance and behaviour.[24]

Nowadays Riis is well known as a pioneer both of social photography and flashlight technique, but during his life he was appreciated more as a writer of the slums and as a philanthropist. Donna Gabaccia considers his works, together with other coeval reportages, as urban tourist guides. The invention of *Little Italy*, according to Gabaccia, was in fact not only connected with Italophobia but also with a high degree of newness, romance, risk and fascination towards the Italian otherness.[25]

Early American pioneers of moving pictures understood the narrative and visual potential of Little Italy. In his studies devoted to the representation of Italy in early US Cinema, Bertellini analyses the relationships between New York's Little Italy and early cinema in great detail; in particular, he focuses on the fascination of the American WASP audience for the picturesque depictions of Italian slums and its inhabitants. The American middle class was familiar with the aesthetic of the picturesque, the visual conventions of which were born in Europe at the time of the early practices of tourism and the *grand tour*, were exported to the USA in the nineteenth century, and served as a form of domestication of unusual and sublime landscapes such as the wilderness of the American west frontier. These conventions later served as a form of domestication of Italian ethnic otherness.[26]

Together with dramas such as *Little Italy: A Tragedy in One Act* (1902) or *The Heart of a Stranger* (1908), Jacob Riis's works and other slum reporters, early US cinema shaped a negative image of New York's Little Italy and Italians in US society. Yet, at the same time, it created a fascinating allure around them. In early cinema, in particular, the racial positioning of Italians appears to be complex and contradictory. In David Wark Griffith's *In Little Italy* (USA, 1909) or in the melodrama *The Italian* (dir. by Reginald Barker USA, 1915), for example, which allowed the director to represent both New York's Lower East Side and a picturesque Venice, the whiteness of the Italian emerges as problematic or even contested.[27]

Later films such as *Little Caesar* (1930) and *Scarface* (1932) established a 'definitive connection between Italian Americans and the gangster film', which depicted Italian criminals in Chicago and their surroundings.[28] These two works were released at the time that Hollywood was formulating the Production Code,[29] after which US film producers were forced to erase or, at least, smooth over ethnic identifiers. The Production Code regulations made it difficult to perpetrate the stereotype of the Italian as a gangster and, more generally, to depict Italian urban clusters, but it did not prevent a number of films from alluding to Italian Americans.

Only with the end of the Production Code in 1967 could the ethnic content be fully restored. After its rules were no longer in force, and in spite of the persistent pressures of different groups of Italian Americans, the 'tragic hero'[30] of the gangster movie no longer had to hide his Italian descent. The Italian American directors of the New Hollywood went back to ethnicity and to Little Italy.

In this period, Italian American directors such as Coppola or Scorsese, to mention only the most famous cases, contributed to the worldwide spread of the myth of Little Italy. The enormous international success of the *Godfather* trilogy (1972, 1974, 1990), the most successful feature film in the history of Hollywood Italians,[31] and in particular of *The Godfather Part II* (1974), with the impressive historical reconstruction of New York's Little Italy, transformed Mulberry Street into the foundational space of Italian American identity.[32]

In a personal essay on Coppola's masterpiece, Tom Santopietro analyses how this trilogy changed the way Italians were depicted in US cinema. Following Santopietro, *The Godfather*, in spite of the criminal activities of its heroes, transformed Italians in the USA into well-rounded characters and helped to Italianize American culture. This film also changed Santopietro's perception of his own identity and made him conscious of his Italian descent.[33]

Italian American directors of the New Hollywood, in general, did not avoid depicting Italian Americans as mobsters or outsiders. They made use of representational stereotypes but they did it with irony or with empathy for their characters in a very different way from, for example, *Scarface* or *Little Caesar*. Italian Americans, in general, experienced an improvement in their condition and their reputation in the USA, and cinema, following Santopietro, contributed to a new self-awareness for many of them. After that, New York's Little Italy has since no longer been a place of misery or slumming, but a place for the re-territorialization of the identity of the community of Italian Americans in the USA.[34]

Little Italy from the USA to Europe

The term *Little Italy* should be considered both a proper noun and a socio-historical concept that describes a spatial concentration of people of Italian origins in an urban context, describing a certain degree of communitarianism and cultural homogeneity.[35] The use of the term, in English or translated, or the application of the concept to describe neighbourhoods of the Italian migration within continental Europe, or outside English-speaking countries, seems to be quite uncommon, at least during the first part of the twentieth century.[36] In Europe, there were various Italian urban clusters between the nineteenth and the twentieth centuries, but their characters were different from those of New York and other North American cities.[37]

Little Italy as a concept for the interpretation of Italian migrant history has also been rarely discussed by European scholars until recently. In this context, in fact, Italian migration was mostly analysed through participants in working-class labour or political movements.[38] Additionally, the historiography of migration in Europe was organized principally around different national identities, while in North America there prevailed a 'vision territorialiste'.[39] The transfer of *Little Italy* as a concept for the interpretation of the history of Italian migration from North America to Europe is quite recent, and has followed the same transatlantic relocation of the term which has taken place in everyday language.[40]

It is difficult to identify exactly when the term *Little Italy* started to be used for districts of European cities as well as those in North America. Further research on the term is certainly in demand if we are to understand fully the history of *Little Italy* and its use. We have some useful information on specific areas or case studies. In the UK, the term *Little Italy* was used at least from the end of the nineteenth century to refer to the Italian neighbourhood of London, in the district of Holborn.[41] In the early twentieth century, George R. Sims edited a well-known book on London and, in one chapter the Count E. Armfelt describes the life in London's Little Italy with a mixture of fascination and moral disapproval combined with concern for its inhabitants.[42] In a manner that borders on racist, the author depicts Italian Londoners in their 'oriental fashion',[43] stressing their otherness and picturesque character, and implying their racial and cultural inferiority. We are not so far from the description of New York's Little Italy made by Riis and his colleagues.

Some Italian intellectuals, who established a contact with the Anglo-American context, also made use of the term *Little Italy* in their writings. Amy Bernardy, for example, an Italian journalist of US origin, a fervent nationalist, in her articles published in Italy between 1907 and 1931 was concerned with the living conditions of Italian migrants in the USA and referred often, through different lexical choices, to Italian urban clusters there.[44] In her writings, she employed the English term, along with the words 'colonia' [colony] and 'quartiere' [district], but she privileged the expression 'piccola italia' [little Italy].[45]

Piero Gobetti also uses the term *Little Italy* in an article devoted to London's Saffron Hill. It describes that district as 'one of the most sordid quarters of London'.[46] Gobetti is among those few Italian writers[47] who came into contact with

Italian clusters in Anglo-American contexts before the Second World War, and who reported their experiences to an Italian public, often with a tone of commiseration. In a certain sense, we are faced with early forms of transatlantic relocation of the term or, in the case of Gobetti, of lexical importation from the other side of the Channel.[48]

In other European countries, the term *Little Italy* seems to not have been in use, at least during the first part of the last century. In France, for example, the recurring definition to indicate urban Italian clusters is that of 'colonie italienne' [Italian colony], and it seems that the expression 'petite Italie' [little Italy] appeared only during the second part of the twentieth century.[49] Marie-Claude Blanc-Chaléard, in her analysis of the urban Italian clusters of the Parisian region, confirms that the term *petite Italie* was established among Italian migrants only after the Second World War. She does not rule it out that the reason for this appropriation may be a consequence of the frequent contact among related Italian migrants in France and the USA.[50] Donna Gabaccia, in her comparative analysis of the Italian diaspora across the globe, confirms the scarce use of the expression in Europe because migrants were not distinguished by race.[51]

What then happened in the later years? The term *Little Italy* also became quite popular in the common languages in Europe and started to be used to label Italian clusters in different countries, both by Italian communities and by host societies. This phenomenon took place in different contexts and with different dynamics. In the next section, we will focus our attention on Switzerland, one of the most important contexts of emigration for Italian inhabitants from the end of the nineteenth century until today.

Ettore Cella and *Bäckerei Zürrer*

In Zurich, in the Aussersihl quarter or fourth district of the city (*Kreis 4*), was located the most important urban concentration of Italian migrants seen in Switzerland in the last century. Aussersihl, which still bears traces of its Italian past, was incorporated into the municipality of Zurich in 1883, as it became bigger than the city itself during the early industrialization of the area. It has always been inhabited by migrant workers from different European countries such as Germany and Austria or from other parts of Switzerland.

Between the end of the nineteenth and the beginning of the twentieth century, Aussersihl was described as a form of urban ghetto. Italian migrants, both seasonal workers and stable migrants, were concentrated in specific streets of the district.[52] The seasonal workers, in particular, were physically segregated into so-called *Massenquartiere*, block of barracks, and lived in miserable conditions.[53] The large-scale presence of Italian workers was a cause of conflict with the Swiss workers. Aussersihl became the theatre of the *Italienerkrawall* in 1896: protracted riots against Italians broke out following a dispute in which a migrant from Alsace had died, probably stabbed by an Italian mason.[54]

Aussersihl was not only an Italian quarter but the presence of Italian migrants — together with that of Swiss Italian citizens from Ticino and the four valleys of

Fig. 12.1. Sign of the Ristorante Cooperativo in Zurich, also known as Coopi.

Grisons — was signalled by visual, auditory, and even olfactory markers.[55] Many restaurants were part of the urban landscapes as well as Italian political associations, political parties, trade unions, and educational and charity institutions.[56]

One of the most important Italian institutions of this district was the Società Cooperativa, founded in early 1905 by a group of Italian socialists living in Zurich. This association opened the Ristorante Cooperativo, which still exists, a school for adults, and a small library for workers. This local became a venue for emigrants, revolutionaries, politicians, and intellectuals. It hosted Benito Mussolini in 1913 and Lenin during his exile in Switzerland. During the fascist era, the Cooperativo became a crucial place of resistance and, after the fall of France, was the headquarters of the socialist newspaper *L'Avanti*.[57]

Enrico Dezza, one of the founding members of the Società Cooperativa, had been manager of the restaurant from the beginning until 1909 and then, together with his partner Erminia Cella, from 1935 to 1952. The couple had a son, Ettore Cella, who became an important actor, director, and writer. Cella grew up in an atmosphere of political engagement and spent his childhood in this quarter full of Italian workers. In 2001, he published two texts which tell the story of the quarter from the beginning of the twentieth century until the end of the Second World War: *Nonna Adele* and *Der Damokle Schwert*. The first is a novel, told from the point of view of Adele, Ettore's grandmother, and documents in an extremely realistic manner the daily and political life of Italian migrants at the beginning of the last century in Aussersihl. The second is a memoir, written by Enrico Dezza and worked up later by his son, which refers to the struggle of fascists and antifascists in the *colonia italiana*.[58]

Ettore Cella's name is linked to Aussersihl and the life of Italian migrants in Zurich for further reasons. At the end of the 1950s, the important Swiss film director Kurt Früh engaged Cella to play an Italian character in his own quarter.[59]

In 1957, *Bäckerei Zürrer* was released and became one of the most popular works in Swiss film history. In this film, the main character Zürrer is a baker, whose sons seem uninterested in continuing the family-owned bakery. The youngest son, in particular, is the greatest disappointment for his father: he wants to make his career as a bicycle racer, and, even worse, loves a young Italian girl, Gina, daughter of Renato Pizzani, an Italian chestnut and fruit seller played by Ettore Cella.[60]

Bäckerei Zürrer was a pioneer in bringing the camera into an urban context, if we consider the locations of the traditional Swiss *Heimatfilm* and *Bergfilm* for countryside or alpine landscapes.[61] In some aspects, the film anticipated the *nouveau cinéma suisse*, with its attention to problems connected with modernity, such as urban culture and the presence of migrants.[62] Kurt Früh was one of the most successful Swiss film directors between the 1950s and 1960s. He was well known in Switzerland for his *Kleinbürger-Drama*, a genre devoted to the realistic representation of urban contexts and its working class or petit bourgeois inhabitants.[63]

In his film Kurt Früh brings out the main characteristics of Aussersihl, its streets and shops, its peculiar atmosphere. When the film was shot, the quarter was populated by many Italians, and Früh makes these residents visible. Italian migrants and Swiss citizens from grassroots classes lived side by side. If we look at the reviews of the film, we can see that the district is labelled as *Langstrassequartier*, from the name of the main street of the area, or *Arbeiterquartier*, from its social milieu. The reviewers also remarked on Ettore Cella's character and the existence of an Italian milieu in the film, but the term *Little Italy*, or *Kleines Italien* or *Piccola italia*, however, does not appear in any piece of criticism.[64]

Cella depicted Renato Pizzani with 'all the clichés of the guy Southern man' and not as a rounded character.[65] Ettore Cella's type is a jovial, generous, emotional, noisy, and vivacious Italian. In spite of his characterization, Renato Pizzani belongs to the group of characters who are open to modernity and to change. In fact, he gives his consent to the intercultural marriage between his daughter and her fiancé, and tries to smoothen out his own conflict with Zürrer. Pizzani is the exact antithesis of the Swiss baker and inaugurates the tradition of Italian characters in Swiss film represented as direct opposites of negative indigenous characters.[66]

Little Italy from USA to Switzerland

Bäckerei Zürrer had great success and entered into the Swiss film canon, and was regularly screened in the following years by movie theatres, film societies, and Swiss television.[67] This and other films by Früh set in Zurich, in particular, have been appreciated a posteriori by the public, not only for their artistic qualities, but for their power of bringing to light the dramatic changes that the city continuously undergoes. Kurt Früh's films are traditionally mentioned in the local press in connection with different urban issues.[68] In other words, they have an enduring impact in the local *Kinoöffentlichkeit*.[69]

Aussersihl, from the release of *Bäckerei Zürrer* onwards, underwent significant changes. From the 1960s, the development of factories, shops, and the red light industry provoked the departure of many Swiss inhabitants. From the 1990s, the

FIG. 12.2. Sign of the Libreria Italiana in Zurich, which is located between two red light venues.

quarter began to attract heroin addicts from other areas of the city and started to become a venue for youngsters of different classes. In those years, many Italians moved to other areas inside or outside the city, or else went back to Italy.

In quantitative terms, Aussersihl lost its Italian character at the end of the last century, but, paradoxically, its 'Italian roots' began to be revalued. At the same time, the definition of the quarter as 'Little Italy' appeared in the language of science, journalism, and marketing.[70]

Recently, Toni Ricciardi, a historian of Italian migration to Switzerland, used the term to describe the urban development of the district during the twentieth century.[71] Additionally, Swiss journalists refer to Aussersihl using the expression *Little Italy*, in particular when they talk about issues related to Italian migration. In an interview in the Swiss Italian newspaper *Azione*, Sandro Cattacin, a prominent Swiss sociologist, is described as a Little Italy-born son of Italian migrants.[72] The term *Little Italy* is used also for marketing purposes, as the related term *Italianità* is a trendy label in Switzerland today.[73]

In the realm of cinema, the description of Aussersihl as *Little Italy* is not uncommon.[74] Many years after its release, *Bäckerei Zürrer* itself is described as a film about Zurich's Little Italy, and Ettore Cella became its most important living witness. In 1992, the actor was interviewed by the local newspaper *Tages-Anzeiger* on Zurich's Little Italy of Aussersihl and Kurt Früh's film is mentioned as *Zeitdokument*, as evidence of the history of the Italian district, which was already 'dead', for Cella, at that moment.[75] The actor had often been interviewed by the Swiss media on the history of the district, and his role as Renato Pizzani followed him around for his entire life.

The connections between *Bäckerei Zürrer* and *Little Italy* are indirectly reinforced through another Swiss film. In 1988, Samir, a Swiss-Iraqi director, shot *Filou*, an experimental fictional work, which tells the story of Max, an artist and rebel,

Fig. 12.3. Piazza Cella in Zurich.

a so-called *secondo*[76] of Italian descent, who lives in Aussersihl. Samir dedicated his film to Kurt Früh and offered a postmodern series of visual cross-references to *Bäckerei Zürrer*. The *Italianità* of Max is not at the centre of the story but only sketched out in some scenes or alluded to through explicit reminiscences to Früh's work. For many reviewers of the film, this was enough to make *Filou* a work set in 'Zurich's Little Italy'.[77]

After Ettore Cella's death, the city of Zurich dedicated a small square in Aussersihl to him and his mother Erminia. For one commentator on this story, the creation of Piazza Cella was intended to act as a reminder of 'Zürich's Little Italy'.[78] The legacy between the district and the history of Italian migration was sealed with this official act, and, in a certain sense, honoured. From the 1980s onwards, Swiss society, after years of Italophobia, radically changed its attitude towards Italians, who started to be considered as an example of perfect integration. Zurich discovered itself to have been Italianized.[79]

The transfer of the term and the concept of *Little Italy* from the USA to Switzerland was favoured by the acknowledgment of the economic, cultural, and political contribution that Italian migrants made to Swiss society in the past. In the context of Zurich, *Little Italy* did not become a familiar and shared expression for all its inhabitants but was introduced for specific purposes. The term lost any negative connotations in Switzerland and turned into an expression linked with the idea of stylishness and, in particular, an instrument of the interpretation and reminiscence of the story of Italian migration in the city.

Notes to Chapter 12

1. The research group funded by the Giovanni Agnelli Foundation chose to call their journal, devoted to the history of Italian migration, *Altreitalie* ('Other Italies'). Similar terms are used to name the programme of the Italian Estate Broadcast RAI, *Community — L'Altra Italia*, or the news magazine *L'Altraitalia*, which are both addressed to Italian citizens living outside Italy.
2. Donna Gabaccia, *Italy's Many Diasporas* (Seattle: University of Washington Press, 2000), pp. 1–13.
3. Robin Cohen, *Global Diasporas: An Introduction* (Seattle: University of Washington Press, 1997), p. 57.
4. For a critical point of view on the use of the term diaspora in relation to the history of Italian migration see: Stefano Luconi, 'The Pitfalls of the "Italian Diaspora"', *Italian American Review*, 1.2 (2011), 147–76.
5. See Gabaccia, *Italy's Many Diasporas*, pp. 1–14. See also *Diaspora and Transnationalism: Concepts, Theories and Methods*, ed. by Rainer Bauböck and Thomas Faist (Amsterdam: Amsterdam University Press, 2010).
6. For the relationships between Italy and early American cinema, see: Giorgio Bertellini, *Italy in Early American Cinema: Race, Landscape, and the Picturesque* (Bloomington and Indianapolis: Indiana University Press 2010). For an introduction to Italian American cinema see: *Mediated Ethnicity. New Italian-American Cinema*, ed. by Giuliana Muscio, Joseph Sciorra, Giovanni Spagnoletti and A. J. Tamburri, Studies in Italian Americana, 2 (New York: John D. Calandra Italian American Institute, The University of New York, 2010).
7. The research project 'Italians everywhere' is an interesting exception. For an introduction on this project see Donna Gabaccia, 'Juggling Jargons: "Italians everywhere", diaspora or transnationalism?', *Traverse: Zeitschrift für Geschichte*, 12.1 (2005), 49–64. See also the research project Transnationalizing Modern Language, <http://www.transnationalmodernlanguages.ac.uk/> [accessed 10 July 2017].
8. From now on, *Little Italy* will be Italicized to denote the concept.
9. For an introduction to the concept of myth in the realm of popular culture during the twentieth century, see also *Filosofie del mito nel Novecento*, ed. by Giovanni Leghissa and Enrico Manera (Rome: Carocci, 2015), pp. 17–38.
10. Philip F. Napoli, 'Little Italy Resisting the Asian Invasion, 1965–1995', in *Race and Ethnicity in New York City*, ed. by Jerome Krase and Ray Hutchison, Research in Urban Sociology, 7 (Bingley: Emerald Group Publishing), pp. 245–69.
11. Jerome Krase, 'Seeing Ethnic Succession in Little Italy: Change despite Resistance', *Modern Italy*, 11.1 (2006), 79–95 (p. 80).
12. Robert F. Harney, 'Italophobia: An English-speaking Malady?', *Studi emigrazione/études migrations*, 22.77 (1985), 6–42.
13. Donna Gabaccia, 'Global Geography of "Little Italy": Italian. Neighbourhoods in Comparative: Perspective', *Modern Italy*, 11.1 (2006), 9–24 (p. 9).
14. See *Little Italies in North America*, ed. by Robert F. Harney and J. Vincenza Scarpaci (Toronto: The multicultural history Society of Ontario, 1981). French Canada seems to be the sole exception outside the English-speaking world. See Bruno Ramirez, *Les premiers italiens de Montreal: l'origine de la Petite Italie du Quebec* (Montreal : Boreal, 1984).
15. See Lucio Sponza, *Italian Immigrants in Nineteenth Century Britain: Reality and Images* (Leicester: Leicester University Press, 1988), and Terri Colpi, *The Italian Factor: the Italian Community in Great Britain* (Edinburgh: Mainstream Publishing, 1991).
16. See Gabaccia, 'Global Geography of "Little Italy"', p. 10.
17. Chain migration refers to the social process by which immigrants from a particular town follow others from that town to a particular city or neighbourhood, whether in an immigrant-receiving country or in a new location in the home country.
18. Jean-Michel Chapoulie, *La tradition sociologique de Chicago 1892–1961* (Paris: Seuil, 2001).
19. *The City*, ed. by Robert E. Park, Ernest W. Burgess, and Roderick D. McKenzie (Chicago: Chicago University Press, 1925).

20. Robert F. Harney, 'Ambiente and Social Class in North American Little Italies', *Canadian Review of Studies in Nationalism*, 2 (1975), 208–24. The most famous New York Little Italy is that of Mulberry Street, but Italians were also concentrated in the district of Harlem. See Judith Rainhorn, 'Paris, New York: deux "Petites Italies" dans l'entre-deux-guerres. Élements pour une comparaison transatlantique', in *Les Petites Italies dans le monde*, ed. by Marie-Claude Blanc-Chaléard, Antonio Bechelloni, Bénédicte Deschamps, Michel Dreyfus and Éric Vial, Collection Histoire, 12 (Rennes: Presses universitaires de Rennes, 2007), pp. 423–36 (p. 424).
21. Giorgio Bertellini, 'Italian Immigrants as "Urban Racial Types" in Early American Film Culture', *Urban History*, 31.3 (2004), 375–99 (p. 388).
22. Peter Bondanella, *Hollywood Italians: Dagos, Palookas, Romeos, Wise Guys, and Sopranos* (New York and London: Continuum, 2004).
23. For an introduction on Riis as a writer and photographer see: Keith Gandal, *The Virtues of the Vicious: Jacob Riis, Stephen Crane and the Spectacle of the Slum* (New York: Oxford University Press, 1997); Bonnie Yochelson, *Jacob Riis* (New York: Phaidon, 2001), and Bonnie Yochelson, and Daniel Czitrom, *Rediscovering Jacob Riis: Exposure Journalism and Photography in Turn-of-the Century New York* (New York: New Press, 2007).
24. Jacob Riis, *How the Other Half Lives: Studies among the Tenements of New York* (Carlisle: Applewood Books, 2011), p. 53.
25. Donna Gabaccia, 'L'invention de la "Petite Italie" de New York', in *Les Petites Italies dans le monde*, ed. by Blanc-Chaléard and others, pp. 25–43.
26. See Bertellini, 'Italian Immigrants'.
27. Valerio Coladonato, 'Italian-Americans' Contested Whiteness in Early Cinematic Melodrama', *MeCCSA*, 7.3 (2014), 5–20 (p. 5).
28. See Bondanella, *Hollywood Italians*, p. 181.
29. See Giuliana Muscio, 'L'era di Will Hays. La censura nel cinema Americano', in *Storia del cinema mondiale. Gli Stati Uniti vol. II, part. 1*, ed. by Gian Piero Brunetta (Turin: Einaudi, 1999), pp. 525–55.
30. Robert Warshow, 'The Gangster as Tragic Hero', *Partisan Review*, 15.2 (1958), 240–44.
31. By 1975, worldwide ticket sales had reached the phenomenal sum of $330.000.000. See Bondanella, *Hollywood Italians*, p. 236.
32. For the relationships between identity, place, and myth see Dario Prola, 'Lo spazio mitico come fondamento dell'identità nazionale. I *Kresy* nella letteratura polacca', in *Il pensiero letterario come fondamento di una testa ben fatta — Contributi*, ed. Geat Marina (Rome: Rome TrE-Press, 2017), pp. 49–64.
33. Tom Santopietro, *The Godfather Effect: Changing Hollywood, America, and Me* (New York: Thomas Dunne Books, 2012). Francis Ford Coppola is not the only one to have contributed to the mythos of Little Italy. Martin Scorsese, a visionary of the city, began his career with films about the neighbourhood where he came from. New York's Little Italy is in fact a recurring motif of his cinema.
34. For a discussion on Little Italy as a space of reterritorialization of identity see Anne-Marie Fortier, 'Re-Membering Places and the Performance of Belonging(s)', *Theory, Culture & Society*, 16.2 (1999), 41–64.
35. Stéphan Dufoix, and Valèrie Foucher, 'Les Petites Italies (et les autres. . .). Élements de réflexion sur la notion d'ethnoterritoire', in *Les Petites Italies dans le monde*, ed. by Blanc-Chaléard and others, pp. 423–36 (p. 424).
36. See Gabaccia, 'Global Geography of "Little Italy"', pp. 9–10.
37. See Judith Rainhorn, 'Présentation: "Petites Italies", le mot et la chose', in *Petites Italies dans l'Europe du Nord-ouest: Appartenances territoriales et identité collectives à l'ère de la migration italienne de masse*, ed. by Judith Rainhorn (Valenciennes: Presses universitaires de Valenciennes, 2005), pp. 7–20.
38. See Gabaccia, 'Global Geography of "Little Italy"', p. 10.
39. See Rainhorn, 'Présentation: "Petites Italies", le mot et la chose', p. 13. See also Judith Rainhorn, *Paris, New York: des migrants italiens — Années 1880 — années 1930* (Paris: CNRS, 2005).
40. See *Les Petites Italies dans le monde*, ed. by Blanc-Chaléard and others.

41. London's Little Italy was better known as Italian Hill or the Italian Quarter in an area delimited by Clerkenwell Road, Farringdon Road and Rosebery Avenue. Over the course of the nineteenth century the Saffron Hill area — as it was earlier known — gained a growing population of working-class Italians. Another historical Little Italy in London was that of Soho.
42. Count E. Armfelt, 'Italy in London', in *Living London: Its Work and its Play, ITS Humour and its Pathos, its Sights and its Scenes*, 3 vols, ed. by George R. Sims (London: Cassell, 1902), I, 183–89. George R. Sims, ed., *Living London: Its Work and its Play, its Humour and its Pathos, its Sights and its Scenes*, 3 vols (London: Cassell and Co., 1902–03).
43. See Armfelt, 'Italy In London', p. 185.
44. See Maddalena Tirabassi, *Ripensare la patria grande, gli scritti di Amy Allemande Bernardy sulle migrazioni italiane (1900–1930)* (Isernia: Cosmo Iannone, 2005). On Bernardy's writings and Little Italy see Carla A. Simonini, 'Re-Visioning Little Italy with Italian Eyes: The Italian Immigrant Experience in Early 20th century America as Portrayed in Melania Mazzucco's *Vita*', in *Constructing Identities: The Interaction of National, Gender and Racial Borders*, ed. by Antonio Medina-Rivera and Lee Wilberschied (Cambridge: Cambridge Scholars Publishing, 2013), pp. 143–61.
45. See Maddalena Tirabassi, 'The Little Italies of the Early 1900s: From the Reports of Amy Bernardy', in *The Routledge History of the Italian Americans*, ed. by William Connell and Stanislao G. Pugliese (New York and Abingdon: Routledge, 2017), pp. 123–35.
46. Piero Gobetti, 'La *Little Italy* londonienne vue par Piero Gobetti (1925)', in *Petites Italies dans l'Europe du Nord-ouest: Appartenances territoriales et identité collectives à l'ère de la migration italienne de masse*, ed. by Judith Rainhorn (Valenciennes: Presses universitaires de Valenciennes, 2005), pp. 69–74 (p. 71).
47. We can mention also Giuseppe Giacosa, *Impressioni d'America* (Milano: L. F. Cogliati, 1908) and Vico Mantegazza, *Agli Stati Uniti. Il pericolo americano* (Milano: Treves, 1910).
48. See Martino Marazzi, *Misteri di Little Italy. Storie e testi della letteratura italoamericana* (Milano: Franco Angeli, 2001), pp. 9–17.
49. Marie-Claude Blanc-Chaléard, 'Introduction', in *Les Petites Italies dans le monde*, ed. by Blanc-Chaléard and others, pp. 13–22 (pp. 16–17).
50. See Blanc-Chaléard and others, *Les Petites Italies dans le monde*.
51. See Gabaccia 'Global Geography of "Little Italy"'.
52. Heiri Gysler, *Einst in Zürich : Erinnerungen an Zürich vor der ersten Stadtvereinigung* (Zurich: author's edition, 1964), p. 181.
53. Luzius Bernet, *Italiener in Zürich 1890–1914. Demographische, soziale und materielle Verhältnisse, Segregation und Emigrantenkultur* (Zürich: Universität Zürich, 1991), p. 61. See also Giuseppe De Michelis, *L'emigrazione italiana nella Svizzera* (Rome: Bollettino italiano emigrazione, 1903).
54. Angelo Maiolino, *Als die Italiener noch Tschinggen waren* (Zürich: Rotpunktverlag, 2011), pp. 41–58. See also Tindaro Gatani, 'L'*Italienerkrawall* di Zurigo', in *Gli italiani in Svizzera. Un secolo di emigrazione*, ed. by Ernst Halter (Bellinzona: Casagrande, 2007), pp. 35–36.
55. See Bernet, *Italiener in Zürich 1890–1914*, pp. 62–64.
56. Ibid., p. 96–110. See also Toni Ricciardi, 'Gli italiani a Zurigo: una presenza significativa', in *Rapporto degli italiani nel mondo 2012*, ed. by fondazione Migrantes (Rome: Idos, 2012), pp. 358–66 (pp. 361–62).
57. See Ettore Cella-Dezza, *Nonna Adele. Das Damoklesschwert*, ed. by Andrea Ermano (Zurich: Tragelaphos, 2001).
58. See ibid. See also the revised and posthumous version of *Nonna Adele* in Ettore Cella-Dezza, *Nonna Adele: Edizione bilingue. Zweisprachige Ausgabe*, ed. by Andrea Ermano (Zurich: Tragelaphos, 2014).
59. Ettore Cella was still popular on Swiss radio thanks to its Italian character Serafino Nostrano, a parody of the broken Swiss German spoken by Italian migrants in Zurich. Some records of his performances are conserved at the Swiss Radio archive of Zurich.
60. For an introduction to Kurt Früh and a bibliography see *Kurt Früh. Ein Schweizer Filmemacher zwischen den Welten*, ed. by Margrit Tröhler (Zurich: Seminar für Filmwissenschaft, 2014),

<http://www.film.uzh.ch/de/research/researchstudies/kurtfrueh.html> [accessed 10 July 2017].

61. For an introduction to Swiss Heimatfilm and Bergfilm in relation to the migration see Mattia Lento, 'Im Bauch des Berges: Der Gotthard-Tunnel im Film', *Cinema Jahrbuch*, 62 (2017), 120–33.

62. For the relationships between Früh's cinema and modernity see Jessica Berry, Noemi Daugaard, and Killian Lilienfeld, 'Zwischen Geistiger Landesverteidigung und 50er-Jahre-Boom. Ambivalenz in den Filmen von Kurt Früh', in *Kurt Früh*, ed. by Tröhler, <http://www.film.uzh.ch/de/research/researchstudies/kurtfrueh.html> [accessed 10 July 2017].

63. For the relationship between Früh's cinema and Neorealism see Marius Kuhn, 'Fahrraddiebe in Zürich? *Bäckerei Zürrer* und der italienische Neorealismus', in *Kurt Früh*, ed. by Tröhler, <http://www.film.uzh.ch/de/research/researchstudies/kurtfrueh.html> [accessed 10 July 2017].

64. A collection of film reviews is available in Cinématheque suisse, documentation centre Zurich, folder 3751. A collection of articles on Ettore Cella is available in Cinématheque suisse, documentation centre Zurich, DDZ3 (Dokumentationsdossiers Personen), folder Ettore Cella.

65. Michele Dell'Ambrogio, 'I viaggi della speranza. L'immagine dell'immigrato italiano nel cinema svizzero', in *Gli italiani in Svizzera: Un secolo di emigrazione*, ed. by Ernst Halter (Bellinzona: Casagrande, 2007), pp. 261–69 (p. 261).

66. See Mattia Lento, '*Les années Schwarzenbach*: Italienische Migranten im Schweizer Film', *Cinema Jahrbuch*, 57 (2011), 146–58. We are far away from the typical representation of US cinema during the classic era.

67. Kurt Früh's work, in addition, has been thoroughly reconsidered by film historians, practitioners and *cinéphiles* in recent years.

68. See Felix Aeppli's interview in Thomas Bodmer, 'Die Stadt war ein Ort der Nichtsnutze', *Züritipp*, 9 July 2016, pp. 4–5; or Miklòs Gimes, 'Wie aus einem Film von Kurt Früh', *Tages-Anzeiger*, 28 August 2014, p. 22.

69. For an introduction to this concept see Miriam Hansen, 'Early Silent Cinema: Whose Public Sphere?', *New German Critique*, 29 (1983), 147–84.

70. It is important to stress the fact that the definition did not become familiar among Italian migrants in Zurich but has been used only in specific contexts or sporadically by single persons. See Pierluigi G. Paloschi's text quoted in Toni Ricciardi, *Associazionismo e migrazione. Storia delle Colonie Libere e degli italiani in Svizzera* (Rome: Laterza, 2013), pp. 222–23.

71. See Ricciardi, 'Gli italiani a Zurigo', p. 361. See also Toni Ricciardi, 'Zurigo-Aussersihl', in *Dizionario enciclopedico delle migrazioni italiane nel mondo*, ed. by Tiziana Grassi, Enzo Caffarelli, Mina Cappussi, Delfina Licata, and Gian Carlo Perego (Rome: Società Editrice Italiana, 2014), pp. 827–28. See also Marina Frigerio Martina, and Susanne Merahr, '. . . und es kamen auch Menschen': *Die Schweiz der Italiener* (Zurich: Rotpunktverlag, 2014), p. 62; and Ernst Matthias Rüsch, '*Conversation über das Eine, was not tut'*: *Evangelisch-reformierte Italienierseelsorge im Kanton Zürich im 19. und 20. Jahrhundert* (Zurich: Theologischer Verlag Zürich, 2010), pp. 47–48.

72. Serena Tinari, 'E la Svizzera divenne italiana', *Azione*, 5 September 2016, p. 26.

73. There was one restaurant in the quarter called *Little Italy: The Osteria Italiana*, in Militärstrasse 76. See also Susanne Wessendorf, *Second-Generation Transnationalism and Roots Migration: Cross-Borders Lives* (London and New York: Routledge, 2013), pp. 65–71.

74. One of the earliest uses of term up to now appears in Bruno Spoerri's album *Langstrasse Zwischen 12 und 12* (1971) as the title of one of its records. This album was composed for the homonymous Gianni Paggi's documentary, which depicts Aussersihl with its tenements, bars, red light locals, and also with its Italian inhabitants and shops.

75. See David Sarasin, 'Die unbekannte Langstrasse', *Tages-Anzeiger*, 25 November 2016, <http://www.tagesanzeiger.ch/zuerich/bellevue/die-unbekannte-langstrasse/story/11300299> [accessed 10 July 2017].

76. A *secondo* is in Swiss-German a person who was born in Switzerland but has migrant origins.

77. A collection of film reviews and press kit materials is available in Cinémateque suisse, documentation centre Zurich, folder 19039/2–3. The connection between *Filou* and Little Italy was suggested by the film production itself through the material addressed to the press.

78. See Redaction, 'Piazza Cella soll an Zürichs "Little Italy" erinnern', *Neue Zürcher Zeitung*, 9 March 2009, <https://www.nzz.ch/die_piazza_cella_soll_an_zuerichs_little_italy_erinnern-1.2165694> [accessed 10 July 2017].
79. Sociologists talk about a mediterranization of Zurich. See Angelo Maiolino, 'La contruction des identités dans le débat politique: du danger de la "surpopolation étrangere" à la méditerranéisation de la Suisse', in *La migration italienne dans la Suisse d'après-guerre*, ed. by Morena La Barba, Christian Stohr, Michel Oris, and Sandro Cattacin (Lausanne: Antipodes, 2013), pp. 129–64.

CHAPTER 13

Italianisms in US English: Past and Present

Laura Pinnavaia

In sailing across the Atlantic and finding a new world, an Italian had in one sense inaugurated 'modern times', and deprived the Mediterranean of its central position in the world. But much earlier, in the fifteenth century, Italy could claim to have given birth to 'modern times' in several other senses.[1]

Introduction

A scroll down the output of entries returned from a bibliographical search on borrowings reveals how much scientific attention has been placed upon English borrowings or Anglicisms in other languages over the last two centuries, owing to the role the English language has had as a lingua franca for roughly the same time. As is well known, however, English has not always held this prime position. For many centuries prior to the twentieth and twenty-first centuries, the principal languages of international communication were Latin, French, and Italian too.

In the sixteenth and seventeenth centuries the Italian language and culture, cradle of ancient and classical studies, enlightened and impassioned the European world. According to the *OED*, the number of Italian borrowings or Italianisms in English reached its peak between the years 1550 to 1650 when a direct line of communication between Italy and England, established through ambassadors, clergymen, diplomats, tradesmen, and teachers took the new humanistic word to England too.[2] Italian life during this century inspired the English social milieu with new ideas, new customs, new styles, and consequently a multitude of Italian lexemes. And even from the 1650s onwards, when Italy with its Catholicism fell into disrepute and England turned to France as a model, strengthened by Charles I's marriage to a French princess, the intake of Italianisms continued steadily until the 1900s in admiration of Italy's artistic and scientific qualities. As studies have shown,[3] the influence that Italy and its language had upon English society, culture, and language from the sixteenth to the twentieth century is significant.

If until the twentieth century by English one basically meant British English, since the 1900s one might also mean one of the many varieties spoken around the world, and most probably US English. It is no surprise in fact that recent lexicographical updates during the revision process of the third edition of the *OED*[4] have shown that the sources that attest to the entrance of Italian borrowings into English from the 1900s onwards are prevalently newspapers and magazines from the USA.[5] By recording the socio-cultural habits along with the scientific and artistic enterprises of a nation directly influenced by the presence of Italians since the first heavy flow of migration between the years 1880 and 1924[6] and a second lighter one in the thirty years between 1945 and 1976,[7] these sources are a clear indication that starting from the twentieth century Italianisms in the *OED* are reported as originating mainly in the USA, where we might say the most popular and influential variety of English is now spoken.

John Simpson claims that the *OED* has become more and more international since the beginning of the revision process that started in 1993.[8] However, to further an exploration of Italianisms in English and in this case in US English, it makes sense to carry out the investigation on the dictionary that — like the *OED* for British English — best represents the US variety, namely the *Merriam-Webster*. Through a quantitative and qualitative examination of the US lemmas of Italian origin recorded in the *Merriam-Webster*, we will show the cultural and linguistic influence of the Italian language upon the US variety of English.[9] The phonetic, orthographic, morphosyntactic, and semantic nature of the Italian borrowings will testify to two types of contact between Italian and US English cultures and societies: an indirect one via the first English settlers and a direct one with the Italian immigrants themselves.[10] Before collating this lexical information, a description of the methodological pursuit will be provided.

Methodology

To retrieve the Italianisms in the *Merriam-Webster*, an advanced search was carried out in the online and unabridged version of the dictionary. The procedure involved, first, typing in the term 'Italian' in the etymology box, which returned a list of 2,547 lemmas; second, an examination of the etymological description of each lemma to select only the lexemes with a direct and exclusive relationship with Italian. It was decided in fact not to take into account (a) lemmas where Italian is the indirect source, such as *ortolan*, described as originating from French *ortolan*, in turn from Italian *ortolano*; (b) lemmas where Italian may be one of two or more foreign origins, for instance *majordomo*, described as stemming from Spanish *or* Italian (my italics); (c) lemmas where Italian is one of multiple origins, for example *apogee* stated as coming from Italian, French, Greek, and New Latin. Our aim was to collect only the lexemes 'borrowed' directly and almost exclusively from Italian.[11]

The theories of some of the major experts in lexical borrowing, such as Haugen,[12] Gusmani,[13] Deroy,[14] all contend that a borrowing is the result of the imitation of linguistic elements that *must* belong to another language. Gusmani's definition is particularly poignant:

> La definizione di prestito spetta solo a quegli elementi che una lingua [. . .] ha effettivamente modellato su un'altra, [. . .] è necessario dunque provare o almeno rendere plausibile il rapporto storico di dipendenza tra l'elemento in

> questione e il modello straniero escludendo per esempio che possa trattarsi di creazione indipendente. Laddove questo rapporto di dipendenza non è dimostrabile o non è verosimile o addirittura va sicuramente negato, non ha senso alcuno parlare di prestito.
>
> [An item can only be defined as a borrowing if it has a model in another language. It is therefore necessary to prove or at least hypothesize that an etymological relationship exists between the item in question and its foreign model, thus excluding the possibility of its being an independent creation. If this etymological relationship cannot be proven, is unlikely, or does not exist, the item cannot be called a borrowing.][15]

He asserts that for a word to be a borrowing a foreign model is needed: more precisely, he emphasizes in his work that for any word to be a borrowing its syntactic and semantic structures must correspond to those of the foreign model, if not completely, at least partially. The extent of the reproduction can in fact result in different types of borrowings: (a) the loanword, where both forms and meanings are fully replicated (e.g. *spaghetti* from It. *spaghetti*); (b) the loan translation, where the meanings correspond, but the form is translated into the target language (e.g. *balsamic vinegar* from It. *aceto balsamico*); (c) the semantic loan, where only the foreign meaning is acquired (e.g. *to invest* (in the sense of money) from It. *investire*); (d) the loanblend, which is either a compound made up of the translation of one of the lexemes and the direct borrowing of the other lexeme (e.g. *Cassini division* from It. *divisione Cassini*) or a derivative, whereby either the root or the affix of a word has been translated and the other borrowed (e.g. *Pescatarian* from It. *pesce* and Eng. *-tarian* as in *vegetarian*). If the lexemes were found to belong to one of these categories, they were selected as Italianisms.

One big question remained whether we should include false or pseudo-borrowings too. Furiassi, who has carried out extensive research on false Anglicisms,[16] and of late has also studied false Italianisms in English,[17] provides this definition:

> False Italianisms — which most English speakers believe to be purely Italian — are created when genuine lexical borrowings from Italian, that is Italianisms, are so reinterpreted by a recipient language, English in this case, that native speakers of Italian would not recognize them as part of their own lexical inventory and would neither understand nor use [them]. Interestingly, the creation of false Italianisms yields to [sic] new insights into the covert prestige attributed to the supposed donor language and culture.[18]

Unlike true borrowings, false borrowings do not have a genuine model in the donor language, but like true borrowings they come into being for the same reasons, the most interesting being the prestige held by the donor language, which Furiassi does not fail to point out. Because the process of imitating words or creating new ones so that they might appear to be foreign has such important cultural implications, false Italianisms recorded in the *Merriam-Webster* were not excluded from this research.[19]

Once selected, the Italianisms were counted, analysed from a structural point of view, and accordingly catalogued in one of a series of sixteen semantic macro categories: (i) arts and learning, (ii) behaviour, (iii) casuals, (iv) clothes, (v) commerce, (vi) crafts, (vii) evaluation, (viii) food and drink, (ix) games, (x) music, opera and dance, (xi) religion, politics, and law (RPL), (xii) science and nature, (xiii) sports, (xiv) transport, (xv) warfare, (xvi) miscellaneous. What follows are the results regarding the number and types of Italianisms in US English as registered by the *Merriam-Webster*.

The Quantitative and Qualitative Nature of the Italianisms

The close analysis of the 2,547 lemmas electronically retrieved from the *Merriam-Webster*, based on the methodology indicated above, led to the exclusion of 818 lexemes (roughly a third of the total number), leaving 1,729 that, owing to the almost exclusive and direct relationship with the Italian language, can be considered Italianisms. The table below accounts for their semantic distribution:

Italianism	*Semantic area*
music, opera and dance	630
nature and science	236
food and drink	216
arts and learning	207
casuals	118
craft	58
behaviour	43
commerce	32
RPL	30
transport	28
games	20
warfare	21
clothes	18
sports	15
evaluation	12
miscellaneous	45

As can be seen, and as might have been expected, the Italianisms belong mostly to the category of music, opera, and dance. Much more equally distributed, but numbering far fewer than 630, are the lexemes that belong to the categories of nature and science (comprising terms in the fields of agriculture, anatomy, astronomy, biology, botany, chemistry, communication, economics, entomology, geography, geology, mineralogy, physics, psychology, zoology), food and drink (including cooking), and arts and learning (including terms that point to architecture, drawing and painting, poetry, language and literature, and sculpture) that all have just over 200 Italianisms each. Particularly interesting is the category labelled casuals, which hosts 118 terms that refer solely to Italian people, places, and lifestyle.[20] All the remaining categories host far fewer words: while craft holds 58 Italianisms that define items principally in the fields of ceramics, fabrics, and glassware, all the others have less than 50 each.

Though numerically lighter, the latter categories are indicative of the way the large majority of the Italianisms made their way into US English. Many of the lexemes referring to human behaviour such as *innamorato* and *furioso* and to evaluations such as *italianate* and *simpatico*; to coins within the category of commerce such as *paolo* and *soldo*; to religious, political, and legislative terms such as *manifesto* and *nuncio*; to different types of sea vessels within the transport category (*argosy* and *felucca*); to terms regarding warfare such as *stiletto* and *vendetta*; to clothes such as *garibaldi* and *mozzetta*; and to sports terms such as *balloon* and *regatta* were present in the English language well before the foundation of the US Republic. Their entrance into US English came via the English spoken and written by the first settlers and founders of the new Republic. Washington, Jefferson, Franklin might have been born in the USA but they were of English cultural breeding and their knowledge of Italy and Italian was scholarly, as was that of Noah Webster, who compiled the dictionary that gave officialdom to the US variety of the English language.

Italianisms of the English Motherland

Although Noah Webster's *American Dictionary of the English Language*, first published in 1828, marks the true beginnings of US English lexicography, like all dictionaries it 'made copious use of existing dictionaries'[21] published in the English motherland. Webster's work was not only based on Samuel Johnson's *Dictionary of the English Language*, but it also relied extensively on the citations of British authors and poets,[22] from whose pens so many Italian words had already smoothly glided into the English of the British Isles. With the successive editions of Webster's dictionaries, these Italianisms would become official members of the new transatlantic lexicon too.

On Webster's death in 1843 the unsold copies and publishing rights of his dictionary were acquired by George and Charles Merriam, who issued a revised edition of Webster's dictionary: the first *Merriam-Webster Unabridged Dictionary*, edited by Chauncey A. Goodrich, in 1847. Successive editions were the *Unabridged* in 1864 (edited by Noah Porter), *Webster's International Dictionary* in 1890 (again edited by Porter), *Webster's New International Dictionary* in 1909 (edited by William Torrey Harris), *Webster's New International Dictionary Second Edition* in 1934 (edited by William Allan Neilson). With *Webster's Third New International Dictionary of the English Language* (edited by Philip Gove) in 1961, a permanent *Merriam-Webster* office staff was established along with a team of over 200 other scholars and specialists, who collaborated in reviewing, revising, and submitting new definitions in subjects in which they were the authorities. While 4,500,000 new examples of recorded usage were added to the 1,665,000 citations already in the files of previous editions, this dictionary also and inevitably included the citations of the *OED*, the largest and most representative of the English language spoken in the British Isles. If so many Italianisms are recorded in the current edition of the *Merriam-Webster*, it is undoubtedly also thanks to the rich treasure of Italian words the *OED* records in testimony of the intricate relationship the British had with Italian culture and its language before the arrival of Italians on North American soil.

Most Italianisms recorded in *Merriam-Webster* with dates of attestation prior to the 1900s seem indeed to coincide largely with the data held in the *OED* — from which many must have been taken — thus reflecting in the US variety the English heritage of much earlier contacts with the Italian language. Defined as *distant* and not *intimate*,[23] the relationship between Anglophones and Italians in Europe was originally of a literary and learned nature. There is cultural and linguistic evidence for this. From a cultural point of view, the fact that the intake of Italianisms covering a wide range of semantic fields regarding music, the arts, science, and nature was so great in the seventeenth and nineteenth centuries underscores English interest principally in the humanistic ideas circulating in Italy during the English Renaissance first and then in Italy's natural beauties and artistic advances during the English Romantic period. From a linguistic point of view, the fact that the Italian language influenced mainly the lexicon of English without impacting on the grammar shows how English contact with Italian was not direct and intimate as it had been with Latin, French, and the Scandinavian languages.

The Semantic Nature of Italianisms

The Italianisms of British English origin recorded in the *Merriam-Webster* that stand out from the total 1,729 are undoubtedly the ones regarding music and opera. Italianisms define musical instruments such as *clavicembalo*, *fagotto*, *piano*, *viola*, *zampogna* and performers such as *basso cantante*, *flautist*, *maestro di cappella*, *prima donna*, *soprano*; musical pieces such as *aria*, *duet/duetto*, *opera/operetta*, *romanza*, *serenata*; and musical directions such as *a cappella*, *crescendo*, *fortissimo*, *presto*, *rallentato*. In the *Merriam-Webster*, just as in the *OED*, the majority are attested for the first time in the eighteenth century when the Italian musical and opera tradition in England had started to bloom, and more precisely with the opening of the Haymarket Theatre in London in 1705.[24]

Another significant number of Italianisms in the *Merriam-Webster* that stem from early English contacts with Italian belong to the macro-semantic category of the arts. We can find terms regarding architecture such as *balcony*, *portico*, *sala*, *villa*, *zocco*; regarding drawing, painting, and sculpture such as *abozzo*, *chiaroscuro*, *relieve/relief*, *seicento*, *torso*; regarding language, literature, and poetry such as *cancellaresca corsiva*, *quattrocentist*, *ottava rima*, *stanza*, *tercet*. Moreover, the precious tapestries, marble sculptures, and stucco ceilings that decorated the wealthy houses of the English nobles[25] explain the number of Italianisms that have been grouped under the category of crafts, comprising principally fabrics (e.g. *armozeen*, *baldachin*, *ferret*, *fustanella*, *mockado*, *mohair*, *organzine*), glassmaking and glassware (*agata*, *calcar*, *latticinio*, *polverine*, *pucellas*, *rochetta*, *smalto*, *vitro di trina*), marble (*cosmatesque*, *giallo antico*, *nero antico*, *palombino*, *parmazo marble*, *pavonazzo*, *rosso antico*, *scagliola*, *terrazzo*), mosaics (*intarsiatura*, *intarsio*, *tarsia*), plaster and dyes (*gesso*, *giallolino*, *indigo*, *terra sienna*, *terra verde*), pottery and ornaments (*albarello*, *bianco sopra bianco*, *bucchero*, *cipolin*, *fioritura*, *majolica*, *mezza-majolica*, *porcelanous*, *tazza*, *terra-cotta*).

The Grand Tour that took many English gentlemen and ladies to Italy in the eighteenth and nineteenth centuries physically but especially virtually — owing to the proliferation of travel books that would describe the landscape, people, cities, sites, customs, and resourcefulness of *il bel paese* — also explains the number of Italianisms classified within the categories of casuals, nature, and science. Some examples of casuals are the terms that define the people and the tongues of different regions such as *Milanese* and *Genovese*; that indicate governmental figures such as *contessa* and *marchese*; institutional posts such as *alpino* and *bersagliere*, urban sites such as *corso* and *piazza*; constructions such as *osteria* and *nuraghe*; and titles such as *illustrissimo* and *signora*. Being terms that pertain to the Italian linguistic community only, the casuals represent terms encountered during the sojourns in Italy, and introduced into the English language by the ensuing travel literature. Consequently, they have remained purely exotic references in British and US English.

On the contrary, the Italianisms regarding nature and science are words that have become essential items of reference in the English lexicon. Some noteworthy examples from this category come from the fields of anatomy and diseases (e.g. *acrophobia*, *influenza*), astronomy (e.g. *new star*, *secchi disc*), biochemistry (*gliadin*, *univoltine*), botany (*belladonna*, *girasol*), communication (*lingua franca*), economics (*del credere*), entomology (e.g. *cicala*, *malmignatte*), geography (e.g. *archipelago*, *marina*), geology (*grotto*, *lava*, *volcano*), mineralogy (*matildite*, *soda*), physics (*Negri body*), and zoology (e.g. *beccafico*, *buffalo*, *giraffe*, *zebra*). Unlike the casuals, these terms truly enriched the English lexicon and, like the ones referring to music and arts listed earlier, filled significant semantic gaps in the English language from the mid-sixteenth to the late nineteenth century.

The Structure of Italianisms

A closer look at the type of Italianisms listed in the section above will disclose a series of loanwords, which reproduce in English the original meaning and form of an Italian word. The loanword is without doubt the most frequent structure among the plethora of Italianisms recorded in the *Merriam-Webster* and is an ulterior sign of the type of cultural contact between the English and Italian languages. As opposed to loan-translations and loanblends, loanwords reflect a distant type of linguistic contact where bilingualism does not really exist,[26] but where interest, curiosity, and awe for the lending country do. The wealthy and educated classes of British society seized a whole series of Italian words to fill social and cultural gaps, phonetically, orthographically, and morphologically integrating them in their language before exporting them to the New World.

Because the Italian and English vowel systems were and continue to be very different, the pronunciation of a significant number of Italian loanwords in British English underwent a phonetic transformation called substitution by approximation,[27] whereby the Italian vowel sounds were replaced by the closest-sounding equivalents in English. *Belladonna* is a case in point: from being pronounced /bellaˈdɔnna/, it became /ˌbɛləˈdɑnə/ (cf. *OED* s.v. *belladonna*) in both British and US English, with the equivalent more open /ɑ/ sound replacing the Italian stressed vowel /ɔ/ and the indistinct schwa sound /ə/, typical of English words ending in vowels, replacing the Italian /a/. Another noteworthy phonetic difference between the original pronunciation of *belladonna* and its new pronunciation is consonantal length,[28] which has been reduced to a single consonant in both varieties of English, shown by the single phoneme /l/.

Another series of phonetic changes that undoubtedly occurred to the Italian borrowings before they left British soil respond to the so-called process of mechanic adaptation,[29] determining such pronunciations as /ˈsmaltəʊ/ in British English and /ˈsmɑltoʊ/ in US English (cf. *OED* s.v. *smalto*) instead of the Italian original pronounced /zmalto/: if in Italian the fricative /s/ is voiced before a voiced bilabial nasal /m/ and a voiced alveolar nasal /n/, in English it is always voiceless. On the contrary, the vowel sound /u/ remains unaltered in Italian regardless of its environment, whereas in English under certain conditions it is delabialized, which explains why Italian *bufalo* /ˈbufalo/ became /ˈbʌfələʊ/ in British English and /ˈbəf(ə)ˌloʊ/ in US English.[30]

Substitution through analogy is the third process which can explain ulterior examples of phonetic adaptations of Italianisms in English.[31] In this case, the pronunciation is influenced by a native interpretation of the foreign orthography. For example, <c> of *cicala* came to be pronounced in English as the voiceless fricative /s/ instead of its original voiceless postalveolar affricate /t͡ʃ/, influenced by the English pronunciation of words beginning with the grapheme <c> followed by <i>; or *matildite* whose suffix became /aɪt/ instead of the original /ite/ through analogy with the pronunciation of this suffix found in native words.

Just as the pronunciation of the Italian borrowings was adapted in British English, so was the spelling. Similar orthographic adjustments of the Italian words in both varieties of English seem once again to endorse the influence of British English upon many US Italianisms. *Girasol* and *acrophobia* illustrate two typical adaptation mechanisms; one phonetically, the other orthographically driven. English *girasol* from Italian *girasole* lost its final <e> influenced by the phenomenon of the mute <e>, typical of English phonetics; the <f> of It. *acrofobia* was replaced by the grapheme <ph> in English to comply with early English orthographic conventions based on classical Greek and Latin. While these two Italianisms illustrate the application of either one or the other adaptation process, some Italianisms exemplify a fusion of both. It is the case of *balcony* from Italian *balcone* and *archipelago* from Italian *arcipelago*. The former shows how the original grapheme <e>, following a phonetic adjustment to an /ɪ/ — presumably in a hypercorrective manner to avoid its becoming muted — became the grapheme <y>, typical of the /ɪ/ sound in final position. *Archipelago* shows the reverse process, in that its orthography caused a subsequent change in the pronunciation: the graphemic string <chi>, chosen to reflect the original Italian pronunciation /t͡ʃi/ represented by the spelling <ci>, led to the new pronunciation /kɪ/ in English, influenced by the pronunciation of analogously spelled words, such as *architect* and *architecture*.

From a morphosyntactic point of view too, most of the Italianisms in the *Merriam-Webster* reflect the same changes undergone by the Italianisms recorded in the *OED*; principally, the elimination or substitution of the original endings. Since the article and the gender ending are two variables that have no reason to be in English, most Italianisms were reproduced without articles (except for *la dolce vita*) and often with inexact gender endings. Unless they refer to Italian people, like *alpino* and *contessa*, the '-a' for feminine nouns and the '-o' for masculine nouns are meaningless in English. This is testified to by Italianisms whose original gender endings were inverted, as in the cases of *romanza* from Italian *romanzo* and *grotto* from Italian *grotta*. The decision to reproduce the gender endings despite their inexactness and semantic irrelevance nonetheless underscores the importance of securing the exotic charm exuding from non-native words.

Indeed, the exotic aura was often maintained even when the morphological suffixes were substituted, because — as is well known — many English nominal and adjectival suffixes have Latin or French origins. The Italianism *porcelanous* stemming from *porcellanoso* exemplifies the substitution of the English -*ous* for the Italian adjectival suffix -*oso*; just as does the Italianism *quattrocentist*, whose original nominal suffix -*ista* in *quattrocentista* was replaced with -*ist*. Thanks to their common Latin denominator, these morphemes in Italian and English are substitutable both formally and functionally. Besides the obvious cultural and historical influence of the French language upon the English, the formal and functional similarity between Italian and French morphemes helps to explain why more French morphemes as opposed to Anglo-Saxon ones were employed in adapting the morphological structure of Italianisms in English. The adjectival suffixes of French origin, -*esque* and -*oon*, readily replace the Italian equivalents -*esco* and -*one*, as shown by *balloon* from It. *ballone* and *cosmatesque* from It. *cosmatesco*. Though foreign, these suffixes are what Hope denominates 'conventional equivalents'[32] because they were the most commonly used to accommodate the new Italian words in British and US English.

In sum, given that many of the Italianisms recorded in the *Merriam-Webster* have the same structures and the same meanings as the Italianisms recorded in the *OED*, with first dates of attestation prior to the arrival of the first Italians in the USA, it is plausible to conjecture that many had already enriched and renewed the English lexicon when its speakers took it to the New World. It is this lexicon that would become the substrate for a new and distinguished variety of English, composed of a whole series of new words from the languages of the new settlers including Italians.

Italianisms in US English

History books tell us that the first immigrants from Italy started to arrive in the USA in the mid-nineteenth century. Romano writes that 9,474,000 Italians predominantly from the central and southern areas of Italy arrived to seek work from 1850 to 1914, creating 'little Italies' in most of the major cities, like New York and Boston on the East Coast and San Francisco and Los Angeles on the West Coast.[33] However, because the Italian immigrants came from humble backgrounds, were almost all illiterate, and only spoke dialect, their linguistic and cultural contribution to the US English language and lifestyle at the end of the nineteenth century and in the early twentieth century was limited. In fact, unlike the Jews who as soon as they arrived climbed the social ladder rapidly, obtaining important posts in the fields of journalism, show business, advertising, and finance, the Italians for a long time did not improve their social status.[34] Living in inner-city areas (called *ghettoes*), running family businesses, marrying their co-nationals, they failed to integrate with other members of US society, by whom they were despised and denigrated (and referred to as *wops*).

Only by discarding their past and concentrating on economic and social advancement, did the Italians of the second and third generations slowly start to become respected citizens whose energies and talents could finally be appreciated.[35] Even though this happened sooner in Las Vegas than in other cities,[36] it is emblematic of how, starting from the mid-twentieth century, Italians began to make a difference in US society. This was heightened by the close alliance between the USA and Italy at the end of the Second World War and with the arrival of a second — albeit minor — flow of Italian immigrants from 1945 to 1976, whose social, cultural, and linguistic standing, owing to better schooling and to the spread of radio, cinema, and television in Italy, was to strengthen further the Italian impact upon US society. Indeed, owing to the conspicuous and constant presence of Italians in the food and drink industry, this sector along with the Italians promoting it began to gain the prestige which now distinguishes Italian food and beverage not only in the USA but all over the world.[37] It thus explains the significant number of Italianisms regarding food and drink recorded in the *Merriam-Webster*.

Italianisms Regarding Food and Drink

There are 216 Italianisms in the *Merriam-Webster* that describe food and drink: more precisely, 176 terms refer to food and 40 to drink. To deal with the terms regarding beverage first:

24 are wines and wine-related items: *amarone, arneis, asti spumante, barbaresco, barbera, bardolino, barolo, brunello, chianti, classico, fiasco, gattinara, lambrusco, malvasia, orvieto, pinot grigio, prosecco, riserva, sangiovese, soave, trebbiano, verdicchio, vino, vin santo*;

8 are liquors or alcoholic drinks in general: *bumbo, fior dell'alpi, grappa, maraschino, negroni, nipa, rosolio, sambuca*;

6 are coffees: *caffè, caffè latte, cappuccino, espresso, latte, macchiato*;

1 is the non-alcoholic sherbet: *granita*.

As might have been expected, the largest group within the category of beverages regards the words that define the wines introduced into the USA by the people of the different wine-making regions of Italy. It is followed by the list of terms pointing to the spirits sold in the liquor stores opened and owned by so many Italians of first and later generations.[38]

As far as the terms referring to food are concerned:

49 describe different types of pasta and pasta dishes: *alimentary paste, agnolotti, angel-hair pasta, bavette, bucatini, cannelloni, cannelon, capellini, cappelletti, carbonara, cavatappi, cavatelli, ditali, ditalini, farfalle, fedelini, fettuccelle, fettuccine, fettuccine Alfredo, fusilli, gnocchi, lasagna, linguine, macaroni, manicotti, mostaccioli, orecchiette, orzo, pappardelle, pasta, pastina, penne, perciatelli, polenta, primavera, puttanesca, ravioli, rigatoni, risotto, semolina, spaghetti, spaghettini, tagliarini, tagliatelle, tetrazzini, tortellini, tufoli, vermicelli, ziti*;

23 are vegetables and vegetable dishes: *artichoke, arugola, broccoli, broccoli rabe, calabrese, carosella, cauliflower, cavolo nero, celery, cipollini, cocozelle, cremini, crimini mushroom, finocchio, minestra, minestrone, parmigiana, porcini, porcino, portobello radicchio, rugola, scarola, zucchini*;

22 are meats and meat dishes: *bollito misto, bologna, braciola, bresaola, cacciatore,*

capocollo, capretto, carpaccio, chianina, coppa, cotechino, mortadella, osso buco, pancetta, pepperoni, piccata, prosciutto, ragù, salami, saltimbocca, scallopini, spiedino;

18 are cheese and cheese dishes: *caciocavallo, caprese, fonduta, fontina, gorgonzola, grana, incanestrato, mascarpone, mozzarella, parmiggiano-reggiano, pasta filata cheese, pecorino, provola, provolone, reggiano, ricotta, romano, taleggio*;

13 are desserts: *affogato, cannoli, cassata, dolce, frangipane, gelato, panettone, spumoni, tiramisu, tortoni, tutti-frutti, zabaglione, zuppa inglese*;

11 are bread produce: *bruschetta, calzone, ciabatta, crostini, focaccia, grissino, muffuletta, panforte, panini, pizza, pizzetta*;

11 are fish and fish dishes: *bottarga, calamari, cioppino, crudo, fritto misto, locust lobster, louvar, petrale sole, scampi, scungilli, fra diavolo*;

6 are fruits: *chinotto, fico, marasca, pignolia, pistacchio, prunello*;

5 are sweets and biscuits: *amaretto, confetti, marchpane, torrone, zeppole*;

3 are vegetables: *fava, borlotti, cannellini beans*;

3 are sauces: *caponata, marinara, pesto*;

2 are condiments and seasoning: *balsamic vinegar, gremolata*;

1 is the cereal: *sorgo*;

1 is the egg-based dish: *frittata*.

Moreover, there are 3 terms regarding cooking techniques: *al dente, to candy, to marinate*.

There are 3 regarding eating habits and places: *brindisi, pescatarian, pizzeria*.

There are 2 regarding food in general: *antepast, antipasto*.

As for drink, likewise for the food category the largest group is not at all surprising: pasta is undoubtedly the biggest novelty introduced to US cuisine, and its many different shapes and sizes are now recorded in the *Merriam-Webster*. Another substantial category is that of vegetables which, along with pasta, characterizes the highly acclaimed Mediterranean diet. That said, also meats and cheeses, typical of certain regions and cuisines of Italy, stand out in the lexicon of US English, along with a series of desserts that might no longer be considered healthy products but that are no doubt appetizing. It is precisely the tastefulness and the overall healthiness of Italian food that has made it prestigious and popular in English-speaking countries. While most of the other Italianisms representing the other semantic categories are of a learned nature and relegated to specific usage, food and drink items are widespread and well known by all members of society. The dates and sources of their introduction into the US variety seem to confirm the fact that, unlike their adoption into the British English variety, they are the outcome of a much more direct and intimate contact between the English and Italian speaking communities in the USA.

Philological Considerations

The examination and comparative analysis of the dates and sources of the 216 Italianisms regarding food and drink in the *OED* and the *Merriam-Webster* seems to support the claim that the Italian influence upon the US variety of English in this category has been largely direct. Well over a half (139 precisely[39]) seem to have entered directly into the US variety of English without the intermediation of the British variety. This is the case of all the words which, firstly, are not recorded in the *OED*. It includes the following 29 terms listed in chronological order with the first date of attestation in the *Merriam-Webster* being 1842 and final one 2000 (*alimentary paste, barbera, fiasco, caciocavallo, barbaresco, bardolino, chianina, cioppino, braciola, broccoli rabe, cipollini, cacciatore, bucatini, fontina, fior dell'alpi, sangiovese, cappelletti, cavatelli, capellini, petrale sole, fettuccine Alfredo, bresaola, bollito misto, angel-hair pasta, porcino, cavatappi, cremini, arneis, crudo*). It also includes the 31 terms not included in the *OED* that have no date of attestation in the *Merriam-Webster*, listed in alphabetical order: *bavette, brindisi, cannellini bean, cannelon, capocollo, capretto, carosella, chinotto, cocozelle, coppa, cotechino, crimini mushroom, ditali, ditalini, dolce* (noun), *fedelini, fettuccelle, fiasco, fonduta, fra diavolo, gattinara, grana, incanestrato, louvar, pasta filata cheese, pinot grigio, provola, scarola, spiedino, torrone, tufoli*. Secondly, it involves the 38 terms whose first date of attestation in the *Merriam-Webster* precedes the first date of attestation in the *OED* (*amaretto, amarone, antipasto, asti spumante, balsamic vinegar, Barolo, caffè, caffè latte, caponata, cappuccino, caprese, cavolo nero, crostini, fava, focaccia, frangipane, frittata, fusilli, lambrusco, linguine, macchiato, orecchiette, pancetta, parmigiana, pizzeria, portobello, puttanesca, radicchio, salami, scallopini, spaghettini, spumoni, taleggio, tortellini, tetrazzini, vin santo, zucchini, zuppa inglese*). Finally it comprises the 37 terms that, either having no date in the *Merriam-Webster* or having the same dates of attestation in both dictionaries, have US publications as their primary sources (see *affogato, arugula, borlotti, calabrese, calzone, carpaccio, cassata, ciabatta, classico, granita, grappa, manicotti, minestrone, mostaccioli, mozzarella, muffuletta, negroni, orzo, panini, pastina, pecorino, penne, perciatelli, pescatarian, piccata, pignolia, primavera, reggiano, rigatoni, romano, rugola, scungilli, soave, tortoni, tutti-frutti, verdicchio, zeppole*).

Clearly, the same procedure of analysis seems to point to 76 food and drink items that might have entered the US variety via British English. It is the case with the following 19 lemmas, whose first attestations in the *Merriam-Webster* and *OED* range from 1516 to 1797: *polenta, marchpane, artichoke, to candy, antepast, fico, bologna, macaroni, mortadella, ricotta, marinate, celery, malvasia, vermicelli, broccoli, ravioli, maraschino, rosolio, semolina*. Because they are attested in both dictionaries well before the migration of the first Italians to the USA, it is more likely these words were introduced by the British settlers. Similarly, the 20 words whose first dates of attestation in the *OED* chronologically precede the ones in the *Merriam-Webster* (*al dente, bottarga, Brunello, cannelloni, espresso, finocchio, gelato, lasagna, marinara, mascarpone, orvieto, panettone, pasta, pepperoni, pizza, prosciutto, provolone, ragù, spaghetti, vino*), or the 37 terms whose first sources are British, when the first dates of attestation are the same or inexistent in the *Merriam-Webster* (*agnolotti, bruschetta, bumbo, calamari, cannoli, carbonara, chianti, confetti, farfalle, fritto misto, gnocchi, gorgonzola, gremolata, grissino, locust lobster, marasca, minestra, osso buco, panforte, pappardelle, parmigiano-reggiano, pesto, pizzetta, porcini, prosecco, prunello, riserva, risotto, saltimbocca, sambuca, scampi, tagliarini, tagliatelle, tiramisu, trebbiano, zabaglione, ziti*) could also be words that might not have been introduced directly by the Italians themselves.

Although these philological observations might lead us to surmise that some of these food and drink Italianisms may have been indirectly transferred into US

English through the British variety, given the nature of these words this might not be necessarily true. Unlike terms regarding music, arts, and science, which tend to be used in literary and specific contexts only, food and drink items are a part of the everyday vocabulary of speakers. It is thus highly possible that many of the food and drink terms of Italian origin introduced into British English first by travel books (such as John Ray's *Observations topographical, moral and physiological in a journey through part of the Low Countries of 1673*), recipe books (such as Eliza Acton's *Modern Cookery of 1845*) or prose in general (such as Charles Dickens's *Pictures from Italy of 1846*) may have independently re-entered into the US variety, through their adoption by speakers *in situ* or through US literary sources. An example of this could be *finocchio*, first attested in the *Merriam-Webster* in 1941; whereas in the *OED* it first appears as *finochio* in 1723. The chronological gap between the two attestations, along with the spelling change, could point to two separate and independent borrowings by the speakers of each variety, just like US English *brindisi* and British English *brendice* (1673 in *OED*), and US English *scarola* and British English *scariole* (1422 in *OED*).

The spelling changes from Italian to English are, however, limited and where they exist they are often indicative of the direct contact with Italian dialects, such as *arugula* and *rugola* from the dialect of Calabria, or *scungilli* from the Neapolitan *sconciglio*. The structures of the food and drink Italianisms are, indeed, generally faithful to the Italian original words. Apart from the loan-translations *locust lobster* and *balsamic vinegar* and the loanblends *cannellini beans*, *pasta filata cheese* and *pescatarian*, the phonetic, orthographic, and morphological adaptations are restricted to a bare minimum, and the loanwords are assimilated into their new environment in the most natural way possible. While this more faithful assimilation endorses an ever more direct exchange between the English and Italian language on US soil, it is also and above all indicative of the continued prestige of the Italian people and the hold of their language in the USA. Just like the literary or learned ones examined earlier, also the food and drink borrowings preserve the original Italian structures, this time in respect of a revered gastronomic culture.

Conclusions

The social prestige that accompanies Italian words in general and above all the ones defining food and drink, causing them to have been absorbed in so many languages, and especially US English, is constant and substantial enough to multiply the creation of false Italian borrowings or pseudo-Italianisms in US English. As Lanzilotti underlines,[40] the need to create new words of seemingly Italian origin (see *caramel macchiato, cinnamon dolce latte, espresso macchiato, frappuccino* in the Starbucks cafeteria menu)[41] shows how Italian is not just a language that fills semantic and cultural gaps, but is also becoming a tool for successful commercial businesses all over the world.

Since the mid sixteenth-century, when Italy was the cultural centre of the world, whose words were being adopted by all its European neighbours, few changes appear to have taken place. For over six centuries Italian words have been entering the English language, defining areas of human experience, in spite of the hegemony of the British and US nations. Although the major direction of borrowings is now from English to Italian, the Italian-speaking world continues to have a significant influence on British and US English, which, with the effects of globalization, are even more difficult to set apart now than they were in the past.

Notes to Chapter 13

1. Harry Hearder, *Italy: A Short History* (Cambridge: Cambridge University Press, 1990), p. 103.
2. See Stephen Lee, *Aspects of European History* (London: Methuen, 1984), p. 3.
3. See Giovanni Iamartino, 'La contrastività italiano-inglese in prospettiva storica', *Rassegna Italiana di Linguistica Applicata*, 33.2–3 (2001), 7–130; Giovanni Iamartino, 'Non solo maccheroni, mafia e mamma mia! Tracce lessicali dell'influsso culturale italiano in Inghilterra', in *L'inglese e le altre lingue europee. Studi sull'interferenza linguistica*, ed. by Felix San Vincente (Bologna: CLUEB, 2002), pp. 23–49; Giovanni Iamartino, 'Italy's unappetizing menu: italianismi recenti nella stampa angloamericana fra giudizio e pregiudizio', in *Italiano e inglese a confronto*, ed. by Anna Vera Sullam Calimani (Florence: Cesati, 2003), pp. 209–19; Anna L. Lepschy and Giulio Lepschy, 'Anglismi e italianismi', in Anna L. Lepschy and Giulio Lepschy, *L'amanuense analfabeta e altri saggi* (Florence: Olschki, 1999), pp. 169–82; Anna L. Lepschy and Giulio Lepschy, 'Italianismi inglesi', in *L'amanuense analfabeta e altri saggi*, pp. 183–207; Laura Pinnavaia, *The Italian Borrowings in the Oxford English Dictionary: A Lexicographical, Linguistic and Cultural Analysis* (Rome: Bulzoni, 2001); Harro Stammerjohann, 'L'italiano e altre lingue di fronte all'anglicizzazione', in *Italia linguistica anno Mille. Italia linguistica anno Duemila. Atti del XXXIV congresso internazionale di studi della Società di Linguistica Italiana (SLI). Firenze, 19–21 ottobre 2000*, ed. by Nicoletta Maraschio and Teresa Poggi-Salani (Rome: Bulzoni, 2003), pp. 77–101; Harro Stammerjohann, 'Introduzione', in *Dizionario di italianismi in francese, inglese, tedesco*, ed. by Harro Stammerjohann, Enrico Arcaini, Gabriella Cartago, Pia Galetto, Matthias Heinz, Maurice Mayer, Giovanni Rovere, and Gesine Seymer (Florence: Accademia della Crusca, 2008), pp. xi–xviii.
4. See *OED: The Oxford English Dictionary*, ed. by John Simpson and Edmund Weiner (Oxford: Oxford University Press, 1989), <http://www.oed.com>.
5. See Laura Pinnavaia, 'From Norm to Usage: Revisiting Italian Borrowings in the *Oxford English Dictionary*', in *Observing Norms, Observing Usage: Lexis in Dictionaries and in the Media*, ed. by Alessandra Molino and Serenella Zanotti (Berne: Peter Lang, 2014), pp. 69–90.
6. See Matteo Pretelli, *L'emigrazione italiana negli Stati Uniti* (Bologna: Il Mulino, 2011), p. 37.
7. See Luca Lanzilotta, 'Il caso Starbucks: l'italiano come lingua di commercio e di cultura negli Stati Uniti', *Italica*, 91.1 (2014), 71–88 (p. 72).
8. See John Simpson, 'The OED and Collaborative Research into the History of English', *Anglia*, 122.2 (2004), 185–208.
9. See *Merriam-Webster: Webster's Third New International Dictionary Unabridged*, ed. by P. B. Gove (Springfield, MA: Merriam Webster, 2002), <http://www.unabridged.merriam-webster.com>.
10. See Hermann Haller, 'Gli italianismi dell'anglo-americano', *Italiano e oltre*, 4.3 (1989), 126–32 (p. 127).
11. Even though the term 'borrowing' might not technically be correct, given there is no two-way transfer in this linguistic and social process, this is nonetheless the traditional term used in English just as its equivalent in French (*emprunt*), in German (*Lehnwort*) and in Italian (*prestito*) are used in the respective languages.
12. See Einar Haugen, 'The Analysis of Linguistic Borrowing', in *Ecology of Language: Essays by Haugen*, ed. by Anwar S. Dil (Stanford: Stanford University Press, 1972), pp. 79–109.
13. See Roberto Gusmani, *Aspetti del Prestito Linguistico* (Naples: Libreria Scientifica Editrice, 1973).
14. See Louis Deroy, *L'emprunt linguistique* (Paris: Les Belles Lettres, 1980).
15. Gusmani, *Aspetti del Prestito Linguistico*, p. 8.
16. See Cristiano Furiassi, *False Anglicisms in Italian* (Monza: Polimetrica, 2010).

17. See Cristiano Furiassi, 'Italianisms in Non-Native Varieties of English: A Corpus-Driven Approach', in *Challenges for the 21st Century: Dilemmas, Ambiguities, Directions. Papers from the 24th AIA (Associazione Italiana di Anglistica) Conference*, II: *Language Studies*, ed. by Gabriella Di Martino, Linda Lombardo, and Stefania Nuccorini (Rome: EdizioniQ, 2011), pp. 447–56; Cristiano Furiassi, 'False Italianisms in British and American English: A Meta-Lexicographic Analysis', in *Proceedings of the 15th EURALEX International Congress. Oslo, 7th–11th August 2012*, ed. by Ruth Vatvedt Fjeld and Julie Matilde Torjusen (Oslo: Department of Linguistics and Scandinavian Studies, University of Oslo, 2012), pp. 771–77; Cristiano Furiassi, 'False Italianisms in English Dictionaries and Corpora', in *Language Contact around the Globe*, ed. by Amei Koll-Stobbe and Sebastian Knospe (Frankfurt: Peter Lang, 2014), pp. 42–72.
18. Furiassi, 'False Italianisms in British and American English', p. 771.
19. False borrowings, such as *alfresco, bimbo, bologna, bravura, cacciatore, confetti, gondola, inferno, latte, macaroni, pepperoni, politico, presto, studio, tutti-frutti* and *vendetta*, have been taken into consideration. Even though the *Merriam-Webster* identifies them as originating from Italian, they do not actually have a precise structural or semantic model in Italian (see Furiassi, 'Italianisms in Non-Native Varieties of English' and Furiassi, 'False Italianisms in British and American English' for a detailed description of each). Particularly interesting is the false borrowing *bimbo*, which in English can be used either to refer contemptuously to a man or to denigrate a woman's level of intelligence, whereas in Italian it has always meant 'child'. It is possible that the new English meaning is a metaphorical extension of the old Italian one, based upon the common ground that links the two in the different languages, i.e. inferiority and weakness.
20. Klajn coins this label 'casual' to refer to foreign words introduced into discourse for 'special and temporary purposes'. They are frequently used in travel books and foreign correspondence to re-evoke the exoticism of the donor country and only rarely are they used to cover new situations in the target language. See Ivan Klajn, *Influssi inglesi nella lingua italiana* (Florence: Olschki, 1972), p. 22. On 'casuals', see also Pulcini's chapter in this volume.
21. See Henri Béjoint, *The Lexicography of English* (Oxford: Oxford University Press, 2010), p. 85.
22. See Sidney Landau, 'Johnson's influence on Webster and Worcester in Early American Lexicography', *International Journal of Lexicography*, 18.2 (2005), 217–29 (p. 227).
23. See Mohammad A. Jazayery, 'Observations on Loanwords as an Index to Cultural Borrowing', in *Studies in Language, Literature and Culture of the Middles Ages and Later*, ed. by Bagby Atwood and Archibald Hill (Austin: University of Texas, 1969), pp. 80–96 (p. 85).
24. See E .H. Thorne, 'Italian Teachers and Teaching in Eighteenth-Century England', *English Miscellany*, 9 (1958), 143–58 (p. 144).
25. See John Rigby Hale, *England and the Renaissance* (London: Harper Collins, 1996), pp. 261–62.
26. See Bruno Migliorini, *Saggi Linguistici* (Florence: Felice Le Monnier, 1957), p. 12.
27. In Italian 'sostituzione per approssimazione': see Roberto Gusmani, 'Interlinguistica', in *Linguistica Storica*, ed. by Romano Lazzeroni (Rome: Nuova Italia Scientifica, 1987), pp. 87–114 (p. 98).
28. In fact, apart from derived or composed words (e.g. *wholly* /həʊllɪ/ or *bookkeeper* /bʊkkiːpə(r)/), the phenomenon of gemination does not exist in English.
29. In Italian 'adattamento meccanico': see Gusmani, 'Interlinguistica', p. 98.
30. What is also noticeable here from the English phonemic transcripts of *smalto* and *buffalo* is the diphthongization of the Italian final vowel sound /o/ to avoid its reduction to the indistinct schwa sound found in other Italianisms. Even though the final phonetic realization of this diphthong differs in British English and US English, the structural adaptations from Italian into both varieties are largely the same.
31. In Italian 'sostituzione per analogia': see in Gusmani, 'Interlinguistica', p. 98.
32. See Thomas E. Hope, *Lexical Borrowing in the Romance Languages* (Oxford: Blackwell, 1971), p. 616.
33. Sergio Romano, ed., *Gli Americani e l'Italia* (Milan: Libri Scheiwiller, 1993), p. 16. See also Mattia Lento's chapter in this volume.
34. Ibid., p. 18.
35. For a complete history of the Italians in the USA see William J. Connell and Stanislao G.

Pugliese, eds, *The Routledge History of Italian Americans* (New York and London: Routledge, 2017).

36. See Alan Balboni, *Beyond the Mafia: Italian Americans and the Development of Las Vegas* (Las Vegas: University of Nevada Press, 1996).
37. For detailed information regarding the role of Italian food in the identity and culture of Italian Americans see Simone Cinotto, *The Italian American Table: Food, Family, and Community in New York* (Urbana: University of Illinois Press, 2013); Simone Cinotto, 'Culture and Identity on the Table: Italian American Food as Social History', in *The Routledge History of Italian Americans*, pp. 179–89.
38. See Balboni, *Beyond the Mafia*.
39. It is worth pointing out that of the 216 food and drink items recorded in the *Merriam-Webster*, five are described as not being of Italian origin in the *OED*. This is the case of the lemmas *nipa*, *cauliflower*, *latte*, *pistachio*, and *sorgo*. However, since space constraints have not allowed for an etymological examination of the data held in the *Merriam-Webster* (as was done for the Italianisms in the *OED*), these lemmas have been considered as being direct borrowings into US English from Italian, even though they will not appear in the following lists.
40. Lanzilotta, 'Il caso Starbucks'.
41. Only *latte*, described as a shortening of *caffè latte* though not etymologically indicated as being from Italian, is recorded in the *Merriam-Webster*; the other words have not been entered yet.

CHAPTER 14

A Century of Americanisms

Massimo Fanfani

When considering the influence of the English-speaking world on the Italian language, one does not usually pay much attention to the country or area from which the influence comes. In particular, Anglicisms coming from Britain and those coming from the USA tend to be treated indistinctly and indicated under the convenient label of 'Anglo-Americanisms'. With the exception of a limited number of terms related to institutions or 'realia' specific to one or the other nation (*tory* and *whig* are English, *grattacieli* 'skyscrapers' and *drugstores* are American), we overlook not only the formal differences between the two areas, which are sometimes a bit unclear, but also their different fields of reference, which would be decisive in determining the connotative field that characterizes Americanisms as opposed to Briticisms — especially since the terms with a clear American footprint generally give rise to a more lively reaction in speakers, whether they are used as words in fashion, or fought off as a danger to the integrity of the Italian language.

It should also be said that, while British Anglicisms have always had free access to Italian to a greater or lesser extent since the Middle Ages, the influx of Americanisms is a more recent phenomenon. From its very beginning it started as an irrepressible avalanche felt by many as a threat, and this has taken place in close parallel to what was happening in the other European languages. This influx is historically linked to the direct presence of the United States of America on European and Italian territories during the two World Wars, from which arose deeper and more stable cultural, political, and economic bonds between the two sides of the Atlantic. Thus, in the past century, the reshaping and modernization of the lexical systems of European languages also involved converging towards the models offered by American English.

In Italy, this considerable presence of American English terms and expressions, especially after the Second World War and in the years of the 'economic boom', led to a revival of purism, directed entirely at English. At first it was just a journalistic and amateur attitude, of a rhetorical and ideological nature rather than a linguistic nature: in fact, novelties have always bothered conservatives and, behind the Americanisms, the shadow of the pervasive power of the USA was felt, especially by the left-wing intelligentsia.[1] But, little by little, intellectuals and renowned linguists joined the fray with their different opinions, and the discussions became more interesting and have been present unceasingly up to the present day.[2]

Back in Time

Although English words, as we said, had been known since the Middle Ages, their existence became significant only in the eighteenth century, when so-called 'anglomania' spread from France throughout Europe, and English began to grow in importance and to widen its influence over other languages.[3] Indeed, a general feeling of admiration was fostered by the colonial and merchant empire that depended on London and that from the sixteenth century on had been increasingly expanding, by the continuous progress made in the industrial revolution, by the modern political system with the parliamentary institutions resulting from the 'Glorious Revolution' of 1688–89, and also by the myth born with the American Revolution of 1775–83 with its young and free federal republic, by the growing cultural and scientific prestige of the two countries, and by their economic and military fortunes (though in truth, during the American War of Independence, all sympathies went to the rebelling colonies). In many aspects, from the organization of their societies to the individual lifestyles, Britain and the USA became then an ideal model and many began to learn their language. Already at the turn of the century, in 1780, in the final phase of the struggle for American independence, John Adams could prophetically state that: 'English is destined to be in the next and succeeding Centuries, more generally the Language of the World, than Latin was in the last, or French is in the present Age.'[4]

In this way, the English language, from being unknown to most and considered barbaric, saw its prestige rapidly rise and gain ever greater influence. Even in Italy, from the beginning of the eighteenth century, people started studying it, as shown by the grammar books written for Italians and two excellent bilingual dictionaries: one by Ferdinando Altieri (1726–27) and one by Giuseppe Baretti (1760), which were reprinted numerous times. It should also be added that, while up until then English was known only for business purposes by merchants, travellers, and diplomats, its literature was starting to be appreciated and its works translated.

As a result, various loans and calques began to emerge in Italian, which were no longer occasional and irrelevant, as they previously were, but started to form clusters. Apart from terms relating to commerce and navigation, typical foods and beverages, there appeared new entries in the intellectual and political lexicon, Latinisms which were very easy to acclimatize since most arrived through French: *adepto, colonia, convenzione* 'assembly', *costituzionale, immorale, legislatura, libero pensatore, opposizione, petizione, sessione, stagnazione,* etc. With the news of the American Revolution came a first significant cluster of Americanisms, here, too, mostly related to the political sphere: *antifederalista, coalizione, confederazione, congresso* 'US parliament', *continentale (armata c.), insorgente, insurrezione, madre patria, presidente* 'president of a republic', etc. However, there also emerged other Americanisms related to different fields: *alligatore, opossum, ranger, schooner,* etc.

French would continue to be the fundamental intermediary for Anglo-American influences throughout the first half of the nineteenth century. Consider the fact that a good deal of the Italian translations of US writers, such as Washington Irving and James Fenimore Cooper, translations which were very rich in Americanisms, were carried out on the basis of French translations.[5] On the other hand, we should not forget that in the nineteenth century there were more and more people who knew English, who travelled to Britain and the United States of America, who had a direct relationship with the language itself. The contingent of Anglicisms increased considerably and the English model gave rise to, or strongly influenced, entire lexical sectors.

In the second half of the nineteenth century, after the American Civil War (1861–65) and especially towards the end of the century, both because of the intensification of trade and diplomatic relations and because of Italian emigration overseas, there was a desire to learn more about the USA and a consequent intensification of translations: Thomas Mayne Reid's adventure novels were extremely popular and Harriet Beecher-Stowe's famous masterpiece, first published in English in 1852, had two Italian translations the same year (in Florence, with the title of *Il tugurio dello zio Tom*, and in Turin) as well as new translations and reprints in the next following years. Several works about the USA (by Alexander Hamilton, Washington Irving, George Bancroft, John Bigelow, etc.) were also translated, while newspapers and magazines frequently had articles about every aspect of the US reality: its natural wonders, the efficient and modern organization of the great metropolises, the positive nature of the political institutions of the federal republic, the adventurous life in the boundless prairies of the West; from the traditions of the 'redskin' natives to the sometimes unscrupulous 'self-made-men' and 'gold seekers'.

Late Nineteenth- and Early Twentieth-Century Americanisms

It is no coincidence that there were more and more Italians publishing significant works about the USA, ranging from mere travel impressions, descriptive works or studies on particular issues, to guides for those who wanted to emigrate. Among the many titles appearing over the nineteenth and twentieth centuries we could mention: *In America* (1875) by the agronomist Francesco Carega di Muricce; the volume by the two journalists Dario Papa and Ferdinando Fontana, *New-York* (1884); *Gli Stati Uniti* (1887) by Dr Carlo Gardini from Bologna; the *Guida all'emigrante agli Stati Uniti del Nord-America* (1892) by Roberto Marzo; the book of memories *Un italiano in America* (1892) by Adolfo Rossi, editor of the New York newspaper *Il Progresso Italo-Americano*; *Impressioni d'America* (1899) by Giuseppe Giacosa; Ugo Ojetti's feature articles for the *Corriere della Sera* collected in the volume *L'America vittoriosa* (1899); *America vissuta* (1911) by the journalist Amy A. Bernardy; etc.

This growing interest in the USA is also reflected by the fortune of the metonymic use of *America* ('È un'*America!* Di paese ricco' [It's an America! With reference to a rich country]: 1887, Petrocchi) and the ethnic adjective and noun *americano* which, in addition to its objective value ('that which is from America or of the Americans'), is also used to indicate what one 'thinks is characteristic of the United States', and therefore something grandiose and sensational, business-like and ruthless. And along with the fortune of these imaginative connotations there are numerous neologisms coming from the same root: *americanamente*, *americanesimo*, *americanismo, americanista, americanità, americanite, americanizzamento, americanizzarsi, americanizzato, americanizzazione, americomania, inamericarsi,* etc.[6] Among them, there are two that will have considerable use: *americanismo* (1876) and, formed with a negative suffix, *americanata* (1888).

The first, *americanismo*, obviously has a number of 'positive' meanings, starting with the consolidated ones: 'an American English word', 'US(-related) doctrine', etc. Yet it must be noted that at the end of the nineteenth century the term indicated above all what was specific to the 'American character' as opposed to the mindset of the old continent, and a strong 'admiration for the United States of America'. Between 1878 and 1879 the economist Francesco Ferrara published in *Nuova Antologia* a series of articles in defence of economic liberalism called *L'americanismo economico in Italia*; in an essay of 1885, Enrico Nencioni argued that Poe's *americanismo* resided 'nel carattere di ardita investigazione, nell'audacia delle ipotesi, nel profondo senso scientifico che gli è compagno fin nelle più strane allucinazioni, nella originalità della invenzione e finalmente nell'odio del *common place* e del *filisteismo* europeo' [in his fervent investigation, in the boldness of ideas, in the profound scientific sense that is a companion even within his strangest hallucinations, in the originality of invention and lastly in the hatred of the commonplace and European philistinism].[7] Instead, for Carlo Gardini (1887), *americanismo* is 'lo spirito pel moderno, e per ciò che si dice progresso' [the spirit for the modern, and for that which one calls progress];[8] while journalist Ernesto Zenuti titled his 1891 booklet: *Americanismo fiorentino: sport, flirtation & marriage*. In short, the semantic sphere of these neologisms was in some way determined by the conceptions, prejudices, and stereotyped images that Italians then held about the United States of America. What is written in the *Piccola Enciclopedia Hoepli* (1913) is enlightening: *americanismo* includes both 'l'iniziativa, l'audacia e la crudeltà del grande affarismo' [the initiative, the boldness and the cruelty of great profiteering], and 'la negazione di ogni eleganza, raffinatezza e buon gusto e anche, spesso, di ogni elementare educazione' [the removal of every elegance, refinement and good taste and also, often, of all basic manners].[9]

The other successful derivative, *americanata*, spreading around the turn of the century, has an analogous function, mainly used to highlight a certain gap in Italian gigantism: 'Il vocabolo "americanata" è un barbaro sostantivo non ancora registrato in alcun glossario. Nondimeno è voce consacrata dall'uso per dinotare cosa strabiliante, non disgiunta da una certa dose di ciarlatanismo' [the term 'americanata' is an awful noun that has still not been recorded in any glossary. Nevertheless it is a specific word used to denote something astonishing, not without a certain dose of charlatanism].[10] The definition in Panzini's (1905) *Dizionario moderno* reads:

> neologismo di formazione popolare, per indicare fatto o impresa esagerata, sorprendente, audace, sfacciata, di cui l'America del Nord sembra avere il privilegio. In questo conviene tener conto del naturale crescere delle proporzioni attraverso l'oceano e della differenza che intercede tra un popolo giovane in terra ampia e vergine, e un popolo vecchio in terra angusta ed augusta per vetustà.

[a popularly created neologism, indicating a fact or an exaggerated, surprising, bold, gaudy undertaking which seems to be the preserve of North America. In this it is worthwhile keeping in mind the natural expansion across the ocean and the increase of the differences that intercede between a young nation in a wide and virgin land, and an old nation in a small land and august by ancientness.][11]

But here we are particularly interested in the many Americanisms that were emerging in the wake of the ever-increasing interest in the USA between these two centuries. Many of these are linked to the most striking and 'sensational' aspects of American life, to the great and frenetic spectacle offered by its major metropolises, beginning with the first and most fascinating encounter for those coming from Europe: New York, with its Statue of Liberty, the world's largest bridge over the East River, its first *grattacieli* (1908).[12] Even before docking, the eyes of each traveller caught the swirling movement of the harbour, with its *elevator* (1875) and its *wharfs*, and with the constant flow of *clippers, schooners, ferry-boats* (1875), *palace-steamers, steam-boats*. And then the 'wonders' of city traffic: the *ferrovia aerea* (*elevated-railroad*, 1884) and the *sotterranea* (*subway*, 1911), the *street-car* and the *stage* 'big horse-drawn carriage' (1884), platforms, *tram* lines, automatic ticket offices. And then Wall Street and Downtown with its *slums* (1911) and its *loffers* (1884); the *avenues* and the streets lined with *bars* (1873), *drugstores* (1911), *groceries* (1892), *apartment-houses* and *tenement-houses*. In the travel reports there are endless descriptions, varying from scepticism to admiration, of the many novelties regarding foods and drinks (*cake, candy, cocktail, drink, ice-cream, peanut, pie*, etc.), dances and shows (*attraction, black bottom, cake-walk, charleston, hop, music-hall, partner, shimmy, show*, etc.), sports and entertainment (*basket-ball, base-ball, bike, camping out, poker*, etc.), education and the university world (*college, common school, graduate, dipartimento, tutore*, etc.).

Every aspect of American life is reported and photographed with its specific name, or sometimes rendered with a calque. Just think of the many terms related to political and intellectual life: *abolizionista, antifederalista* (1899), *Casa Bianca* (1875), *congressman, espansionista, imperialismo, imperialista* (1899), *indesiderabile* (1903), *linciare* (1877), *linciaggio* (1891), *piattaforma* 'programme of a political movement' (1890), *pragmatismo* (1890), *proibizionista* (1884), *speech*, etc. Or consider these items from the language of journalism: *advertisements, cartoons, chief editor, editoriale* (1875), *intervista* (1899), *linotype* (1893), *magazine* (1892), *giallo* as 'sensational' (1899), *reporter* (1875), *scoop* (1911), etc.

Numerous terms refer to the organization of society and business: *boss* (1892), *boy* as messenger (1875), *business* and *businessman* (1875), *color line* (1884), *contractor, coolie* (1875), *depressione* 'economic slump' (1892), *foreman, high-life, manager* (1875) *messenger-boy, self-made man* (1892), *stock, timekeeper* (1892), *trust*, etc. Many are also related to new technical inventions, appliances, means of transportation: *cow-catcher, fonografo* (1874), *monitore* 'warship' (1866), *pullman* 'type of railway carriage', *sleepers* 'sleeping car', *westinghouse* 'kind of brake', etc.

Widespread as well, thanks to travel books and translations of adventure novels, were the many terms referring to the *Far West* (1875) and the courageous life of *pionieri, cercatori d'oro, cowboy* (1890), *farmer* (1899), *trapper*.[13] We can note animal names like *grizzly*, the areas called *prateria* and *riserva*, *ranch* and *saloon*; and then concerning the native *pellerossa* world: *squaw, papoose, mocassini, totem*, etc.

The examples could be multiplied, but it is already clear from the ones above that the wave of Americanisms that influenced the Italian language at the end of the nineteenth century is of considerable magnitude, although only some of these have permanently entered the Italian language. It should also be noted that most of these terms are non-adapted or 'integral' linguistic loans. This is mainly due to the fact that (like other nineteenth-century Anglicisms) they almost exclusively appear on written pages, on which they are reproduced exactly as they are, without even those minimal graphical adjustments that are common in loans from languages structured in a similar way to Italian. Instead, for those loans that have penetrated more deeply into Italian usage we witness, as is natural, adaptations and assimilations at the phonetic and morphological level, often with repercussions on their written form, and we also witness the emergence of calques such as *Piccola Italia* (from *little Italy*).[14] In some cases, the Anglicism is accompanied by a calque or a synonym that may or may not prevail: *congressman* (1856)/*congressista* (1899); *meeting* (1819)/*comizio* (1830); *steamer* (1837)/*vapore* (1857).

Twentieth-Century Americanisms

With the new century, and especially after the Great War, the relationship among European languages changed and consequently the inter-lingual interferences shifted. In particular, French began to give way to English as the language of international culture and communication. Already in the preliminaries of the Peace Conference in Paris (1919) involving the nations that had taken part in the conflict, the American President Wilson had succeeded in imposing English as an official conference language, after more than two centuries during which French had been the only language used in diplomacy. Moreover, with its intervention in the war, the USA had considerably expanded its influence in Europe and successively strengthened it further, in spite of the 1929 crisis and its consequent depression. The international position of the USA would be reinforced by trade expansion, by the efficiency of increasingly 'automated' and 'standardized' production, by the free development of mass culture, and by Roosevelt's 'New Deal'.

Soon American English became the 'lingua franca' for economic-financial exchanges and political and scientific relations between nations, while new waves of Americanisms spread everywhere: in writing (newspapers and periodicals, complete translations of popular 'thriller' series, 'science fiction' books, essays), and through increasingly powerful and fast-spreading media (radio, cinema, television) which were able to cross barriers, address people of every social level, and were effective in transmitting word sounds and linking them to a context of images and situations. Given its increasingly prominent position, it was the USA that now conveyed exoticisms and foreignisms of any origin, creating a transnational lexical network of internationalisms.[15]

The scenario of this inversion of linguistic influence can be noticed, among others, in the Italian dictionaries of neologisms which already in the first decades of the twentieth century showed a sharp drop in Gallicisms and a continual expansion of Anglicisms. A barometer of these changes is undoubtedly the *Dizionario moderno* by Alfredo Panzini which, from 1905 to 1963, with the appendices of Bruno Migliorini, recorded through its ten editions the stratification of lexical novelties.[16] As noted, while the Gallicisms still comprise two thirds of all the foreignisms in Panzini's first edition, in the 1918 edition they are already reduced to half, and they decreased even more in later editions. On the other hand, Anglicisms doubled from edition to edition reaching 11% of headwords in the tenth edition (1963): more or less the same percentage found today in similar repertories of neologisms.[17]

The *Dizionario moderno* also illustrates something else: unlike the French and German loans, English is accompanied by the indication of pronunciation that leads us to understand how English was still known by few people, while Anglicisms were nonetheless being used in common speech. Moreover, unlike most other linguistic foreignisms and the many neologisms of the 'nuova lingua italiana' that are branded by Panzini with more or less ironic comments of puristic or moralistic censorship, Anglicisms, and especially Americanisms, are almost always welcomed with indulgence, even apparently superfluous ones: *bluff 'folata di vento. Nel senso di vanteria, smargiassata, è un americanismo'* [*a gust of wind*. In the sense of *boasting* or *bragging* it is an Americanism]; *flirt '(floet) significa l'amoreggiare, ma più per arte, ozio e desiderio di piacere che per amore. [. . .] Civettare, frascheggiare son voci press'a poco corrispondenti; ma una dama si offenderà del verbo civettare, e non troverà nulla a ridire del verbo flirtare'* [means *to seduce* but more for art, idleness and desire of pleasure rather than for love. [. . .] *To play the coquette, to dally with* are more or less equivalent words, but a woman will be offended by *to play the coquette*, and will find no fault with *to flirt*]; *girl '(gherl): la fanciulla o ragazza americana, bella, sana, forte, allegra, indipendente. È un tipo!'* [the American *young lady* or *girl*, beautiful, healthy, strong, happy, independent. Really something!].[18]

Americanisms in the *Dizionario moderno* are quite numerous and belong to different fields, from political and intellectual life (*brain trust, dry bill* 'alcohol ban', *patto Kellogg, Ku-klux Klan, macchina elettorale, money-making-man, Rotary club, strenuous life, uomo rappresentativo*, etc.) to films (*atmosphère, miss America, movietone, sex-appeal, studio, talkie, taxi-girl, vamp*; and also *Charlot, Hollywood, Laurel e Hardy*, etc.); from music and dance (*banjo, cake walk, fox-trot, jazz, jazz-band, ukulele*, etc.) to games and pastimes (*jò-jò, parole incrociate, puzzle, toboga*, etc.); from means of transportation and techno-industrial inventions (*bus, clacson, elevator, flit, Ford, Gillette, Kodak, Morse, radiovisione, rayon, runabout, timer, zip*, etc.) to organized crime (*gangster, g-men, gun-moll, kidnapper, mani in alto*, etc.).

Even in Italy, and even in the years between the two wars when puristic campaigns for the defence of the national language were being promoted, the presence of Americanisms became increasingly dense, not only in the press or in 'snobbish' conversations but also in popular usage, as is well seen in the case of sports. Here, even though for the most popular sports adaptations, calques and substitutions spontaneously emerged, many integral loans became firmly rooted despite official proposals for Italianization (*base-ball, bob, break, cross, K.O., round, soccer, sprint, uppercut*, etc.).

We can also consider the cinematographic terminology, which after its first loans — starting with the word *film* (1889) — was enriched by numerous American technical terms and jargon, especially between the two wars and then more so after the Second World War: *ampex, box office, camera* 'cinecamera', *cameraman, cartone animato, cast, censura Hays, cinemascope, cinerama, documentario, drive-in, flash back, gag, happy end, mixage, moviola, musical, play-back, remake, serial, set, story, studio, stunt man, talent scout, star, suspense, thriller, western*, etc. The movie world contributed primarily to making several loan terms popular, sometimes already in the titles, which were destined for large circulation: *baby doll, cowboy, gang, gangster, killer, motel, okay, partner, racket*, etc. In addition, through the dubbing of films, several calques of American expressions were introduced, some of which are now ingrained in the language: *assolutamente* (from *absolutely*) and *esatto* (from *exactly*) used as affirmative adverbs; *non c'è problema* (no problem), *ci puoi scommettere* (you can bet on it!), *dacci un taglio* (cut it out!), etc. In the same way, especially through the radio, new musical genres were introduced (*blues, country, gospel, rock and roll, soul, spiritual, swing*, etc.) and different dances that had originated in the USA (*boogie-woogie, charleston, slow, tip-tap*, etc.).

After the Second World War

In the post-war period, the influence of American English, in addition to being substantial, started taking on different characteristics. Now, compared to integral loans, it was the semantic and structural calques that increased exponentially. Loans were still naturally adapted to the local pronunciation, but with greater adherence to the model. Graphic adaptations tended to disappear almost entirely; on the other hand, some phenomena showing the progressive impact of English at the level of word formation and syntax began to emerge more clearly. Interferences, in fact, were not only transmitted through writing, but now mainly exploited the new spoken communication channels (such as radio-television), which favoured the assimilation of pronunciation. Furthermore, the number of Italians who now knew English was also increasing. And, for those who did not, the media offered various types of aid, such as those 'didactic' advertisements of the 1960s: for instance, 'Si scrive Colgate, si pronuncia Colgheit' [you write Colgate but you pronounce it Colgheit]. However, the first thing to point out is that now almost all Anglicisms were of American origin and also spread from the bottom up, through the networks and powerful channels of mass culture.

This fact should not be surprising: with the return of freedom to Italy after 1945, the American Dream, which in the 1930s had been cultivated by intellectuals such as Pavese, Soldati, Vittorini and Cecchi, became a popular myth. The USA became a boundless world to discover and imitate starting from that 'American way of life' based on widespread well-being, individual success, and consumerism. A number of factors increased the popularity of a cultural model that was also a linguistic model. These included the political, military, and economic primacy of the USA, the closer relationship with Italy created by the Marshall Plan and the Atlantic Alliance, the ongoing advances in scientific research and 'human sciences', technological innovations, Hollywood films that fascinated the public after the forced blockade of the war years, light music, juvenile fashion, and some new customs that overcame ancient traditions ('Santa Claus' and decorated trees in the place of the traditional nativity scenes and, more recently, *Halloween*). On the other hand, the profound transformations affecting Italian society during the post-conflict reconstruction years and the economic boom, the rising education levels, migratory movements, European integration and international development made the Italian language more permeable to external interferences, developing more flexibility in the language and an unimaginable ability to react to innovation and to accommodate different communication needs.

In addition to these elements, the media, as mentioned, has played a decisive role in the penetration of Americanisms starting from the traditional ones to the newer ones that since the 1990s have gravitated around computers and the Internet. The linguistic models offered by them, and their particular communicative ways, have provided resources that have never been seen before. The population is repeatedly subjected to the same messages, the same slogans, the same words, from which it is often possible immediately to absorb what is needed to make them indelible: from the 'referent', to the graphic form, to the pronunciation, to the meanings in diverse contexts. And since almost everything in the sphere of the media comes from the USA, from technologies to the ideological schemes, from consumer background to its very content, it is clear that this entails a process of cultural homologation and hence, on a linguistic level, the diffusion of lexical networks strongly modelled on the American frame of reference.

There is no field, from politics to economics, from commerce to advertising, journalism, science, technology, music and sports, where the influence of American English is not felt. In addition to the allure of the USA, there is the new, anti-traditional mindset of the economic boom years and, above all, of the season born with the '1968' phenomena: in the US reality, the new aspirations of Italian society found a source of inspiration for technocratic modernization and the forms and words to represent it.

An important role in the interference patterns of the last decades of the twentieth century is played by the greater knowledge of English. While until the middle of the last century foreign language study was reserved to restricted circles of people, from the late 1960s, with the rise of the compulsory schooling age and with new linguistic skills required in almost every field of activity, English became the second language for an ever growing number of Italians.[19] It should also be said that, on the one hand, this has favoured interference phenomena (and has established an approximate phonetic system for integral Anglicisms, parallel to Italian); on the other hand the increased knowledge of English functions as a sort of filter that tends to eliminate casual loans and to transform part of necessary loans into calques or translations.

This is easily perceived in the attitude of specialists and technicians who, knowing English and using it habitually in their environment, when they resort to Italian, are quite fond of using Anglicisms. The case is different with journalists, advertisers, marketing managers and professionals in the media, for whom Anglicisms have a special stylistic and evocative function. So even 'luxury' Anglicisms, seemingly superfluous, can be used in the news or in advertising slogans, just for their connotative aura. In other cases, a foreignism serves as an easily identifiable label: in a television broadcast, for example, certain recurring foreign terms (think of current expressions such as *competitor, devolution, fiscal drag, mobbing, spending review, stalking*, or the pseudo-English *jobs act*) can attract attention to a given topic far better than the Italian equivalent or a synonym. It is for this reason that in media language there is always a need for new foreignisms which, in addition to adding colour, have a spotlight function. This is also apparent in sports news: if in the first half of the century several Anglicisms were popularly replaced with Italian terms, during the second post-war period terms began to be taken fully from English, not only for the diffusion of new sports (*basketball, hockey, rugby*, etc.), but also for already popular sports, with the Anglicization of different expressions: *allenatore* became *trainer* and then *mister* or *coach*; instead of *squadra*, *team* is also used, etc.

It should not be surprising, therefore, that in newspapers and other media the rate of integral Anglicisms, especially those coming from American English, is rather high. Just to give some examples of entries that spread through the media in the 1950s and 1960s, we can mention *audience, audiovisivo, baby, babysitter, beat, best seller, bingo, boy, by-pass, candid-camera, chips, clip, disc jockey, doping, drink, drive in, fall out, fan, feedback, flash, flipper, freezer, gossip, hostess, hot, hot dog, identikit, jam session, jeans, jet, jet set, jolly, juke box*, etc. In those same decades, characterized by the opposition between the USA and the Eastern bloc, there were many Americanisms which concerned the political lexicon, starting with *guerra fredda* (calque of *cold war*): *bipolarismo, deterrente, escalation, establishment, ponte aereo, superpotenza, welfare state* (perhaps a Briticism), etc.[20]

In the last thirty years, the influx of Americanisms has mainly concerned sectorial languages that have an international character and function. In many cases the expansion of such 'global' Anglicisms was largely foreseeable, starting from the economic-financial jargon: *benchmark, capital gain, credit card, fixing, franchising, home banking, insider trading, job sharing, joint-venture, junk bond, just in time, leasing, new economy, project financing, spread, swap, trading*, etc.[21] Anglicisms (including calques) are also found in the sideline fields of business and publicity: *advertising, brand, call center, copywriter, customer care, discount, front line, gadget, label, megastore*, etc. A very recent addition is *Black Friday* to mean 'the day that marks the start of the Christmas shopping season, with heavily discounted prices'. In the language of politics we find *bipartisan, blind trust, election day* (that led to a widely used noun + *day* pattern), *exit poll, politically correct* (an interesting expression as regards its socio-cultural implications), *question time*, etc.

Definitely the field in which Americanisms are most numerous is that of computer science: this was inevitable, given its origin and progress. Although a part of this terminology has been Italianized (*cartella, formato, incolla, salva, sito, stile*, etc.), the entire contingent is remarkable and constantly expanding: *backup, bug, byte, chip, click, cd, data, database, default, desktop, digitale, directory, display, driver, file, font, formattare, gigabyte, hard disk, ipertesto, laptop, link, monitor, mouse, multitasking, network, password, query, reset, scanner*, etc.[22] These terms are flanked by those related to the world of Internet and social media: *account, allegato* (attachment), *banner, browser, chat, cookie, download, emoticon, follower, hacker, hashtag, homepage, link, login, mail, mailing list, navigare, nickname, online, provider, router, selfie, twitter*, etc.

Beyond these areas subjected to significant linguistic interferences, it is quite surprising to find Anglicisms even in areas that have usually been well protected from foreign influences, such as legal or administrative language. In the legal lexicon, for example, we increasingly find English words and expressions (*money broking, rating, stalking, swap*), because they are more precise and univocal than the Italian counterparts, and because there is an immediate parallel with the legal terminology of other languages, starting with the legislative dispositions of the European Union.[23]

Something similar has happened in the language of public administration, the so-called 'burocratese'. Initiatives aimed at simplifying or making it clearer do not exclude the use of the now common foreignisms. In fact, their substitution with Italian equivalents would make the text more obscure: for example, the term *locazione finanziaria* for many is less clear than its English counterpart *leasing*; *open access* or *open data* is preferable in certain contexts to *accesso aperto*; *performance*, despite its various Italian synonyms (and beyond the uncertainties about the position of the word-stress), is not easily replaceable in the administrative language. Moreover, for this sector, too, as a result of the process of European unification, there has been the need to adapt to EU norms and provisions, thus incorporating many Anglicisms that are nothing more than Europeanisms. And you can be sure that this will continue even after Brexit.

Beyond Lexical Influences

In the analysis of Anglo-American influence, it is not enough to record linguistic loans and reconstruct their history. It is also necessary to investigate further the repercussions they have on the Italian lexical system. In fact, the semantic integration of a loan always involves some change or restructuring within a given semantic field, not only when it comes to 'technicisms' or with entirely new terms, but especially in the presence of so-called 'luxury loans' (i.e. words which have not been borrowed simply to fill a gap in the recipient language). In this case, the foreign word is accompanied by Italian words and expressions that have the same value or indicate something very similar. Consequently, this leads to an inevitable lexical overlap which, after a more or less long period of rivalry, will lead to the fall of one of the two elements, or to a specialization of their expressive connotations, or to the differentiation of their respective areas of use or, finally, to their semantic polarization. For instance, simply compare the different connotations of *barista* and *barman*, *dirigente* and *manager*, *diva* and *star*, *modella* and *top model* (the English term has completely replaced the previous Gallicism *mannequin*). Instead, between *bibita* and *drink*, there has been a semantic specialization: the Anglicism refers only to an 'alcoholic drink' in Italian.

In addition to the lexical sphere, English influence has also affected the innermost Italian structures, favouring innovations that have evolved in all the other European languages. In spelling, for example, Anglicisms have led to the use, in Italian neoformations, of graphemes foreign to the traditional alphabet (*k, y, x, w*), the habit of young people to Anglicize spellings (*briosha*), the iconic use of letters (*u-turn > inversione a u, v neck > scollo a v, T-shirt*). In phonetics, we can see a greater tolerance for some consonant clusters typical in English but not in Italian, and for the definitive adoption of words ending with a consonant, present not only in loans and acronyms, but now also in emerging Italian usage, as in truncations (*prof*) and in the adverb *non* before a pause. Hence, as was mentioned, a parallel phonetic system has formed which, despite adaptations and assimilations, tends to approach the Anglo-American one when in the presence of Anglicisms, a system that sometimes tends to even phase out old pronunciations based on the way a word is written ([bus] > [bas], in an attempt at reproducing [bʌs]).

At the level of lexical morphology, English models have offered the Italian language new formative resources and reactivated some old modules, making the whole sector more versatile and modern. Thus, new compounds can now employ, even in hybrid forms, elements of the most diverse types: Greek-Latin formants, foreign terms, abbreviations, lexeme clipping, acronyms. And increasingly often, Italian is adopting the English *determinans–determinatum* sequence (*baby killer, project manager, reality show*, etc.), now appearing alongside traditional compounds with the opposite order. There are now countless abbreviations of all kinds: word contractions (*demo, info, neocon* 'neoconservative'), elliptical uses (*talk* for *talk show*), morphemic reductions (*tecno* 'technomusic'), acronyms (*dvd, pc, pdf*).

Certain cases of English patterns in the use of prefixes are now found as well, such as the use of *co-* even before a consonant (*cobelligerante, copilota*) and *non-* (*no-*) with nouns, a use deriving from calques such as *no-profit, nonsenso, non violenza*, etc.[24] Numerous formative elements have been obtained through clipping: *e-* from *electronics* (*e-mail, e-books*), *cyber-* from *cybernetics*, *docu-* from *documentary*, *net-* from *internet*, *servo-* from *servomechanism*, etc. As regards 'suffixes': *-matic* from *automatic*, *-cam* from *camera*, *-gate* from *Watergate* (with the meaning of 'political scandal'). Following US models, the suffix *-ese* has been used to indicate linguistic varieties or styles: *aziendalese* 'language of business', *giovanilese* 'language of young people', *politichese* 'language of politicians'.

The influence of American English is also visible in the diffusion of the compositional type consisting of a first element (adverb, adjective or noun) followed by an adjective (or participle) that functions as the *determinatum* within the compound: *lungodegente, videodipendente, sieropositivo*, and so on. The same has happened also with the attributive juxtaposition of two nouns, one of which qualifies the other, both in the traditional *determinatum–determinans* order (*fine settimana, ragazza copertina*), and in the English order (*zero consumi, Obama-pensiero*). In several cases, the individual composing elements tend to become new suffixes and prefixes, and thus become available for new, autonomous lexical creations.

In syntax there are several Anglicisms, including the use of the indefinite article in predicative function, especially in titles (*Una cultura classica nella scuola*);

constructions such as *grazie di non fumare*; the tendency of the adverbial use of adjectives (*pensa positivo*); constructions with double detached prepositional syntagms (*per mezzo e in difesa della teoria*);[25] the use of the *e/o* disjunction; and multiple interrogative clauses.[26]

These innovations, while being less apparent than the assortment of full loans or single lexeme calques, are much more decisive because they act upon the deeper structures of the language, showing the increased penetration of American linguistic models at the beginning of this new millennium.

Concluding Remarks

As we have seen from this synthetic overview, the influence of American English has progressively increased since the middle of the last century. This influence has not stopped in recent years, despite the fact that the prestige of the USA has dampened with the 2008 crisis of *subprime*, *hedge fund* and *OTC* (*over the counter*) derivatives. Indeed, with the Obama presidency and now with that of Trump, Americanisms, especially those of politics, have multiplied. Examples range from *storytelling* to *jobs act* (abbreviation for *Jumpstart Our Business Startup Act* in a 2012 law, which has been taken up in Italy with a different meaning), from *whistleblowing* to the *fake news* of *post-truth politics*. Moreover, it is certain from various indications that the current flourishing of Americanisms will not be exhausted soon.

Notes to Chapter 14

1. Tullio De Mauro reports on some of these journalistic interventions; see *Storia linguistica dell'Italia unita*, 2nd edn (Bari: Laterza, 1970), pp. 364–68. The discussion started up again after René Etiemble's work was published, *Parlez-vous franglais?* (Paris: Gallimard, 1964): among many others see Franco Fochi, *Lingua in rivoluzione* (Milan: Feltrinelli, 1966), and Giacomo Elliot's [Roberto Vacca] work, *Parliamo itang'liano. Ovvero le 400 parole inglesi che deve sapere chi vuole fare carriera* (Milan: Rizzoli, 1977), which mostly dealt with the Americanisms used by managers, pointing out that 'l'itangliano fornito qui aiuta certamente di più a parlare con americani, piuttosto che con inglesi' [the Itangliano provided here certainly helps more with speaking with Americans than with British people] (p. 194).
2. Cf. Claudio Marazzini, 'Perché in Italia si è tanto propensi ai forestierismi?', in *La lingua italiana e le lingue romanze di fronte agli anglicismi*, ed. by Claudio Marazzini and Alessio Petralli (Florence: Accademia della Crusca, 2015), pp. 14–26.
3. For a historical description of English influence on the Italian language, see the paragraphs devoted to foreignisms in Bruno Migliorini, *Storia della lingua italiana* (Milan: Bompiani, 1994), first published in 1960 (in particular pp. 164, 220, 279, 383, 523–24, 597–98, 658–59, 663–64); cf. also Paolo Zolli, *Le parole straniere*, 2nd edn (Bologna: Zanichelli, 1991), pp. 71–117; Gabriella Cartago, *L'apporto inglese*, in *Storia della lingua italiana*, 3 vols, ed. by Luca Serianni and Pietro Trifone (Turin: Einaudi, 1994), III, 721–50; Giovanni Iamartino, 'La contrastività italiano-inglese in prospettiva storica', *Rassegna italiana di linguistica applicata*, 33.2–3 (2001), 7–130. See also Pulcini's chapter in this volume.
4. Letter by John Adams to the President of Congress (Samuel Huntington), 5 September 1780, no. 6, in Adams Papers, National Archives; a digital copy of the letter can be viewed in the National Archives website at https://founders.archives.gov/documents/Adams/06-10-02-0067 [accessed 5 November 2019].
5. On Cooper's novels see Anna-Vera Sullam, *Il primo dei Mohicani. L'elemento americano nelle traduzioni dei romanzi di J. F. Cooper* (Pisa: Istituti editoriali e poligrafici internazionali, 1995).

6. With *America* and *americano* we refer not to the central-southern part or to the whole American continent, but to the United States of America, according to a use that was established after the American Revolution. For the metonymic uses of these terms and for their derivations cf. Wolfgang Schweickard, *Deonomasticon Italicum*, 4 vols (Tübingen: Niemeyer, 1997) I, 70–77.
7. Enrico Nencioni, *Saggi critici di letteratura inglese* (Florence: Le Monnier, 1897), p. 101.
8. Carlo Gardini, *Gli Stati Uniti. Ricordi*, 2 vols (Bologna: Zanichelli, 1887), II, 267.
9. Gottardo Garollo, *Piccola Enciclopedia Hoepli* (Milan: Hoepli, 1913), p. 233.
10. Giuseppe Sormani, *Eco d'America* (Milan, 1888), p. 32.
11. Alfredo Panzini, *Dizionario moderno* (Milan: Hoepli, 1905), p. 15.
12. *Grattacielo*, as is known, is a calque of *skyscraper* (in Fr. *gratte-ciel*, in Ger. *Wolkenkratzer*): Italian at first alternated between *schiaccianuvole* (1899, Ojetti) and *grattanuvole* (1911, Bernardy), which perhaps might have been affected by the German calque. (The dates that accompany each individual term in the text are almost all derived from my own original research.)
13. See Cottini's chapter in this volume.
14. Cf. Lento's chapter in this volume.
15. On the twentieth-century expansion of English as a universal language, see David Crystal, *English as a Global Language*, 2nd edn (Cambridge: Cambridge University Press, 2012).
16. Alfredo Panzini, *Dizionario Moderno. Supplemento ai Dizionari Italiani* (Milan: Hoepli, 1905, and then 1908, 1918, 1923, 1927, 1931, 1935, 1942, 1955, 1963). On the importance of Panzini's work, see Luca Serianni, 'Panzini lessicografo fra parole e cose', in *Che fine fanno i neologismi? A cento anni dalla pubblicazione del Dizionario Moderno di Alfredo Panzini*, ed. by Giovanni Adamo and Valeria Della Valle (Florence: Olschki, 2006), pp. 55–78; Arturo Tosi, 'Dictionaries of Neologisms and the History of Society', in *Languages of Italy: Histories and Dictionaries*, ed. by Anna Laura Lepschy and Arturo Tosi (Ravenna: Longo, 2007), pp. 249–68, especially pp. 258–62; Marianna Franchi, 'Deonomastica panziniana fra antonomasia e tendenze enciclopediche', in *Lo spettacolo delle parole. Studi di storia linguistica e di onomastica in ricordo di Sergio Raffaelli*, ed. by Enzo Caffarelli and Massimo Fanfani (Rome: Società Editrice Romana, 2011), pp. 545–58.
17. Cf. Gaetano Rando, 'Anglicismi nel *Dizionario Moderno* dalla quarta alla decima edizione', *Lingua nostra*, 30 (1969), 107–12.
18. Alfredo Panzini, *Dizionario moderno*, 4th edn (Milan: Hoepli, 1923), pp. 67, 246–47, 274.
19. Cf. Schirru's chapter in this volume.
20. See Ingrid Furlan, 'Termini della politica inglese e americana entrati in italiano nel decennio 1951–1960', *Lingua nostra*, 39 (1978), 64–68; Diego Zancani, 'Anglo-American Linguistic Borrowings 1947–58', in *Italy in the Cold War: Politics, Culture and Society*, ed. by Christopher Duggan and Christopher Wagstaff (Oxford: Berg, 1995), pp. 167–87.
21. Cf. G. Rando, '*Capital gain, lunedì nero, money manager* e altri anglicismi recentissimi del linguaggio economico-borsistico-commerciale', *Lingua nostra*, 51 (1990), 50–66.
22. Cf. Fabio Marri, 'La lingua dell'informatica', in *Storia della lingua italiana*, 3 vols, ed. by Luca Serianni and Pietro Trifone (Turin: Einaudi, 1994), II, 617–33.
23. Cf. Federigo Bambi, 'Il linguaggio giuridico tra semplificazione, rispetto delle tecnicità e anglofonia', in *Manuale di comunicazione istituzionale e internazionale*, ed. by Raffaella Bombi (Rome: Il Calamo, 2013), pp. 29–44.
24. Cf. Alessandro Carlucci, 'Per la storia degli influssi alloglotti: fr. *cogestion* e it. *cogestione*', *Lingua nostra*, 78 (2017), 56–58.
25. See Carlucci's chapter in this volume.
26. Concerning these and similar interferences see Lorenzo Renzi, *Come cambia la lingua. L'italiano in movimento* (Bologna: Il Mulino, 2012), pp. 70–76.

CHAPTER 15

Contact, Change, and Translation: A Theoretical and Empirical Assessment of Non-Lexical Anglicisms*

Alessandro Carlucci

Much of the existing scholarship on the influence of the English language in Italian focuses on lexical borrowing, especially on (graphically) non-adapted items such as *film, jazz, hard disk*, and on closely related aspects of semantic borrowing (as in the case of *salvare*, which has acquired the extra meaning of 'safely storing data on a computer'). Far less attention has been devoted to phonology, morphology and syntax — or, to use a cover term, to 'grammatical' influences. Another aspect of this predominantly lexical focus is our relative ignorance of the impact that English has had on the Italian language as used and recognized by the Italian-speaking community at large. Linguistic contact does not have the same effects in all communicative domains, and lexical influences are nowadays particularly strong in those 'area[s] of Anglophone culture (for example sport, technology, business) [which] effectively lend not only words but indeed the concepts those words represent'.[1] While a significant body of scholarship has therefore described Anglo-American influences in these and other domains (from trademarks to advertising, to the Italian used by economists or politicians), the impact on non-domain-specific Italian is yet to be adequately explored.

Only in recent years has the balance begun to be redressed.[2] This chapter aims to move further in this direction by following three major orienting criteria. Firstly, I will shift the focus of attention from the 'bricks' of language to the architectural patterns used in combining bricks — according to a metaphor that linguists commonly use in order to foreground the grammatical structure of a language, as opposed to its vocabulary. Secondly, I will endeavour to avoid as much as possible those grammatical borrowings which remain confined to special types of text or particular varieties of Italian. Results would be different if one chose to focus on micro-contact between English and the Italian of migrant communities in English-speaking countries, but such a choice would hardly be representative

* I would like to thank the John Fell Fund of the University of Oxford, whose funding has made this chapter possible.

of the behaviour of the Italian-speaking community as a whole, of which Italy's population remains a numerically and culturally pivotal section. Thirdly, I will focus on English influences which have given rise to permanent changes in the functioning of the Italian language, thus excluding cross-linguistic transfers which are essentially a matter of performance. Put in plain (and somewhat simplistic) terms, speakers with various degrees of familiarity with English may introduce some of its features into Italian, especially when suddenly having to switch from the former into the latter, and something similar occasionally happens, for instance, in the dubbing of American films and TV series — but this does not mean that Italian has actually changed.[3]

The first section of the chapter summarizes the historical and sociolinguistic background to the diffusion of the English language in Italy. The second and third sections explain the most relevant notions from the existing literature on linguistic contact and change, so that in the remaining sections of the article I can proceed to apply those notions to two features of Italian grammar which are under English influence: progressives and coordination. I conclude by returning to theoretical and methodological notions; in doing so I refer to language and translation, but I hope to provide food for thought for all those interested in the historical study of how — and why — cultures change.

What Kind of Contact?

It is said that when the US author William Saroyan visited Elio Vittorini, shortly after the Second World War, the two men had to write little notes to each other: Vittorini was unable to have a conversation in English, despite the fact that he was a gifted intellectual and one of Italy's leading translators from English.[4] Whatever the accuracy of this anecdote, it is a well-known fact that during the first half of the twentieth century many literary texts were not even directly translated from English into Italian. French was still the dominant foreign language in education, as well as in Italian society at large, and French editions were often used — either as a source text, or as a close point of reference — when producing the Italian version of a British or US text.

Contact with English became more significant during the second half of the century,[5] even if mastery of this language remained confined to small groups of the Italian population. The ability to read was generally more common than active competence in the oral use of the language. Contact with texts in English and direct interaction with its speakers became more regular in special sectors of trade and business, as well as among executives, scientists, diplomats and other members of geographically mobile, socio-cultural elites. But within the rest of the population, English was either not used at all, or only used infrequently, usually in a basic manner and for a limited set of purposes. In either case, English remained detached from everyday communicative practices, in which the local languages (or dialects), and increasingly also the national language, were regularly used. Foreign publications in the original language were relatively expensive and not always easy to find. Dubbing was the norm for films and television programmes. The main exceptions were music — where lyrics, however, were seldom the focus of listeners' attention — and advertising.

Especially in the language of advertising, the other side of the coin of Italians' scant familiarity with English was the proliferation of Anglicisms, pseudo-Anglicisms, and other superficial manifestations of a growing fascination with this language — from Anglo-American interjections and fixed phrases (*okay, last but not least*) to commercial names and slogans such as Nike's untranslated 'Just do it'. As shown by sociolinguistic research conducted in the 1980s and 1990s, those Italians 'who are not fluent in a foreign language feel gratified by the use of easily-comprehensible foreign words (for example *no limits, action, style, stop, best, show, view, new*)'.[6] In the case of pseudo-Anglicisms (a famous example being *recordman* for 'record holder'), words which were almost meaningless and even ungrammatical in English were presented in iconic contexts (such as hoardings, shop windows and signs, newspaper headlines and captions), thus making them meaningful without requiring a sound knowledge of the language. Most of these innovations have permanently entered the Italian lexicon thanks to the perception of English as the new language of social advancement, and to the prestigious status of the transnational elites who regularly used it with native or near-native bilingual competence. In contrast, the Americanisms carried to Italy by returning migrants have usually remained confined to their own linguistic variety, or have at best spread to the local dialect of their province. For instance, while *store* 'large shop, online shopping site' has recently become part of the Italian lexicon, the *storo* 'shop' of Sicilian migrants did not.[7]

The twentieth century also saw passionate puristic reactions against the linguistic corruption allegedly caused by the English language, notwithstanding the limited extent of its influence. These reactions, which were officially supported during the Fascist regime and still present in more recent years, are typically triggered by sentences such as 'Da Tossic Park una class action contro i pusher' [literally: From Tossic Park a class action against pushers] (from the title of a newspaper article) or 'formatta il floppy clickando col mouse' [format the floppy (disk) by clicking with the mouse].[8] From a sociolinguistic point of view, these sentences show that Italian journalists have become quite prone to use English words and phrases, and that Italian is borrowing much of the technical terminology of Information Technology from English. From a linguistic point view, however, what these sentences reveal is in fact an unswerving adherence to the structure of the Italian language (perhaps with a few phonological exceptions concerning word-final consonants in [ˈtɔsːik], [ˈpark], [ˈklas] and [ˈmauz]). At least in these cases, English influences are restricted to spelling (*sh, ck, y*, silent *-e* in *mouse*) and lexicon.

The number of Italians claiming to know English began to increase significantly only in the last few decades of the century, when English acquired a dominant role in education. In the 1990s, the average knowledge of foreign languages among young people was four times higher than among the over-45s.[9] One in four lower secondary school leavers, however, still admitted that three years of compulsory training in a foreign language had led them to acquire no knowledge at all in this field.[10] Since then, the sociolinguistic context has further evolved. English–Italian bilingualism has been reinforced by young Italians working for companies where English is frequently used; many Italians have also moved to English-speaking countries, where Italian is in turn studied as a foreign or heritage language.[11] The number of people using Italian is 92,200 in the UK (possibly a restrictive estimate, given that there are now 324,368 Italian citizens in this country),[12] 438,000 in Canada, and 300,000 in Australia.[13] Figures for the USA vary from 'nearly 800,000'[14] to 723,632,[15] with a standard source recently indicating 724,000.[16] However, these are relatively small figures compared to the estimated total of 67 million speakers of Italian worldwide. Finally, the number of people currently living in Italy who come from predominantly English-speaking countries can be estimated at approximately 50,000.[17]

On the whole, Anglo-American influence on Italian is still to be ascribed to what most linguists call 'remote' or 'virtual' contact, in that it does not predominantly rely on 'physical contact between speakers'.[18] In what follows, I will refer to it more generally as 'mediated contact'.[19] This kind of contact has expanded in modern societies, due to changes in information and communication technology. In Italy, in particular, an important channel for mediated contact continues to be provided by dubbing — whose potential impact can hardly be overestimated for a country where television is watched for many hours a day, and where '[a]bout 80%' of films and TV series 'are imported from English-speaking countries, predominantly from the USA'.[20]

What Kind of Change?

Historical linguists have developed complex theoretical and methodological notions for studying the relationship between contact and change. In this chapter it is not possible to do justice to this impressive set of notions,[21] but it is probably helpful to clarify some basic and long-established distinctions. First of all, linguists differentiate between *internal* (or, more precisely, endogenous) *change*, whereby a language changes in ways which are entirely explainable by referring to its grammatical and lexical structure and to the history of the community that uses it, and *contact-induced* (or exogenous) *change*, whereby the language in question changes in ways which can only be explained by referring to contact with (communities using) other languages.

Broadly speaking, most linguists would further differentiate between: (i) contact situations involving high levels of bilingual competence and frequent, large-scale speaker interaction; and (ii) situations in which frequent interaction between speakers of the source and recipient language is not a mass phenomenon, while much of the contact takes place through translation, interpreting, dubbing, language learning and other similar practices. Mediated contact, as described in the previous section of this chapter, is clearly part of the latter type.

The two types of contact situation are traditionally expected to correlate with two different types of change. Bearing in mind that contact rarely leads to the exact reproduction, in the borrowing language, of a model from the source language (an outcome that some scholars even deny in principle),[22] situations of the former type (i) are normally expected to result in the borrowing of basic vocabulary and potentially also grammatical features at the level of phonology, derivational morphology and syntax. With prolonged and increasingly intense contact, these situations can eventually lead to changes in inflectional morphology (although these may be constrained by the structural difference, or typological distance, between source and recipient language). In general, this kind of contact situation is capable of producing non-peripheral changes in the recipient language, from both a linguistic and a sociolinguistic point of view — that is to say, changes that reach core grammatical structures, and which do not remain confined to certain lexical strata or to particular varieties or registers of the recipient language.

Most linguists predict that contexts of the other type (ii) will instead result in peripheral changes, typically at the level of non-basic vocabulary and with little or no impact on grammatical structures. A relevant example is the use of *-trone* in *positrone, ciclotrone, sincrotrone* and so on, which Klajn ascribes to the influence of English *-tron* (cf. *positron*).[23] This development is essentially confined to the specialist variety of Italian used by professional physicists, and perhaps to the special languages of science popularizers or medical practitioners.[24] Likewise, the phrasal type 'Robert Redford come Gatsby' instead of 'nella parte di', as reported by Dardano,[25] almost exclusively appears in the special language of film criticism. While the occasional transfer of a morphological device such as the so-called Saxon genitive might point towards unexpectedly strong grammatical influence (as in the title of *Occidentali's karma*, the winning song at the 2017 Festival di Sanremo), there is no indication of its widespread adoption by the Italian-speaking community, let alone of its fully productive embedding into Italian grammar. This is not the whole story, though. As we shall see, Anglo-American influences have in some cases gone beyond small, domain-specific innovations. But in order to appreciate fully the wider picture, we now need to say a few more words on recent developments in the study of contact-induced change.

Recent Approaches to Contact-Induced Change

The most innovative scholarship has recently moved beyond the distinctions that we have seen in the previous section.[26] Such a move has been inspired by dissatisfaction with traditional approaches that underplayed the significance of contact as a source of change. As Sarah Thomason (a leading expert in contact linguistics) stated in 2010,

> there is a strong tendency to consider the possibility of external causation for a change only when the search for an internal cause has failed to produce a plausible result. This tendency has weakened in the past 20 years or so, but it has not vanished.[27]

In other words, if abstract structural analysis can explain a linguistic change, the influence of other languages should not be taken into consideration. These traditional views especially underplayed mediated contact, which, *on its own*, is unlikely to produce far-reaching grammatical change.

A crucial premise in rejecting this reductionism has been the definition of contact as *a* source, rather than *the* source, of particular grammatical changes, based on 'a growing body of evidence suggest[ing] that multiple causation — often a combination of an external and one or more internal causes — is responsible for a sizable number of changes'.[28] This premise has various interesting implications. For instance, in traditional approaches the emergence of similar constructions in closely related languages (as in the case of *essere* + gerund in Sardinian, quite similar to the Italian progressive periphrasis to be discussed below) undermined contact explanations. But in multi-causal approaches, the similar development of related languages A and B does not rule out contact: the emergence of a construction in B may still have been favoured by contact with other languages, even if a similar construction emerged in A as an entirely internal development.[29]

Through the notion of multiple causation, the contrast between major types of contact-induced change loses part of its appeal and is replaced by a continuum with various intermediate possibilities. At one end of this continuum we find those structurally disruptive changes which modify the borrowing language in an unprecedented and largely unexpected way, and which would arguably be unlikely in the absence of contact (for example, the appearance of suffixation in languages that previously only had prefixes). At the opposite end of this continuum we have those contact-induced developments which typically capitalize on pre-existing diachronic trends within the recipient language, introducing new items or patterns, or simply changing the frequency and productivity of existing ones. The role of multiple causation becomes especially important as we move towards this end of the continuum, where some scholars prefer to speak of 'contact-influenced' rather than 'contact-induced' change.[30]

In a previous publication, I reviewed the most likely cases of English influence on Italian grammatical structures.[31] My conclusion was that, far from introducing radical innovations into core structures, Anglo-American influences have mainly led to the extension of minority patterns, or have in other ways exploited pre-existing possibilities. In the remainder of this chapter I would like to substantiate this argument further by focusing on two of the (ten) grammatical features discussed in my previous publication. This close observation of a smaller number of cases should make it easier to move beyond considerations solely based on linguistic analysis, or on sociolinguistic dichotomies concerning the situation in which contact takes place. In other words, I hope to produce a deeper empirical assessment of contact with English as a cause of change in the recent history of Italian, in line with the latest approaches to the study of linguistic contact and change.

First Case Study: The Progressive Periphrasis

The emergence of a progressive meaning for a string such as 'sto leggendo' is an example of what historical linguists call 'grammaticalization', a diachronic process which is often responsible for the emergence of new verb forms. Although it has some antecedents already in late Latin, progressive *stare* + gerund is a Romance innovation which has especially expanded in modern Italian. Although Italian *stare*

+ gerund is not fully grammaticalized, later in this section we will see that it has probably reached that stage in the diachronic development of verbal periphrases where they are still 'put together according to the rules of syntax but they often have special shades of meaning such as intent or progression and involve contrasts with fully morphological forms, so that they function as members of the verb's extended paradigm'.[32]

The story begins with a purely compositional meaning: *sto* retains its lexical meaning of 'I stand' or 'I stay', or at least some locative value, and so 'sto leggendo' means something like 'I stand reading' or 'I stay reading', or perhaps 'I am standing and reading'. From a structural point of view, the next step involves the semantic bleaching of *stare* and the emergence of a meaning of duration for the periphrasis with the gerund. A third step gives this periphrasis its current meaning, which is well exemplified by a sentence such as 'quando sei arrivato stavo leggendo' [when you arrived I was reading]. Here, *stare* + gerund presents the dynamic unfolding of an action ('I was reading') as if observed from a single, intersecting point in time ('when you arrived'), creating that instant-focused situation which is the trademark of progressives. With this last step, *sto leggendo, stavo leggendo* etc. have essentially become periphrastic forms of the verb *leggere* in much the same way as *I am reading* etc. are periphrastic forms of *read*. From a historical point of view, examples of the durative meaning have been identified in various authors, from Boccaccio ('e quasi storditi stavano riguardando, non sappiendo che fare' [as though stunned, they just looked and did not know what to do], *Filocolo*, v, 6) to Manzoni ('Il Griso non rispose nulla, e stette aspettando dove andassero a parare questi preamboli' [Griso did not answer but just waited to see where all this was going], *I promessi sposi*, XXXIII), whereas the progressive meaning became dominant during the twentieth century. This expansion was not purely quantitative, but also had structural implications. The rise of progressive *stare* + gerund was accompanied by a decline in the frequency of related structures, such as *venire* + gerund and *andare* + gerund (known as continuous periphrases): forms such as *vengono aumentando* or *vanno aumentando*, for instance in 'i prezzi vanno aumentando' [prices are increasing], are nowadays perceived as highly formal and somewhat old-fashioned. But the twentieth century also witnessed an expansion in the types of verb to which the progressive periphrasis can be applied, including previously excluded punctual and transformative verbs, as in *sto partendo* [I am leaving] and *sta succedendo* [it is happening], and also meteorological verbs as in *sta piovendo* [it is raining] — previously nonsense, as long as *sta* retained something of its original meaning '(s)he stays'.

Despite this vigorous expansion, the incomplete grammaticalization of *stare* + gerund makes this Italian periphrasis different from English progressives. While in a sentence such as 'I am reading the newspaper right now' the progressive is obligatory in English, most scholars and native speakers agree that 'in questo momento sto leggendo il giornale' and 'in questo momento leggo il giornale' are interchangeable variants in Italian. Another difference is that while in English the use of the progressive periphrasis 'can be extended to non-progressive contexts, in Standard Italian the construction appears to be limited to instant-focused situations'.³³ Unlike English, moreover, Italian does not allow the combination of the progressive periphrasis with perfective tenses (*sono stato leggendo*, *stetti leggendo*) or with the passive forms of the verb's paradigm. Finally, while English tolerates sentences such as 'John is being silly' (which could be rendered as 'John sta facendo lo stupido'), one cannot say *'sta essendo stupido' — not because of a purely formal, arbitrary constraint on the combination of *stare* and *essere*, but because of semantic motivations: the progressive meaning of *stare* + gerund makes this periphrasis somehow incompatible with 'stative' predicates which describe a quality or ability of the subject (as in the case of 'essere stupido', whereas 'fare lo stupido' forces the interpretation of the subject as an agent intentionally and dynamically doing something).³⁴

What I have said so far is largely based on the works of Durante,³⁵ Bertinetto,³⁶ Brianti,³⁷ and others. If we focus on recent data, however, we see that the expansion of *stare* + gerund is progressing further. Based on his own judgement as a native speaker, Cortelazzo finds 'ieri **stavo passeggiando** nei dintorni dell'Università, quando ho incontrato un vecchio amico' [yesterday I was taking a walk near the university when I met an old friend] less formal and more natural than 'ieri **passeggiavo** nei dintorni dell'Università, quando ho incontrato un vecchio amico' [yesterday I was walking near the university when I met an old friend],³⁸ which might signal the end of full interchangeability and perhaps the firming up of the contrast between periphrastic and non-periphrastic forms (along progressive vs generically imperfective aspectual lines). On the other hand, Squartini records the use of *stare* + gerund outside instant-focused situations, in sentences denoting habitual actions: 'in questo periodo sta leggendo un romanzo francese' [these days he is reading a French novel], 'in questo periodo sta studiando spesso con Olga' [these days he is often studying with Olga].³⁹ Passivization is also becoming less exceptional, as in this subtitle from the website of the Italian newspaper *Il Foglio*: 'Quando gli universitari protestano, è sempre buon segno: vuol dire che sta venendo proposto qualcosa di interessante' [When university students start protesting, it is always a good sign: it means that something interesting is being discussed].⁴⁰ We have already mentioned Italian journalists' well-known proclivity for Anglicisms, and it is clear that some of these latest developments are making Italian verbal structures more similar to their English counterparts. Yet, it would be unwise to assign a role to Anglo-American influence solely on these grounds.

We clearly need to turn to more empirical considerations. In order to do so, I have built a specifically designated corpus of written Italian, consisting of approximately half a million words evenly spread across four periods: 1874–1917, 1918–45, 1946–88, and 1989–2014. The corpus contains both literary and non-literary texts. The latter range from a letter that the Italian anti-fascist intellectual Gaetano Salvemini wrote in 1935, while living in the USA,⁴¹ to the Italian edition of the American magazine *National Geographic*; from travel journals, to speeches and interviews published in Italian magazines and newspapers (especially *La Stampa* and the *Corriere della Sera*) at various stages during the twentieth century. I have attached tags to all the texts: IT for texts with no particular relation to Anglophone culture (mostly written by

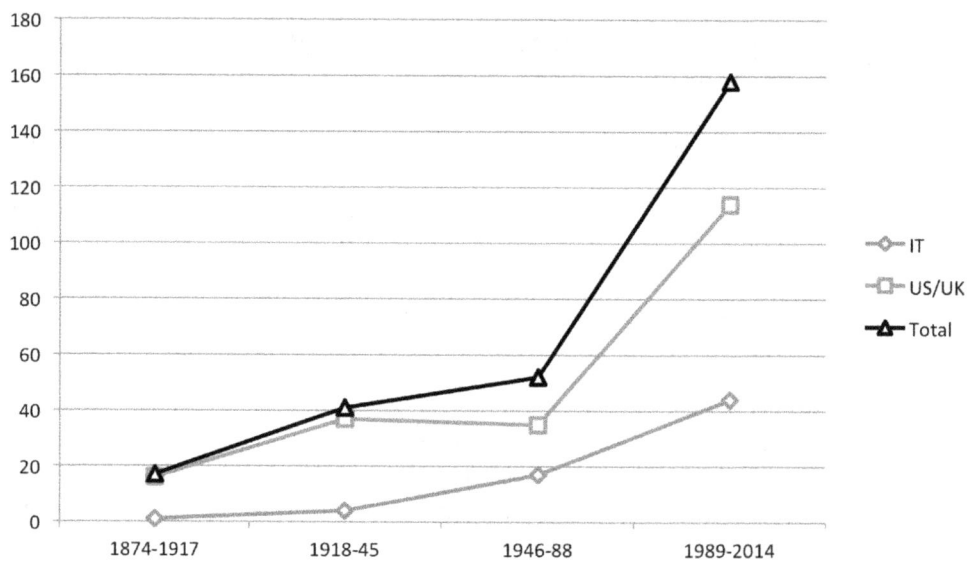

FIG. 15.1. Occurrences of progressive *stare* + gerund (y-axis) across time (x-axis).

Italians living in Italy); UK for texts linked to the United Kingdom in terms of internal content and/or external context of production; US for texts linked to the United States in terms of internal content and/or external context of production; TR for translations from English.

Some UK/US texts belong to advertising and news translation — that is to say, to two of the most likely channels for grammatical borrowing.[42] In order to produce a representative sample, however, care has been taken to avoid including only texts where cross-linguistic transfer is particularly intense. Moreover, the need for sufficient internal diversification has been combined with that for homogeneity — especially in the sense of avoiding text types and genres, as well as linguistic registers, which are less representative because of their predilection for uncommon forms, marked stylistic choices, regional variants, or other non-standard features (for instance, poetic texts have been excluded, as well as particularly experimental or elevated forms of literary prose).

On this material I have tested the hypothesis that Anglo-American influence may have favoured the expansion of the Italian progressive periphrasis. That 'l'influenza dell'angloamericano' [Anglo-American influence] only became 'notevole e profonda' [noteworthy and profound] in Italian after the Second World War is an independently and abundantly observed fact.[43] Therefore, we shall have an argument in favour of our hypothesis if progressive *stare* + gerund appears mainly in written texts that were exposed to English influences, and if it does so increasingly and especially during the second half of the twentieth century. But if progressive *stare* + gerund turns out to be more frequent in typically Italian texts with little or no contact with English, or if it was more frequent at the beginning of the century, when Anglo-American social and cultural influence was less strong,

Fig. 15.2. Progressive *stare* + gerund in translations from English and in other texts (% of all occurrences, y-axis).

then we must reconsider the status of progressive *stare* + gerund as an Anglicism. Figure 1 shows my findings, which are compatible with the hypothesis of contact-influenced change.

Only in the oldest text have I found an occurrence of *stare* and a gerund in close proximity to each other but without progressive value.[44] It is also interesting to note that translations, which account for approximately 48% of all the words in the corpus, are a constantly dominant source of progressive *stare* + gerund, peaking to 70% of the occurrences in the period 1989–2014. This sample of written Italian suggests that contact with English has helped to boost progressive *stare* + gerund at the expense of *venire* + gerund and *andare* + gerund. While these two alternatives still appear in literary texts from the first part of the twentieth century, they become rare in more recent periods, especially in TR texts. Such changes in relative frequency are an expected outcome of contact at the syntactic level.[45] This outcome is probably linked to the well-known role of translation in producing texts where features unique to the target language are under-represented, while constructions which bilinguals perceive as common to the source and target languages (in this case *be* + *-ing* and *stare* + gerund) are over-represented.

The hypothesis tested here is essentially based on the views of scholars (such as Durante and Degano) who attribute the increased frequency and productivity of the progressive periphrasis to Anglo-American influence; however, many others deny (Cortelazzo, Brianti), or do not say (Renzi),[46] that this increase has been caused by contact with English. From what we have seen in this section, there is no reason to question the idea of a gradual, internal process of grammaticalization largely explaining the recent expansion of *stare* + gerund; but bearing in mind the theoretical and methodological premises set out in the third section of this chapter, there is also no reason to rule out a combination of endogenous and exogenous causes. In fact, my data confirm that contact with English most probably *has* played a role in favouring the expansion of progressive *stare* + gerund.

Second Case Study: Coordination

The appearance of 'régimes à double préposition' [government by two prepositions] was already attributed to English influences in French in the 1960s,[47] when it was denounced as part of puristic attacks against the 'américanisation du langage' [Americanization of usage] and other similar targets.[48] In Italian, the spread of this syntactic feature would not seem to have been detected until the 1980s. Since then, its status as a borrowing from English has been generally accepted — in contrast to the much more contested case of English influence on the progressive periphrasis. Prepositions have been the main focus of attention also among Italian linguists, who speak for instance of 'duplice reggenza preposizionale' [double prepositional government]:[49] 'da e per l'aeroporto' [literally: from and to the airport] exemplifies this simple and fairly common construction, in which two prepositions governing the same constituent are coordinated. However, their discussions often include more complex examples, such as 'affascinato dalla, e invischiato nella, regola' [fascinated by, and entangled in, the rule],[50] and even sentences in which the coordinated elements are not two prepositions. Anglo-American influence would therefore seem to have been responsible for the emergence of wider patterns of coordination, including 'delayed right constituent coordination'. 'In this construction the constituent which in basic coordination would appear as the rightmost element of the first coordinate is held back until after the final coordinate',[51] as in 'scopre inizialmente la (o viene scoperto dalla) dialettica dell'influenza'. This last example translates 'first discovers (or is discovered by) the dialectic of influence' in the Italian translation (1983) of Harold Bloom's *The Anxiety of Influence*.[52]

Focusing on the simplest construction, Renzi defines it as 'coordinazione di preposizioni con ellissi del S[intagma] N[ominale] uguale' [coordination of prepositions with ellipsis of an identical noun phrase] and states that its model 'è l'inglese di espressioni come *to and from the airport*' [is to be found in English expressions such as *to and from the airport*].[53] But apart from the different order (typically 'da e per', as opposed to 'to and from'), from a purely linguistic point of view it may not be necessary to refer to contact: a functional explanation is traditionally available for the emergence of elliptical constructions, namely the search for economical means of expression.[54] Sociolinguistic factors, too, are probably ambivalent in this respect. Although it has spread into spoken Italian (typically in formal, considered registers), the construction in question was first observed — and is still predominantly attested — in newspapers and academic writing. Both are indeed under English influence, but they are just as often characterized by a sophisticated style and painstaking avoidance of repetitions.

A cursory empirical exploration allows us to add a few details which further problematize the role of contact. Confronted with 'to and from the city' in the third chapter of Francis Scott Fitzgerald's *The Great Gatsby*, translators opted for conservative solutions: the first Italian translation (1936) has 'dalla città al castello e viceversa' (but as evidenced by the title, *Gatsby il magnifico*, this was almost certainly based on the French translation, where we find precisely 'de la ville au château, et *vice-versa*') and subsequent translations have 'dalla città e ritorno' (1950) or other similar solutions.[55] Only very recent translations display the coordination of prepositions and, at least in one case, even the order of the source language: 'da e per la città' (2011), 'da e verso la città' (2011), and 'per e dalla città' (2016).[56] This suggests that, while academic translations were probably a fast-acting source of Anglo-American influence,[57] literary translations may have lagged behind. In any case, at an earlier time than any of the translations cited thus far, coordinated prepositions already appeared in special varieties and types of text where brevity is a crucial requirement. While going through the written corpus that I used for the progressive periphrasis, I have found examples of the 'da e per' type in guidelines issued by Italy's national railways in the 1920s (i.e. an IT text).[58] One could therefore argue that Anglo-American influence has simply favoured the generalization of this construction beyond special varieties of Italian.

In sum, it seems almost impossible to separate external influences from internal evolution in this case. The overall picture is, however, compatible with a multi-causal explanation, whereby the emergence of 'da e per l'aeroporto' and other similar constructions is the result of a combination of internal and external factors.

Conclusions

In the first case study we considered a structural feature which many linguists refuse to link to contact with English, and we found that mediated contact is in fact a plausible factor for explaining its recent expansion. In the second case study, we turned instead to a feature that is generally regarded as an Anglicism, and found that indigenous factors may well have favoured its appearance. The lessons to be learned from this reassessment of the progressive periphrasis and of coordination might bear some relevance not only to the study of linguistic change, but of cultural change as a whole.

Historical linguistics was born in the nineteenth century (under the distinctive name of 'comparative philology' or *Sprachwissenschaft*) and its methods were decisively shaped by the preoccupations that the discipline had in its budding years, when it rapidly built a huge reputation thanks to its unprecedented, lasting advancements in reconstructing the early stages of Indo-European languages, for which we have little or no written evidence. With similar objects of study, contact explanations can easily lead to circular reasoning: analogous changes in languages A and B may be attributed to contact, but there may not be any other substantial evidence of contact between A and B except for their analogous development. Especially for prehistoric periods, it may be difficult to exclude accidental similarity or a common remote origin. Among comparative philologists and their structuralist successors, the risk was usually averted by invoking contact only in the absence of any internal explanation. Language historians are still instinctively attached to these methodological principles, which also involve underplaying mediated contact as an especially fuzzy explanatory factor.

For more recent periods, however, we often have sufficient historical knowledge allowing us to trace contact independently and produce a detailed understanding of its interaction with internal factors. From this privileged viewpoint, change no longer needs to be attributed to a single cause, which should necessarily belong either to indigenous evolution or to contact with other cultures. Secondly, especially in contemporary societies, mediated contact is neither irrelevant, nor necessarily less important than more intimate types of contact involving human proximity and/or mobility. My chapter confirms this second point — which has been highlighted by some of the latest work in contact linguistics. Finally, recent scholarship includes various forms of translation into mediated contact, and sees them as a pertinent component of empirically validated, multi-causal explanations of linguistic change. As this chapter has confirmed, translation is not only a channel of contact, but can also be a source of contact-influenced change.

Notes to Chapter 15

1. Christopher Pountain, 'Syntactic Anglicisms in Spanish: Innovation or Exploitation?', in *The Changing Voices of Europe*, ed. by Mair Parry and others (Cardiff: University of Wales Press, 1994), pp. 109–24 (p. 110).
2. See especially *Italiano e inglese a confronto*, ed. by A. V. Sullam Calimani (Florence: Cesati, 2003); Chiara Degano, 'Influssi inglesi sulla sintassi italiana: uno studio preliminare sul caso della perifrasi progressiva', in *L'italiano delle traduzioni*, ed. by Anna Cardinaletti and Giuliana Garzone (Milan: Angeli, 2005), pp. 85–105; Michele Cortelazzo, 'La perifrasi progressiva in italiano è un anglicismo sintattico?', in *I sentieri della lingua. Saggi sugli usi dell'italiano tra passato e presente* (Padua: Esedra, 2012), pp. 31–39; Mairi McLaughlin, 'News Translation as a Source of Syntactic Borrowing in Italian', *The Italianist*, 33 (2013), 443–63; and Lorella Viola, '*Stai scherzando?* "Are you kidding?": Investigating the Influence of Dubbing on the Italian Progressive', *Italian Journal of Linguistics*, 28.2 (2016), 181–202.
3. Widely studied cases include the frequent, pragmatically exotic recurrence of *bene* and *prego*, on the model of *well* and *please*, the literal translation of idiomatic expressions (e.g. 'non è come andare in bicicletta' for 'it's not like riding a bike', when the context requires 'non è come bere un bicchier d'acqua') and other well-documented examples of interference in translations from English (e.g. 'domestico' instead of 'nazionale'). Because of what I have said above, my approach also differs from the one taken by McLaughlin ('News Translation'). She focuses on translated news dispatches, seeing them as a source for potential changes in the structure of Italian and therefore exploring innovations that 'can enter the language' (p. 446), even when these innovations have not yet spread through the Italian-speaking community at large.
4. See Ettore Vittorini (Elio's nephew), 'Vittorini e i "pizzini" a Saroyan', *Corriere della Sera*, 23 July 2008. See also the testimony of another prominent translator: 'conosco traduttori ottimi, dall'inglese, che portati a Londra morirebbero di fame, perché non saprebbero farsi intendere nei ristoranti' [I know very good translators from English who would starve in London because they would not be able to make themselves understood in restaurants]. Luciano Bianciardi, 'Il traduttore' [1969], in *La solita zuppa e altre storie* (Milan: Bompiani, 1994), p. 181.
5. See Gabriella Cartago, 'L'apporto inglese', in *Storia della lingua italiana*, 3 vols, ed. by L. Serianni and P. Trifone (Turin: Einaudi, 1994), III, 721–50; and also Fanfani's and Pulcini's chapters in the present volume.
6. Arturo Tosi, *Language and Society in a Changing Italy* (Clevedon: Multilingual Matters, 2001), p. 212.

7. See e.g. Leonardo Sciascia, 'La zia d'America', in *Gli zii di Sicilia* (Turin: Einaudi, 1958), pp. 9–60, and the studies of Alberto Zamboni ('Gli anglicismi nei dialetti italiani', in *Elementi stranieri nei dialetti italiani. Atti del XIV Convegno del Centro di studio per la dialettologia italiana* (Pisa: Pacini, 1986), pp. 79–125), Pier Vincenzo Mengaldo (*Storia della lingua italiana. Il Novecento* (Bologna: Il Mulino, 1994), p. 131), and Arturo Tosi (*Language and Society in a Changing Italy*, pp. 229 ff.).
8. I take both examples from Beccaria's chapter, 'Lingua madre', in Gian Luigi Beccaria and Andrea Graziosi, *Lingua madre. Italiano e inglese nel mondo globale* (Bologna: Il Mulino, 2015), pp. 79–122 (p. 92).
9. Tullio De Mauro, *Minima Scholaria* (Rome: Laterza, 1998), p. 184.
10. Tullio De Mauro and Patrick Boylan, 'L'incidenza dell'apprendimento di una lingua straniera sull'apprendimento e l'uso della lingua materna nella scuola italiana', in *L'universo delle lingue*, ed. by P. Desideri (Florence: La Nuova Italia, 1995), p. 8.
11. See *L'italiano nel mondo*, ed. by Claudio Giovanardi and Pietro Trifone (Rome: Carocci, 2012), and *Stati generali della lingua italiana nel mondo* (Rome: Ministero degli Affari Esteri e della Cooperazione Internazionale, 2016). Various types of research have shown that Italian as used in Italy remains a prestigious point of reference for the teaching and usage of Italian abroad. In particular, in communities of former Italian migrants, 'subsequent generations appear to take an attitude towards their heritage language and will either progressively abandon it or learn it normatively' (Mari Jones and Christopher Pountain, 'Romance outside the Romània', in *The Cambridge History of the Romance Languages*, 2 vols, ed. by Martin Maiden, J. C. Smith and Adam Ledgeway (Cambridge: Cambridge University Press, 2013), II, 361–99, on p. 369), thus converging on usage norms which essentially come from Italy.
12. See *Ethnologue: Languages of Africa and Europe*, 20th edn, ed. by Gary F. Simons and Charles D. Fennig (Dallas: SIL, 2017), p. 356; but cf. *Annuario statistico* (Rome: Ministero degli Affari Esteri e della Cooperazione Internazionale and Sistema Statistico Nazionale, 2018), p. 92.
13. See *Ethnologue: Languages of the Americas and the Pacific*, 20th edn, ed. by Gary F. Simons and Charles D. Fennig (Dallas: SIL, 2017), pp. 76 and 191.
14. Anna De Fina and Luciana Fellin, 'Italian in the USA', in *Language Diversity in the USA*, ed. by Kim Potowski (Cambridge: Cambridge University Press, 2010), pp. 195–205 (p. 195).
15. Susan Tamasi and Lamont Antieau, *Language and Linguistic Diversity in the US: An Introduction* (New York: Routledge, 2015), p. 204.
16. See *Ethnologue*, p. 158.
17. Based on <http://dati.istat.it/> [last accessed 15 October 2017].
18. Mairi McLaughlin, *Syntactic Borrowing in Contemporary French: A Linguistic Analysis of News Translation* (Oxford: Legenda, 2011), p. 14.
19. I am indebted to migration historian Donna Gabaccia for suggesting this terminological choice.
20. Viola, '*Stai scherzando?*', p. 187.
21. For detailed surveys of the issues involved, including different ways of defining the stages and sub-components of linguistic change, see Henning Andersen, 'Actualization and the (Uni)directionality of Change', in *Actualization: Linguistic Change in Progress*, ed. by Henning Andersen (Amsterdam: John Benjamins, 2001), pp. 225–48; Sarah Thomason, 'Contact as a Source of Language Change', in *The Handbook of Historical Linguistics*, ed. by Brian Joseph and Richard Janda (Oxford: Blackwell, 2004), pp. 686–712; William Labov, *Principles of Linguistic Change*, 3 vols (Oxford: Blackwell, 1994–2010), III, 303–75; and Gillian Sankoff, 'Linguistic Outcomes of Bilingualism', in *The Handbook of Language Variation and Change*, ed. by J. K. Chambers and Natalie Schilling (Oxford: Blackwell, 2013), pp. 501–18.
22. See e.g. Roberto Gusmani, *Saggi sull'interferenza linguistica* (Florence: Le Lettere, 2015 [1986]), ch. 1.
23. Ivan Klajn, *Influssi inglesi nella lingua italiana* (Florence: Olschki, 1972), pp. 168–69.
24. On the difference between *specialist language* and *special* (or *sectorial*) *language* see Gaetano Berruto, 'Varietà diamesiche, diastratiche, diafasiche', in *Introduzione all'italiano contemporaneo. La variazione e gli usi*, ed. by A. Sobrero (Rome: Laterza, 2000 [1993]), pp. 37–92, and Alberto

Sobrero, 'Lingue speciali', 237–77. Note that specialists, too, may sometimes use a special language when addressing a wide audience, yet this kind of variety coincides only in part with specialist varieties, which are defined by their avoidance of polysemy and connotative meanings, by explicit rules for the use of technical terminology and the creation of new terms, and often by conventional ways of making an argument and structuring a text.

25. Maurizio Dardano, 'The Influence of English on Italian', in *English in Contact with Other Languages: Studies in Honour of Broder Carstensen*, ed. by Wolfgang Viereck and W. D. Bald (Budapest: Akadémiai Kiadó, 1986), pp. 231–52.
26. The traditional distinctions and related predictions about the outcomes of contact can be traced back to Leonard Bloomfield's (*Language*, New York: Holt, 1933) distinction between 'intimate' and 'cultural' contact. Attempts at constructing borrowability scales (which go further back to William D. Whitney, 'On Mixture in Language', *Transactions of the American Philological Association*, 12 (1881), 5–26) are essentially rooted in this tradition. The new approaches are instead more akin to notions such as 'appui', introduced by Yakov Malkiel ('Critères pour l'étude de la fragmentation du Latin', in *XIV Congresso internazionale di linguistica e filologia romanza. Atti*, 5 vols (Naples: Macchiaroli, 1978), I, 27–47) with reference to derivational morphology, and especially Christopher Pountain's 'exploitation' ('Syntactic Anglicisms in Spanish').
27. Sarah Thomason, 'Contact Explanations in Linguistics', in *The Handbook of Language Contact*, ed. by Raymond Hickey (Oxford: Blackwell, 2010), pp. 31–47 (p. 34).
28. Ibid., p. 32.
29. See also Alberto Varvaro, 'La frammentazione linguistica della Romània', in *Identità linguistiche e letterarie nell'Europa romanza* (Rome: Salerno, 2004), pp. 74–108 (pp. 83–84).
30. See McLaughlin, *Syntactic Borrowing*, p. 109.
31. Alessandro Carlucci, 'English Influences in Contemporary Italian: Innovation or Exploitation?', *Modern Language Review*, 112 (2017), 381–96.
32. Nigel Vincent, 'Non-Finite Forms, Periphrases, and Autonomous Morphology in Latin and Romance', in *Morphological Autonomy: Perspectives from Romance Inflectional Morphology*, ed. by Martin Maiden and others (Oxford: Oxford University Press, 2011), pp. 417–35 (p. 424).
33. Viola, '*Stai scherzando?* ', p. 187.
34. Mario Squartini, *Il verbo* (Rome: Carocci, 2015), p. 95.
35. Marcello Durante, *Dal latino all'italiano moderno. Saggio di storia linguistica e culturale* (Bologna: Zanichelli, 1981).
36. Pier Marco Bertinetto, 'The Progressive in Romance, as Compared with English', in *Tense and Aspect in the Languages of Europe*, ed. by Östen Dahl (Berlin: De Gruyter, 2000), pp. 559–604.
37. Giovanna Brianti, 'La perifrasi progressiva "in progress": confronto tra italiano e inglese', in *Letteratura e filologia fra Svizzera e Italia. Studi in onore di Guglielmo Gorni*, ed. by M. A. Terzoli, Alberto Asor Rosa and Giorgio Inglese (Rome: Storia e letteratura, 2012), pp. 351–62.
38. Cortelazzo, 'La perifrasi progressiva', p. 36.
39. Squartini, *Il verbo*, pp. 60–69.
40. Antonio Gurrado, 'A Firenze vogliono far pagare di più gli universitari fuoricorso. Giusto', <http://www.ilfoglio.it/scuola/2017/06/06/news/a-firenze-vogliono-far-pagare-di-piu-gli-universitari-fuoricorso-giusto-138240/> [published 6 June 2017, last accessed 13 July 2017]. The author often writes about the UK, where he previously lived (according to his biographical blurb). Gaetano Berruto (*Sociolinguistica dell'italiano contemporaneo* (Rome: Carocci, 2012 [1987]), pp. 82 and 123) discusses a few similar examples (including one from *La Repubblica*, 19 May 1987). See also Cortelazzo, 'La perifrasi progressiva', pp. 35–36.
41. Gaetano Salvemini to Mary Berenson, 15 March 1935, in Iris Origo, 'Lettere inedite di Gaetano Salvemini a Bernard e Mary Berenson', *Nuova Antologia*, 551 (1982), 146–51 (I am grateful to Alice Gussoni for providing me with a scanned version of Salvemini's hand-written original).
42. See McLaughlin, *Syntactic Borrowing*, pp. 10–14, and also Degano, 'Influssi inglesi'.
43. Massimo Fanfani, 'Per un repertorio di anglicismi in italiano', in *Italiano e inglese a confronto*, pp. 151–76 (p. 174). Cf. note 5 above.
44. 'Incrocio le braccia e lo guardo; egli incrocia le braccia e mi guarda; e stiamo così guardandoci qualche momento' [I crossed my arms and stared at him. He crossed his arms and stared back.

So we stared at each other for a few moments] (Edmondo De Amicis, *Ricordi di Londra* (Milan: Treves, 1909 [1874]), p. 4; Edmondo De Amicis, *Memories of London*, trans. by S. Parkin (London: Alma Classics, 2014), p. 7). I will not go into the question of whether this sentence contains a periphrasis at all (a late survival of durative *stare* + gerund?) or is a purely compositional string put together according to syntactic rules (in which case it should be translated roughly as 'we stood like that, staring at each other').

45. As already pointed out, for instance, by Vladimir Ivir, 'Contrastive Methods in Contact Linguistics', in *Languages in Contact and Contrast: Essays in Contact Linguistics*, ed. by Vladimir Ivir and Damir Kalogjera (Berlin: De Gruyter, 1991), pp. 237–45 (p. 244). A prevalence of progressive *stare* + gerund in translations was also observed by Ondelli and Viale in a corpus of 1963 newspaper articles written in Italian or translated predominantly (but not exclusively) from English during the years 2001–08: see Stefano Ondelli and Matteo Viale, 'L'assetto dell'italiano delle traduzioni in un corpus giornalistico. Aspetti qualitativi e quantitativi', *International Journal of Translation*, 12 (2010), 1–62.
46. Lorenzo Renzi, *Come cambia la lingua. L'italiano in movimento* (Bologna: Il Mulino, 2012).
47. Pierre Guiraud, *Les mots étrangers* (Paris: Presses universitaires de France, 1971 [1965]), pp. 113–14.
48. René Étiemble, *Parlez-vous franglais?* (Paris: Gallimard, 1964), pp. 200–01.
49. Berruto, *Sociolinguistica dell'italiano contemporaneo*, p. 103.
50. Ibid. Cf. Andrea Fabbri, 'Un costrutto di recente diffusione nell'italiano: il tipo "affascinato dalla, e invischiato nella, regola"', *Lingua nostra*, 48 (1987), 17–19.
51. Rodney Huddleston, John Payne and Peter Peterson, 'Coordination and Supplementation', in *The Cambridge Grammar of the English Language*, ed. by Rodney Huddleston and Geoffrey Pullum (Cambridge: Cambridge University Press, 2002), pp. 1273–1357 (p. 1343).
52. Quoted by Fabbri, 'Un costrutto di recente diffusione nell'italiano', pp. 18–19. Renzi quotes a real example which seems even more complex: 'per sedersi accanto a, una volta riconciliato con, i molti compagni' [in order to sit next to, once reconciled with, his many companions] (*Come cambia la lingua*, p. 73). This example resembles the ones which Huddleston, Payne, and Peterson use to support the following statement: 'Delayed right constituents occur predominantly in coordination, but they are found in some subordinative constructions too' ('Coordination and Supplementation', p. 1344).
53. Renzi, *Come cambia la lingua*, p. 72.
54. Structurally similar examples from the first part of the twentieth century include: 'la rivoluzione si fa con Ø o senza sindaco?' (Antonio Gramsci, 'Domani' [1917], in *Scritti. 1910–1926* (Rome: Treccani, 2015), p. 291), 'con Ø o senza frutto e vantaggio' (Giovanni Gentile, 'Introduzione a Leopardi', *Nuova Antologia*, 1 November 1927, pp. 5–20, 9). Following Renzi's interpretation, I use 'Ø' to indicate the omitted constituent(s). As I pointed out in 'English Influences in Contemporary Italian', the alternatives would be the repetition of, for instance, 'sindaco', or the equally uneconomical use of a pronoun: 'con il sindaco o senza di lui' [with the mayor or without him].
55. I have quoted the relevant passage from: *Gatsby il magnifico*, trans. by Cesare Giardini (Milan: Mondadori, 1936), *Gatsby le magnifique*, trans. by Victor Llona (Paris: Simon Kra, 1926), and *Il grande Gatsby*, trans. by Fernanda Pivano (Milan: Mondadori, 1950). In the first two translations, 'château' and 'castello' refer contextually to Gatsby's house, but do not correspond to a particular English word in the original sentence. See also 'fra la villa e la città' (trans. by Tommaso Pincio, Rome: Minimum fax, 2011) and 'faceva la spola dalla città' (trans. by Franca Cavagnoli, Milan: Feltrinelli, 2011).
56. Quoted from the translations by Bruno Armando (Rome: Newton Compton, 2011), Roberto Serrai (Venice: Marsilio, 2011) and Alessandro Ceni (Florence: Giunti, 2016).
57. As confirmed by the data discussed by Fabbri, 'Un costrutto di recente diffusione nell'italiano'.
58. See 'Bollettino commerciale delle Ferrovie dello Stato', *Rivista delle comunicazioni ferroviarie*, 15 February 1929, pp. 35–48 (e.g. 'da e per la Francia' on p. 38).

INDEX

Acton, Eliza 228
Adams, John 233
advertising 36, 40, 43 n. 10, 45 n. 37, 70 n. 13, 93, 94, 109, 116, 125, 224, 236, 239, 240, 241, 246, 248, 254
African-American 8, 73, 79, 144, 146, 147, 148, 149, 150, 152, 154 n. 39, 156, 160, 169, 179, 188–90, 201
Agee, James 67, 71 n. 35
Agnelli, Giovanni 114–18
Ainsworth, Catherine Harris 24, 27, 28
Ajello, Nello 137 n. 19
Alberini, Filoteo 94
Alessandrini, Goffredo 128
Alfieri, Dino 134–35
Alighieri, Dante 34, 108
Altieri, Ferdinando 233
Alvaro, Corrado 146
Ambrosio, Arturo 105, 107, 108, 109–13, 118, 121 n. 22
American dream 5, 69, 72, 82, 84 n. 7, 239
Americanismo (philosophy) 93, 101 n. 17
Americanisms 10, 59, 66, 123, 127, 159, 161, 162, 232–45, 248
Americanization 3, 6, 31, 32, 42, 47–58, 89, 118, 135, 157, 256
American revolution 32, 92, 233, 245 n. 6
Amici, Marina 24
Ammer, Christine 176, 192 n. 12
Anderlini, Elios 23, 24
Anderlini, Virginia 23, 24
Anglicisms 6, 10, 33, 34, 35, 36, 37, 38, 39, 40, 41, 42, 44 n. 22, 216, 218, 232, 234, 237, 238, 239, 240, 241, 242, 243, 246–61
Anglo-American 6, 31–46, 49, 184, 187, 188, 189, 195 n. 55, 205, 206, 232, 233, 242, 243, 248, 249, 250, 251, 253, 254, 255, 256, 257
Anglomania 31, 32, 41, 42, 233
Aprile, Renato 26
Arbasino, Alberto 185
Arendt, Hannah 68
Arlìa, Costantino 34
Assuntino, Rudi 158, 162, 166, 167, 168, 169, 170
Attala-Perazzini, Elena 7, 73, 74, 75, 80, 81, 82, 83, 85 n. 29
autarchy 35, 49, 123, 126, 136, 160

Baez, Joan 164, 168
Balboni, Paolo 50
Bambara, Toni Cade 177, 178

Bancroft, George 234
Bandello Caesar Enrico 65, 66
Baretti, Giuseppe 233
Barnum, Phineas 91
Baroncelli, Flavio 186, 193 n. 30
Bartolini, Francesco 108
Basile, Giambattista 25
Bazin, André 67
Beban, George 62, 64, 68
Beecher-Stowe, Harriet 234
Belasco, David 98
Benjamin, Walter 104
Beraducci, Anna Maria 19, 24, 25, 27
Berlinguer, Luigi 52
Bermani, Cesare 162, 163, 167
Bernardy, Amy 205, 213 n. 44, 234, 245 n. 12
Bernstein, Richard 179, 194 n. 34
Bertellini, Giorgio 4, 7, 103
Bertinetto, Pier Marco 253
Beynet, Michael 124
Bianco, Carla 29 n. 19, 30 n. 39
Bigelow, John 234
Bilingualism 41, 222, 233, 248, 249, 255
Bloom, Allan 179, 180, 181
Bloom, Harold 256
Bloomfield, Leonard 260 n. 26
blues 158, 159, 160, 164, 165, 167, 169, 170, 239
Boccaccio, Giovanni 252
Boito, Arrigo 110
Boldini, Giovanni 104
Bolelli, Tristano 33
Bollati, Benito 150
Bonelli, Sergio 89
Bonsaver, Guido 8, 59
Borgnetto, Luigi Romano 108
Bosio, Gianni 161, 169
Bradley, Harold 162, 163
Brianti, Giovanna 253, 255
Britain 2, 5, 9, 10, 31, 32, 44 n. 22, 92, 105, 118, 157, 167, 175, 202, 232, 233, 234, 254
Budd, Edward G. 122 n. 31
Buffalo Bill, see Cody, William
Bulwer-Lytton, Edward 108
Buonomo, Leonardo 189
Burgess, Ernest 202
Burnett, L. D. 177, 178
Burnett, W. R. 65
Burt, A. S. 91

Bush, George (Sr) 181, 194 n. 45

Cain, James 126
Calvino, Italo 21
Camonte, Toni 66
Capone, Alphonse 11
Caprettini, Gian Paolo 21, 26
Caproni, Giorgio 146
Carega di Muricce, Francesco 234
Carlucci, Alessandro 10, 59
Carnevali, Emanuel 79
Carpitella, Diego 157, 158, 159, 161
Carrera, Alessandro 167
Cartosio, Bruno 188
Caruso, Enrico 97
Casati, Gabrio 48, 49
Cassai, Judith 25, 26
Cassola, Carlo 145
Castellani, Arrigo 33
Castronovo, Valerio 121 n. 28
Cavour, Camillo Benso di 48, 57 n. 2
Ceccherini, Silvano 146
Cecchi, Emilio 126 127, 239
Cella, Ettore 207, 208, 209, 210, 213 n. 59, 214 n. 64
censorship 37, 59, 123, 126, 129–30, 147, 148, 149, 180, 238
Cesaroni, Giancarlo 162, 163
Charles I 216
Chase, Ezra B. 192 n. 17
Cherchi Usai, Paolo 106
Ciarchi, Paolo 162, 166, 168
Cioni, Federico 102 n. 45
Cirese, Alberto Mario 157, 161
civil rights 8, 148, 156, 160, 161, 164, 168, 181
Civinini, Guelfo 97
Coburn, James 104 n. 1
Cody, William (aka Buffalo Bill) 7, 8, 89–102
Cohen, Robert 201
Cold War 90, 158, 167, 241
colonialism 90, 93, 95, 97, 113, 123, 158, 186, 233
comics 89, 90, 99
contact:
    direct 3, 31, 32, 34, 217, 228, 247
    indirect 2, 3, 31, 34, 157, 217
    mediated 249, 250, 257, 258
    zone 2, 8, 73, 148, 149, 151, 152
Cooper, Gary 89
Cooper, James Fenimore 233
Coppola, Francis Ford 66, 204, 212 n. 33
Cortelazzo, Michele 253, 255
cosmopolitan 63, 65, 76, 77, 101 n. 14
Cossio, Carlo 99
Cottini, Luca 7, 8
Crawford, Joan 127, 134
Credaro, Luigi 104
Crivelli, Filippo 159

Croly, Herbert 70 n. 13
Cugnot, Nicholas-Joseph 113

D'Annunzio, Gabriele 104, 109
D'Arpe, Gustavo 145
D'Souza, Dinesh 180, 181
Dana, Jacqueline 151
Dane, Barbara 156, 167, 169
Dardano, Maurizio 250
Davis, Miles 78
Davis, Shelby 102 n. 47
De Amicis, Edmondo 97, 101 n. 17, 102 n. 36
De Certeau, Michel 80
De Céspedes, Alba 146
De Chomòn, Segundo 110
De Grazia, Victoria 135
De Gregori, Francesco 99
De Martino, Domenico 33
De Martino, Ernesto 157
De Mauro, Tullio 38, 41, 51, 52
De Santis, Giuseppe 147
De Seta, Vittorio 159
Deed, André 107
Degano, Chiara 255
Deleuze and Guattari 78
Deroy, Louis 217
Devoto, Giacomo 37
Dewey, John 49, 70 n. 13
Dezza, Enrico 207
Di Franco, Manuela 8
Diaspora 74, 81, 83, 105, 185, 186, 201, 202, 206
Dickens, Charles 228
Dietrich, Marlene 131, 133, 134
Disney, Walt 11
Drago, Antonietta 128–30, 138 n. 31
drink 43 n. 10, 76, 219, 225, 226, 227, 228, 231 n. 39, 236, 241, 242
dubbing 239, 247, 248, 249
Durante, Marcello 253, 255
Dylan, Bob (Robert Allen Zimmerman) 166, 167–69

Eastwood, Clint 89, 100 n. 4
Eco, Umberto 165
Edison, Thomas 106, 107, 108
education 4, 6, 7, 18, 23, 28, 33, 37, 40, 41, 42, 47–58, 73, 75, 104, 136 n. 3, 179, 192 n. 13, 194 n. 33, 207, 236, 240, 247, 248
emigration 32, 83, 93, 94, 95, 97, 99, 101 n. 17, 158, 206, 234
English 31–46, 47–58, 246–61
    American English 32, 42, 43, 175, 176, 177, 182, 184, 188, 191, 216–31, 232, 235, 237, 239, 240, 241, 243, 244
    British English 5, 9, 10, 13, 42, 43 n. 9, 216, 217, 221, 222, 223, 224, 226, 227, 228, 229, 230 n. 30

Fabbri, Franco 188
Fabre, Marcel 107
fairy tale, *see* folk tale
Faloppa, Federico 9
family 17, 18, 19, 20, 21, 22, 23, 24, 25, 26, 27, 28, 49, 76, 77, 80, 81, 86 n. 30, 104, 114, 119, 152, 208, 224
Fanfani, Massimo 10
Fanfani, Pietro 34
Farber, Manny 67
Fascism 8, 36, 49, 59, 118, 135, 136, 143, 146, 148, 159, 160, 171 n. 16, 180, 186
feminine 63, 223
Ferrara, Baladino 20, 21, 28
Ferrara, Francesco 235
Ferroni, Giorgio 147
Fersen, Nicholas 151
Fiaba, *see* folk tale
fiction 4, 72, 74, 78, 83, 89, 90, 97, 99, 125, 209, 237
Fiore, Teresa 7
Fiorentino, David 101 n. 17
Fiori, Umberto 167
Fo, Dario 159, 161
folk:
  culture 159, 160, 161
  music 2, 8, 158, 162, 163, 164, 166
  tale 6, 17–30
Fonda, Henry 100 n. 4
Fontana, Ferdinando 234
food 10, 22, 27, 37, 39, 219, 225, 226, 227, 228, 231, 233, 236, 247
Ford, Henry 115–18
Ford, John 89, 99 n. 1
Forgacs, David 135
Fortini, Franco 161
France 8, 32, 103, 104, 105, 106, 107, 112, 113, 114, 115, 118, 175, 206, 207, 216, 233
Franklin, Benjamin 220
French 6, 7, 12, 32, 34, 35, 36, 37, 39, 45 n. 44, 47, 48, 49, 50, 52, 55, 56, 57 n. 2, 93, 103–22, 125, 127, 151, 189, 192 n. 7, 211 n. 14, 216, 217, 221, 224, 229 n. 11, 233, 234, 237, 238, 247, 253, 256, 257
Früh, Kurt 202, 207, 208, 209, 210
Fucilla, Joseph 18, 19, 20, 24, 27
Furiassi, Cristiano 218
Futurism 95, 96, 104, 105

Gabaccia, Donna 105, 201, 202, 203, 206, 259 n. 19
Galleppini, Aurelio 89
Galli de' Paratesi, Nora 186
Gandolfi, Alfredo 110–11, 121 n. 16
Garbo, Greta 127–28, 131
Garcia Lorca, Federico 78
Gardaphé, Fred 27
Gardini, Carlo 234, 235
Garibaldi, Giuseppe 32, 101 n. 18

Garret, Peter 33, 43 n. 10
Gelmini, Mariastella 52
gender 63, 72, 106, 185, 188, 192 n. 12, 192 n. 13, 223, 224
genres 59, 73, 107, 158, 160, 239, 254
Gentile, Emilio 135
Gentile, Giovanni 49
George, Harrison 177
German 32, 39, 41, 47, 49, 50, 51, 55, 56, 113, 114, 116, 125, 137 n. 15, 137 n. 16, 148, 149, 175, 192 n. 7, 206, 213 n. 59, 238, 245 n. 12
Giacosa, Giuseppe 234
Giammanco, Roberto 188
Giannini, Amadeo 11
Gilpin, William 62
Giovanardi, Claudio 33, 39
Gobetti, Piero 205, 206
Goethe, Johann Wolfgang von 32
Goldoni, Carlo 98
Goldsoll, Frank Joseph 112
Görlach, Manfred 39
Graf, Aturo 32
grammar 40, 85 n. 20, 184, 189, 218, 222–24, 237, 239, 241–44, 250
  affixation 223, 224, 235, 243, 251
  coordination 247, 256, 257
  progressive periphrases 251, 252, 253, 254, 255, 256, 257
Gramsci, Antonio 2, 104, 157
Granata, Ivano 124
Great Depression 11, 60, 65, 169, 236, 237
Great War, *see* First World War
Griffith, D. W. 112–13
Gualdo, Riccardo 33, 39
Guazzoni, Enrico 108, 109
Gundle, Stephen 135
Gusmani, Roberto 217
Gussoni, Alice 260 n. 41
Guthrie, Woody 162, 164, 165, 169

Haley, Alex 188
Hall, Stuart 2, 193 n. 30
Hamer, Fannie Lou 156
Hamilton, Alexander 234
Hammett, Dashiell 65, 126
Harney, Robert H. 202
Haugen, Einar 217
Henabery, John 113
Hillery, Mable 156, 169
Hobsbawn, Eric 3
Hollywood 8, 11, 37, 60, 63, 66, 67, 68, 89, 100, 105, 113, 119, 123, 124, 126, 127, 128, 129, 130, 131, 132, 134, 201, 204, 238, 240
Hope, Thomas 224
Howe, Herbert 64
Hughes, Geoffrey 177

Iamartino, Giovanni 34
identity 2, 3, 17, 27, 34, 41, 75, 76, 78, 79, 81, 82, 83, 113, 121 n. 23, 182, 204, 212 n. 32, 231 n. 37
illiteracy, *see* literacy
illustrated magazines 123, 124, 125, 136 n. 3, 137 n. 16, 137 n. 17, 137 n. 18
immigration 61, 63, 73, 74, 81, 85 n. 12, 85 n. 17, 186, 187, 202
Internet, *see* technology
Irving, Washington 223, 234
Italian American 4, 11, 12, 17, 18, 20, 22, 23, 24, 27, 28, 65, 69, 74, 79, 84 n. 7, 86 n. 36, 119, 166, 201, 202, 203, 204

Jefferson, Thomas 220
Johnson, Richard 176
Johnson, Samuel 220
journalism 32, 40, 41, 45 n. 37, 51, 70 n. 10, 72, 74, 83, 85 n. 29, 94, 101 n. 18, 116, 126, 128, 137 n. 15, 137 n. 17, 145, 175, 186, 194 n. 33, 195 n. 45, 203, 205, 209, 224, 232, 234, 235, 236, 240, 244 n. 1, 248, 253

Kelly, Megyn 191 n. 3
Kimball, Roger 179, 180, 194 n. 33
King, Martin Luther 156
Kirkpatrick, Frederick Douglass 156
Klajn, Ivan 34, 44 n. 18, 230 n. 20, 250
Kleine, Geore 108–13, 121 n. 16
Kohl, Herbert 177, 193 n. 22

La Guardia, Fiorello 11
Lafitte, Paul 106
LaFrate, Deborah 26, 27, 28
Lajolo, Davide 145
Lakoff, Robin Tolmach 176, 181
language policy and planning 33–36, 41, 44, 45 n. 47, 47, 49, 52, 57 n. 7, 120 n. 2, 180, 186, 189–91, 238, 248
Latin 41, 103, 104, 190, 216, 217, 221, 223, 224, 233, 243, 251
Latin American 73, 85 n. 17
Lattuada, Alberto 147
Lavinio, Cristina 25, 26
Le Corbusier (Charles-Édouard Jeanneret) 116
Le Pen, Marine 175
Lead Belly (Huddie William Ledbetter) 164–65
Leavitt IV, Charles L. 3, 8
Lee, Shelton Jackson (Spike) 187
Lento, Mattia 9
Leo XIII, Pope 93, 101 n. 17
Leone, Sergio 89, 90, 100 n. 4
Lépine, Charles Lucien 107
lexical borrowing 9, 10, 32, 33, 34, 36, 37, 39, 41, 45 n. 37, 184, 216, 217, 218, 222, 223, 228, 229, 230, 231 n. 39, 232–42, 246

Leydi, Roberto 9, 157, 159, 160, 161, 162, 163, 164, 166, 168, 169, 170
Lippman, Walter 70 n. 13
literacy 18, 19, 20, 24, 27, 28, 29 n. 7, 31, 37, 105, 120 n. 3, 224
Little Italy 9, 62, 201–15, 224
Lomax, Alan 9, 157, 158, 159, 160, 161, 162, 164, 169
Longanesi, Leo 8, 123, 124, 134–35
Longone, Riccardo 145
Love, Rachel E. 8
Lucetti, Piero 151
Luisi, Luciano 146
lyrics 156, 160, 169, 248

Machado, Antonio 78
magazines 8, 64, 123, 124, 125, 126, 127, 128, 130, 134, 136 n. 3, 137 n. 16, 137 n. 17, 137 n. 18, 137 n. 19, 138 n. 35, 162, 179, 180, 181, 211 n. 1, 217, 234, 236, 253
Maggi, Luigi 108
Malaparte, Curzio 151
Mancina, James 21
Mancini, Enzo 147, 151
Mancini, Marco 38
Mandel, Carlotta 146, 151
Mangione, Jerre 22, 24
Manzoni, Alessandro 252
Maraschio, Nicoletta 33
Marazzi, Martino 188
Marchelli, Chiara 7, 72, 73, 74, 75, 76, 77, 78, 82, 83, 84 n. 11
Marchionne, Sergio 4, 119
Marinelli, William 26, 27, 28
Marinetti, Filippo Tommaso 8, 90, 95–96, 99, 104, 105–06
Marini, Giovanna 9, 158, 162, 163, 164, 165, 166, 167, 169, 170, 171 n. 8
Marshall Plan 157, 239
Martí, José 78
Marzo, Roberto 234
masculine 63, 106, 184, 185, 223
Massey, Doreen 2
Matté-Trucco, Giacomo 116
Mayer, Jane 181
Mazzini, Giuseppe 32, 101 n. 18
McCarthyism 158, 160, 164, 179
McKenzie, Roderick 202
McLaughlin, Mairi 258 n. 3
Méliès, George 107, 110
Merriam, Charles 64, 220
Merriam, George 220
Micheli, Silvio 143, 144, 145, 147, 152
Migliorini, Bruno 36, 37, 238
Milani, Lorenzo 51
Minutiello, Michael 186, 187
Mito americano/American Myth 8, 32, 90, 100 n. 5, 127, 135, 161, 239

Modigliani, Amedeo 104
Mondadori, Arnoldo 11, 12
Monelli, Paolo 35, 36
Montanelli, Indro 40, 124, 125, 145
Moratti, Letizia 52
Moravia, Alberto 126, 146, 147
Mori, Giorgio 121 n. 28
Moro, Aldo 50
Morricone, Ennio 104 n. 1
Morrison, Toni 181
Mucci, Umberto 73
music 2, 8, 9, 37, 42, 65, 78, 96, 102 n. 47, 109, 157, 158, 160, 161, 162, 163, 164, 166, 167, 168, 169, 170, 219, 221, 222, 228, 236, 238, 240, 243, 246, 248
Mussi, Fabio 52
Mussolini, Vittorio 129, 138 n. 28
Mussolini, Benito (Duce) 12, 63, 64, 65, 69, 118, 129, 135, 207
myth 32, 78, 89–102, 127, 135, 160, 161, 201–15, 233, 239

Navarra, Anthony 28, 29 n. 7
Nencioni, Enrico 235
neologisms 34, 36, 38, 39, 41, 114, 234, 235, 236, 237, 238
neorealism 60, 67–68, 71 n. 40
newspapers 35, 36, 38, 93, 94, 101 n. 18, 125, 129, 145, 149, 150, 151, 174, 175, 179, 181, 192 n. 7, 207, 209, 217, 234, 237, 241, 248, 252, 253, 256, 261 n. 45
Nixon, Richard 156

Oakley, Annie 91, 98, 100 n. 10
Obama, Barack 243, 244
Ojetti, Ugo 234, 245 n. 12
Omegna, Roberto 105

Padoan, Adolfo 108
Pannunzio, Mario 128–29, 130, 134
Panzini, Alfredo 34, 35, 235, 238, 245 n. 16
Papa, Dario 234
Park, Robert Ezra 202
Pascoli, Giovanni 97
Pasolini, Pier Paolo 51, 159
Pastrone, Giuseppe 107–08, 109
Pavese, Cesare 135, 145, 159, 239
Pea, Enrico 146
Pellegrini, Ferdinando 156, 168
Perry, Ruth 177
Petrocchi, Policarpo 234
photograph 62, 67, 68, 78, 80, 100 n. 11, 124, 125, 126, 130, 131, 132, 135, 137 n. 16, 137 n. 17, 162, 203, 236
Pianta, Bruno 162
Pinnavaia, Laura 9, 10
Pintor, Giaime 126, 127
Pivano, Fernanda 135, 261 n. 55

Pizzetti, Ildebrando 109
Poe, Edgar Allan 78, 235
Portelli, Alessandro 156, 158, 160, 161, 164, 168, 169, 170
Pratt, Mary Louise 8, 73, 148
Praz, Mario 126, 127
Presley, Elvis 166, 167
pronunciation 39, 40, 44 n. 18, 147, 186, 222, 223, 237, 239, 240, 242, 243, 248
propaganda 36, 127, 129, 160
Puccini, Giacomo 8, 90, 94, 95, 96, 97, 98, 99, 102 n. 47
Pulcini, Virginia 6, 7
Puzo, Mario 66

Rabinowitz, Dorothy 179
racism 148, 166, 179, 181, 195 n. 45
Radio 27, 34, 124, 158, 160, 163, 213 n. 59, 225, 237, 238, 239
Raffaelli, Sergio 36
Ragusa, Kym 79
Rando, Gaetano 38, 44 n. 22
Rawick, George P. 188
Ray, John 228
Redford, Robert 250
Reid, Thomas Mayne 234
Renzi, Lorenzo 255, 256, 261 n. 52 and n. 54
Répaci, Leonida 145
Reza, Matthew 6, 59
Ricciardi, Toni 209
Ricolfi, Luca 174, 191
Rinaldi Castro, Tiziana 7, 72, 73, 74, 75, 78, 79, 82, 83, 85 n. 21, 86 n. 37
Rizzoli, Angelo 135
Robinson, Cedric 154 n. 36
Rondolino, Gianni 105
Roosevelt, Franklin Delano 123, 132, 237
Rossellini, Roberto 68
Rossi, Adolfo 234
Russo, Luigi 147

Sabatini, Alma 190
Sabatini, Francesco 33, 37, 45 n. 29
Salgari, Emilio 8, 90, 94, 95, 96–98, 99, 109
Salvemini, Gaetano 253
Saroyan, William 126, 131, 132, 247
Savinio, Alberto 134–35
Scarpino, Cristina 33
Schillace, John 151
Schirru, Giancarlo 7
Schoonover, Karl 68, 71 n. 40
Schultz, Debra L. 178
Schwamenthal, Riccardo 162
Sciascia, Leonardo 78
Scorsese, Martin 204, 212 n. 33
Scott Fitzgerald, Francis 257
Second World War 3, 6, 7, 8, 12, 31, 32, 33, 34, 39, 42,

49, 52, 53, 67, 89, 90, 114, 148, 157, 158, 160, 169, 206, 207, 225, 232, 239, 247, 254
Sedgwick, Eve Kosofsky 194 n. 33
Seeger, Pete 160, 162, 163, 164, 165
semantic borrowing 38, 44 n. 22, 182, 218, 239, 246
Sienkiewicz, Henryk 109
Simpson, John 217
Singer, Ben 60–61
Sloan, P. F. (Philip Gary Schlein) 167, 168
Sociolinguistics 33, 37, 247, 248, 249, 250, 251, 256
Soldati, Mario 126, 127, 239
Sordi, Alberto 100
Spanish 39, 47, 50, 51, 52, 55, 56, 63, 78, 93, 110, 217
sports 36, 43 n. 10, 219, 220, 236, 238, 240, 241
Squartini, Mario 253
Staglieno, Marcello 124
Stammerjohann, Harro 32
Stead, William 32
Stefano, Joan 22
Stevani, Mario Alberto 100–13, 121 n. 16
Storero, Luigi 114
storytelling 2, 4, 17–30, 244
Strachey, John 177
Strezza, Jacques 151
subtitles 34, 125, 253

Tasso, Torquato 108
Taylor, Frederick W. 115
technology 3, 37, 34, 42, 61, 100 n. 11, 113, 118–19, 240, 242, 243, 248, 249
television 24, 27, 34, 89, 157, 160, 166, 189, 208, 225, 237–41, 247–49
Thomason, Sarah 250
Torelli, Milziade 145
Toscanini, Arturo 98
Tosi, Arturo 32, 39
translation 10, 11, 12, 26, 32, 52, 58 n. 17, 85 n. 11, 125, 126, 130, 132, 138 n. 35, 158, 160, 162, 167, 182, 184, 188, 218, 222, 228, 233, 234, 236, 237, 240, 246–61
Trump, Donald 42, 174, 175, 181, 191 n. 3, 244
Tse-Tung, Mao 177
Turturro, John 4

Valentino, Rudolph 11, 63–65
Verga, Giovanni 68, 104
Vietnam 162, 164, 165, 168
Visconti, Luchino 68
Visentini, Gino 127
Vittorini, Elio 126, 127, 131, 135, 159, 239, 247
Volontè, Gian Maria 104 n. 1
Voltaire 32

Walker, Alice 181
Warshow, Robert 59, 66
Washburne, Carleton W. 49–50, 57–58 n. 10
Washington, George 220
Wayne, John 89
Webster, Noah 220
Wendt, Rainer 175
West, Mae 131, 133
Western (film) 89, 100 n. 3, 100 n. 5, 100 n. 11, 160, 239
Whyte, William Foote 202
Wild West 89–102
Williams, John 149
Wilson, Woodrow 4, 237
Wilson, James 176
women 7, 20, 36, 63, 64, 72–86, 91, 124, 126, 128, 131, 132, 134, 144, 149, 150, 152, 175, 178, 179, 186, 195 n. 45
Wright, Richard 148

Zampa, Luigi 147
Zangarini, Carlo 97
Zavattini, Cesare 67, 124
Zenuti, Ernesto 235

www.ingramcontent.com/pod-product-compliance
Lightning Source LLC
Chambersburg PA
CBHW080541090426
42734CB00016B/3170